The Darjeeling Himalay

New Jalpaiguri – Darjeeling

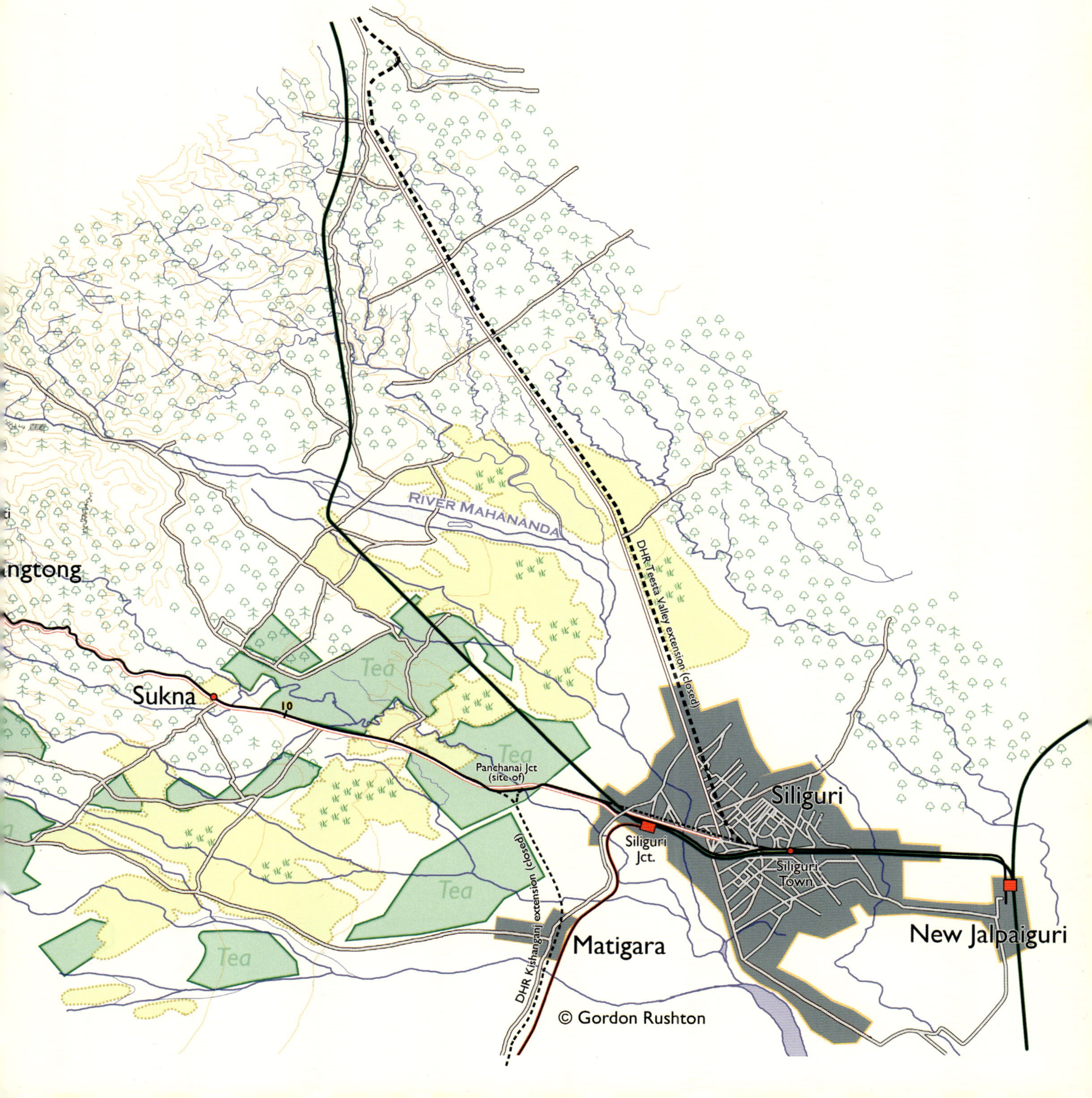

The Iron Sherpa

VOLUME 1
The History

Rail Romances
Specialist Publishers

P.O. Box 85, Chester CH4 9ZH
United Kingdom

The Iron Sherpa

VOLUME 1
The History

by

Terry Martin

The Story of
The Darjeeling Himalayan Railway
1879–2006

© Terry Martin and Railromances 2006
© Gordon Rushton–Maps 2006
© David Charlesworth–Jacket 2006

All rights reserved. No part of this publication may be reproduced in any form or by any means, electronic or mechanical, photocopying, recording, or by any information storage or retrieval system including the Internet, without the written permission of the Author and the Publisher and, where appropriate, other copyright holders.

ISBN-10: 1-900622-10-6 (Hardback)
ISBN-13: 978-1-900622-10-3 (Hardback)

British Library Cataloguing in Publication Data

A catalogue record for this book
is available from the British Library
Catalogue Reference No.385'.095414

Publishing, Typesetting and Design by:
RailRomances, PO Box 85
Chester CH4 9ZH

Special Graphics by:
John Milner

Maps by:
Gordon Rushton

Bureau Services by:
Lazertype,
Unit 6, Clwyd Court Two,
Rhosddu Industrial Estate,
Wrexham LL11 4YL

Printed by:
HSW Print,
Cambrian Industrial Park,
Tonypandy,
Rhondda CF40 2XX

Acknowledgements

The Club was an integral part of British life in India, and what could be more appropriate than belonging to those that have since been formed to represent the interests of the railway. Members of the Darjeeling Himalayan Railway Society, and the Narrow Gauge Railway Society in the United Kingdom, the Darjeeling Himalayan Railway Supporters Association in Australia, and the Indian Steam Railway Society based in India have given me every support with this book, as have the British Association for Cemeteries in South Asia and the Friends in British India Society.

I would particularly like to thank Rajesh Agrawal, Bill Aitken, Nick Anchen, Peter Bailey, David Barrie, Terry Barringer, Michael Bishop, Steve Blackmore, Colin and Joyce Blunt, Malcolm Brown, Benedict Cadbury, Jill Cartwright, David and Gwen Cattermull, David Chase, John Clemmens, Derek Cobby, Hazel Craig, Douglas Darby, Nilina Deb Lal, Dr Joydeep Dutta, Sheila Feeney, John Flower, Alan Gilbert, Sir William Gladstone, Tim Hadfield, Bernard Holden MBE, Mike Jackson, Peter Jarvis, Judith Jones, Peter Jordan, David Joy, Patrick Keef, Eddie Lambert, Peter Lee, Andrew Lemin, Peter Lemmey, Cedric Lodge, Beryl McConville, David McNeill, Tim McDonald, Laurie Marshall, O.K.Mathews (of SAN Engineering), Michael Melbourne, Murdoch Nicolson, Sandra Noel, Pat Orr, Elizabeth Oxborrow Cowen, Nigel and Ann Plackett, Dr Michael Powell, Julian Rainbow, Peter Richards, Peter and Elona Rogers, Paul Rowland (of the splendid *Indiaman* magazine), Andrew Savage, Betty Shaw, Adrian Shooter, Claus Simon, James Sinclair, Hugh Smith, Paddy Smith, John Snell, Keith and Mary Strickland, Peter Summers, Carol Tanner, Keith Thompson, Don Townsley, Sir Mark Tully, Harsh Vardhan, Dr Ken Walker, Charlotte Wallis, Harvey Watkins, Miss Vyvian Wells, Jeff Welter, Andrew and Shirley West, Paul Whittle, Jack Willis MBE, Barry Winston, David Wooton, and Teddy Young. I must add that I would have no hesitation in offering work as a detective to David Churchill, who has had the knack of ferreting out some superb leads with research and helped me unravel a number of the more devious elements of the DHR story.

I would also like to express my appreciation to Nick Trudgian, who arranged for the survival of the unique collection generously given to the Darjeeling Himalayan Railway Society by Wing Commander R.C. Cresswell. Whilst on the matter of collected works, I thank George Garner of the Glasgow University Archives, Enda Ryan and Lynne Vezza of the Mitchell Library, Dr Kevin Greenbank of the Institute of South Asian Studies, and Carol Morgan of the Institution of Civil Engineers, for they have given me every help I could wish for. The same must be said for Nick and Deki Rhodes with their detailed knowledge on the early history of Darjeeling, and for Peter Tiller and Marilyn Metz with helping me to understand the intricacies of more recent developments. Indeed their help and assistance with proof reading and guidance with accuracy has been greatly appreciated, whilst their work in identifying and preserving the historical aspects of the Railway has been an invaluable contribution to this unique World Heritage Site.

Hands-on research in India today can present its own set of challenges, but they were made so much easier and enjoyable by the assistance I was freely given by (in alphabetical order) Mr R. Baid, Mr R. Bali, Mr B.M.S. Bisht, Mr B. Dikshit, Mr S. Dikshit, Mr R. Lochan, Mr N. Petrie, Mr T. Rabha, Mr N. Roy, Mr H.P. Sharma and Mrs Sheela Verma. Mr Baid also generously made available Uttam Gurung, his excellent driver, who never flinched from a series of bizarre requests that ranged from photographing the train deep in the *terai* forests at the dead of night, with heaven-knows what prowling around, to fleeing from gangs of drunken bandits in Bihar whilst tracing the old Kishenganj line.

Many friends have freely offered their photographs without the demand for grace or favour, and their generosity has been greatly appreciated; any illustrations not credited have come from my own camera or collection. The question of copyright did not appear to exercise the mind in India in past times, and photographs taken by residents and visitors would often turn up as prints and postcards for others to buy; I apologise should any be found between the pages of this book without the correct acknowledgment. The superb maps in the book have been drawn by Gordon Rushton with preparatory work by David Charlesworth, and I thank them not only for their kindness but their tolerance with my requests to change contours, reverse sidings and all the other difficulties that Nature and mankind inflicts on the DHR. There is also much to be found in the many videos that have been made of the railway in more recent years, but I am hesitant to single out those that may have been a direct source of reference for fear of offending others who have covered the same ground. Nevertheless, the superb cinematography of Nick Lera's *'Toy Train to the Clouds'* captures the very spirit of the DHR, and not to mention this would be a travesty.

It may seem somewhat perverse to acknowledge the Internet, but it is only through cyberspace that I was able to become acquainted with records and information that could easily have evaded my research. It also introduced me to a network of correspondents whom I have never met but whose names have become so familiar that I feel an overwhelming sense of concern if one of them does not appear on my screen when I switch on my computer of a morning. I hope the day will come when I can personally thank them, but until then I raise a *burra peg* to Brinds, Cathy Day, John Feltham, Jill Grey, Doreen Grezoux, Pratik Kanjilal, Samir Metha, Sylvia Murphy, S.K. Pande, Dileep Prakesh, Nicholas Shreeve, Sally Stewart, Maria Suffolk and Betty Vanerstrom.

Whilst on matters of IT, the scanning of the photographs has involved technologies that I could not begin to spell, let alone understand, and I am in awe of John Milner for agonising over the mixes of magentas, cyans, yellows and blacks whilst being mindful of all manner of complications brought on by Newton rings and computer compatibilities; my eyes glaze over at the mere thought of it. Committing the research to the word processor would not have been possible had it not been for the patience of Fabien Raymondaud, who sorted out a temperamental computer that was made infinitely worse by my inability to understand how one should cope with its electronic moods.

It is with heavy heart that I must also recognise that there are some who did not live to see this edition in print, and the passing of Peter Bawcutt, Harold Bowtell, Derek Gordon, John Handover, Fred Pinn, Peter Pryke, Michael Seymour, Dr Sprigg, Mrs Phurpa Lhamu (Mary) Tenduf La and Conrad Todd have become particularly poignant for me. Their spirit and reminiscences have been woven into the story and live on for others to savour and enjoy.

The faith and encouragement that I have received from everybody with this project has been magnificent, but it would not have matured to a revised publication had it not been for the foresight and support from John Milner of RailRomances. His help and assistance has been unstinting and, as with the original edition, the quality of the production before you is a reflection of the supreme standards he achieves with consummate skill.

Even with such a wealth of help and information to hand, it is inevitable that mistakes, misunderstandings, and errors of judgement can creep in, and for these I place all responsibility firmly at my own doorstep.

Sukna Station.

By Way of Explanation

There is no single language as Indian, and most of those that are generally used today have their own script, which becomes immediately apparent when it is noted that fourteen are expressed on the banknotes for five rupees and higher. English became understood as the influence of the East India Company spread, and many still regard it as the one language that is common to all, even though the British left India in 1947.

The English spelling of place names has been very much a living process and has changed considerably over the last hundred years, its evolution being not so much a science as more a question of compromise. To illustrate the point, the final section of the railway runs in the shadow of the third–highest mountain in the world. It is referred to as *Kinchinjunga* in the 1898 guide and as *Kinchenjunga* in 1920; most of the travel books for India published today spell the name as *Kanchenjunga*, whilst a guard on the DHR refers to his mountain as *Kanchan Janga*, and he should know if anybody does! A text in the 1920s would refer to the station of *Nuxalbarie* on the extension line that ran to *Kissengunge*, whereas ten years later the towns would be recorded as *Naksalbāri* and *Kishanganj*, and today as *Naxalbari* and *Kishenganj*. The valley of the river *Tista* on the other extension line has similarly metamorphosed into that of the *Teesta*, and its terminus at *Gielle Khola* is now listed as *Geljhora* ... and so the list goes on.

Until the demise of the British Raj, the maps published by the Surveyor General of India took great care to include the use of ā and ī in the spelling, whilst in more recent times there have been changes to de-Anglicise some of the better–known names (e.g. *Calcutta* is now *Kolkata*, *Bombay* is *Mumbai*, etc). A similar change has also become apparent to personal names, for Mr *Chakroborty* is Bengali but when anglicised becomes Mr *Chakravarty*, whilst pronunciation has become a minefield in its own right. Care should be exercised by the visitor, for the railway passes through many cultures, and each has its own vernacular enunciation. For the purpose of continuity, the spelling in the text has been kept to that which is generally known and understood, and it is hoped that those who have felt strongly over the question will accept that there are already enough confusions within this narrative, and that no offence is intended if it does not appear as one might wish.

It is inevitable that a number of Indian terms have been used, and a brief explanation of their meaning may be helpful at this stage. Some may appear a little insensitive today, but they have been included because of their relevance to the culture of the time, and in no way reflect the opinions of the author or publisher.

Agent: ....Although an English word, it was a term used in India for the position of a Chief Executive of a railway, and in particular one in charge of the administration side of the Company. A Managing Agent would be a Company appointed to handle the administrative, legal and financial affairs.
Anna: ....pre-1957 sub-division of the rupee (16 annas = 1 rupee)
Beldar: ....Generic term in Western Bengal for a wandering caste of earth workers and navvies
Budhiman: ....One of a number of generic names for Tibetans and the people of Bhutan
Butcha: ....Child
Cantonment: ....Administrative and military area of a town during the British Raj
Caste: ....Hindu hereditary class that determines social status and occupation. It originates from the belief that there are four main groupings (varnas) that come from a primordial being. The Brahmans (priests and teachers) come from the mouth, the Kshatriyas (rulers and military) from the arms, the Vaisyas (merchants and traders) from the thighs, and the Sudras (labourers) from the feet. Each varna contains numerous castes and subcastes with its own hierarchy. There is a fifth group that has not been acknowledged by the primordial being; as such are regarded as so polluted as to be untouchable (achuta)
Chogyal:..............Sikkimese King (literally King of Religion)
Chota: ....Small
Chota peg: ....Small measure of drink
Chowkidar: ....Watchman or janitor
Chula: ....Clay oven/pot
Coolie: ....Hired native labourer

Crore: Ten million
Cutcherry: Court house or office building for public business
Dak: The Mail, Post
Dak bungalow: Travellers' rest house
Dak gari: Mail coach
Darbar: Reception given by a ruler in British India, or by an officer of rank; also a royal court
Dharma: Hindu/Buddhist code of moral conduct
Godown: Warehouse
Gompa: Small Tibetan Buddhist monastery
Goompties: Turning point
Gorkha: One of the dominant races of Nepal, often referred to by the anglicised form Gurkha. The name was taken from a small town to the west of Kathmandu, and has become synonymous with the fearless soldiers of Nepal. In 1768 the warrior Prithvi Narayan Shah conquered the Malla kings of the Kathmandu valley and took the title of King of Nepal. He continued to extend his territory until he died in 1774, after which his descendants continued their expansion into the area that is now Darjeeling.
Jemadar: A native junior officer belonging to a local regiment of the British Army, although it is occasionally used to describe a sweeper (to grant the task some importance). However, the term was used on the railway to describe a member of staff with a position of authority, e.g. a *jemadar* brakesman would be the person in charge of the team working the brakes on a train.
Karma: The law of cause and effect, founded on the principle of justice based on past deeds
Khansamah: Butler
Lakh: Hundred thousand (i.e. 10 lakh = 1 million)
Maund: Unit of weight; varies according to place, generally approx. 37 kilos = 82lbs
Maya: An illusion
Paise: The current sub-division of a rupee (100 paise = 1 rupee)
Palanquin: Box-like carriage carried on a central pole by four men
Palki: As palanquin
Peon: Messenger, office boy
Pice: Pre-1957 sub-division of currency (4 pice = 1 anna)
Pie: Pre-1957 sub-division of currency (3 pie = 1 pice)
Pukka: Proper, solid (often a term used during the British Raj era)
Quintal: Indian unit of weight (formerly 1 cwt but now 100 kilos)
Resident: In the early days of the Raj it referred to a head of the East India Company's commercial interests, and for a short time to the European head of a district. Latterly it applied to a representative of the Governor-General at important native courts.
Rupee: Basic unit of Indian currency, generally shown as Rs
Sahib: Respectful title for gentlemen
Sear: Sub-division of Indian weight (40 sears = 1 maund)
Shri: Short for Shriman, an honorific title with its nearest equivalent being Mr
Smt: Short for Shrimati, an honorific title with its nearest equivalent being Mrs
Sirdar: Leader, commander, officer (e.g. the head of a set of palanquin bearers or the leader of a hill tribe)
Terai: Forest jungle
Tiffin: Lunchtime snack
Tonga: Two-wheeled carriage pulled by horse or pony
Wallah: Suffix used for a man to denote occupation (chai-wallah = teaman)

A number of organisations will be noted in the text that are frequently referred to by their initials:

AIGL — All India Gorkha League
BJP — Bharatiya Janata Party
CPI — Communist Party of India
CPI (M) — Communist Party of India (Marxist Group)
DGHC — Darjeeling Gorkha Hill Council, now DGAHC Darjeeling Gorkha Autonomous Hill Council
DHRS — Darjeeling Himalayan Railway Society
DHRSA — Darjeeling Himalayan Railway Supporters' Association
GLO — Gorkha Liberation Organisation
GNLF — Gorkha National Liberation Front
ICOMOS — International Council on Monuments & Sites
UNESCO — United Nations Educational, Scientific & Cultural Organisation

The DHR also used its own set of abbreviations for stations and sidings, and these have been included in the text after the full name (New Jalpaiguri – NJP)

The Indian system of numbering is recorded as tens,

hundreds, thousands, hundred thousands and ten millions, with the latter two units being a *lakh* and a *crore*; thus, one million is referred to as ten *lakh* and 1,000,000 would be written as 10,00,000.

The culture of compromise becomes acute with regard to the matter of weights. The unit most frequently quoted is the *maund*, which is subdivided into 40 *sears*. English dictionaries define the *maund* as a measure of weight in India with a value varying in different places from about 25 to 85lbs, approximately between 11 and 39 kilos; the travel guides to India quote the going rate as 1 *maund* roughly equalling 20 kilos. The informative Indian book entitled 'Railway Policy in India' was written by Horace Bell in 1894 and helpfully advises that a *maund* is the weight of 3,200 tolas, each tola being a weight of 180 grains; with a grain being defined as 1/7000th of 1 lb, a *maund* would calculate as 82$\frac{1}{4}$ lbs. The equally helpful Indian book entitled 'Railway Statistics' published in 1978 by N.B. Bagchi (the former statistical officer of the Eastern Railway) records that 1 *maund* = 37 kilos, which would calculate as 81$\frac{1}{2}$ lbs. These latter two references more or less agree, and it is this I have used to give some propriety in the text. However, just to throw a spanner in the works, the *quintal* also appears as another measure in some of the reference works, and the English dictionaries explain this as formerly being 1cwt, but is now 100 kilos, a matter which Mr Bagchi has tactfully avoided.

The question of currency values must also be considered, for it may mean little to read that a particular project cost Rs100,000 when there is no measure of its comparative worth. As may be expected with matters Asian, the problem to overcome is not as simple as it appears, for the value of the rupee fluctuated against the British pound. The cost of living in India compared to that in contemporary Britain must also be considered, and there are enough factors inside that equation to be taken into account to make a book in its own right! The monthly salary in the 1880s for an assistant supervisor in a tea garden could amount to Rs100, whilst a *khansamah* (butler) or a *bawarchi* (cook) in domestic service would be paid Rs10 and a *bheesti* (water carrier) was considered lucky to earn a meagre Rs5; the exchange rate for 1 rupee was approximately 10 pence. The wages paid for comparable work had doubled by 1930 and the rupee was valued at approximately 1/6d = 7$\frac{1}{2}$ pence; the ability to pay for domestic staff may be judged by a young civilian with 9 years' service as a district officer, married and with 1 child would have earned £120.00 a month (Rs600). To simplify matters, I have reduced many of the costs quoted to decimal.

The distances on the DHR were originally measured in miles from Siliguri and marked in red on small oval discs attached to iron stanchions along the route, whilst those on the Cart Road were painted in black. All Indian Railway timetables today, and indeed most road maps, denote distances in kilometres, although there appears to be an indiscriminate use of imperial and metric when it comes to heights above sea level. The maps produced by the Surveyor General of India during the time of the Raj recorded Siliguri as being 393 feet above sea level. More recent documents have argued the case that the correct height when converted from metric should be 500 feet, and I was persuaded to use this measurement in the original book. The strategic sensitivity of the area and the threat of terrorist insurgency makes detailed maps of the area now extremely difficult to obtain, and the consensus of opinion has reverted to accepting the details as recorded on the earlier ones.

The custom in the UK of classifying trains running to the capital as 'Up' and those leaving as 'Down' was not applied by the Raj to India, which had established its own capital in Calcutta before moving it to Delhi in 1911. Each Province and State also had its own capital city, and with the railways crossing such a patchwork of administrations, it would have been a nightmare to try and apply the same terminology. The broad–gauge 'Darjeeling Mail' from Sealdah (Calcutta) to Siliguri was always referred to as the Up train, and it followed suit with the DHR service to Darjeeling. When it came to the two extension lines, trains that ran from Siliguri to Kishenganj were the Up service, as were those climbing the Teesta Valley to Gielle Khola.

The station layouts that appear in the book are not drawn to scale; they show the railway as recollected in the 1940s and have been constructed from the hand-drawn maps of Mr Dikshit and a few faded photographs. The map of the DHR (2005) and those of the Extensions and towns (circa 1930) are closer to scale, and the symbols used conform with those used by the office of the Surveyor General of India.

Foreword

I first travelled on the DHR in 1941. I was a mere five-year-old making my way to a boarding school in Darjeeling, a hill station renowned for growing 'the champagne of teas'. Because of the war we British children could not be sent 'back home' for our schooling, but something had to be done because Doctors did not advise keeping Children in Calcutta through the hot weather. The answer the parents found was to set up a special school for us in cool, and at times of year bitterly cold, Darjeeling.

I remember weeping copiously as we drove to catch the broad–gauge Darjeeling Mail from Calcutta's Sealdah Station. Spurred on by the fear of appearing to be a 'sissy', I managed to curtail this to the occasional snivel as we rattled through the night. By the time we reached Siliguri to board the DHR for the climb up to Darjeeling I was ready to enjoy one of the world's most remarkable journeys, my status considerably enhanced by the fact that my father was a director of the railway. I still have the gold tiepin shaped like a Kukri or Gurkha knife which is engraved on the back 'DHR Pass No.73 Director'.

One of the older children who travelled in our special train remembers that the DHR carriages were 'quite out of date and looked old and worn out'. But apparently this had been put right by the time we came down the mountain. I do remember my astonishment when the train stopped and went backwards at the first zig-zag designed to overcome a particularly steep section of the climb. The older children got out and scrambled up the mountainside to board the train again after it had completed this complicated manoeuvre. For much of the way we were accompanied by young boys running alongside the train laughing and shouting 'baksheesh'. Vendors jumped on and off too. When we stopped for refreshments at Kurseong we slipped away to see a chemist's unusual way of attracting business. He kept a two-headed lamb preserved in a large bottle of formaldehyde in his shop window.

On the journey back home the train was sometimes held up by monsoon landslides. One of the children at school with me remembers the train proceeding even more slowly than usual over some very unstable track relaid through the rubble of a landslide. Labourers were lying on their stomachs and shouting to their overseer the number of any sleeper which wobbled. My strongest memory of coming down the mountain is reaching the plains and the final short flat section of the DHR. It was dark, the frogs were croaking, the crickets clacking, the train seemed to be going at a vast speed after its laborious descent from Darjeeling, and we knew we really were on the way home now – only one night to go.

Even in those far–distant days road transport was threatening the DHR. Some parents booked seats for their children on the Mail Bus, which took half the time, and some even hired taxis. Since then of course road transport has turned the DHR, which once earned higher receipts per mile than almost all the mighty broad-gauge lines, into a financial burden on Indian Railways. It goes greatly to their credit that they have nevertheless kept the DHR running. Now UNESCO has recognised this pioneering mountain railway as a World Heritage Site and Indian Railways have committed themselves to making it worthy of that status. So it looks as though this will be one narrow-gauge railway that road transport won't be able to kill off. But if Indian Railways are to allocate the resources required to return the DHR to its former glory, it's up to all of us who love railways to support them. So I am delighted to write the introduction to another book by Terry Martin, which will deepen all his readers' commitment to the DHR.

Sir Mark Tully

Introduction

There is no gradual approach to the Himalaya. It is sudden and immediate, and as if by way of defiance, there is the *terai* that must be crossed before the awesome ascent begins. A dripping, vaporous forest sown together by entangling vines, it provides a home for the elephant, tiger and panther, as well as a multitude of things that fly, slither and crawl across its hot, damp valleys. They guard the gateway to the highest mountains on earth, and it was with good reason that the area struck fear into the heart of early travellers.

If a railway was to be built to Darjeeling, then it would have to pass through the *terai*, and it was essential that the track was laid as quickly as possible with the minimum of fuss. The work was undertaken simultaneously at several sites alongside a road, which had already been constructed for bullock carts and provided a route through the steaming jungle. Travellers' reports from the early days on the train recalled that a log of resinous wood would be attached to the locomotive chimney to light the way at night, whilst fearless coolies riding at the front would be armed with buckets of stones to ward off stray animals. It was said that a lost race of giants also lived in the area and that it was the haunt of the *churail*, a ghost that had taken the female form and fallen in love with one of the locomotive drivers. The phantom used to wait for the train and travel with him, sometimes riding at the front of the locomotive and on other occasions by sitting on the roof of the guard's carriage, depending on her mood. And if that was not enough there were *nats* to avoid, the spiritual beings that lived in the trees and were said to be always on the lookout to obtain possession of the human body.

It was therefore with some misgivings that I ventured into the *terai* one February night in 2005 to photograph the evening dining-car special that had been chartered by the Darjeeling Himalayan Railway Society. The drama and mystery of the forest had come alive after dusk, but Uttam, my driver, refused point blank to leave the car and busied himself rearranging the plastic gods and offerings that dangled from the mirror or were glued to the dashboard altar.

The darkness fell like a net as I left the car and walked along the silent track, lit only by the moon and a few stars that had come out. The anxious exhaust of No. 780 could be heard in the vague distance, panting and breathless before it delved into a cutting or disappeared behind a bend with its train, leaving only the sounds of the forest to take over. It was not long before the whistle cut through the gossip of the cicadas and whatever was rustling the leaves and, when the train came into view, a flare of crimson cast spectacular shadows through the trees as the firebox door was opened and more coal was laid on the flames. There were no lights on the locomotive, for any watts that were being generated by the steam turbine were being directed to the carriages, leaving one of the sanders at the front to rely on a flickering torch to contest any territorial dispute that might arise with the wildlife. With a gathering excitement the train pounded past me, the sparks from the chimney racing into the night sky as it worked its way up the darkened slopes to Rangtong. I knew at that moment there was no place better to be in the world.

It was my research into this extraordinary railway that had brought me back to India, for the original edition of *'Halfway to Heaven'* had been a key that opened the door to more long-forgotten archival material, as well as many delightful and evocative recollections from those whose lives had been woven into its history. But then I had also shared the agony with others over the frustrations of more recent times, for the answers to the problems the DHR was enduring seemed so simple from the comfort of my own desk. It is the way with India, and I was making the fundamental mistake of putting my values and aspirations into another culture. I knew the Railway, but I had yet to understand it.

The decision had to be made from which point the story should begin ... and from when. Siliguri was the original terminus of the three lines, but the history of the settlement has remained elusive, although references on maps can certainly be traced back to the early part of the 19th century. The mountain terminus at Darjeeling is the best known, but there were in fact two Darjeelings, the first being a small and thriving community built round the monastery founded by the Sikkimese monk *Dorje* in 1756. It had been abandoned by 1827, and was reclaimed by the forest until the British found the overgrown site three years later. The terminus of the branch line that ran up the Teesta valley was at Gielle Khola, but that fell short of anywhere that could lay claim to be a natural point by 1½ miles, and at its busiest evolved into little more than a collection of wooden huts that shared a name. It is not mentioned in any books today, let alone those from the past, and the nearest town with any historical reference was 3,000ft higher and 6 miles away at Kalimpong.

For the earliest date one must turn to Kishenganj, the terminus of the branch that was so vernacular, none of its travellers had the inclination to photograph it. Over the years it had become too easy to dismiss the sun-burnt villages of the plains in favour of the mountains, for how could such dust-blown scrub be of any interest other than to the native farmer scratching a living? Here too the story would have been lost but for James Sinclair, whose family history in the area can be traced back to 1555. He had been sent to Darjeeling for his schooling in the 1950s, and his affection for the train that took him there each term led him to the first edition of this book. Kishenganj is therefore my *terminus a quo*, the point at which the story begins, and it falls conveniently close to the time the British first made their tentative steps into India with trade.

Indeed, it has been the account of James' remarkable family that led me to appreciate I could not divorce the story of the Railway from that of the British Raj and its demise, nor of the challenges that were to be faced by India as a self-governing nation. It therefore seemed only right to consider how the political changes affected the fortunes of Darjeeling and its railway, which often became a battle of wills if not arms. Such a contest of principles inevitably impacted on daily life, and the personal experience of everybody who has come into contact with the DHR is part of its history.

The help that everybody has given me with the research has been profound, and my appreciation is recorded in the acknowledgements at the start of this book. But for those who never knew British India, it can be difficult to understand the impact that the Railway had for those living in the hills, and with this in mind it is fitting that I should also mention Betty Shaw here. Her husband James was arguably one of the greatest General Managers who worked on the line, and she has recalled the life and times of those who saw the DHR through the Second World War and when India smelt the sweetness of independence. Her first-hand knowledge of events during this period has been quite exceptional, whilst her friendship has been symbolic of the incomparable bonds this railway can forge.

The same must be said for Nigel Plackett, for his father Geoffrey was the General Manager who proceeded Jimmy Shaw, and it was his quiet and determined resolve that enabled the railway to survive and modernise itself in the face of the encroaching war. It is a testament to the respect that his staff held for him that they corresponded by post long after the family had returned to the UK. It would be equally iniquitous if I did not also mention Gwen Cattermull, whose father Bruce Ellis moved his family to Kurseong in 1924 to escape the gruelling heat of Calcutta. He worked on the DHR as the Assistant Traffic Superintendent until 1936, when the economic climate caused staff to be laid off and he obtained employment on the South India Railway. One can imagine the surprise when Gwen received a telephone call over sixty years later from her childhood friend in Kurseong, Pat Orr, whose father George Batterbury had joined the DHR in 1911. Pat has been able to breathe life into his memories, for he became the Assistant Engineer responsible for the construction of the lines to Kishenganj and up the Teesta Valley. He rose to the position of Resident Engineer by 1924 and held the post until 1942, when he moved to Burma to work under Lt. General 'Bill' Slim on the Rangoon–Mandalay Railway.

No history of the DHR would be complete without reference to Mr Banshidhar Dikshit, an extraordinary man who had worked for the Railway as a Permanent Way Inspector from 1942 to 1972; at the age of 92, he readily accompanied me on forays into the Teesta Valley to exhume buried treasures of the extension line that once ran up that stunning valley. Ably assisted by his son Sushil, he enthusiastically answered a barrage of questions that anybody half his age would have grown weary from, and the station layouts and track plans for the two extension lines would have been lost for ever had it not been for the sketches he kindly undertook for the book. His recollections have been of immense value, and I thank both him and Sushil with great affection.

Before the outbreak of hostilities, British parents would often send their children back to the UK for their education, but this practice was brought to an abrupt halt by the theatre of war that was raging in Europe. The best schools in India were invariably regarded as those up in the hills, but they were already full and unable to accommodate the influx of children now having to return from Britain. It led to the establishment of the New School in Calcutta in 1940, but barely a year had passed when even that had to withdraw to the safety of Darjeeling, as a precautionary measure against the Japanese army advancing through the Burmese jungle. So it was that a young Mark Tully travelled with his two sisters on the train to their boarding school, immensely proud that their father was a Director of Gillanders Arbuthnot, the Managing Agents of the DHR. After completing his studies at Cambridge University in the UK, Mark Tully returned to the country of his birth to become the India correspondent of the BBC, a position which he held for the next 22 years. It was through his reports and writing that his deep understanding of the complexities of life in the sub-continent became legendary, and from where he brought the heart of India to the conscience of the world. The applause for his knighthood in the New Year's Honours list was heard across the land, and I was very moved when he kindly agreed to contribute the Foreword to this revised edition. It appears in two volumes, the first focusing on the history of the railway, leaving the second to concentrate on a description of the line, its operation, the locomotives and rolling stock.

It is with immense pride that in 2006 Indian Railways celebrated the 125-year anniversary of the opening of its remarkable railway to Darjeeling, and it is to this date that I have arrived at my *terminus ad quem*, the point at which the story must close.

Dedication

To Betty Shaw and the memory of my two great mentors
Peter Bawcutt and Fred Pinn.

Contents

Acknowledgements	5
By Way of Explanation	7
Foreword	10
Introduction	11
Chapter 1 – A Monarchy of Merchantmen	15
Chapter 2 – Rails on the Road	33
Chapter 3 – The Iron Sherpa	59
Chapter 4 – Nature Takes Revenge	87
Chapter 5 – Investment & Improvement	111
Chapter 6 – Summits of Achievement	143
Chapter 7 – War & Attrition	175
Chapter 8 – The Restless Dream	207
Chapter 9 – The Pendulum of Politics	235
Extending the Lines – An Introduction	259
Chapter 10 – The Kishenganj Extension	265
Chapter 11 – The Teesta Valley Extension	291
Chapter 12 – Great Expectations	321
Afterword	353
Bibliography	361
Index	362

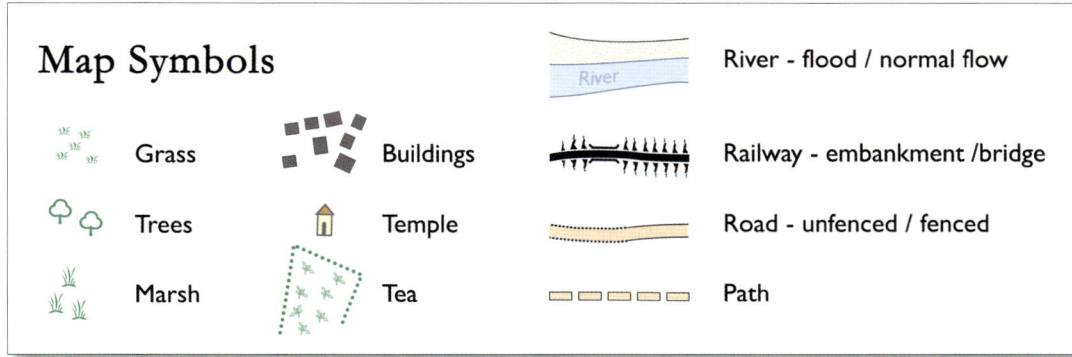

Chapter 1
A Monarchy of Merchantmen

India has never been easy to understand, and over the centuries its ever-changing face has been obliged to adapt to the rule of empires based on religion, superstition and commerce. It has survived them all, whilst most of the controlling dynasties have become little more than echoes of its history.

The second of the great Mughal Emperors was Humayan, who ruled India from 1530 until his defeat in 1539 by the Afghan opposition led by Sher Shah. Revered by some and dismissed by others as a soldier of fortune, Sher Shah held on to the Delhi throne until his death in 1545. There followed a period of disorder and confusion as his descendants fought over who was to rule, until at the bequest of Humayan, the Shah of Persia sent an armed force to restore the former ruler to the seat of power in 1555.

The Persian army was led by Syed Khan Dastur and after the successful campaign was asked by the Emperor to sort out a long-standing problem of lawlessness in the *pargana*[1] of Surajpur, which lay on the east bank of the Mahananda River. It had fallen into Nepalese control under Rana Sukhdeo, and was known for the merciless outlaws who robbed and terrorised anybody who ventured into the area. Khan Dastur established his headquarters in what is now Kishenganj, and successfully drove the Nepalese back into the hills of Mowrang. In recognition of his valour, the Emperor granted him the 729 square miles of conquered territory free of revenue, and conferred him with the title *Raja* and the appointment of being the *Kanungo*, the dictator of the law.

The eventual decline of the Mughal Empire in India did not lead to its being immediately replaced by another dominating power. However, it had enabled European traders to extend their authority, and none had grasped the nettle with so much determination as the English. A Royal Charter had already been granted by Elizabeth I for the formation of the East India Company in 1600, and as long as there was a profit to be made, it was of little concern to them who worshipped what and when.

Nevertheless, a considerable part of India was now coming directly under its influence, and the business of the Company was not without its jealousies and resentments. Indeed, it came under severe criticism with its failure to recognise the customs and beliefs that had evolved over countless generations, believing that British education and values were the answers for India and her problems. It also had to recognise that the Dutch, Portuguese and French still had their fingers very much in the pie; whilst some of the Princely States stood fast and retained their independence, some were simply not worth the trouble of pursuing for trade, and some were in the Himalaya, the highest mountain range on Earth.

Sandwiched between Nepal, Tibet and Bhutan, the wild mountains of Sikkim had been invaded and occupied by everybody who thought it was possible to rule over its proud and courageous people. The eastern lands were eventually lost to the Bhutanese in 1706 and the Gorkhas overran the rest in 1780, after establishing their control and sovereignty in Nepal. The Gorkhas (often referred to by the anglicised form Gurkha) had taken their name from a small town to the west of Kathmandu and became one of the dominant races of

---

[1] A division of an administrative district in India.

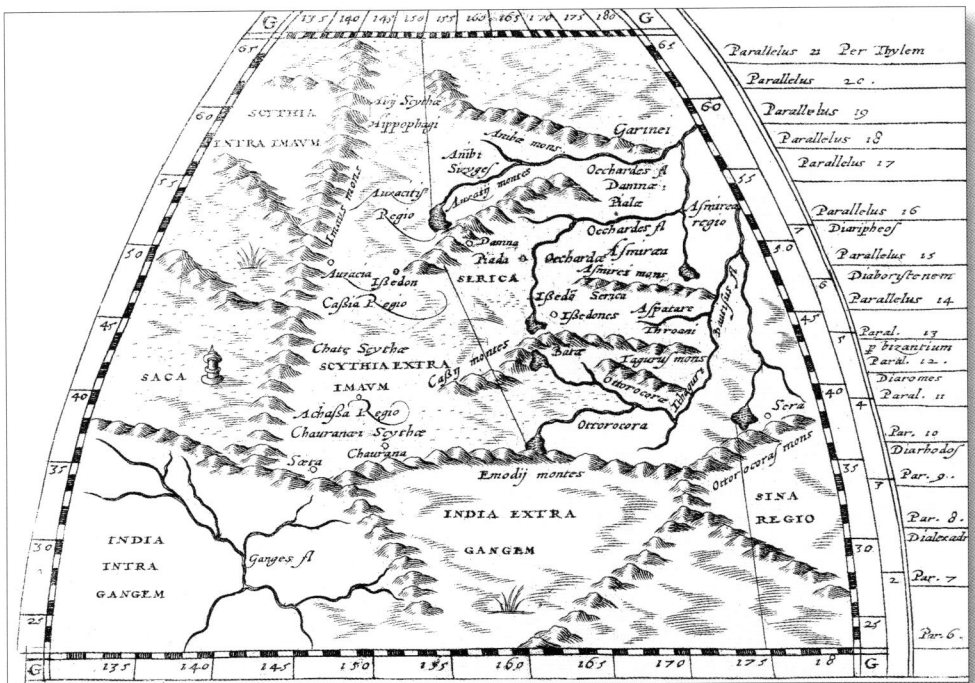

Taken from the earliest printed pocket-size atlas to show India and the Himalayan source of the Ganges, this map from the Magini/Porro edition of Ptolemy's Geographia was published in Köln by Petrus Keschedt in 1597. Although produced some 1,450 years after its creator, it still referred to a landlocked Indian Ocean and the north-south range of mountains in Central Asia that Ptolemy called 'Imavm' (placed nearly 40° too far east) which divided the ancient country of Scythia in two.

Collection: (The late) Fred Pinn

Nepal. In 1768 the Gorkha warrior Prithvi Narayan Shah conquered the Malla kings of the Kathmandu valley and claimed the title King of Nepal. He continued to extend his territory until he died in 1774, after which his descendants continued a policy of expansion. They had their eye on Tibet but were held in check by the Chinese, and as a consequence turned their attention south. This brought them into conflict with the British in 1813, which resulted in their defeat after a number of battles over the following three years, and the land was finally returned to the Chogyal of Sikkim under the Treaty of Titalya, signed on 10th February 1817.

History has remained silent regarding the first approach made by the British to the area, but one of the earliest references is to be found in the mid-1820s from the diaries of a Mrs Fenton. Bessie Campbell had married a Captain by the name of Fenton, but within five months of arriving in India became widowed and sought refuge with a visit to her cousin Frank Gouldsbury, the Magistrate of Malda.[2] Mrs Lamb was the local doctor's wife, and as such was well placed to introduce Bessie Fenton back to the sectarian delights of society life within the British Raj. It was on such an occasion that she met the Commercial Resident, Captain James Grant, confiding to her diary her admiration for him and of the time he had spent painting in the 'hills'. Grant was to later write of his expedition in 1826, when he took his daughter to a place where she could see the mountain of Kanchenjunga. Nepal was a closed country, as was Bhutan, leaving the only remaining area that he could have visited being around Darjeeling, a name that makes claim to a number of explanations.

It is widely accepted that it came from the Tibetan words *Dorje* (the thunderbolt of Indra, the Hindu god of the firmament and rain) and *ling* (place), the belief being that Indra's sceptre fell on the summit now known as Observatory Hill. A Buddhist Gompa had been built in 1756 on the flattened part of the mountain ridge close to the summit as a branch of the Dorling Monastery in Sikkim, it being named after the founder Lama, Dorje-Ling-pa. Indeed, it is possible that the name may be traced further back in time, for Dorje Lingpa was the name of a Nyimapa Lama from the Tang Valley in Bumthang (central Bhutan) who became a famous *Terton*, a 'treasure revealer' who lived during the 14th century.

The original inhabitants of Sikkim are the Lepchas, and it is not unreasonable to expect they also hold claim to the name. Their legend states that Rum (God) created a boy and a girl from two handfuls of snow taken from the summit of Kanchenjunga, and though technically brother and sister, divine intervention had allowed them to become the mother and father of the Lepchas, the Rong-pa. A less spiritual account divides the Lepchas into two families, the Rong and the Khamba, the tradition being the Rong were natives of Sikkim and the Khamba having come across the

---

[2] A town that had given its name to an administrative district some 350 kms north of Calcutta.

snowy ranges from Tibet at the beginning of the 17th century. Rong is the language of the Lepchas, in which the word *Dar-Zu-Lyang* translates as '*the abode of the heavenly goddess of beauty*'.

A Lepcha village had certainly grown around to the northwest of the Dorje-Ling monastery, and developed into quite a sizeable community with a small bazaar. It subsequently became a Gorkha cantonment after the Nepalese established their control over the area in 1788 under the command of Jar Singh, and appointed the Lepcha chief known as Roop Chiring as their local governor and tax collector. The monastery was destroyed, and when later rebuilt was moved to its current site at Bhutia Busti during the time of Pon-lop Lhon-dhup. The ruins became a place of great sanctity for Buddhists, and to this day are marked by prayer flags and offerings to the guardian of the temple who was supposed to have lived there before Man.

The hill has also become known as Mahakal Baba Ko Sthan in more recent times, and it has been claimed that the larger of the two caves found on the western side has been an auspicious site for Hindu pilgrims since at least 1815. Sardar Bahadur S.W. Laden La was the great-grandnephew of Dorje-Ling-pa and drafted a report on 9th May 1912 regarding the founding of the Buddhist monastery. He recalled that in the mid-1880s very few other than Buddhists would worship at the old site, although an occasional Nepalese would be seen sacrificing goats and pigeons, the practice being strictly against Buddhism. By the turn of the century he noted that three Hindu *jogis* were occupying the upper cave and were turned out by the police for reasons that were not made clear. Soon afterwards Marwaris, Biharis, Bengalis and other plainsmen were seen offering sweets, pan leaves and nuts, whilst others were seen placing money in front of the figured stones, after which many began to visit of a night to worship Mahakal Baba.

It is contended that the cave contained a stone that represented the destructive aspect of the god Shiva, which was revered as Mahakal the Great Destroyer, or Durjaylinga the Unconquerable. This led to the claim that the town owes its name to the latter, but on examination it appears that the word is indeed a fabrication that was concocted during the 1940s.

This has cast a suspicion over the story, and it probably arose from Hindu fundamentalists setting out their stakes for ownership of the territory in the fading days of the Raj as India was approaching independence. It was said that the stone was subsequently taken from the cave and resited on a mound close to the top of the hill, which some have suggested would have made it convenient when searching for a suitable rock to worship. A much older legend held that the entrance led to a secret underground passage, the three sacred caves of Sikkim and eventually to Lhasa, although it seems nobody has been that intent on disturbing the myth and undergrowth by actually trying it.

Although there are shadows over the early records, it is probable that the Lepchas were still there in 1826 when James Grant was in Darjeeling, but they soon abandoned the settlement in fear of the reputation the Chogyal had for inflicting cruelty and suffering. In 1828, Captain Grant was sent back to the Darjeeling area by the Governor General Lord William Bentick, and was to be accompanied by Captain Lloyd to assess and report on the potential it had as a sanatorium for the military employees of the East India Company. Captain Lloyd was the British Representative, and had been given the brief to sort out a border dispute that had flared up between Sikkim and Nepal.

Although it was not openly declared at the time, it was recognised that the Darjeeling site had a strategic importance with the frontier of Tibet, whilst there would be the additional bonus of its being an ideal mountain retreat for the officials of Calcutta to escape from the summer heat. The British had previously made an attempt to use Cherrapunji in Assam as a sanatorium, but many saw its failing by being the wettest place on Earth with an average annual rainfall of 1,150cms (just over 37ft),[3] whilst others recognised the indigenous right of property and wealth passing through the female line of families as potentially contentious!

Grant was asked to return to Darjeeling in February 1830 with Captain James Dowling Herbert to make a geological evaluation. Herbert had served with the Bengal Infantry in the Nepalese Wars, after which he established a respected career surveying the Himalaya and the upper sources of the Ganges, which culminated in his promotion to the position of Deputy Surveyor General in 1829. It took thirteen days for Grant and Herbert to get to the overgrown site from Calcutta, travelling by *dak*, elephant and finally on foot. They found the village still deserted, but learned of the twelve hundred Lepchas who were now living in the supposed sanctuary of Nepalese territory. Led by their chief Eclatoe, the community had been branded as outcasts, for the ruling Gorkhas were strict Hindus and had subjected them to acute prejudice and many prohibitions. Anxious to return to Darjeeling, the

---

[3] The United Kingdom has an average of 61 cms/24 inches per anum.

Lepchas endeavoured to seek a guarantee of safety from the British, but the Gorkhas realised their value and prevented them from establishing any dialogue.

To add to their problems, the pitiless Chogyal had Cazi Barajit (the brother of Eclatoe) and his family murdered. One son was spared, and he was held in confinement as bait to lure the Lepchas back. It was an act of betrayal and treachery, for Cazi Barajit had provided the Chogyal with protection and provisions when previously invaded by the Gorkhas. It only served to make the Lepchas more resolute in returning to Darjeeling, for they now claimed to have sufficient numbers to drive the Chogyal out of the country. It was a brave statement, but they were not convinced of British impartiality with the problem and were understandably nervous of any dealings with Sikkim over the territory.

Grant and Herbert spent two days at the site, but the weather was not in their favour. Clouds obscured most of the area and it was difficult to map out the exact nature of the surroundings. Despite the conditions, they were convinced the climate would be the perfect antidote to Calcutta and reported that '… *water was plentiful and not too distant*', and that they '… *found ample room, even for a small town*'. Their only disappointment was not being able to take sightings and readings of the mountains, particularly with Kanchenjunga, which had been previously

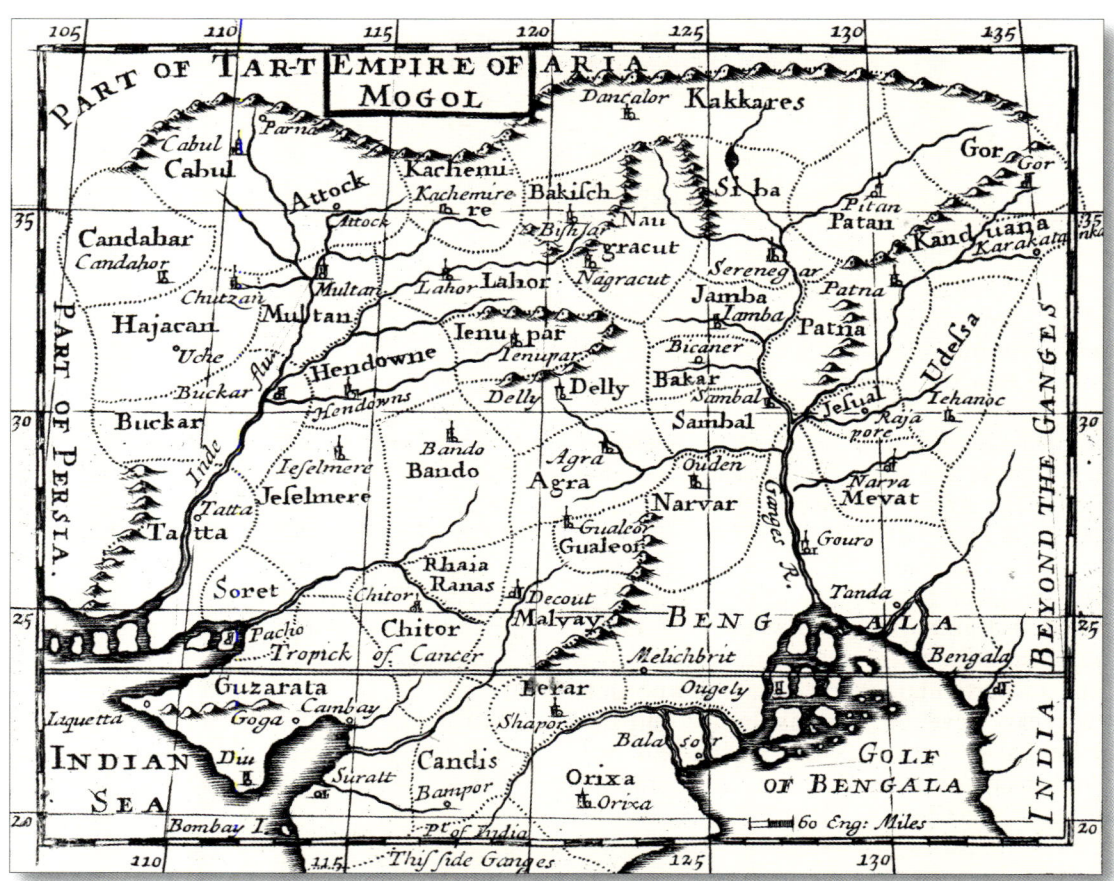

Drawn by John Seller in 1679, this map of the Mughal Empire in India shows there had been considerable progress with cartography since the arrival of the Europeans. The location of Delhi, Agra and other towns on the plains was beginning to be identified with some accuracy, but the whereabouts of known sites in the mountainous north were highly speculative and often misplaced. Details based on hearsay were liable to misinterpretation, whilst the English direction to bear left or right was mystifying to many natives and some Indian language directions did not translate adequately into English. Note that Calcutta had not yet been established, for it was not until 1686 that the British moved their warehouse downstream from Ougely (Hooghly) to the three unmarked villages of Kalikata, Sutanuti and Govindpur and set up a trading base.

Collection: (The late) Fred Pinn

A very early photograph of Observatory Hill, with the remains of the monastery built in 1756 still in evidence close to the tree on the flattened part of the ridge. The building had been destroyed in 1788 after being overrun by the Nepalese and was later resited at Bhutia Busti.

Collection: Nick Rhodes, ex Das Studios

speculated as a 27,000 ft-high volcano! However, they could see Darjeeling would be an ideal stage for the British sanatorium and submitted their findings to the Directors of the East India Company in Calcutta.

Lloyd was given the authority to negotiate with the Chogyal to purchase the site or grant available land in exchange for the strip of territory, which included the villages of Kurseong and Darjeeling. Sikkim wanted the area around Debgong in return, but this had already been given to the Rajah of Jalpaiguri. The Chogyal would not be moved, and went on to make an additional claim for the return of slaves who had escaped, and in particular one accountant who had fled with two years' revenue. The East India Company could not be party to this as the slaves had not offended English law, and saw the matter as a domestic dispute between the Chogyal and his servants. The situation reached a position of stalemate and Lloyd, as the British Representative, was instructed to cease negotiations.

However, Colonel Lloyd (as he now was) was apt to overshoot his authority with his boundless enthusiasm for the area, and turned a deaf ear. He arranged a further meeting with the Chogyal, which was somewhat cautiously conducted as both parties took up residence on their respective sides of the riverbank forming the border between their two lands. It became a game of bluff and assumption, which resulted in the Chogyal agreeing to hand over Darjeeling in the belief that he would be granted his original demands.

Lloyd produced a document that determined the boundaries within which he intended to build the sanatorium, but it was without the sanction of the British Government. It was made on the premise that the Chogyal would change his mind and opt for something else in return besides Debgong and the hapless servants. Lloyd had previously been instrumental in sorting out the frontier trouble between Sikkim and the Nepalese, and was hopeful he could now call in a favour and pave the way for a deal to secure Darjeeling.

The Chogyal sent the document back in February 1835, some six months after the negotiations had began. It was endorsed with his official seal, and surprisingly handed over the Darjeeling area free of charge. The motives behind this unexpected move are not clear, but it was probably an attempt by the Chogyal to twist the arm of the Company into agreeing to his terms by playing on the custom of exchanging presents. Lloyd kept the document for a further six months before submitting it to Calcutta, presenting the situation as a *fait accompli* and having obtained the territory for nothing.

The British Government was taken aback, for it had assumed the instruction to cease all negotiations had been observed. There had been a change of Governor General at the time, and the new holder of

An engraving from 'The Journal of a Tour in India' by Captain Mundi in 1832 captures the spirit of travelling by 'dak' as would have been experienced during the expedition undertaken by Captains Grant and Herbert from Calcutta to the overgrown site of Darjeeling.

Collection: (The late) Fred Pinn

the position had not been briefed on the custom of exchanging presents. In the winter of 1836, the East India Company sent Lloyd with a Dr Chapman back to Darjeeling for a year, and from their experience to compile a report on what life was like and assess its suitability for the convalescence of its military and civilian personnel. They endured severe cold during their early days, but it was no surprise to find their submission in 1838 recommended that a sanatorium should be set up. Invitations were made for private developers to build property and the Government of India directed that all quit rents[4] paid by settlers would be deposited into an account known as the Location Fund and used to improve the area.

Lieutenant Napier of the Royal Engineers (who later became Lord Napier of Magdala) was given the task of aligning a forty-mile road to connect Darjeeling with the plains. The construction began in 1839 and was completed by 1842 at the cost of Rs800,000 and many lives, for there had been scant regard for the provision of food and accommodation for the workers. The road climbed steeply from the deadly *terai* forests near Sukna by a route that crossed nearly three hundred bridges before reaching Kurseong, after which it ran along the mountain ridges to Jor Bungalow and Darjeeling. It was known as the Military Road, although the section to Kurseong was often referred to as the Pankabari Road after the *pankas*, the leaf-fans used at the *dak* bungalow.

The entrepreneurs were not slow in seeing the potential offered by the clearing of the forest and the construction of the road, and work began immediately in 1839 with the building of a hotel for visitors. Known as the Darjeeling Family Hotel, it had 14 single and 7 double rooms, with the advertisement promising that '... *it would be conducted upon the same principle as those of the fashionable watering places of Europe, and our charges will be for Board at the Table d'Hote and Lodging, 150 rupees per month per person (excluding wine)*'. It was managed by D. Wilson & Co., who had been so inspired by the introduction of the horse-drawn bus in London that

---

[4] Small rents paid by freeholders or copyholders in lieu of service; in effect a ground rent.

they made plans to introduce a similar service to the new hill station. However, the *dak-ghari* was little more than a four-wheeled box pulled by ponies in ten-mile stages across the Indian plains, and although it was relatively fast, it occasionally took bundles of straw to be lit underneath the animals to induce them into action! Even with such drastic measures, the Military Road was way beyond their capabilities, and Wilson's notion for a bus service faded on the wind.

Lloyd's eagerness remained unchecked, and on his own authority he issued a proclamation in the name of the Governor General to invite all those who had fled to Nepal in 1827 to return to Darjeeling. Calcutta was furious, and was pushed to breaking point when he sanctioned approximately Rs8,000 of Government money to set up a bazaar without keeping any accounts of the finances. He was sacked from his position in June 1839 and returned to his Infantry unit, after which he was sent to China.

Although Darjeeling consisted of barely thirty private houses at the time, Dr Campbell of the Indian Medical Service was transferred from Kathmandu as the first Superintendent and British Agent for the new settlement. It fell to Campbell to attract new settlers, and it is said that a Nepalese nobleman named Sri Dakman Rai arrived in Darjeeling with a caravan of twenty pack-ponies loaded with food and a retinue of servants. The evidence is yet to be corroborated, but it is claimed that he met Campbell and agreed to help by encouraging thousands of immigrants to come from Nepal as the unskilled labour for the development of the new road and town. In return for his help he was granted the freehold of land that was to later become the tea estates of Soureni, Phuguri and Samripanee.

The progress of building in Darjeeling appears to have been slow, and in November 1840 a correspondent for the *Bengal Hurkaru* reported that:

> *'The only public building is the Superintendent's Cutcherry on the Dorjeling Hill, a neat wattle and daub bungalow with an iron roof. There is an allotment for a Church and spaces for public purpose but no appearance of appropriating them. A small fort or neat stockade on the crest of Dorjeling Hill, where there yet appears the remains of an old monastery, would be ornamental and useful. A good clock is much wanted to regulate the time of the station ... if Government cannot afford a good clock a good sundial would be very acceptable, and a morning and evening gun would be useful.'*

The suggestion to build a fort was not adopted, although it was interesting to note that the site was again being seen in terms of its strategic location. Quite what use a sundial would have been in view of the moods of the weather is unclear, but one was later presented to the town by a generous visitor, and a clock finally appeared when St Andrew's Church was rebuilt after being struck by lightning in September 1867.

It was not long before Dr Campbell noticed that nobody had actually bothered to translate the document issued by the Chogyal to Lloyd, who had previously told the Government he would have given Rs12,000 for the area. However, Lloyd did not reveal that he been nurturing his private intentions of planting tea, and with the Military Road now opening up the land for the British to develop its cultivation into a viable

'The Governor General having expressed a desire for the possession of the hill of Darjeeling on account of its cool climate, for the purpose of enabling the servants of his Government suffering from sickness to avail themselves of its advantages.

I, the Sikkimputee Rajah, out of friendship to the said Governor General, hereby present Darjeeling to the East India Company, that is all the land south of the Great Rangeet River, east of Balasum, Kahail and Little Rangit Rivers, and west of the Rungpee and Mahanuddy Rivers.'

Seal of the Rajah

Dated 9th Maugh, Sambat 1891 (A.D. 1835)

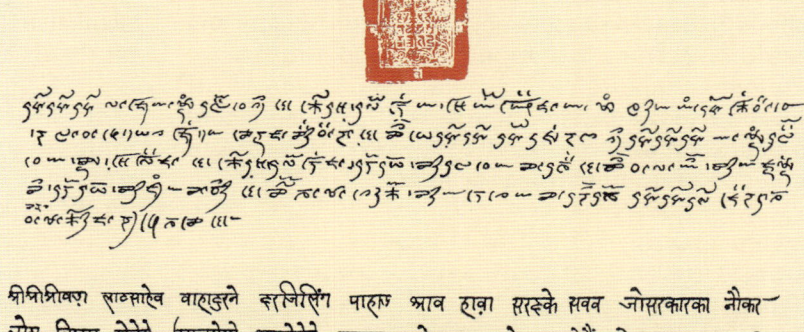

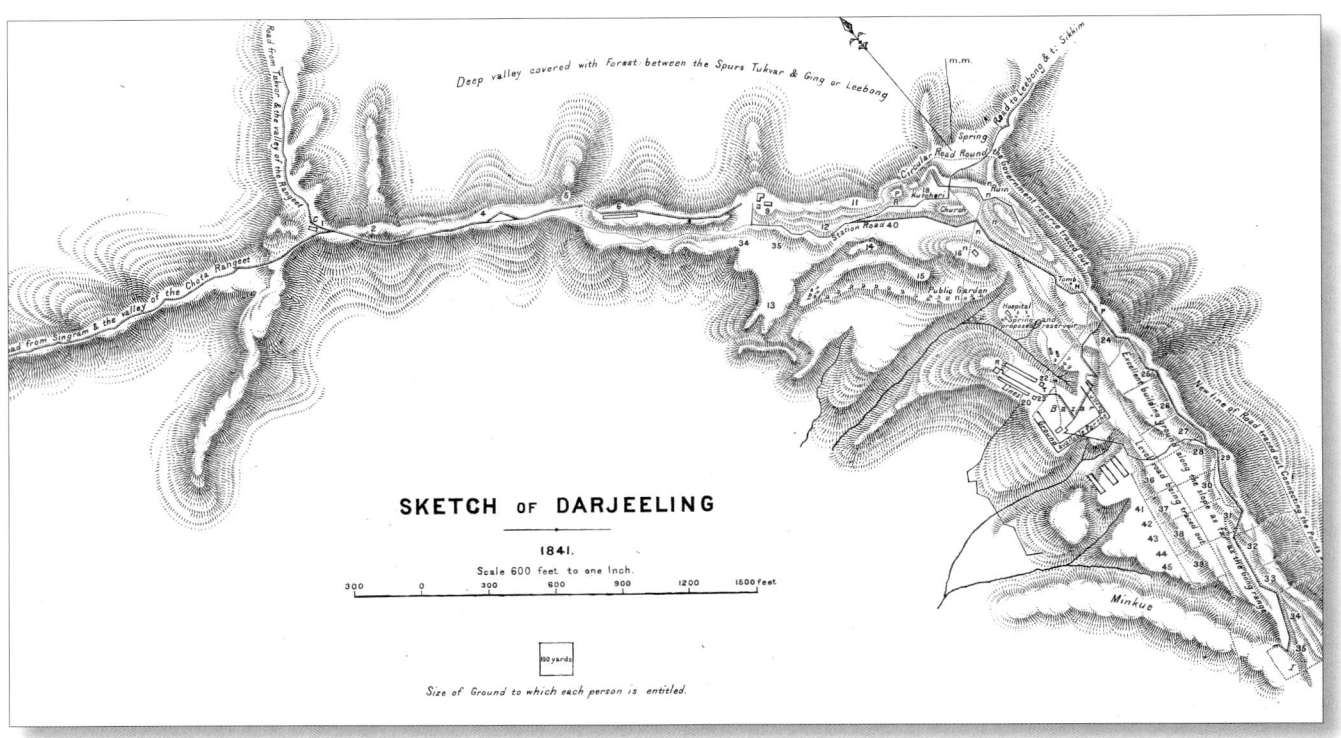

The demand to build houses in Darjeeling was slow at first, this map published in 1841 showing there were 45 plots of land, of which 43 had been taken by 32 settlers. Wilson's hotel was at site 6 and Dr Campbell's house at 26, although he spent the greater part of his life at 'Beechwood' built on sites 44 and 45. Current landmarks to assist with the orientation would include the DHR station in the bottom right-hand corner, Chowrasta at 'P' just above plot 24, and 'Ruin' being the site of the former monastery on Observatory Hill.

Collection: (The late) Fred Pinn

industry, more Nepalese workers were being attracted to the area in search of employment.

Tea bushes had been found growing wild in Assam in 1820, but it was the Chinese seeds from the Kumaon hills of northern India that Campbell brought to Darjeeling in 1841 and first planted in his garden at 'Beechwood'. Although it was not appreciated at the time, the consumption of tea had been making a considerable contribution to the health of the United Kingdom. The development of steam power during the Industrial Revolution had taken labour from the field to the factory, and the opening of the first railways enabled raw materials to be transported from the mines and ports to the new centres of production. As a consequence there was an alarming growth in the population of cities, but there had been little progress with an infrastructure to cope with the sewerage. Waterborne diseases were endemic, and the living conditions had made such an impact on the young Franklin Engels whilst visiting Manchester as a student from his native Germany, that it shaped his political vision for a utopian future. But despite the seemingly appalling situation, the health of workers in British cities was substantially better than their contemporaries on the European mainland. In fact it could only be compared to Japan, which paradoxically had shunned any industrialisation and had even rejected the use of the wheel for transport in its cities. The answer was found with the two countries being the major consumers of tea. It was not the boiling of the water, which would take a minimum of five minutes to kill the bacteria, but the powerful antiseptic properties the Chinese had long recognised the herb possessed.

Tea was vital for Campbell's ambitions, and he sought to appease the ageing Chogyal with the gesture of his long-awaited present, which comprised a double-barrelled gun, a rifle, a twenty-yard bale of cloth and two pairs of shawls. It was in everyone's interests that the matter should be amicably settled, and the Government agreed to an annual compensation payment of Rs3,000 for any revenue lost. Sikkim had received virtually no income from the land in the first place, but now the Chogyal wanted gold, not rupees, which prompted an exchange of letters from Campbell that were addressed in less than diplomatic terms. The Government recognised the potential that Darjeeling had and doubled the compensation payments to

Darjeeling in 1852 with Kanchenjunga dominating the skyline. A number of features can be identified from the 1841 map shown opposite, with Observatory Hill being noted centre right in the middle distance.

By permission of The British Library P389; 640(25)

Rs6,000, and at the same time forbade Campbell to issue any further correspondence without it going through them first.

Although settlers were hesitant in coming to Darjeeling, the population in the region was growing and by 1849 it had reached 10,000. The rise in fortunes brought jealousies and renewed tension with the Sikkimese, which came to a head when the naturalist Dr Joseph Hooker visited the area to pursue his botanical research. The Governor General specifically asked the Chogyal to grant him every assistance, but his brother-in-law Namgoway who was the *Dewan*,[5] placed every obstacle in his way that he could. Campbell joined Hooker to seek an interview with the Chogyal at Toomlong (then the capital of Sikkim) on 3rd November, but they were ignored and promptly arrested four days later. The Chogyal was not disappointed with the opportunity to settle his personal animosity with Campbell by having him imprisoned, although Hooker was still allowed to move around quite freely.

The British issued demands for their release, and sent troops to sort the matter out. The First Minister of Sikkim became anxious as soon as the military crossed the frontier at the Rungeet river in February 1850, and arranged for Campbell to be released and both men to be allowed home. Calcutta was incensed and felt that a lesson had to be taught by annexing 640 square miles of land around Darjeeling and terminating all further payments being made to the Chogyal, it being reported that four policemen from the Company had entered the Treasury and found it contained only six rupees!

The post of Governor General of India had been given to Lord Dalhousie in 1848, and one of his first acts was to create a Public Works Department to advance the construction of roads. However, mountains, vast rivers and chaotic weather impeded much of the progress and the Government saw the advantages that a railway system could make. The military could be moved

---

[5] The revenue collector, often referred to as the *Pagla Dewan*, the mad collector.

much more quickly than any road transport would allow, whilst the commercial implications would be enormous for crops and coal. The scourge of famine could also be challenged by relief trains, although in reality it was only of value if it occurred at the railhead as it was found that the oxen would eat more food than they could transport to the outlying villages, which somewhat defeated the objective!

The first steam locomotive to arrive in India came from England in 1851, and started work on 22nd December transporting clays and other materials from Piran Kaliar to Roorkee, ninety miles north–east of Delhi. It ran on the British standard gauge of 4ft 8½in and was used to assist with the construction of a canal aqueduct over the Solani river. The engine was named '*Thomason*' after the executive engineer who conceived the idea of employing steam traction. Its two wagons were loaded to a capacity of 180 to 200 tons, and it was said to cover the 2½ mile journey in 38 minutes. It remained operational for about 9 months until it caught fire one day in 1852, although to the relief of the engineers the aqueduct at least had been completed.

The Government was keen to attract private investment to railways that would open up India, and was obliged to adopt a policy of guaranteeing a percentage return to prospective shareholders. The land was often provided free as an added incentive, for there was some understandable reluctance with investing money into schemes where the profits could only be a vague guess. However, the Government insisted on clauses that would protect its interests by ensuring it would receive a half-share of any profit that exceeded 5% and that it had the right to purchase the railway after 25 or 30 years. The Great Indian Peninsular Railway Company was the first to be formed and was subscribed by British investors, the inaugural train running on 16th April 1853 from Bombay to Thana '*amidst the loud applause of a vast multitude and to the salute of 21 guns*'. The East Indian Railway Company was close on its heels, and by February 1855 was connecting Calcutta to the Raniganj coalfield.

The new railway companies were registered in London and most of the shares held in the UK. As such, the investment in the railways brought handsome profits for the British, and even by 1868 there were only 400 Indians who were shareholders. The romance of speculation had certainly attracted a number of investors in Calcutta with the formation of the Central Bengal Railway, but they had not been amused to read the local news report that: '*A splendid entertainment was given at the Town Hall by the promoters to celebrate the event. Shortly afterwards, the promoters and the money both disappeared.*'

The East India Company dictated the style and nature of the new lines to be built, and Lord Dalhousie wanted them laid with double track and wide spaces for the rivers to flood. It must be said that his wishes were not always complied with, and there had been problems with the wooden sleepers being enjoyed by

From its earliest days in Darjeeling, it was essential for the British Raj to maintain contact with Calcutta and the plains. The mail was initially carried in relays by dak-wallahs, and though the responsibility was subsequently passed to the DHR, the runners were invaluable when the weather caused landslides and suspended the train service.

Collection: (The late) Fred Pinn

an increasing population of white ants, although it was claimed that they were now being shaken out by the passing trains. Experiments were made with metal sleepers, but these tended to buckle in the extreme heat, and spikes had to be inserted to the base of telegraph poles to prevent them being pulled out by elephants who had learned they made excellent back-scratchers!

It appeared that India would reflect the industrial progress of Britain, but there were too many changes happening too quickly for a land that was steeped in centuries of traditions and beliefs. It was one thing changing the means of governing law and order, and India had been used to that long before the British had stepped on her territory, but now her physical appearance was being altered by public works, and in particular the railways. The seeds for social unrest had been unwittingly sown with land becoming annexed into the British sphere of administration, threatening the power and influence of many rulers. The reasons behind the Mutiny in 1857 are complex and beyond the scope of this book, but the outcome made a profound effect on the ways and means Britain was to exercise its power. It resulted in the East India Company being brought to an end, and the British Government taking direct control under a new system.

And so, with the stroke of a pen, the British Raj was created, and with Queen Victoria firmly in the driving seat, she appointed a Viceroy to replace the position previously held by the Governor General; it was a deliberate move that stated the significance with which the Monarch now regarded India. But her austerity was to give way to vanity when her eldest daughter married Frederick III, the future Emperor of Germany. As an Empress she would outrank her mother, a situation that would be unimaginable for the British Queen. As Prime Minister, Disraeli was to later proffer his devotion to his Monarch by manoeuvring the Royal Titles Bill through a reluctant Parliament in 1876, and thus elevated her status to being the Empress of India.

The development of public works took on a new impetus, and with the Military Road to Darjeeling having proved to be too narrow and steep for bullocks

The original road to Darjeeling was simply too steep for bullock carts, and anybody intent on travelling there in some degree of comfort was dependent on the dandy and palanquin.

Collection: (The late) Fred Pinn

to haul the loads, the authorisation was given in 1861 for a new road that would be suitable for wheeled traffic. A completely new route was surveyed and it took eight years to build the twenty-five-foot-wide Hill Cart Road from Siliguri to Darjeeling at a cost of £6,000 per mile.

The opening of the East Indian Railway from Howrah (Calcutta) to Sahibgunj in 1860 also made a distinct improvement to the journey for Darjeeling, although from there on it remained dependent on the moods of the Ganges and the ponderous nature of the bullocks. The first obstacle was the two miles from Sahibgunj station to the river crossing, which passed through a dense jungle inhabited by tigers and equally predatory robbers. Crossing the Ganges to Bhavanipur on the opposite bank would take a further five hours, followed by two miles on foot over a wide sandy bank to Karagola Ghat. From here most travellers secured the services of the Darjeeling Bullock Cart Train Company or its rival Bird & Company, both of whom operated caravans of ten to twelve bullock carts. They were often run together to offer mutual support for the many difficulties encountered along the way, and would be accompanied by an armed guard equipped with armour and spikes. Departing Karagola at 4.00pm, the convoy was expected to arrive at Purnea at 10.00am the following morning, and after crossing the Mahananda River, be in Kishenganj the same evening. Siliguri would be reached around 11.00am on the second morning with an overnight stay at Gayabari, before passing through Kurseong during the middle of the third day and finally pulling into Darjeeling by nightfall.

The completion of the Eastern Bengal Railway from Sealdah (Calcutta) to Kushtia via Poradah Junction in 1862 nearly halved the distance to the Ganges, and the Government decided that more investment could be attracted by subsidising the railway contracts instead of guaranteeing a fixed rate of return.[6] Franklin Prestage, as Agent of the EBR, was contacted in 1864 to consider the viability of advancing the broad-gauge towards Darjeeling, and his investigations concluded that the line should be run from the north bank of the Ganges and pass by way of the Teesta and Rungeet valleys to get as close as was possible to the hill station. He envisaged that his route would not only pass through the highly productive districts of Dinagepore and Rungpore, but be the most favourable to serve the trade anticipated from Sikkim and Tibet. Although the Directors were delighted at the spiralling prosperity of their existing lines, they became nervous of promoting extensions as it was felt their dividends would be diluted, especially when the Government had made its opposition felt to railways as commercial undertakings.

In 1868 the Secretary of State suggested a new strategy for railway development that classified the projects as being of commercial or political value, the former attracting the guaranteed system and the latter being built by a Government Agency. However, the Viceroy Lord Lawrence contested that if a railway was a commercial proposition then it was capable of making a profit, which in turn should be taken by the Government and used for further railway development. He won the argument, but the policy later foundered when the Government became embroiled in the second Afghan War (1878–80) and India was plagued with a series of famines. The finances were quite simply not there for the railways, and the Government was obliged to return to the system of private investment with a tighter control over the guarantees.

Trials were held in 1872 with the Government Steam Train on the Grand Trunk Road,[7] and such was the success that it appeared to be a serious rival to the railways. The service was provided by the *Chenab, Ravee* and *Indus*, three 100 HP road-engines designed by Colonel R.E. Crompton and constructed by Ransome, Simms & Head of Ipswich in the UK. They were shipped to Calcutta and were soon able to demonstrate their

Travelling on the Cart Road by tonga was indeed arduous and not without its own perils, particularly on the steep descent to Darjeeling. It is not difficult to see how the idea of a tramway became a very attractive proposition.

Collection: (The late) Fred Pinn

---

[6] The line was extended in 1883 from Poradah Junction to Damookdeah Ghat on the southern banks of the Ganges, which served as the ferry terminal until the opening of the Hardinge Bridge in 1915.

[7] This ancient trade route dates from the 4th century and runs from Peshawar (now Pakistan) to Calcutta. It originally followed the sweeping bend of the Ganges through Bengal (now Bihar) but the British realigned the route to make a more direct connection between Calcutta and Varanasi.

The bullock-cart trains first using the Hill Cart Road would require an overnight stay at Gayabari for the climb to Darjeeling. To this day they can be seen working individually in India, although this illustration taken from an early postcard is now a rare sight on the Hill Cart Road.

Collection: Nick Rhodes

superiority over the ponderous two miles per hour averaged by the bullock-cart trains. Their ability to move troops at three times this speed attracted the support of the military, and Crompton believed his vehicles would contribute more effectively to the development of new countries than narrow-gauge railways. Demonstrations were held during a series of Government experiments to show one of his machines hauling 19 four-wheeled carts up a gradient of 1 in 18 at five mph, but one can only speculate whether such transport would ever have been seriously considered as a viable option for the Hill Cart Road and Darjeeling.

The Institution of Civil Engineers held a meeting in 1873 to discuss the proposition made by the Government of India to introduce narrow-gauge railways on future extensions, for there were some 5,326 miles laid on 5ft 6in gauge, but only 17 miles on metre gauge and 27 miles on sub-metric. The cost for laying the metre gauge was estimated at £5,880 per mile, which was thought to be £200 – £1,000 per mile less than a comparable line on the broad gauge.

Further surveys for a railway from the Ganges to the hills were made, but it was a devastating famine later in the year that precipitated the order for the construction of the metre-gauge Northern Bengal State Railway.[8] The Engineer-in-Chief was Major Lindsay RE, and the intention was for the line to run from Sara Ghat on the northern bank of the Ganges to Adulpore at the foot of the Himalaya. Such was the sense of urgency that engineers were drafted in from many parts of India, although the order was equally explicit that the labour was not to be imported but recruited locally. The preliminary work began in February 1874, but the heat soon put a stop to this and construction could not start in earnest until the four-month 'season' of 1874–75. Sanction to commence the bridging was not received until the following year and this was not completed until the end of 1877.

The contractors for the first 52 miles were Messrs Burn & Co., and it was recorded that the work

---

[8] The Northern Bengal State Railway and the metre gauge lines of Assam were merged with the Eastern Bengal Railway on 1st April 1887 to form the Eastern Bengal State Railway.

was exceptionally heavy, with 101 million cu.ft of embankment being constructed and 18 million cu.ft of brickwork laid. This section ran across the flood basin of the Ganges and the foundations of the works had to withstand the loose sand and shifting nature of the soil. The permanent way and materials for the 112-mile section from Halullia to Jalpaiguri had to be transported by river, which was possible only between July and October, and it was a testament to the workforce that with the exception of two small bridges, it was laid in one four-month season. The longest bridge crossed the Burrul on 15 spans, each being 164 feet long, and the cost of the railway amounted to approximately £7,400 per mile. The section to Jalpaiguri was opened on 18th January 1878 by the Lieutenant Governor of Bengal, Sir Ashley Eden (the grandfather of the British Prime Minister, the late Sir Anthony Eden), and the service extended to Siliguri on 10th June 1878. It was decided that the line should terminate here and not continue to Adulpore, for that would entail passing through the *terai* forests where malaria was endemic.

As with many such settlements, the history of Siliguri appears to have vanished on the wind and can only be pieced together from fragments written in contemporary diaries and references on maps. It has been recorded that the town came into being with the coming of the metre gauge and that the origin of the name came from the shingle and stones brought down by the nearby Mahanandi River. However, the settlement certainly pre-dates the railway, and some residents in Siliguri hold the belief that the name came from '*Shaligree!*' (Attack), the battle cry of the invading Lepchas, who were subsequently defeated under the terms of the Treaty of Titalya in 1817. It is an engaging explanation, but does not stand up to scrutiny as a map has been traced of the area that was drawn in c1805 and has the settlement as Siligari. There are also accounts of the name being derived from its being the place where logs of the sal tree (known as '*sills*') were transported by the '*gari*' (bullock carts), but the word also appears in the patois of the *Koch*, the forest race that founded nearby Cooch Bihar. It refers to 'the stony place', the outermost limit where pebbles from the Himalayas appear on the surface, which lends credibility to the provenance of the name. Further variations have been found with the spelling on later maps, including Sileegory in 1820/21, and both Silligoree and Selleegoree in 1845. Sir Joseph Hooker refers to the Siligoree bungalow in his 'Himalayan Journals' published in 1849, whilst Major General D.F. Newall opts for Silligóri in '*The Highlands of India*' in 1873.

The reason behind the new railway to Siliguri and others being laid to a metric gauge was also a matter of some mystery for many, particularly when all else in India was measured to the Imperial standard. There had been a number of heated debates and exchanges of learned views for some time, and Lord Dalhousie had actively promoted the cause of 5ft 6in being

the standard gauge. He had been President of the Board of Trade in Britain prior to his appointment as Governor General of India (1848–56), and in this position had witnessed the chaos with the battle of the railway gauges in the UK. However, the costs of developing a broad-gauge network across India would have impeded the progress being encouraged by the Government, and active consideration had to be given to an alternative standard for the secondary lines. Lord Mayo was appointed Viceroy in 1869, and he was emphatic that India would benefit from the introduction of the metric system. To address the question of a narrower gauge, he calculated that the minimum external width of a carriage necessary to accommodate four passengers sitting abreast was 6ft 6in. On the advice that the gauge should not be less than half the body width, he advocated this should be 3ft 3in, which conveniently translated into being one metre.

The name of Charles Easton Spooner from the Festiniog Railway in North Wales (UK) also began to feature on many contemporary submissions to the technical press. The Welsh line was the first narrow-gauge railway in the world of any engineering distinction, having been constructed by James Spooner to a Royal Assent granted in 1832 and opened in 1836. It had provided an economic means of transporting slate over the fourteen miles from the Ffestiniog quarries to Portmadoc by a line that had been built to very high engineering standards and laid to a gauge of 1ft 11$^{5}/_{8}$in.

The route traced a course that climbed 700 ft from the seaport to the quarries by a steady gradient, which enabled horses to haul the empty slate wagons up, and ride back in 'dandy' cars at the rear of a loaded train that descended by gravity. Such was the success of the railway that James Spooner was to seriously consider steam traction, but the mantle for its adoption was passed to his son and successor, Charles Easton Spooner. No locomotives had previously been built for such a narrow gauge, but the first that arrived in 1863 acquitted themselves well and soon gave the Festiniog aspirations of introducing its own passenger service.

However, the law at that time in Britain did not permit this on any gauge less than the accepted standard of 4ft 8$^{1}/_{2}$in, but undaunted, the Festiniog applied to the Board of Trade to legalise the situation. The line was duly inspected in 1864 by Captain Tyler, and he was so impressed that his report stated:

> 'The cheapness with which such a line can be constructed, the quantity of work which can be economically performed on it, and the safety with which the trains run over it, render it an example which will undoubtedly be followed sooner or later in this country, in India and in the Colonies where it is desirable to form cheap lines for small traffic, or as a commencement in developing the resources of a new country.'

Charles Spooner saw India as a natural repository for his ideas, and it is not surprising to find that Lieutenant General Sir William Baker and his colleagues from the India Office were included on the guest list of dignitaries present at the locomotive trials of the articulated Fairlie locomotive staged on the Welsh line in 1870. Spooner also commented that it was fortuitous that Colonels Dickens and Strachey, two principal advisors of the Indian Government in matters of Public Works, happened to be in the country at the time and were able to form a committee to reflect on the question of gauge for India.

Spooner argued at length that the secondary railways of India should be laid to a gauge of 2ft 9in, i.e. half 5ft 6in, before producing his statistics in 1869 to show that the Festiniog, at 1ft 11$^{5}/_{8}$in, had conveyed

The Government Steam Train was seen as a distinct improvement over the bullock trains for the movement of troops, but despite the success of the 'Ravee' seen here undergoing trials on the Grand Trunk Road, it would never have been a serious contender for the climb to Darjeeling.

An engraving of tea cultivation in British India in 1876. The illustration shows (not in the order of process) the plantation (1) weighing the leaf (2) plucking the leaf (3) rolling by hand (4) withering in the sun (5) rolling by machinery (6) withering in the factory (7) and sorting by machinery (8).

Collection: (The late) Fred Pinn

eleven times the weight of goods per annum than the broad-gauge Indian lines! To underpin his case he quoted the report on the proposed State railways of India that the broad gauge was to be constructed for traffic working at a speed of 15 mph, whilst the Festiniog had proved that a speed of 30 mph could be run with ease and safety. These figures turned out to be somewhat spurious, as most of the traffic on the Festiniog involved the transportation of slate by gravity and the matter of free energy did not appear in the equations, but his precepts regarding earthworks and civil engineering, with the obvious reduction in costs, were completely valid.

The Secretary of State for the Colonies sent Guilford Molesworth, the Consulting Engineer for the Indian State Railways, to the Festiniog Railway with the brief of examining the claims made by Spooner. His antagonism for a break of gauge was well known, and when holding his previous position as Director General of the Ceylon Railway, he had successfully discouraged the Governor from extending the line on the 3ft 6in gauge. His opinion was not moved by the indifferent reception he received at Portmadoc, where it appears that no special trains were laid on for him and for some curious reason the double-Fairlie engine was not working. He returned to India intent on recommending that any gauge other than the standard 5ft 6in should not be adopted.

Lord Mayo was still adamant that the metre gauge was viable, and as Viceroy he had the last say. Molesworth was overruled and given the task of supervising its construction, going to great lengths to save face by differentiating between the economies gained by its use and the folly of breaking gauge. *The Engineer* could not contain itself, and commented in its editorial on 12th May 1871 that the Indian Government had recently published the recommendations for adopting the metre gauge as the new standard, and that is ... *'the reasons were not very clear'*.

However, the reasons for the railway coming to Siliguri were very clear indeed. In 1869 the sea journey from India to Britain was reduced from three months to three weeks with the opening of the Suez Canal, and with it came a reduction in the cost of transporting the tea that was now flourishing around Darjeeling. The first commerical tea garden had been the Steinthal plantation laid down by the German missionary family of Stolke in 1847, and within five years a number of small and medium-sized estates had been established. The industry developed rapidly, and by 1866 there were 39 gardens producing an annual crop of 46,000 lbs of tea. Within a year of the canal opening this number had increased to 56 gardens yielding 156,000 lbs, and by 1874 over 20% of the population was employed in 113 estates harvesting some 3,928,000 lbs of tea.[9]

But getting to the hill station from Siliguri by *tonga* (the two-wheeled horse carriage) and transporting goods by bullock cart was still a long and costly process. Rice that sold for Rs98 a ton on the plains escalated to Rs238 by the time it had been carried to Darjeeling, and this was a staple food for the workers in the tea plantations. It was also hard going for the soldiers being sent to the sanatorium for convalescence, and was a two-day trek even for the fittest of travellers. It could take a day simply to get to Chunbatti, as the Reverend W. Urwick recalled, having arrived at Siliguri about ten o'clock in the morning:

'Here, with much difficulty, and after some hours' delay, we obtained wretched ponies to take us to Kursiong, halfway to Darjeeling; but the ponies travelled so slowly across the Terai, or swamp of low lying jungle, the seat of malarious fever, which forms a deadly belt along the foot of the hills across the north of India, separating the Himalayas, that darkness came on before we began to ascend, and we rode in faith along the road, which at the time was undergoing repair, till we reached the Dak Bungalow of Chambattie, where we put up for the night.

The Dak Bungalow is an Inn or Rest House, provided by Government for travellers, one-storied, with verandas, often perched on a knoll; with scanty furniture and scantier fare. It is in charge of a native called a Khansamah, who locks it up when empty, and appears on the ground to open it when you call. A tariff of prices, very moderate, a list of rules, a list of articles provided, and a carefully drawn map of the district, hang on the walls. After some delay we got candles and chocolate and bread; but it was too late to procure the usual repast of roast fowl, or 'sudden death', as this dish is called in the East, the creature being usually killed and dressed within half-an-hour of your arrival. We turned in after giving directions to

---

[9] The Darjeeling Tea Research & Development Centre reported in 2005 that there were around 70 gardens still in operation producing an annual yield of approximately 23,000,000 lbs. At the time the industry was employing over 52,000 people on a permanent basis, with an additional 15,000 engaged during the plucking season (March to November). Over 60% of the workers were women, and the employment was mainly on a family basis.

the khansamah to look after our ponies, and to prepare an early morning meal. The silence of the hills was impressive; here and there a firefly, here and there across the valley, or through the trees, the twinkle of the light of a native hut.'

Franklin Prestage, the Agent for the East Bengal Railway, travelled to Darjeeling in 1878 whilst on privilege leave with his brother-in-law Sulyard Bernard Cary.[10] He no doubt reflected on the speech made by the Lt Governor with the opening of the Northern Bengal State Railway, particularly when he read that amongst its benefits it would bring:

'... the wearied and exhausted citizen of Calcutta within a short journey of what I have no hesitation in saying is the finest scenery and almost the purest air in the world. It brings the rapidly developing tea interests of Darjeeling and the Dooars into direct communication with the ports of export ... the cotton goods, metals and salt of Europe and the indigo, tobacco and tea of India to be exchanged with the gold dust and wool of Thibet, and the silks of China. I even hope that his dreams of social intercourse with Lhasa, may be so fully realized that we may have, some day, the honor of carrying the Grand Lama to exchange religious views with the Bishop of Calcutta.'

Prestage epitomised the entrepreneurial spirit that was associated with the British Raj in India, and conceived the idea that a steam tramway running alongside the cart road would be far superior to the *tonga* that had spent two laborious days taking them to the sanatorium. Cary was working as a civil engineer for the Eastern Bengal Railway at the time, and Prestage asked him to make plans for a preliminary project.

There could be no better opportunity for him to submit his scheme to the Lt Governor and Colonel Stanton RE, the Director General of the Railways.

Franklin Prestage, the man whose vision, drive and determination was to lay the tramway to Darjeeling.

---

[10] The marriage records show the name spelt as Carey, although it is Sulyarde Cary on documents signed in his own hand. His sister Eliza Amelia married George Hawes in 1857, but it was not long before he tragically died, and the young widow subsequently married Franklin Prestage on 14th August 1860. It throws light on Cary's association and recruitment to the DHR project and the family animosities there must have been when he left. It comes as little surprise that he only accepted the position of General Manager in 1889 after Prestage terminated his involvement with the railway. The family connections continued with Sulyard's brother James Cary marrying Sophia Hawes in 1858.

Chapter 2

Rails on the Road

Despite the original intention by Prestage '*that steam power should somehow be used on the road*', he was later adamant that the line never was a tramway but a railway, although where the distinction lies confuses travellers to this day. Nevertheless, it was the Darjeeling Steam Tramway Company that was formed with Franklin Prestage as the chairman. The capital of 1,400,000 rupees (£140,000) was mainly subscribed within India, and Lord Lytton, the Viceroy, promptly put his name down for shares. The Lt Governor stated he was prepared to give a guarantee from Provincial resources as he felt that the scheme was not only financially sound and commercial, but that it would defray the spiralling cost of maintaining the Cart Road. This was now suffering from the pounding of the carts and annual landslips brought on by the monsoon rains; the expense had amounted to Rs70,305 a year. He felt that the mail should be carried free of charge with troops and Government stores transported at a reduced price. He also recommended that the Company and train timing should be under Government control, and that the Director of the State Railway of the North Eastern System should be ex-officio a Director of the Tramway.

However, the ink was barely dry on the contract between the Government of Bengal and Prestage when the Government of India, through its Public Works Department, objected to the advance made and felt that Bengal had exceeded its authority. Representations were made in mitigation to show that the bulk of the money had been subscribed or was forthcoming, as were the agreements for material and supplies. Prestage responded that the estimates for receipts did not include the conveyance of troops, the transport of Government stock nor those for the stores at the intermediate bazaars. The tramway, he advised, would give greater speed and create much traffic, and assuming that it was necessary to run two trains a day, a considerable portion of the receipts would be for maintenance purposes. He listed the advantages by stating the tramway would *(sic)*:

- *Maintain the Hill Cart Road.*
- *Bring cheaper and more regular communication between the North Bengal State Railway and Darjeeling.*
- *Serve the tea gardens.*
- *Improve the alignment of the Hill Cart Road including doubtful bridges.*
- *Improve all the property in the district and offer lower rates of food, reducing the cost of living in the hills.*
- *Render health-restoring sanatoria to the capita of India and allow a much larger number of European troops who could be returned more promptly in case of emergency.*
- *Be a boon to poorer classes of Europeans in Calcutta to visit the hills.*
- *Stimulate goods, parcel and passenger traffic.*
- *Reduce the cost of fuels.*
- *Nine miles of* terai *between Silligoree and Sookna could be traversed with the minimum of discomfort in little more than half an hour.*
- *Bring self-supporting communication of the most useful kind almost up to our frontier.*

Prestage also stated that he had already ordered the rails and other materials required to advance the work without delay, but the Government was obdurate and insisted on the cancellation of the

Despite claims that the line was never really a tramway, this superb early photograph of a Down freight passing Tindharia shows the intimacy of the rails and the road. The hut seen on the far right of the photograph is on the site now occupied by the Railway's workshop.

The ability to move troops quickly to the cantonments near the hill station was a powerful selling point to the Government. The depot at Jalapahar (7,701ft) was about 1½ miles before Darjeeling and close to the crest of the ridge that rose up from the railway. It was completed in 1848, and by 1863 it included a hospital, church and accommodation for 150 men. This photograph dates from the turn of the century and by the end of the First World War the depot had expanded to accommodate 550 soldiers.

contract. Lord Lytton subsequently withdrew his name as a shareholder, which greatly concerned Prestage as he felt his enthusiasm for the tramway had influenced many others, and in particular the native subscribers. Indeed the Viceroy had stated he was pleased of the *'intelligent departure'* made from railways being purely commercial undertakings and constrained by contracts and routine, which he felt had motivated influential natives to take the lead with the development of railways on the plains. However, the British Government had its hands tied by London financiers, and the opportunities for investment evaporated.

A new Agreement for the tramway was drawn up which stated that Government land and the right to use the Cart Road would be given free of cost, whilst any additional land required would be obtained at cost price. It was stipulated that the tramway was to be completed within eighteen months and equipped with a minimum of eight locomotives and sufficient stock to carry the traffic to meet the estimated gross receipts of two *lakhs*. Should the work not be completed in time, or the service not maintained for six consecutive months, the Company would be obliged to restore the road and land to its former condition. The maintenance and repair of the Cart Road was to be sub-contracted to the Company and paid for by the Secretary of State, the details of work to be executed and the rates of payment being itemised in the contract. The Government would have undertaken the work in any case, but it was a positive and encouraging sign.

The contract allowed the tramway to use the Siliguri terminus and all the accommodation and appliances of the Northern Bengal State Railway free of charge until it could pay a clear dividend of 7½% of paid-up capital, and thereafter agree or arbitrate to a rent. All the construction and maintenance materials were also to be carried by the NBSR at rates not exceeding 60% of the lowest rates charged for similar goods, which equated to the actual cost. It was agreed that after the tramway had been opened for its entire length for five years, one-half of any net profits over 5% on the paid-up capital would be used to offset the subsidies it had previously made and given to defray the costs of maintaining the Cart Road. The agreement also obliged the Government to pay the value of the line as a dividend earner, plus an additional bonus of 20% over and above that value should it decide to take over. It was an attractive financial proposition, and the tramway was to become the first great public work built by money wholly subscribed in India.

Not everybody was happy, especially Guilford Molesworth, the Consulting Engineer for the Indian State Railways, who was still smarting after being sent halfway round the world to the Festiniog Railway to reflect on the gauge question. His reception there had been perfunctory at best, and it had done nothing to overcome his declared antagonism of adopting the narrow gauge for India. He thought the Agreement for the Darjeeling Tramway was most objectionable, raising concern that the Company could fall into the hands of unprincipled Directors who might secure a dividend of 5% by keeping the capital expenditure low through having an inefficient railway and doing everything to discourage traffic.

Major Luard, the Consulting Engineer to the Government of India for Guaranteed Railways, stated that it should be borne in mind that the Darjeeling Tramway, owing to physical circumstances, would distinctly be a monopoly. He felt that the Government

Lebong (the tongue-like spur) was 5,970ft above sea level and situated about 1³/₄ miles north of Darjeeling. The area was taken over by the military authorities for barracks in 1888 and the photograph (circa 1900) shows the settlement well, with the parade ground in the centre. In 1910 plans were being considered for a rail connection with the DHR, which would have involved laying the track for 4¹/₂ miles along the New Lebong Road as it rounded Birch Hill.

should have some power to revise the rates and fares, as there would be no competition to reduce them, which indeed turned out to be the case. The contract had determined there would be two classes of travel for passengers, Upper and Lower, for which the Company was empowered to charge fares at 6 *annas* and 15 *pies* per mile. Freight was classified as 1st, 2nd or 3rd Class and the rates for its transport were 3, 4 and 5 *pies* per *maund* per mile respectively, whilst parcels and excess luggage was charged at 1 *anna* per *maund* per mile. An allowance was made to increase the rate for goods by 50% during the months of July, August and September, presumably to reflect the difficulties of transport during the monsoon period. It was also stipulated that all the mail, parcels and articles in charge of the Post Office authorities, along with their staff in charge of them, would be carried by the tramway in return for an annual payment of Rs10,260.

The Agreement was finally signed for the construction of the tramway on 8th April 1879, which set out the estimated costs for clearance and construction, along with the proposals for motive power, rolling stock, fares and conditions of operation. It was stipulated the tramway was to interfere as little as possible with other traffic on the Cart Road, and between Siliguri and Sukna it was to be laid only on one side of the highway. Stations or sidings were to be provided every seven miles to enable trains to pass, and it was stated that the sidings should total to a minimum of one-fifteenth of the length of the line. Signalling was to be erected in accordance with that used on other steam tramways, but quite what lines they had in mind is not clear as there were none in India at the time.

There were to be eight locomotives capable of hauling nine tons at seven mph, along with twenty tramway 'cars' that could each accommodate six passengers and three tons of goods, along with four 1st Class 'cars' with seating for eight passengers. It is interesting to note that the bridges and culverts were to be strengthened to allow locomotives weighing eight tons to cross, but with the first engines being nine tons in working order, it is clear how the problems began so quickly for the enterprise in its earliest days.

The government passed the Bill for the tramway on 12th April 1879 and it was formally agreed by the Lt Governor on 16th April. Prestage lost no time with the work, and in his role as Managing Director of the Company appointed I.J. Whitty as the Chief Engineer and H. Edwards as his assistant. Irwine John Whitty was born at Kilrush in County Clare (Eire) in 1839, and after completing his education at Queen's College in Cork, served his time as an apprentice with P.R. Roddy in the construction of the Cork & Bandon Railway. He sailed to India at the age of 24 and obtained employment with the East India Railway Company in the surveying and construction of the Chord line. His work continued through a number of posts as the system expanded over the following 16 years, during which time he qualified as a Member of the Institution of Civil Engineers in 1877. He eventually became the General Manager of the extensive collieries of the East Indian Railway at Giridhi, which he left in 1879 to take up the appointment of constructing the tramway to Darjeeling. Unfortunately little is known about his partner Mr Edwards, or if there was a connection with the Calcutta civil engineering company of Marillier & Edwards who advertised their services as contractors and Agents for the Bengal Iron Works.

The concept of a mountain line was still very new at the time, and the principles of construction as laid down by Charles Easton Spooner would have had some influence over the planning of the tramway. The civil engineering business of Spooner & Company, of Portmadoc in North Wales, had been established since 1870 and his precepts were enjoying wide acclaim with pioneering railways in difficult terrain. The interests of the Company as consulting engineers were independent from the running of the Festiniog, although the experience gained from it was undeniable. But Spooner's thoughts had been turning to horizons far beyond Portmadoc, as his submissions to the Press for developing sub-metric railways in India had shown.

George Percival Spooner took over the post from his father Charles Easton in 1872, and became responsible for the designs of arguably its most successful locomotives and some of the more capricious rolling stock. He dissociated his connection with the Festiniog in 1879 as family difficulties began to show on account of his affair with a domestic servant from which a child was born. Disgraced in the eyes of his father, he fled to India in 1880 and may well have sought absolution with an inspection of the construction work being undertaken to Darjeeling. His name does not appear on the records until 1882, by which time he held the post of Assistant Locomotive and Carriage Superintendent at Khandwa on the recently constructed metre-gauge Holkar & Sindia Neemuch State Railway in Madhya Pradesh. Within a year he rose to being the District Locomotive Superintendent of the Rajputana-Malwa affair, which was worked by the Bombay, Baroda & Central India Railway and had coincidentally employed Robert Fairlie in the 1860s.

The problems with surveying in the Himalayas. The agreement to have the construction of the tramway to Darjeeling completed within 18 months was based on the assumption that it could simply be laid on the road without the need of heavy earthworks. The detailed survey subsequently undertaken revealed a different story, for the gradient of the road was found to be 1 in 20 for 15 miles. However, with the budget already determined and the work under way, there was no alternative but to complete the project as stipulated.

Collection: (The late) Fred Pinn

Prestage understood that the Cart Road to Darjeeling had been built to a ruling gradient of 1 in 30 and a maximum of 1 in 25, and that with a few exceptions, curves of no less than a 70ft radius could be attained for the tramway with little additional cost. The original intention had been to lay the track alongside the road without the need of heavy earthworks, a notion that may have amused Spooner if not impressed him. However, once the funds became available for detailed surveys, Whitty found to his horror that 15 miles were actually inclined at 1 in 20, but the Company had been formed and the work was already under way, with the agreement that the tramway would be laid to Darjeeling within eighteen months. With this in mind, and the ever-present demands to stay on time and within budget, there was little opportunity to consider alternative alignments away from the road on a more sympathetic grade.

A report that appeared in *The Englishman* on 2nd May 1879 voiced some caution:

'Owing to the zigzag nature of the present road, the tram will frequently have to cross and re-cross it. What provision will be made to protect, not only the local traffic, but the trains en route, has not been made known; this is a special feature that certainly requires the attention of all concerned. The projectors believe they will command from 70 to 80 per cent of the present traffic, and their calculations are well within the mark, for the increased facilities the tram will offer must augment the traffic. At certain points, such as the intermediate stations that will be opened, the cart traffic too will necessarily be much larger than at present, and it is highly necessary that a system of fencing

and protection at points where the tram may cross from side to side of the common road should be insisted on.'

The contract for the construction of the tramway to the specifications and design laid down by Whitty and Edwards was given to Herbert Rumsey and Thomas Mitchell & Co. of Calcutta. Their task was to organise and manage the workforce who would physically build the line, and with it came the responsibility for profiling the earthworks, building the bridges, ballasting and laying the track, and the construction of the stations. Mitchell & Company had been established as civil engineers and contractors since 1875 and was originally based at 4 Commercial Buildings in Calcutta before moving to 137 Bow Bazaar Street in 1879.

Little is known about their early business enterprises, although the Company's work with steam sawmills was sufficient to attract the attention of the official directory for the city. The contract for the construction of the tramway to Darjeeling was a major coup and Tom Mitchell moved to an office in Kurseong and his partner W. James based himself in Darjeeling.

Herbert Gordon Rumsey was born at Twickenham in England on 6th April 1848 and served his apprenticeship as a civil engineer at Crewe. He was drawn by the attraction of India and the heavy investments being made to finance railway construction. He bought a one-third share in the Bagadogra Tea Estate, near Siliguri, to supplement his income, and settled in Kurseong where the more temperate climate made life less disagreeable than on the plains. It was there that he met his future wife Elizabeth Anne Heal, who was known to her family and friends as Lily.

The Heals lived in the Irish town of Enniskillen, where tragedy hit the young family when Lily's father died at an early age. In time her widowed mother Margaret became attracted to the charms of an Army sergeant by the name of Roberts, and was intent on following him after he was posted to Darjeeling. It took her and Lily nine months to get there, the ship being wrecked on the way by all accounts. They married and Lily adored her new stepfather, who was an accomplished musician and had formed a band that was well known at the

Above: *Herbert Rumsey who, with Thomas Mitchell, was the contractor responsible for the construction of the tramway.*

Right: *Lily Rumsey, the wife of the contractor, who it is said was responsible for the concept of the reverse sidings. They raised six children in Kurseong before moving back to England in 1890, although Herbert was to return to India many times by himself.*

Dr Michael Powell

The contract to build the tramway stated that the Hill Cart Road was metalled across its full width of 20ft on the lower section of the climb. This early photograph, believed to have been taken on the climb to Tindharia, shows that on some sections the road was barely wide enough for the rolling stock and that passing places were necessary for the bullock carts to wait. Note the boards laid between the tracks to assist the carts in crossing.

Collection: Nick Rhodes

balls and public functions held at Dunn's Assembly Rooms in Darjeeling. It was there that he taught Lily to dance, a seemingly innocuous pastime that is said to have later provided the solution to serious engineering difficulties with the railway!

Roberts became the manager of the Delaram Tea Estate and subsequently bought the Woodlands and Drum Druid Hotels in Darjeeling, along with the Clarendon in Kurseong; they were collectively known as the Roberts' Hotels. In 1880, Lily met Herbert Rumsey at a function staged at the Clarendon for the Viceroy's visit to celebrate the opening of the tramway to Kurseong, and after a brief elopement, they married and settled in Kurseong to raise a family of six children. The family finally moved back to England in 1890, although Herbert was to return to India many times by himself.

The task of building the railway to Darjeeling was formidable for Mitchell and Rumsey. Their position as contractors placed the responsibility for the training and coordination of the technical skills firmly in their hands. They had to understand and manage the complexities of the Indian caste system with its sub-divisions of labour and its strict rules of conduct, and for this they had to rely on a tier of native sub-contractors. These would often be local headsmen, who recruited the labour from nearby villages for work that was often new to them. Their role was to facilitate and co-ordinate the native workers, whose entire lifestyle was governed by an intricate pattern of behaviour that exerted control on all the permutations of existence, whilst at the same time seeing everything in this life as *maya*, an illusion. Indeed, the overriding concern was not so much one of economic standing but the ability to regenerate on a higher plane of existence during each successive life.

Entire families would undertake the unskilled work, which was hard manual labour using only the simplest of tools. The men were engaged on the more physically demanding tasks of digging the earth and rock, which gave them status and a slightly better pay than the women and children who were delegated to transport the excavated soil. The earth would be carried in baskets on their heads and used for the construction of the embankments and realignment of the curves. The women and children were also responsible for fetching and carrying the materials to the work site, and were expected to lift the bamboo scaffolds and timbers for building the stations and bridges. However, they were all unskilled hands and were liable to vanish into the fields for agricultural work as soon as the season advanced. As such, the native sub-contractors would often prefer to engage the *beldar*, a generic term in western Bengal for a wandering caste of earth-workers and navvies who earned their livelihood from the soil and would build and move their grass huts alongside the line as the tramway progressed.

The division of labour with the construction workers was broken down into numerous sub-castes, from bridge builders, carpenters, stonecutters and bricklayers to ironsmiths, hammer men, lifters of heavy weights, bellows boys, water carriers, storekeepers, timekeepers, interpreters, platelayers, trumpeters for mobilising people, quarrymen, brickmoulders, riveters and bullock-cart drivers. They were all part of a self-policing social system that did not always make it spiritually easy to work alongside each other. Nevertheless, the tramway was laid down at an amazing rate, which was a testament to the skills of Mitchell and Rumsey, who overcame many of the problems by treating the question of caste with respect and kindness as they directed and inspected the work.

The partition of tasks into such specialisms, from which the station in life was indelibly drawn, may seem to have lacked compassion, but then the class system and the eternal flames of damnation threatened by a religion in Victorian Britain were not seen as *that* beguiling. The caste system had survived for a thousand years, for it had created a series of sub-communities within which each could identify themselves in a potentially terrifying land. By making each caste exclusive, it gave each member a sense of belonging and purpose in every stratum of Indian society; the lower the caste, the greater the possibilities were for improvement in the next cycle of rebirth by leading a virtuous life, although it appeared nothing featured in the equation about efficiency. The probity was assayed by your *karma* and the acceptance of the situation was your *dharma*, which perhaps provides an insight to the cultural resignation that poverty is not seen as a failure of this life, but the heavenly troubles brought on as a consequence of deeds in a previous existence.

The construction of railways was uniting India in a way that no dynasty, however competent or cruel, could ever have achieved. The tramway to Darjeeling was only the second narrow-gauge line to be built in India, and it must be said that the first had not been an outstanding success. It had opened in 1862 and was built at a time when the Government was being asked to extend rails across some of the Princely States. Run by the Gaekwar of Baroda, the first section of this twenty-mile 2ft 6in-gauge line from Dabhoi to Miyagam was laid with 13lbs/yd rails, which had been adequate at the time with bullocks as the motive power but hopeless when the three 0-4-0 saddle tanks arrived in 1863. They wobbled so badly over the track that His Highness had been obliged to return to animal power until the rails were upgraded to 30lbs/yd in 1873, after which the locomotives were converted to carry their fuel and water in a tender to give the permanent way a chance. As a senior native ruler, the Gaekwar was the first to own his own train and went to the point of having a throne installed in a special carriage.

The estimates prepared by Prestage for the Darjeeling line show that he intended to use 35lbs/yd rails and would require 55 tons per mile @ £6.00 a ton to be sent from England, which along with the fish-plates, spikes, nuts and bolts, would bring the cost for 49 miles of main line and 2 miles of sidings to £18,703.30. However, a correspondent for *The Englishman* submitted a report on 2nd May 1879 that the steam tramway had obtained a contract from England for steel rails at £4.15.0d a ton (£4.75), and reflected that quotations for rails four or five years earlier had been given at £15.00 a ton. The report continued to inform that:

> '*The gauge of the tramway will be 2ft 6ins and to facilitate the movement of the trains round the curves, the whole of the rolling stock will be fitted with Cleminsons' radial axles. The Projectors have also secured the services of Mr Owen as Chief Engineer, and he will be assisted by Mr Bradley. Both are gentlemen of experience, who have been connected with some of the leading railway enterprises in India.*'

It was the popular fiction of journalism, for the gauge was incorrect and so was the ability of Cleminson's carriages to negotiate the curves, whilst it was Whitty and Edwards who took the responsibility for the line as Resident Engineer and his assistant. The names of Messrs T.E. Owen and P. Bradley did not feature again and their employment appears to have remained with the Northern Bengal State Railway, with the former as the Executive Engineer at the permanent-way depot of the Mahanandi division and his assistant as Sub-engineer of the p.w.d. of the Kurto sub-division.

Mitchell & Rumsey were obliged to use the flat-bottomed rails Prestage had already ordered from England. The sleepers were obtained locally, and it was estimated that 1,980 would be required for every mile, but it is not clear just what rails were actually used, as the records serve only to confuse. The contract stated the rails were '*to weight not less than 30lb to the yard on the level portion and 40lb on the hill road*' and that '*when the rails weigh 40lb per yard or more, not less than seven sleepers per rail of 24 feet are to be used on the straight and nine on curves. Where rails weigh less than 40lb, nine sleepers per rail are to be used.*'

The Government Inspector's report, made by Colonel Taylor prior to the opening of the line, appears to

Most of the stations along the new tramway were roadside halts and did not need a great deal of civil engineering. However, the terminus at Darjeeling would require a lot more work, and was estimated to cost Rs25,000 to complete. Photographs of the original building are a considerable rarity, but this one is dated 4th January 1891 and shows the overall construction of the large canopy covering a rake of four-wheeled trolleys. The uncoupled closed coach in the open is thought to be either a Cleminson six-wheeler or one of the two 3rd Class closed vehicles with longitudinal seating and entrances fitted in the end bulkheads.

Courtesy: The University of Queensland Library, Fryer Library, Papers of the Hume Family, UQFL 10, Image 537.

have been lost or destroyed, but a report submitted by Sulyard Cary in 1883 to the Institution of Civil Engineers stated that the weight of the rails was 40lbs/yd, which he thought many may have regarded as very heavy, and that each 24ft length was spiked to nine sleepers cut from oak and chestnut to 4ft 6in x 8in x 4in. Bearing plates were used on all the curves up to 150ft radius with two spikes on the outside and one on the inside of the rail, whilst fang bolts were inserted through the sleepers at the joints to prevent the spikes shearing by the thrust of the wheels.

However, the DHR was also used as a model for comparison with a Ceylonese railway in 1886, and the findings were based on statistics relating to its construction and working for 1884. The report advises that the two weights of rail in use and the spacing of sleepers were as stipulated in the contract. It may have been that Prestage based his estimates on an average of the two weights he intended to use, but he was not an engineer and saddled those with the responsibility with an order he was not qualified to make.

Spooner had previously stated in his thesis that track weighing 30lbs/yd would not bear the weight of a locomotive that exerted $2^1/_2$ tons on each wheel, even with sleepers having bearings of 2ft 6ins and 1ft 6ins at the joints. Prestage could be criticised for not reflecting on this, as the first of the No.1 Class four-wheeled tank engines weighed 10.1 tons in working order, and with the weight increasing with each batch delivered, it left no working margin. Spooner went on to state that the $48^1/_2$ lbs/yd rails that were in use on the Festiniog were not at all too strong, although in mitigation, the network of 2ft gauge tramways later built from Howrah adopted 30lb/yd rails and E.R. Calthorpe used 35lbs/yd track for his acclaimed Barsi Light Railway. However, these were totally different concerns; the Calcutta lines trundled across the flood plains of the Hooghly River and the axle loadings on the Barsi affair were less than the Darjeeling line, although the spacing of the wheels did cause a greater pressure on each sleeper. There were mountains to climb to Darjeeling by a route nobody would have previously experienced with a railway, and the clarity of hindsight would only become apparent with experience.

Three main stations were to be built, with estimated costs for Siliguri and Kurseong each being Rs7,500 (£750) and Darjeeling Rs25,000 (£2,500). The work at Siliguri was limited, as it had already been established as the terminus of the Northern Bengal State Railway, whilst Kurseong was a through station adjacent to the Clarendon Hotel. Darjeeling on the other hand was the hill terminus and would require considerable sculpturing of the land to accommodate the buildings and service sidings. The Ceylonese report later described the masonry used as '... *being very rough and having cost 4 rupees per cubic yard*'. There were also to be five intermediate stations, which were listed as being 3rd Class and would account for Rs1,500 (£150) each.

The work began on the plains by laying sleepers and rails at the side of the road from Siliguri to Sukna, and it was reported that approximately 3 miles had been completed by June. The wooden bridge that spanned the Mahananda River was built in 1868 to a cost of Rs70,000 and was now in a very shaky state. However, many of the native carpenters had seen the fortunes of Darjeeling rising with the coming of the tramway, and with that came a demand for new properties to be built. They had taken advantage of the situation by moving into the hills, where they were now able to charge premium rates for their skills. The contractors for the tramway were obliged to replace them with Chinese labour, whose families had originally come to the area with the first seeds of tea. They had shown the planters how to cultivate the crop, but were now without work and willing to accept employment at lower rates. The Oriental workers strengthened the bridge by inserting a number of wooden crossbeams, but it was not long before the Mahananda became gorged with the monsoon rains. Rumsey was unfortunately laid up in Kurseong with fever, and the work was placed in the hands of two native clerks who seized the opportunity of a scam by imposing a levy on all those desiring to use *their* bridge. They now held the monopoly, and should anyone protest, were not against pulling the wheels off the carts and casting them into the river.

The first 2½ miles of rails had been secured to the sleepers by July and continued for a further 2 miles with the track placed *in situ*, beyond which the bare wooden sleepers ran for another mile. However, the contractors were soon deprived of any more as the Forestry Department was smarting with not receiving the sole concession for their supply. The Press were not impressed, and suggested that the Department pocketed their jealousies and helped the railway in order to remove Darjeeling from the scare of starvation. The matter appears to have been resolved by the August, as good-quality oak and chestnut sleepers were being taken in great numbers up as far up as Chatakpur (39 miles from Siliguri). Those blackmailing on the bridge were not too distressed with having to wait for the timber to complete the reinforcements against the floodwater, which in its embryonic state at Pagla Jhora had brought a boulder down the mountain and crushed three coolies to death on the Cart Road. The *Darjeeling News* felt '... *the cheapest way would be to bridge over the difficulty, certainly were it in American hands they would act so. But that wants more spec. than the powers out here seem to have.*'

The work with laying the track had barely started when the steam engines arriving on the metre gauge began to challenge the cosmic vibrations of the Gods. A traveller at the time recalled the tale from a servant he met at a staging post bungalow, which claimed that:

> '... *two limbus[1] who had been to Siliguri returned with the news that they had seen a great fire eater. It walked on lines emitting shrieks, and each time it shrieked, the stomach of those nearby burst open.... Then the news came that the railway was to be laid into the hills. This, at first, we did not believe, but a day came when the Engineer Sahibs came for the survey. Those who could leave Darjeeling left and went to the places where the dreaded shriek could not be heard, and those who did not leave did puja, but Bhawani[2] demanded blood! blood! blood!.*'

The challenge for the contractors came as the Cart Road steepened in the forests of the *terai* beyond Sukna (the dry place). Borrowed from a Persian word for damp, the area was infamous as a malarial jungle and a favourite haunt of tigers, panthers, elephants and the less obvious life in the undergrowth.

The construction of the tramway was now being carried out at a number of unconnected sites, one of the first being the spur at Chunbatti, some 16 miles from

---

[1] Natives of an area between Sikkim and Nepal.

[2] The offering of prayers and respect to Bhawani, one of the many forms of Kali, the most terrible of the female deities, who appears clasping weapons in her ten hands, a garland of skulls around her neck, and has blood dripping from her tongue as she rides a tiger trampling over the demons of the unenlightened.

Siliguri. It was not quite as haphazard as the Press was to report, for the contractors had planned the construction of the line in stages and commenced work on the various sections that would require the most amount of labour. The theory allowed for the work in each section to be completed simultaneously, with temporary tracks laid on the road for the contractors' wagons servicing the construction of the embankments and earthworks. The *Darjeeling News* reported in July that:

> '... *until you reach Panchkella there is very little evidence of the Tram, but just before reaching the site of the Dak Bungalow, a number of coolies are there employed levelling off and cutting a more suitable gradient than the road. Sometimes the proposed track of the Tram is outside the boundary walls of the road. It is being made on the right, or outer side coming up. Immediately after leaving the Dak Bungalow, where they have succeeded in laying another 300 yards or so of tramway, wherever they have come to bridge the spanning of it is deferred I suppose, till they get heavy timbers, or until the heavy rains stop. This remark refers to below also. The last sign of the future iron horse is at Choonbuttee Dak Bungalow. They have been obliged to bring the track right through the compound, and clean through the centre of the cook-house. The Khansamah showed me, with wailing and weeping, the stake driven into his cooking chula* [large clay pot]. *When I was there I saw one of the Assistant Engineers, who seemingly has not been long up, being pulled up by a Sirdar* [leader from a hill tribe], *one of the great unsoaped. Knowing their customs, as I do, it was a truly amazing spectacle.*'

There was no loop at Chunbatti when the tramway was first built, the track being laid through the compound of the 'dak' bungalow. The double loop was constructed in 1882 to ease the gradient, with the lower section running behind the bungalow and the upper in front. This very early view shows a No.2 Class hauling a rake of trolleys at a location much favoured by photographers over the years.

Changes with the buildings and vegetation can already be seen in this second early photograph of the Chunbatti loop. It was originally the third spiral, but such is the restless nature of the land that the first two were later washed away by the monsoon rains. The track follows the same profile as initially laid, although subsequent earth-slips and encroachments have considerably altered the rest of the scene today.

Collection: Nick Rhodes

A No.2 Class leads a short Down train of trolleys close to the point where the Viceroy's train foundered in 1880. The first of the zig-zags was constructed here in 1882, the track of the reverse climb disappearing into the trees of the centre foreground. The locomotive works at Tindharia was moved in 1913 to the flattened spur seen in the top right corner of this early photograph.

Das Studios

No.1 of the No.1 Class, the Works No. 2869 and date of construction 1880 being just discernible on the original photograph. These locomotives were designed to be fired on either wood or coal, but in this rare photograph the bags of fuel stored close to the chimney suggest the former was soon found to be impractical. The sandbox originally placed behind the dome has been removed and the whistle re-sited from the cab roof to the dome.

Courtesy: George Eastman House

Prestage had stated that he saw no reason why the line should not be partially opened for public service by the end of the year and through to Darjeeling by the beginning of the next hot season. However, the work appeared to be done in fits and starts, and by the February of 1880, the correspondent for the *Darjeeling News* reflected:

> *'Now all the strength is put on near Kursiong, and, in a day or two, the same is transferred to Choonbutty, and so on. There is an order to get up a muster of coolies, and when they arrive, there are no working implements, or they have come too late, or some other excuse. The up-shot is that the great unsoaped are beginning to fight shy of the Mountain Railway.'*

The report in *The Englishman* was more encouraging, for it advised its readers on 16th February that two of the new engines specially designed for the tramway were due to arrive at Calcutta within a few days. Indeed, it stated that considering the construction work had begun at the time of the monsoons and was laid through the fever-ridden *terai*, it reflected a credit on all concerned.

There was a very definite need for encouragement; the Viceroy and the Lieutenant Governor were to visit Darjeeling at the beginning of March and reviewing the progress of the tramway was high on the agenda. On Saturday 26th February Colonel Stanton RE, the Director of the North Eastern State Railway, Franklin Prestage, the Resident Engineer and the Locomotive Superintendent, made an inspection of the line. There was much concern as the new locomotives from Sharp, Stewart & Co. had not yet arrived and the tram for the Viceroy would be dependent on *'Tiny'*, the diminutive 0-4-0 saddle-tank being used by the contractors. It was steamed over the severest gradients to the 15th milepost and managed to haul three of the four-wheeled trolleys, which could at a pinch carry a total of 18 passengers. The inspection party found that the friction could be reduced on the sharp curves by lubricating the flanges of the leading wheels of the engine and trolleys with copious supplies of water, which left them satisfied that the Viceroy and his entourage could be carried to the 20th milepost.

The occasion of Lord and Lady Lytton's visit a week later on 4th March did not pass without complication. It took *'Tiny'* three hours to struggle and wheeze up the gradients with the hopeless task of hauling the Viceroy and his party with their vast amounts of luggage wedged into the three trolleys. The engine foundered and brought the train to a halt near the 18th milepost shortly before Tindharia, whereupon an army of coolies were immediately press-ganged to assist with large hawsers and dragged the load uphill to the awaiting *tongas*. The Viceroy finally arrived at the Clarendon Hotel in Kurseong, which was owned by Roberts, the stepfather of the contractor's future wife. Lady Lytton wrote in her diary:

> *'We left Calcutta at 5pm., for Darjeeling, with Sir Ashley Eden, Mr Bewick his A.D.C., Mr & Mrs Hope, Col St John, Col Dalrymple, and Mr Kitson, A.D.C. and after 4 restful hours in the train, we got to the river Ganges, which is very wide, so we took half an hour to cross it, and dined during this time with a nice refreshing breeze blowing on us. Then we got into another train for the night. The next day we were up at 7, and breakfasted at Siliguri, and started by 8 in the little new tramway with two or three light cars, but only a small engine. The air was delicious as we passed through very pretty jungle ground, then the engine puffed us gaily, up, up, up, to fresher air. At 11 we changed into Tongas, which were very rough and dusty – but there was plenty of beauty all round to distract one, and as we neared Darjeeling lovely tree-ferns appeared in the forest. About 2pm. we were allowed a rest. The reception at Darjeeling was a very cordial one, and at the entrance the Sirdars and big people of the place were all dressed in Chinese dresses of varied shape and colours, looking so picturesque. One in an orange dressing gown riding on a mule was particularly effective.'*

The stop at the Clarendon appears to have warranted no more mention than *'a rest'*, but the Viceroy seemed delighted at the dinner laid on in his honour at Siliguri on the way back to Calcutta. It was attended by a number of the principal officials of the Northern Bengal and Eastern Bengal Railways, and toasts of prosperity flowed to the success of the Darjeeling Tramway.

The spirit of optimism continued in the Press as *The Englishman* reported:

> *'The works are being rapidly pushed forward, and rails and sleepers are sorted in quantities at different points along the road to Darjeeling, and, as the natural difficulties to be encountered on the rest of the line are, apparently, not of a formidable character, there is every prospect that the contractors will be able to complete the undertaking within the prescribed period, a*

result which, it appears, will be advantageous to these gentlemen as well as to the Company and the public.'

The new locomotives from Sharp, Stewart & Co. arrived just in time to miss the Viceroy, for the passengers who arrived at Siliguri on 25th March by the morning mail train from Calcutta were given an unexpected trip up the tramway to the 19th milepost to test them out. Not only was it free but it was at *9 mph* and a correspondent for *The Englishman* who happened to be present, reported that the journey was:

'... made without any halts or mischances of any kind, the engine and the few carriages attached to it going round the sharpest corners smoothly and with the greatest ease. The line is not yet open for traffic. On the occasion the authorities good-naturedly allowed the public to avail themselves of the special train put on for Messrs Martin, Hall and Kennedy.[3] The tongas ordered were sent on to the 19th mile beforehand, there to await the arrival of the passengers. I was one of the lucky public on the occasion, and, having a painful and protracted experience of the tongas on the road, I can testify to the marvellous success of the tramway so far as it has gone. There was something absolutely exhilarating in the sensation of going calmly, swiftly, almost unconsciously by the well-known landmarks and 'difficulties' of the ascent. How often have I been compelled to associate these landmarks with apparently hopeless stoppages and blocks; with pushing wheels, dragging of ponies by the head, with fever fits of despair, hope, excitement, desperation; with any amount of strong language from the coachman to the ponies, language which conveyed injurious reflections on their parentage, and sullied the snow of their mothers' fame. Even to the unprofessional eye, it is obvious that the engineering difficulties to be surmounted were very great — but they have been surmounted, and the success of the tramway is an achievement, which reflects the greatest credit on all concerned in the undertaking.'

As a public-relations exercise, it was a success, but Prestage was anxious to start running trains and making a profit as soon as possible. The pressure was on for the contractors to complete the work, and despite the reassurance from the Viceroy and the Press, the next 12 miles to Kurseong followed one of the most difficult sections of the line. The engineers made a conscious decision not to bore tunnels, for it was suggested they would *'detract the traveller from his comforts and of the scenic pleasures of the line'*. The truth was they were laying the track on the Cart Road wherever possible, whilst literally cutting some corners with the construction costs in order to keep within the working budget.

An engine was finally tested up to the 29th mile at Kurseong, on 22nd May, and ballast trains were working flat out on the section in preparation of the obligatory Government inspection. A spell of heavy rain held back the completion of work, but the ever-optimistic tramway felt the weather had done much good in helping to consolidate the new construction. Not everybody shared the view, as the Chief Mechanical Engineer and his wife found to their cost. Mr and Mrs Annand were descending this section by trolley when they saw a boulder had been deliberately placed across the tracks. Unable to stop, the trolley crashed into the rock and badly injured the couple as they were thrown off. Further reports were received of the rains bringing rocks crashing down the mountainside and knocking the track out of gauge. The repairs were soon sorted out, and allowed the Company to place an advertisement on the front page of *The Englishman* to announce that the steam tramway would be open for the conveyance of passengers, parcels and goods to Kurseong on 23rd August 1880.

The tramway now terminated at the Clarendon Hotel in Kurseong, the Press reporting the following month that the trains were working in a most satisfactory manner and run with great punctuality and despatch. It was also noted that the natives were said to be warming to the idea of the tramway, and on the section below Kurseong there was scarcely a bullock cart to be seen. No further major earthworks were deemed necessary beyond Kurseong and the work in laying down the track progressed rapidly, it being within two miles of Sonada by the end of October. There was a demand for the Company to invest in some storage facilities for the goods transported, but on the whole the tram settled down favourably despite the heavy downpours of rain. Indeed during one night in October, the Northern Bengal mail train was so overloaded that it arrived at Siliguri 1½ hours late, but the tram rose to the occasion and, by confining its load to passengers only, was able to make up an hour during the climb to Kurseong.

---

[3] W.R. Martin was a manager with the Kurseong & Terai Tea Company, B. Hall held a similar position with the Singell Tea Company at Kurseong, as did J. Kennedy with the Runjo Valley Tea Association in Darjeeling.

An early scene of the railway in Kurseong (note the open goods shed in the right distance). The first hotel was built by Mr H.M. Low, to which the Bengal and Agra Annual Guide and Gazetteer of 1841 was led to comment ... 'is let to Mr F.D. Bellow, who, aided by his wife, a very intelligent and businesslike dame, manages generally to give satisfaction. This is certainly the quietest and most comfortable place for a family who intend to remain a season in the hills.'

Collection: (The late) Fred Pinn

The New Year had barely dawned when a delighted correspondent from the *Darjeeling News* reported that:

'... we had the pleasure of a run down the line from Sonada to Kursiong [sic] and back again last Friday (1 January 1881). The down trip was done in a trolley, and, including several stoppages to inspect work going on at different portions of the line, the nine miles were covered in five minutes under the hour. The line seems to be exceedingly well laid, as hardly any jolting was felt throughout the journey, although wherever there was a straight bit of road, the pace could not have been less than fifteen miles per hour. From Kursiong upwards the journey was done on a material train and it was really wonderful to see the way in which the small, but powerful, contractors' engine pushed a heavy load of sleepers and rails up the steep inclines, and round the sharp turns met with on this portion of the road. With the completion of the line to Sonada, the really serious engineering difficulties in the construction of the line may be considered as having ceased, as the Cart Road from thence to Jor Bungalow presents no very steep gradients or comparatively sharp curves; while, from

An early photograph of an 'A' Class locomotive leading a train bound for Siliguri through Jor Bungalow. The topee, bow-tie and pocket-handkerchief worn by the third man on the footplate would not have identified him as one of the crew! Note the European-style street lamp.

Collection: (The late) Fred Pinn

The Clarendon Hotel in Kurseong. The Viceroy and his party stopped here on their way to Darjeeling in 1880, and it was at the reception given in his honour that the owners' stepdaughter Lily met Herbert Rumsey, one of the two contractors responsible for the construction of the tramway. They subsequently became engaged and married, and the new Mrs Rumsey is said to have inspired the design of the reverse sidings from the ballroom dancing she was taught by her stepfather. The hotel became the station for Kurseong until the site was moved to its current location in 1894, after which its status was reduced to a halt until the hotel closed for business in 1938.

Collection: Nick Rhodes

the latter place to Darjeeling, the line will run down hill all the way. As an instance of the difficulties successfully overcome in the construction of the line it may be mentioned that at one point near Chuttackpore, the rails cross the road from side to side no less than thirteen times in a quarter of a mile. It is calculated that, with anything like favourable weather, a mile of rail can be laid down in four days, and it is confidently expected that the Tramway can be completed the whole way to Darjeeling by the end of March at the latest.'

Unfortunately, the area suffered some heavy falls of snow and it was not until February that the first official passenger train arrived at Sonada. The contemporary guide to Darjeeling described it as *'a small dirty native bazaar'* and the next village along the line fared no better, for Jor Bungalow was dismissed as *'a collection of filthy tumbledown huts'*. However, its annexe at Ghum, being the highest point of the line at 7,407 feet above sea level, was given the title of *'the highest station in the Old World, if not the Universe'*!

It would take a further five months before Darjeeling would witness the arrival of its tram, but that did not dampen their aspirations. It was seen that the line would bring a fall in the price of food and all the other imports the town was dependent on, whilst the transportation of tea to Siliguri and the Calcutta markets was seen as crucial to the prosperity of the district. The Press had indeed warned that there would be no progress made in the town until something was done to combat the excessive cost of labour and goods, feeling that the tramway was destined to be a great success and should in time be able to change all this.

It appeared that not everybody was sharing the sense of excitement, for some of the less urbane residents of Darjeeling were trapped inside their own personal torment with the coming of the tram. The alarm bells rang during the population census conducted on 17th February, when it was found many of the coolies would not be shaken from the belief that a child was to be taken from each house and laid on the tramway as a sacrifice. As a consequence no infant was ever left in the house when the parents were out at work in case it should be spirited away in their absence. Many of the workers refused to stay in their homes on the night of the census and preferred the sanctuary of the jungle, as they had it fixed in their minds that a man from each house was also to have his right arm cut off!

The panic abated by the time the tramway had advanced to Ghum on 4th April, but it also appeared the enthusiasm of the Press was beginning to decline and the nightmare of the journeys by *tonga* and bullock cart had been quickly forgotten. There was now a new target, and reports began to appear of lost carpetbags and singed babies arriving with parents blinded by cinders from the locomotives. The fear of landslips had not interrupted traffic, but the tendency for the train to run off the line had become something of a standing joke. A correspondent with a gentler pen wrote in the *Calcutta Gazette* on 18th April 1881:

'The train very seldom goes off the line now, but when it first started it used to go off very often indeed. And what happens when it does go off? Nothing. It is lifted on again, and speeds away as merrily as ever. I once made a downward journey from Karseong to Siligoree when the train went off the line three times, and yet we arrived at Siligoree only four minutes late. It is great amusement for some of the old hands like myself to come up from Siligoree with some of the newcomers from Calcutta who have never seen the tramway before. The other day I came up with two elderly gentlemen who saw visions of one another and a better World at every bend in the road, and who once, when the train stopped suddenly and with something of a jerk, clung to each other with frantic energy, as if they were determined at all events to die together, and a lady opposite to a friend of mine, in a sudden inspiration of alarm, crooked the handle of her umbrella into his waistcoat, resolved to have something to hold by in case of emergency.'

The Lt Governor later countered that the Company had been eager to please the public by providing a service as each section opened, and consequently had been obliged to use temporary carriages run up for the occasion. He reprimanded the public for its somewhat ungracious impatience with such a pioneering line and said they had yet to show the appreciation it deserved. Darjeeling had become the summer headquarters for the Bengal Government and was becoming popular with visitors before the line was fully completed, although there appeared to be a certain reluctance from the residents in providing accommodation to rent. The hotels and boarding houses were often crowded to suffocation, whilst private houses were lying empty for the season.

The truth was that many of the derailments were due to the tramway having, for some curious reason, invested in twenty of the patented six-wheeled carriages advocated by the engineer James Cleminson, but there could not have been a more unsuitable line to be put at the mercy of these lamentable vehicles. Cleminson was closely involved with the Spooner social circle at the time and his London offices in Westminster Chambers almost shared the same staircase with Robert Fairlie in Palace Chambers. Fairlie's patented double-engine had been highly applauded on the Festiniog line and Cleminson had been appointed the Engineer of the North Wales Narrow Gauge Railway after Edwin Spooner had resigned in 1878. This had given him the opportunity of introducing three of his carriages into service, although the Festiniog had drawn the line at just one, and that was only for freight. How he convinced the Darjeeling line to adopt twenty of them remains a mystery, but it must have been a testament to his marketing skills and perhaps the distance of the customer.

The final stretch of the tramway from Ghum to Darjeeling took but a further three months to complete; it had been a remarkable achievement. Indeed the entire forty-nine miles of track from Siliguri had taken barely eighteen months to lay, but despite the economies employed, the actual cost had risen by Rs300,000 to 1,700,000 (£113,330).

The grand opening was set for 3rd July. It was to be a lavish affair attended by the Lt Governor and all the local dignitaries Prestage could muster for the ceremonies. The inaugural train was to depart from Siliguri at 6.05, and the engine was dressed in garlands of flowers and evergreen whilst the guests were treated to a sumptuous breakfast in the station. The Hon W.E. Gladstone was amongst the dignitaries, a relative of the British Prime Minister and a useful name to have as the Chairman of the tramway. The crowds were out in force, and the locomotive steamed out of

'A collection of filthy tumbledown huts' was how Jor Bungalow was described in a contemporary gazetteer. Nevertheless, it was the junction with a route that led to the Teesta Bridge, passing close to the former cantonment at Senchal (8,163ft). Although detachments of invalid soldiers had been quartered here in daub–and–wattle structures as early as 1844, construction of the barracks did not begin until 1857 and was only partially completed by 1860. Work was terminated three years later owing to the excessive isolation and bitter cold driving many soldiers to suicide, and by 1867 the cantonment had been abandoned and moved to Jalapahar.

An early photograph of the railway descending from Ghum to Batasia. With a gradient that averaged 1 in 20 (and steepening to 1 in 16 at one point), this section of the line to Darjeeling was the most demanding for the locomotive crews. The track laid on the outer edge of the area seen on the top bend is still extant, but the flattened area has been built on and borders the railway.

Below: *As an 'A' Class leads with a short freight bound for Siliguri, a trolley pauses for the photographer to capture this 19th-century scene of the railway on two levels near Tindharia. The sense of adventure with the journey can be appreciated, with no signs of habitation and the absence of any traffic on the cart road.*

Siliguri at the head of three new Cleminson carriages specially brought up for the occasion. There was a great fanfare, with cheering crowds waving flags as the fog detonators attached to the rails exploded.

The train ran into mist near Chunbatti, but spirits remained high and another reception awaited the party at Tindharia. More fog detonators accompanied the departure, and when the train steamed into Kurseong in record time at 9.30, it seemed that nothing could stand in the way of a most successful day. The guests were given another huge breakfast to toast the success of the tramway, but the tributes were all a little premature, for the train had barely left the celebration when the last carriage jumped the track. No sooner had it been put back on the rails than the second Cleminson wandered off, and indeed it did so again before reaching Jor Bungalow. By now the guests had become quite proficient with manhandling the coaches back to the rails, and the only real casualty was a certain amount of bruised pride. Indeed, it caused great amusement with some of the passengers, and a contemporary report reflected that '... *it sounds for all the world like a toy railway.*'

Meanwhile, Sir Ashley Eden and his entourage were patiently waiting at Jor Bungalow to open the final section, and two additional trains had been marshalled to reduce the possibility of mishap. The passengers rearranged themselves according to their order of precedence, the leading train comprising but two carriages for the Lt Governor and his immediate party, with the second transporting guests regarded as having less importance, which left the third to bump along with their servants and baggage.

The station at Darjeeling was packed, and the first train arrived in grand style with the assembled band thumping away to stirring music and the crowds cheering .... and there they waited. Unfortunately the second train had fallen off the rails, and after the crew managed to lever the errant stock back on the line, it began a very cautious descent towards Darjeeling. It was not long before it ground to a halt again, whereupon the Lt Governor sent his train back up the line to sort things out and rescue those now stranded. As if matters could not get any worse this also derailed, and now blocked any other train that might have stayed on the track.

It must have been a magnificent nightmare, and quite what the hill people were now making of the purple-faced crews heaving the trains back on the rails can only be imagined, but one thing for sure was that their children were being kept well away in case a sacrifice was required! The old servant, who had previously reported on the fire-eater seen on the metre gauge at Siliguri, claimed that men had said the tramway locomotive:

> '... *was a small thing, the butcha* [child] *of the larger evil that came to Siliguri. It did not burst the bellies of men, but its shriek brought on sickness, and many of those working on the line were down with malaria. The line crept forward, and one day when the engine came to Darjeeling, all were filled with fear. Men heard the distant rumble of the wheels from behind trees and watched the monster creep into the station.*'

The marooned guests, dressed in top hats, morning suits and crinoline dresses, attempted to maintain some form of silent dignity as they picked their way over the track and waited for the Governor's train to be dragged back on the rails, determined at all costs to make a glorious entrance into Darjeeling. Indeed they did, as the train arrived at 15.30 to the roar of approval from the crowds and, as the band played on, the welcome drowned out all the embarrassments.

A splendid banquet was laid on and Franklin Prestage opened the speeches by reminding the party that the railway could not have been built without the support of Colonel Stanton. He then went on to lavishly praise the Viceroy, and toasted his health before paying tribute to the Governor of Bengal. Prestage recalled the achievements of the Province in recent times, and extolled the virtues of private enterprise advancing the construction of its railways, whilst Sir Ashley Eden was acclaimed for removing the official barriers he had encountered on the way. The Governor responded that advisors to the Indian Government had been of the opinion that the railway might be constructed as a toy and would never be a useful paying line. However, along with Colonel Stanton, he had a strong belief in the Darjeeling Tramway, which he hoped would soon be renamed the Himalayan Railway and be accepted with pride by the residents of Darjeeling.

Prestage gave the concluding speech and commented on his anxieties:

> '... *although I had implicit faith in the professional opinion of Colonel Stanton, and I hope I have satisfied you that I have the proper regard and respect for the judgement and opinions of our late Viceroy and His Honour, yet many professional men whose opinions were*

With the photographer standing with his back against the original locomotive works at Tindharia, this early view looks towards the bluff of rock on which the bungalow had been built for the Locomotive Superintendent (and later under IR occupied by the Assistant Mechanical Engineer). The first of the grand receptions held on the opening day of the tramway is believed to have been held in the rather opulent office behind the trolley. It can be seen that the foundations on the outer edge were subsequently torn away, and the subsidence was noted by Colonel Le Messurier RE during his inspection (published in 1888). Note the supporting rails he referred to embedded in the embankment below.

Courtesy: Library of Congress, World's Transportation Commission Photograph Collection, (reproduction number LC-D426-572)

entitled to more respect, thought we should not get our engines up the Hill; many more thought we should not get them round the curves, and almost all agreed we should not haul a fare paying load. Well, all this has now been set at rest and will, I believe, be more thoroughly so by results in the way already indicated by His Highness.... What are occasional derailments, and I must confess I do not see why they should occur when the line is in working order, when compared with a long wearisome journey of days gone by? The Press, I am afraid, has been too prone to listen to the carpings of indignant passengers who have grievances, imaginary or true. Let those who are unbelievers judge for themselves and make a journey on the line. With ordinary care and moderate speed we ought never to hear of an accident.'

Many of the invited guests stayed on at the hill station for the next few days and the records show that the return trip was no less of an adventure. Some of the party elected to travel in an unsprung open trolley, but Darjeeling can experience four seasons of weather in one day and the rain began to fall like stair-rods. Those departing were wrapped in waterproofs and sheltered under their umbrellas on the trolley, desperately trying to enjoy whatever was in sight. Any derailment was now regarded as being perfectly normal, and when they ran into a landslide after Kurseong, the passengers simply scrambled over the rubble and scree. Mrs Herbert Reynolds later recalled in her memoirs that it had been:

'... a proceeding I rather enjoyed as it enabled me to fill a small basket with ferns and begonia roots which grew abundantly on the rocks.

Once on the other side we again took train and arrived in Calcutta without further mishap, feeling considerably refreshed both in body and mind by our pleasant jaunt!'

It had to be admitted the opening had been high farce, but the novelty of a train scaling the flanks of the Himalaya had outweighed the humiliation of it falling off the track. However, if it was to gain respect, the Company now had to show it was capable of running a service and providing a return for its investors.

An early photograph of the wooden bridge across the Mahanandi river (now known as the Mahananda). The train is hauled by a No.1 Class side-tank locomotive, which were soon superseded by the No.2 Class well-tanks. However, four were retained until the bridge was strengthened in 1894, as it was regarded as too weak to support the weight of the new engines. The same scene today would show the concrete dual carriageway road bridge engulfed by the growth of Siliguri. This is one of the many Bourne & Shepherd photographs taken of the DHR.

From the opening day, the four-wheeled gravity trolleys proved to be highly popular, enabling a party to descend at their own pace and stop wherever they chose. The Hill Cart Road appears more as a convenient place to stretch the legs rather than providing an alternative means of travel.

Chapter 3

The Iron Sherpa

The new Darjeeling Steam Tramway Company was now up and running and published its first staff list in Thacker's Business Directory for Bengal:

Headquarters Kurseong:

Resident Engineer:	I.J. Whitty	(Kurseong)
Personal Assistant:	R. O'Flaherty	(Kurseong)
Assistant Engineers:	H. Edwards	(Kurseong)
	J. Bibra	(Gayabari)
Sub. Assistant:	J. Nash	(Gayabari)
P.W.Inspection:	J. Sharpe	(Gayabari)
	W. Marsden	(Siliguri)
	T. Lloyd	(Chunbatti)
	W.R. Williams	(Chunbatti)
Overseers:	R.K. Mookerjee	(Kurseong)
	Bunsgopal	(Chunbatti)
	R.B. Claudius	(Sonada)
Sub.Overseer:	J.G. Chatterjee	(Gayabari)

Resident Engineer's Office:

Accountant:	M.L. Ghosal	(Kurseong)
Clerks:	S.N. Burrat	(Kurseong)
	K.N. Banerjee	(Kurseong)
	M.L. Chatterji	(Kurseong)
Cashier:	K.C. Bhuttacharjee	(Kurseong)
Draftsman:	Golam Ruhman	(Kurseong)
Sub. Store Keeper:	M.L. Chuckerbutty	(Siliguri)
Traffic Superintendent:	W.H. Robinson	
Guard:	D.J. Gore	

Locomotives:

Loco Superintendent:	A.E. Annand
Clerk:	G.C. Roy and native staff

Drivers:	G. Rouhrey	Firemen:	J. Miller
	W. Monro		J. Martin
	W. Nelson		C. Martin
	W. Allen		A. Khan
	J. Phillips		

Stationmasters:

Darjeeling	T. Crimson
Jore Bungalow	K.N. Chucrobutty
Sonada	N.L. Mookerjee
Kurseong	J.N. Dutta
Gayabari	J.N. Ghose
Tindharia	R.G. Chowdry
Sukna	L.N. Banerjee
Siliguri	F.H. Harcourt (Darjeeling Steam Tramway/North Bengal State Railway)

But it was not to last for long; the posts remained, but soon many of the British who held positions moved on. It was still pioneering country and however romantic the notion sounded, the health of those not used to the climate suffered as they tried to cope with the rawness of the Himalaya. Darjeeling was indeed a sanatorium, but at least as a guest one could pick and choose the season to visit and depart when conditions changed.

The climate could not have helped to heal the serious differences of opinion that appeared to be forming between Prestage and the engineers, and for some it was time to make sure the sun would never set somewhere else in the Empire. In fact the year had barely closed when the Locomotive Superintendent left and the Company sought the services of James Houghton to fill the vacancy, whilst only one of the

A splendid early photograph of No.9 on a Down freight at Agony Point. Built in 1882 as a well-tank to a cost of Rs12,350 by Messrs Sharp, Stewart & Co. of Manchester, it was the first of the No.2 Class locomotives. These engines were fitted with an additional saddle tank in 1886 and referred to as the 'A' Class following the introduction of the 'B' Class in 1889. The first wagon is one of the original Cleminson six-wheeler carriages converted to carry goods.

Darjeeling-Himalayan Railway Co.,
LIMITED.

Travel to Darjeeling by the
MOUNTAIN RAILWAY
and for the Downward Journey use the
SERVICE TROLLIES.

The best way to view the
GORGEOUS HILL SCENERY.

No Additional Cost to First Class Passengers.

original locomotive drivers still remained by 1882. Irwine Whitty vacated his post shortly after the tramway opened and took up an engagement with the construction of the Bengal-Nagpur-Tirhoot line, from which he retired in 1889.

The journey to Darjeeling in the 1880s was not for the faint-hearted and the published timetable advised the journey would take 7 hours 23 minutes from Siliguri, with an additional hour for the stop at Kurseong. A contemporary report relates the journey by the metre gauge to Siliguri from Sara Ghat by the Northern Bengal State Railway as an absolute nightmare:

'It was noisy, bumpy and shaking in all directions, it plodded its way towards the Himalayas, regardless of passengers' comforts. It had to get there and it got there, though many parted with their dinner and sleep – and then remained but fifty-two miles by the DH Railway, which had just cast off its appellation of a steam tramway to take on that of a railway. The journey over those fifty-two miles absolutely put in the shade the discomforts endured on the NBSR.'

The report continued that whilst the metre gauge shook the passengers in all directions, the line to Darjeeling:

'... did a sort of Charleston - an up and down movement – which still clings to it between Siliguri and Sukna. By the time travellers reached their destination they were pale and limp, and the commiseration of their friends on their enforced residence in the horrid plains fell on deaf ears.'

It appears that the pleas from Prestage for more reasoned comments had yet to be heard, and it was no wonder, for the abominable Cleminson six-wheelers must have left a trail of havoc over the light track for the four-wheelers to cope with.

The Company appointed Messrs Gillanders Arbuthnot & Co. of Calcutta as its agent to handle all the legal and financial sides of the operation. Established in 1820, the main focus of this highly respected company lay with their trade as bankers and merchants. Such an Agency usually managed several businesses of the same type, for example tea estates, as it was more economical to sell their output in Calcutta than each garden trying to do so alone. Over the years, Gillanders Arbuthnot became responsible for the management of many different companies' including jute mills and coalmines, and received their income from a percentage of the profits rather than owning any shares in the concerns. In time they also came to control the affairs of a number of other Indian railways as their commissioned agents, including the Raipur Forest Tramway, the Hurdwar Dehra Branch Railway and the Southern Punjab Railway.

The House of Gladstone, which gave Great Britain one of its finest prime ministers of the time, became strongly identified with Gillanders Arbuthnot & Co. throughout the life of the DHR in private ownership. The core of the business was directed by the Partners at the London office of Ogilvy Gillanders & Co. with 'd.o.l's' (demi-official letters) being dispatched weekly from Calcutta to appraise the situation. Many members of the Gladstone family served on the Board of Directors, and indeed held the position of being the first and many of the later Chairmen of the railway. It was to prove a fruitful working relationship, and

Although the location of this early rake of trolleys was not recorded, it appears to be on the plains section and probably at Sukna. The four-wheelers were hastily put together to relieve the passengers and track from the peripatetic Cleminson six-wheeled coaches.

Collection: Mrs Tenduf la

A mixed train of one six-wheeled Cleminson and five four-wheeled freight wagons plus seven passenger trolleys pauses on the descent to Darjeeling. This would have been the maximum load for the No.2 class locomotive, which appears in its original form without the additional saddle tank and bunker, and thus dates the photograph before 1886. The severity of the gradient can be seen on the following bluff.

Collection: Hugh Ashley Rainer

a policy was maintained that ensured a close liaison was always kept between the Manager and Engineer's offices on the railway, along with the Mechanical Superintendent of the workshops at Tindharia. The day-to-day running of the railway took place in Darjeeling and later Kurseong, but the agent was responsible for the overall management and, as a public company, it was quoted on the Calcutta Stock Exchange. A Director of Gillanders later recalled the accounts submitted from Kurseong were without exception well maintained and that an annual budget was always prepared in advance for the agent, a common practice in business today but something which was quite unknown in India as nobody ever thought about such things!

The tramway changed its name to the Darjeeling Himalayan Railway Company on 15th September 1881 and it was now expected to deliver its promises. The traffic was encouraging, with the report that 8,000 passengers were carried in its first full year of operation along with 380 tons of goods. However, a letter from a tea planter printed in *The Englishman* only a week later complained bitterly over the time taken to transport tea to Calcutta and stated:

> *'I beg you to understand that I am not talking of the Tramway; delays of course must be expected by those who are foolish enough to entrust to it.'*

The Press warned in early October that:

> *'The climate and scenery of Darjeeling may be all that the most fastidious dweller of Calcutta may require at this time of year for a change, but man cannot live on ozone and scenery any more than on bread alone.'*

The food supply was rapidly running out and the prices were escalating rapidly. By 13th October it was reported:

> *'There was a very near approach to utter famine in Darjeeling last Sunday. Coarse rice was selling at the rate of only 8 seers for the rupee and fowls were almost unprocurable at any price while Rupees 1/4 [1 Rupee 4 Annas] per dozen was being asked and paid for eggs. A sort of modified millennium[1] for house keepers in Darjeeling was expected to set in when the railway had been completed and the Teesta bridge opened, but as far as results have gone at present, what with the increased cost of food and fuel, the millennium appears to be further off than ever.'*

The love affair with the Press was over. The railway was no longer news and, as with the way of so many others, little was to appear in the newspapers apart from it being held accountable for its failings. The fun was now in the province of the travellers and in the reading of their hardships.

It was clear that the priority for the new Company lay with sorting out the severity of the curves and gradients, particularly on the section up to the 24th milepost. Prestage turned to his brother-in-law Sulyard Bernard Cary, who had accompanied him to Darjeeling in 1878, when the idea of laying a tramway on the Cart Road was first mooted. Cary had trained and worked his articled pupillage as a civil engineer for Rowland Brotherhood of Chippenham, a railway engineering company that had previously secured contracts from Brunel for constructional work on the GWR. The company was concentrating its business on building components for railways and bridges across the British Empire by the time Cary joined and, after three years' employment, he left in September 1868 and sailed to India the following year.

Cary worked for two years on the Eastern Bengal Railway with the building of the Gorai Bridge and subsequently became Assistant Engineer in 1872, using his skills mainly on protective works and flood repairs. Prestage had him transferred to the tramway project as soon as the contract had been signed, where he became the Assistant and Deputy Resident Engineer in May 1879. He left in September 1880 to return to the EBR in the capacity of Acting Superintendent of Way & Works, and one can only surmise if it was coincidence that his departure was only days after the tramway had advertised that it was to open for business to Kurseong. He certainly would have felt that his professional principles had been compromised by the hasty construction, and when the line was opened to Darjeeling the following year all the iniquities were exposed for all to see. Prestage desperately needed Cary to sort the nightmare out and offered him the post of Manager and Resident Engineer, no doubt hoping that family loyalties would keep the causes of the embarrassments quiet.

There was also an urgent need to improve and increase the locomotive stock, and two machines of a new design were ordered straight away from Messrs Sharp, Stewart of Manchester. The most noticeable change was a 250-gallon well-tank set between the frames and two supplementary 10-gallon wing-tanks suspended

---

[1] A term used in this context to describe a time of peace and happiness.

beneath the cylinders, both of which gave them a much lower centre of gravity than the original engines. A contract was agreed in 1882 to supply a further six machines, four of which were sub-contracted to the Hunslet Engine Company to speed up the deliveries. Two from the Sharp, Stewart order and two from the Leeds manufacturer arrived later in the year, with the remaining four following soon after in 1883.

With this work under way, Cary was able to focus his attention on the challenge of the civil engineering. The work required on the plains section was relatively straightforward, for that involved widening and upgrading the wooden bridge over the Mahanandi near Siliguri, which along with the others on this stretch was estimated to require Rs25,000 (£2,500). However, it was the gradients beyond Sukna where the principal difficulties lay, and new surveys were made to consider the options. The solution was found by constructing a series of loops that would enable the train to gain height by the track circling round and passing over itself on a bridge. This could be achieved by following the natural contours at the end of the spurs that rippled so much of the land, and thus would allow the line to climb on a ledge around the lower section before winding in on itself as the profile of the hill tapered.

A No.2 Class locomotive heading an Up goods at the top of loop No.2. There were problems with soil creep in the deep cutting from the time it was first cut, and a substantial construction of wood was needed to prevent the stone sets from collapsing.

The first loop was constructed 11½ miles from the terminus at Siliguri, where the road and railway rounded one of the numerous small promontories on their climb through the *terai* forest. The engineers maintained a workable gradient by cutting the trackbed at a lower level to the road, and by following a more sympathetic contour, it was able to swing back on itself and pass under the road at right angles. This led the train into a cutting on a tightening curve until it met the road on the level and crossed the bridge it had just passed under. The new earthworks had barely time to settle before the monsoon rains of 1883 washed the soil and rocks into the cutting, and the railway had no option but to close down the service until the rubble was cleared. The geology of the *terai* comprises beds of shale and boulders brought down the mountains, alternating with layers of sand from the plains, which makes for a cocktail that becomes particularly troublesome when full of water.

A second loop was laid at milepost 14, which described a more complicated spiral as it scaled the mountain near the Kulong bend at the end of a long spur from Selim Hill. It was approached almost in a southerly direction at a height of 1,743 feet above sea level, and the engineers were obliged to design a route that would follow the meandering contour before doubling back on itself. From this point, the track passed into a cutting that would lead the train beneath a gantry of timbers that trussed a bridge across an outcrop of rock, the sides of which were reinforced with stone sets. The running curve tightened to a 100ft radius until it became parallel to the original course, before wrapping back on itself by a 75ft-radius curve. The track was now lined up to climb the embankment and cross the wooden bridge, having gained 138 feet in all, although the lower and upper courses were barely 50 yards apart in plan view and running in opposite directions.

The gradients of the road eased out over the next two miles and it was comparatively easy for the engineers

In 1889 it was hoped that the problems with loop No.2 would be resolved by filling in the cutting and forming a tunnel for the train to pass through, after which it would climb and subsequently cross by an embankment. It was never a really satisfactory improvement as the blast from the locomotive was to cause problems inside the confines of the tunnel. The loop was severely damaged in 1942 and replaced by a reverse siding.

to follow the route to Chunbatti, where a third loop was cut into the side of another spur. The layout was a more straightforward plan of the previous spiral, describing a double circle that followed the perimeter, the lower track running behind a *dak* bungalow before tightening in on itself. This led the train under a road bridge to a rising loop that passed in front of the bungalow to meet the road and bridge.

It was shortly beyond here that the surveyors were faced with the gradients that had brought the train carrying the Viceroy to grief in 1880. The line had been carved into the side of the mountain and there was nowhere that a loop could be constructed. It appeared there was no way to ease the climb and the skills of the engineers and contractors were pushed to exasperation. It is said that Herbert Rumsey (the contractor) confided in his wife Lily of the impending defeat one evening as they sat down at the tea table, whereupon she offered an unlikely but glaringly simple suggestion. She told him that whilst learning ballroom dancing from her stepfather in Darjeeling, she had been taught that it was permitted to make a reversal when faced with a tight corner, and by carving out her idea on the side of a fruit cake, she demonstrated that the same principle could be applied if the railway backtracked up the hill. So the first of the reversing stations was constructed near the 18th milepost, and it took the train forward to the lower limit on a gradient of 1 in 28, whereupon it reversed up the hillside on a 1 in 33 climb to a siding at the second level. A change of points at this junction would then permit the train to resume its forward journey at the higher elevation.

It must be stated that it was not the first use of reverse sidings, for the principle had been established just over twenty years earlier with the climb from Bombay over the Bhore and Thal Ghats. This staggering accomplishment of civil engineering allowed the trains to scale the 1 in 37 by a single reverse, the locomotive changing ends at the mid-way point. In 1869, the engineer John Whitton also designed the Great Zig-Zag on the western line of the New South Wales Railways. It was the only financially viable option that could take the line into the Lithgow Valley, and for the first time provided access by rail to the interior of Australia. Henry Meiggs adopted the design of double reverses for construction of the Oroya Railway in Peru during the late 1870s, and one can only speculate if the achievements in Australia and South America had reached the ears of the tramway contractors in the *terai* forests of Bengal. Thacker's guide to Darjeeling published in 1883 advised these reverses were known locally as *goompties*,[2] whilst the late and highly respected Mike Satow, who was an honorary adviser to the National Railway Museum of India, recalled that the railway staff often referred to the sidings as *jet curves*.[3]

A second reverse siding was the only solution to gain height at the 20th milepost, beyond which the engineers were faced with the prospect of constructing a fourth loop. In plan view it was the simplest in profile by being a single spiral, but the civil engineering literally required the removal of the top of a hill and laying the track round the elliptical perimeter. It was a spectacular diversion, with the track tightening to a mean radius of barely 59ft and constricting to 44ft at the most acute point. Such was the sensation from the overhang of the carriages that early passengers talked of their exhilaration of being poised in the air and referred to it as 'Agony Point'. A third reverse was carved into the mountainside three miles beyond the loop shortly before the line approached Gayabari, and the fourth and final reverse siding appeared soon after leaving the village.

The Rt Hon.W.E. Baxter MP made an account of his journey on the railway just after the first loop had been constructed. He recalled travelling with a party overnight on the metre gauge:

> *'... and was astonished when a man shouted in my ear at 6 am, 'next station Siliguri'. Here we breakfasted, and took our seats in perhaps the most extraordinary and toy-like tram railroad which exists on the face of the earth. An American said of it the other day to a friend of mine: "I guess I have seen a good many queer things in the shape of railroads in my country, but this is the cheekiest little concern that ever I came across." The rails are two feet apart; the carriages are like low tram-cars; and so steep is the gradient – often 1 in 17 – that little boys, seated on the engine, jump off at places where the sun has not melted the dew, to put sand on the rails, the tiny engine meantime puffing and blowing until the wheels can get a grip. At one place there is an actual loop, the train passing over a bridge, which it has passed under a few minutes before.*
>
> *I am one of those unfortunate people who become easily giddy looking down from great heights, and my friends had prepared me for a terrible experience on this line; but except at four or five unprotected curves close to Darjeeling, it was not nearly so bad as I had expected it would be. In many of the most dangerous places there is a substantial parapet, and trees and shrubs cover the sides of the steep hills, so, that you are not sensible of the sheer precipice. .... It would amuse a London-and-North-Western man to see the miserable hut which serves as the first station-house on the Darjeeling-Himalaya line. At this point it begins rapidly to ascend through a forest of exceeding beauty, many of the trees being very lofty, some of them having a canopy of flowers, and others covered with creepers of strange and weird-like shapes. There is a cart-track alongside the train-line, and every now and then you come upon stations to permit of conveyances passing each other, like those on the Suez Canal. There are a good many villages and shanties for the workmen who are employed in great numbers in repairing and altering the line. Occasionally you steam through a crowded bazaar, and the curves well merit the American description.*
>
> *Khersiong, surrounded on all hands by tea gardens, is a bustling place; and we found the bazaars crowded by men, women and children of all the multifarious races, which inhabit this part of Central Asia. The main street is only a few feet wide; but the steam-car puffs along the centre of it; and it would be difficult for a person who has never been out of Europe to imagine the scene at the market-place when we started after breakfast.*
>
> *Nepaul, Thibet, Sikkim and Bhotan were all within sight from points on these lofty*

---

[2] Ghoom or ghoomna is a vernacular term used for turning or rotating, and the term used on the railway grammatically appears in the female gender, which indeed many friends in India suggest the train is!

[3] The explanation has so far remained elusive, although the ballet term jeté, a leap from one leg to the other, may have been bequeathed by amused ladies of the Raj seeing their train jumping from one level to the next. A relatively modern claim could also be made by the engine storming up an incline in reverse resembling the backward force of a jet!

Encroaching vegetation and building have made the reverse sidings more difficult to photograph in recent years. This early illustration shows the layout of the original No.1 reverse, close to where the Viceroy's train foundered in 1880.

Collection: Nick Rhodes

Below: *The scars of construction and the erosion of the topsoil by torrential rain are evident in this early photograph of the third reverse siding at Gayabari. The course of the railway and Hill Cart Road can be seen slowly rising in the distance, with the Pagla Jhora (Mad Torrent) in a quiet mood to the left of centre. Note the semaphore signal on the lower approach to the reverse.*

Travelling by a gravity trolley was the undoubted highlight for most travellers returning to the plains, Mark Twain having described it as 'the mixed ecstasy of deadly fright and unimaginable joy'. They were permitted to descend at 25mph and were usually controlled by two coolies, who either applied the brake to check the speed or pushed when passing through the bazaars and on level sections.

elevations; and hundreds of the races which dwell there are to be found employed on the railway, or on those great plantations of tea which are accomplishing almost a revolution in this remote portion of British territory. Our engine had to stop several times, in consequence of bad coal, and it was nearly 6 o'clock in the evening when we arrived at Meadow Bank, one of Mr Doyle's hotel-bungalows....

.... A great treat was awaiting us this morning. Mr Prestage, the managing director of the tramline, had arranged that we should be 'trollied' down the mountains instead of going in the train; so at Ghoom station, which is higher than Darjeeling, and from which to the plain there is a continuous descent, we found two little tramcars fastened together, and Mr Walker, one of the officials – a Scotchman, of course – who managed the brakes, and took us down in the most skilful manner, at the rate of fifteen miles an hour, stopping an hour for breakfast at the charming little Clarendon hotel at Khersiong, from which we had our final look of the gigantic Kinchinjunga. The motion of the trollies was the most delightful I ever experienced in travelling, and without the locomotive you see the scenery far better. Its grandeur and variety struck us more than when going up.

At Siliguri station I saw a considerable quantity of very superior jute, which had been brought on ox-carts for forty miles. We found here waiting us an excellent dinner, and three large sleeping carriages for our night journey on the Northern Bengal Railway. The East Indian Company refused to give us any facilities whatever, but the managers of all the other railroads were exceedingly polite, and their liberality will certainly be an encouragement to travellers.'

It is not clear whether the railway was preoccupied with its civil engineering or still sorting out the business relationship with Gillanders Arbuthnot, but the fact that it had not published its half-yearly reports was attracting comment in the Press. No dividends had been paid, causing a letter being sent to *The Statesman* on 11th October 1882 from a *'Shareholder of 170 Shares'*:

'Sir, – We are now in the middle of October, yet has no half-yearly report of the Darjeeling-Himalayan Railway been furnished to the shareholders. Surely it cannot be a very difficult matter to bring out the half-yearly report for a small line of 50 miles in length, within two months after the close of the half year. It is hard for shareholders not only to see the market value of their property decreasing, but also to be kept out of the dividend on their shares for so long a period.'

Cary left before the civil engineering work was completed, and one can only speculate about the tensions that had been mounting behind the scenes. The urgent need for improvements with the track so soon after opening must have strained their relationship, for Cary would have advocated investment for sound construction whilst Prestage was anxious to open as quickly as possible and earn a profit. Cary subsequently made a submission in 1883 to the Institution of Civil Engineers in London to qualify as an Associate Member, with Whitty as one of his backers. Prestage refused to release any papers to assist with the paper Cary was writing on the construction work undertaken, stating he did not wish his name to appear in any way, and declared he was adverse to the Institution itself. Indeed, Prestage would have had the final say on the submissions that were made to Thacker's Directory, and the entrepreneur was not going to let anybody steal his thunder. Only the names of the Deputy and Assistant Resident Engineers were published, and with the search being on for a scapegoat, it looked as though one had been found.

Anxious to rescue credibility, Prestage decided to release one of the new locomotives from service and entered it into the Calcutta Exhibition. Staged from 4th December 1883 to 10th March 1884, it was a major show for its time, and today would be the equivalent of a 'World Expo'. It was organised by Mr Joubert, a private operator who was French by birth but had since been granted citizenship to New South Wales in Australia. The exhibition was a remarkable event, for the presentation of the concept, the planning and its staging all occurred within twelve months. Special buildings were erected on the maidan between Chowringhee and the Hooghly, and the categories for display covered almost every conceivable facet of life and industry from foodstuffs and machinery to education and surveying, with exhibits coming not only from India, but Britain, Europe and North America. Merit awards were given in numerous classifications, and the DHR locomotive No.15 was honoured with a silver medal. It was just the sort of tonic Prestage needed, for the railway had its hands more than full with the civil engineering and was now hastily hammering together some closed four-wheeled

Although there had been a small bazaar in Darjeeling long before the British acquired the area, it became a focal point for trade after the opening of the railway. This early photograph shows the extension of the line from the passenger station to the main bazaar passing by the ubiquitous shacks and stalls that have become synonymous with life on Indian railways.

carriages to release the Cleminsons from service.

The new rolling stock and reconstruction work doubled the costs of the railway to Rs2,800,000, but it was a sound investment as it finally made it possible to run a viable train service. The figures for 1884 showed that 36,500 passenger train miles were run and a new Class had been introduced, with 2,274 travelling by 1st Class, 4,903 by 2nd Class and 24,000 by the lowest Class. The maximum pay-load for the new No.2 Class locomotives was stated to be twenty tons and the standard make-up of a passenger train was thirteen four-wheelers, comprising one luggage van, one 1st Class carriage and two 1st Class trolleys, four 2nd Class carriages, four 3rd Class trolleys plus a mail or brake van. Passengers were charged fares of 72 *pies*[4] per mile for 1st Class, 36 *pies* per mile 2nd Class and 15 *pies* for the lowest Class, which was between four and six times that on other Indian railways. An analysis of the statistical returns had been made and demonstrated that each 1st Class passenger was travelling an average of 45.12 miles, those in 2nd Class 34.18 miles and the lowest Class 30.65 miles, which any railway would have been delighted with as it showed that the majority were travelling the full distance.

The new locomotives were an undoubted improvement over the original machines, which were found to be rough riders on account of the boxing motion caused by their short wheelbase. This in turn had created a wave effect with the water in the side tanks, and when originally obliged to haul the Cleminson six-wheeled stock, it had been a miracle of physics if the train ever got to Darjeeling without leaving the rails. The internal valve gear set between the narrow frames of the engines added to their misgivings and the arrival of the No.2 Class soon made them redundant. It was

---

[4] 100 pies/paise = 1 rupee.

decided to sell four of them in 1884 to the Ferozepore Tramway in the Punjab, the others being retained for working trains over the Mahananda Bridge. This had yet to be upgraded and there was some doubt whether or not it could bear the weight of the new engines.

The freight returns for the same year were equally promising, with 86,705 train miles being run to transport 16,730 tons of goods. The new locomotives were capable of hauling five loaded freight wagons with a gross load of 39 tons for the climb and twelve for the downhill run. Freight trains were well patronised in both directions, and the figures showed the majority of this traffic was being carried right through to the termini. It was sufficient encouragement to lay a quarter-mile extension from the passenger station at Darjeeling to the bazaar, and this opened for traffic on 16th June 1885.

The freight charges made by the railway were based on the classification of the merchandise to be carried. The cost of transportation for each mile of 1st Class goods was calculated at 3 *pies* per *maund*, 2nd Class at 4 *pies* per *maund*, and 3rd Class at 5 *pies* per *maund*. These charges were six to ten times the average for other railways, and the highest income was earned from transporting 3,598 tons of tea down to Siliguri (Rs68,170), followed by the 3,829 tons of grains and pulses being carried uphill (Rs50,398) for the workers. The remaining freight comprised mainly coal and coke, manufactured metals, manufactured cotton and the general provisions of salt, sugar and spices – and not forgetting the 394 tons of liquor!

The railway worked hard to ensure the salubrity of Darjeeling was no longer compromised by the journey, but the following letter from Eustace Kenyon, written

However innocuous the terai may have seemed at first sight, its name was enough to strike fear into the hearts of those who knew the area. It was the haunt of tigers, panthers and elephants, whilst the more secretive life in the undergrowth was venomous and equally deadly. No.2 Class locomotive No.15 pauses for the photographer with a short freight train in the forest.

Collection: Nick Rhodes

to his mother from Kurseong on Friday, 12th June 1885, reveals there were problems that are no less valid today!

'Yesterday morning about 8 we reached Siligori at the foot of the hill, stopped half an hour for breakfast then got into the tramway that goes up the hill. It is really something between a railway and tramway. Gauge two foot. First Class carriages supposed to hold six, cannot seat more than 4 comfortably. Rate supposed not to exceed 7 miles an hour but I should think it went up to ten sometimes. The road seems much like ours between Tavoy and Siam; but broader, and instead of sticking to the same level as a rule of 50 to 100 ft above water level, is constantly rising. Sometimes one describes a sort of figure eight to get on to a higher level, the train going round a complete loop and re-crossing the line over which it has just come at right angles or so only at a higher level. Then again one goes up a regular zigzag; the train stops then backs up upwards for a short distance and then stops and goes forward again still upwards. Sometimes you look down and see the line along which you came some time ago some 100 ft or more below. The hills are extremely steep and sometimes you twist on an extra sharp corner you think how exceedingly awkward it would be if a carriage were to be derailed there. Then on the other side one must be careful how one puts one's nose out of the window as it may get scratched by jungle or almost bruised by rock.

The journey however gets monotonous; the officials are very casual and waste a lot of time at the stations, where nobody gets in or out; then the train constantly stops at watering stations for the engine to drink, and once the engine ran almost dry before it got to the tank, so left us behind for half an hour or so while it went on to liquor. The result was that we were 3/4 of an hour late here. The view coming up is said to be very pretty but I couldn't see it, the whole being buried in heavy damp mist, which still continues here.

I had telegraphed for a room at the hotel here the morning I left Calcutta; but on arrival found no room and the manager knew nothing of my telegram, though a sort of sub-manager owned to having rec'd it. However, I and three others were put in a detached bungalow up a fearful bit of hill. This would be all right in fine weather and if I were not still a little weak, but as it is to toil up and down the hill in a damping mist or rain for every meal is too much of a good thing, so I have telegraphed Darjeeling for rooms this evening and go on by train today on the chance of getting them, though I hear Darjeeling is very full. I had a fire in my room last night for the first time since I left home. I must say even this mist is infinitely better than the heat of Calcutta.'

Franklin Prestage became the Chairman of the railway in 1885, the same year that the name of Spooner entered the records for the Darjeeling line. Thomas John Spooner was the younger brother of Charles Easton and worked as a solicitor in Leicester, although it is said his skills were more often required to defend allegations made about his own financial probity! His son Thomas John (junior) was born in 1862 and at the age of 17 was sent to work for his uncle Charles at Portmadoc. George Percival had already fled to India, and after four years in North Wales, young Thomas also became attracted to the sub-continent and followed on the heels of his errant cousin.

The interests of Spooner & Co. were no doubt an item on the agenda, and there would have been one of two wry smiles in Portmadoc when he became the Sub-Assistant Engineer of the DHR at Tindharia. He worked on the railway for three years, during which time he shared the duties with a D.L. Prestage, leaving one to speculate if the introduction of a family member to shadow the work of Spooner served to influence the theories of the strong-willed Chairman. It appears that Thomas John may also have directed the design of some of the rolling stock built to replace the ghastly Cleminsons. Many of the early four-wheeled carriages that appeared certainly bore a close resemblance to those on the Festiniog, whilst some of the wrought ironwork displayed definite elements of Spooner frippery. Thomas John moved on to build himself a distinguished railway career, becoming a District Engineer for the Madras State Railway before turning his attentions to East Africa to take up a similar post in Uganda. He eventually returned to India before retiring to England in Seaford, Sussex, where he died on 17th June 1937.

There were other elements of patronage and business interest between Prestage and Spooner. William Williams was Manager of the Boston Lodge Works on the Festiniog Railway and had worked closely for many years on the engineering side with James Spooner, whilst Charles Easton later became dependent upon him after the hasty departure of George Percival. The

An Up freight hauled by a No.2 Class fitted with the tapered coal bunker and 75-gallon saddle tank, the latter making for a more balanced weight distribution between the axles. The design for the 'B' Class was now emerging, and although these early machines were less powerful, the load in this photograph shows what a properly maintained steam locomotive on the railway is capable of.

Courtesy: George Eastman House

lure of India in Victorian Britain was endemic, and his own son John Williams set sail from Liverpool soon after and secured work on the East Bengal Railway, of which Franklin Prestage still happened to be the Agent.[5]

The circle did not stop there, for George Mingay Garrard, the consulting engineer for the DHR in Britain, had London offices that stood almost in the same shadows of those occupied by Fairlie and Cleminson. Based in Great George Street, his Westminster address also gave him easy access to the Institution of Mechanical Engineers and the Houses of Parliament. His name became closely associated with the construction of the engines and running frames of the rolling stock, having the responsibility for the inspection of the materials manufactured before despatch to India. He had previously worked as an Assistant Engineer for the Eastern Bengal Railway, where he was in charge of the construction from Choadangah to the Koomar River, followed by the position of a gazetted officer with the Public Works Department of the Bengal Government. Returning to Britain, Garrard became a partner with E.R. & F. Turner of Ipswich, before acquiring two further partnerships with foundries in Banff and Carmarthen. He finally set himself up in private practice, and in 1886 published detailed plans for a patented double engine for the DHR that he called *'The Climber'*. It never matured beyond the drawing board, and although it must have flattered Prestage by reflecting his original desire for a twin locomotive, one can only surmise what was going through Fairlie's mind at the time!

On a more prosaic level, it was decided that the situation with the motive power already in use could

---

[5] It is also interesting to note that the memorandum and plans of the Darjeeling Himalayan Railway were later to be presented on 16th March 1901 by John Hughes to the Cape Government Railways. As a trained civil engineer and a Fellow of the Geological Society, he had become the official surveyor with the Welsh Slate Company and in 1874 entered into partnership with Spooner & Co. In 1889 he was made the Engineer and General Manager of the Festiniog Railway on the condition he relinquished all other interests, which included his involvement with Spooner & Co.

An Up train of four-wheelers at Tung (5,656ft). Five miles beyond Kurseong and 800ft higher, it was the next watering stop (the tower being in the middle distance) on the climb to Darjeeling. The attractive passenger waiting room was on the opposite side of the road, and work has been undertaken in more recent times to restore the decorative fretting on the station roof, seen on the left-hand side of this early photograph.

Collection: (The late) Mrs Tenduf la

be quickly improved by upgrading the No.2 Class locomotives with saddle tanks to increase their water capacity. Coal bunkers were also fitted above the fireboxes to carry additional fuel, and the design was now evolving into what was to become the most successful class for the railway.

Prestage produced a paper in December 1886 entitled 'Notes on the Progress, Construction and Working of the Darjeeling Himalayan Railway' and submitted ten copies to the Institution of Civil Engineers in London, an organisation he had previously been adverse to. No reasons for his change of heart were given, but he must have been smarting with his brother-in-law Cary being made an Associate Member for his work on the railway whilst he had not received so much as a nomination; perhaps it was now time to try another strategy. The doubling of the investment in order to overcome the problems with the civil engineering had been an embarrassment, and he sought to justify the glorious folly of building the line without a proper survey. He also recommended that the gauge should be widened to 2ft 6in, subject to the minimum curve having a radius not less than 100ft, and suggested that it would enable the line to carry four times the traffic without strain. He was even able to put a spin on the question of flange friction, advising that it could be used to gain the necessary adhesion required for the proposed Nilgiri Railway in southern India, which was still undecided whether to go with the Riggenbach or Abt rack systems. Prestage was clearly delighted with the solution offered by the reverse sidings and advocated that: *'In selecting the route for a Mountain Railway, if it can be arranged, particularly in a country where the rainfall is heavy, economy would be shown in all important directions by ascending by a number of zig-zags up one even slope or face.'*

The Darjeeling line was now settling down to the business of running a railway, but it was still a cruel and desperate land where life was hard, fever endemic, and only the fittest were able to survive the disease, the damp and the drink. The *terai* forests on the plains between Siliguri and Sukna were being cleared for tea plantations, and as the tiger and elephant retreated, so the mosquito and red spider held life to ransom. The tea-planter made the law, became the judge, the jury, and inevitably the dispenser of justice. Alcohol was seen as a welcome retreat from the rasping climate, and stories have been passed on of planters riding through the night after orgies of serious drinking. Visitors from the cities in search of the benefits of the hill station were seen as ready targets for practical jokes, and the reputation of the planters spread as far afield as Calcutta, where they were known as the 'Blue Devils'.[6]

Although one suspects the story could be apocryphal, it is said there were records that showed Messrs Hurt and Feltwell were not the assumed names, but those of two such jokers riding on a down train to Siliguri. They were having great fun passing along the carriages at stations collecting tickets from passengers and offering the advice of where to change trains for Paddington, Euston and the like. The driver decided to get his own back and departed rapidly from one station, leaving the pair chasing the train. Hurt fell and could have indeed been killed had it not been for Feltwell grabbing him, and the train was stopped to put an end to the caper. The railway staff asked for their names and addresses, whereupon the first replied *'I am Hurt'* and despite reasoning, would not change his answer. Tempers were not soothed when the other was asked if he was injured and replied *'I, Feltwell'*, whereupon the two were promptly placed under arrest and subsequently fined 25 rupees for boarding a train in motion!

Gradually the land became tamed, and consequently the spirits of the early traders subdued and life sobered to a more structured society, with schools and health institutions being established and some semblance of legal rights being granted to the workers. It did not stop the pranks, and the tale is told of one old planter encouraging a new arrival to drink 'tiger's milk' to prevent malaria, the brew being no more than the local hooch. He was laid in his alcoholic haze between the corpses of two coolies who had died earlier that day, and when he awoke the following morning was told that the widows may be placated with a payment. Nursing a fierce hangover, he fled to the railway station in a fit of panic and vanished on the departing train.

It was perfectly possible for those travelling on the railway to dismiss such antics, as to them India was seen to be riddled with strange happenings. Darjeeling was the ideal escape from the heat, and one learned not to notice such behaviour and look the other way. Lord Beveridge recounted that his mother Annette found the journey to Darjeeling in 1887 had now *'... improved immeasurably, although was hardly luxury ... but to enjoy it, one should not have travelled all the previous night'*.

However, the mischief of the men on the plains was replaced by the more vixenish social life of the ladies in the hills, for she observed:

> *'Everyone knew everyone and all were continually in and out of one another's houses, in which anything that happened to anyone was the subject of concern to the rest. Everybody, reported Henry to Annette, is distressed to see pretty Mrs Joll growing so stout and coarse looking. Of course, kind friends supplied the malicious explanation.'*

Lord Curzon, who was later to become Viceroy, noted in his diary on 21st December 1887, whilst on a world tour:

> *'... The train passed through flat cultivated land and palm groves. Five garrulous Frenchmen got in the carriage with me. I was amused at one incident; At a wayside station the natives were jabbering at the tops of their voices, one being louder than all his fellows; "Quel vociferateur!" exclaimed one of the Frenchmen. Now was not that characteristic of French idiom? No Englishman would have said "What a vociferator ....!" He would have exclaimed "What a damned row!" But the Frenchman with his ingrained civility and hyperbole glosses it over and is polite even when he swears.'*

An inspection of the railway made by Colonel A. Le Messurier RE, in his capacity as the Officiating Consulting Engineer for Railways in Calcutta, revealed that there was also no shortage of hyperbole and gloss with the claims Prestage had made. The report of the inspection published on 11th August 1888 in *Indian Engineering* noted that there were no proper plans and sections of the railway for inspection or record, whilst those that were with the Resident Engineer that showed the alignment from Sukna to Kurseong were not correct. Indeed, he went on to state:

> *'Other essential records are also apparently not available for reference – notably a diagram of moving dimensions, a standard section to which the Railway is to be maintained; a specification of the nature of the ballast, etc. The lithographed maps, which have lately been prepared on a scale of $1/2$ mile to an inch, are inferior. The impressions were too much mixed up with unimportant detail and give but a poor idea of such an interesting engineering*

---

[6] The name probably came from the indigo planters, whose lifestyles were just as notorious.

undertaking. Moreover the locations of the stations Ghoom and Tindharia are wrongly shown, and nearly a mile out of position.'

The goods shed at Siliguri was noted as being a large temporary structure of corrugated iron containing an office, and being flanked on both sides by carriage sidings it was not only inconveniently placed, but more than liable to accident from fire. The wooden bridge over the Mahanandi was under heavy repair at the time of the inspection, but this was exacerbated by having to maintain a train service at the same time. It was estimated that the work since 1884 had amounted to Rs24,000, and it was recommended that the railway should be diverted during the cold season to a temporary crossing whilst a new iron bridge was constructed in its place. The Colonel was clearly not impressed, for he stated that: *'The supervision of this reconstruction should not, however, fall on the Resident Engineer, as he has plenty to occupy his constant attention on other parts of the line.'* He felt the Panchanai bridge should also be replaced and the old timber retained for the repair of small bridges and culverts. Although a section about 1/4 mile south of the station had been replaced with 40lb rails, the report reflected that nothing else appeared to have been done in upgrading the rest of the 30lb track. The concern must have been compounded by his observation that there was no weighbridge to ascertain the tare of the stock or of the load the wagons were carrying.

Mention was also made of a previous inspection undertaken by the Chief Engineer of Bengal, which included the recommendation that the track should be upgraded to 40lb at the rate of two miles a year.[7] Cary's report to the Institution of Civil Engineers in 1883 advised the track was indeed 40lb, but he had left the railway before the work was completed. Statistics relating to the construction and working of the railway in 1884 were used in 1886 to make a comparison for a Ceylonese railway (see Chapter 2), and these stated that 30lb rails were used on the plains section and 40lbs for the climb. Prestage stated that 41lb rails were used throughout in his submission to the Institution of Civil Engineers in 1886. The report made by Colonel Le Messurier not only casts a shadow over the accuracy of the figures submitted by the railway, but is perhaps also an indication of the compromises Cary felt were still being made and the reason behind his leaving.

A certain amount of precautionary work had been undertaken at Loop No.2 against earth slips in the cutting by the construction of a 12ft x 12ft timber trestle, and mention was made of the suitability of the design for a tunnel as a permanent solution.

Although surface water had been diverted at Tindharia, settlement had added to the catalogue of troubles, necessitating supporting rails to have been driven into the embankment below to prevent the railway buildings from toppling over. It seemed to get worse in the blind valley that led to Pagla Jhora, for the report claimed that:

'The line in many places is not maintained to any standard, that is to say, the line is permitted to approach and crown the crest of a slope, so much so that in places the ends of the sleepers project into the air, and to a certain extent overhang the hillside. This evil is also in some places aggravated by villagers, whom in making short cuts, have worn away or trodden down whatever little formation may have existed at the ridge of the spurs. These omissions, and many others of minor detail, indicate clearly the necessity for a strict observance of some standard plan of construction.'

But despite such obvious problems, the railway was proving to be a good business venture, and it gave the investors a healthy return on their dividend by paying 8% in 1886. This had given Prestage the charge of adrenaline he needed for his proposal to extend the railway into Nepal to develop a trade with Tibetan wool. There had been previous ambitions to introduce Indian tea to the Nepalese and Tibetan markets, but these were closed lands and there were strict controls on any articles sold by foreign traders privileged to deal in Kathmandu. Tea was not on the list, and the Chinese were ready to frustrate any attempts that were made, for theirs had long been available in Darjeeling. It had also been suspected that a number of trade returns from Nepal had misrepresented the Chinese brick tea[8] as Indian, and the Government of India was urged to *'relax the total exclusion of tea from the Nepalese market'*.

Politics stood in the way and nothing was achieved, but it did not prevent Prestage from promoting his own bold and imaginative scheme. The Government of India

---

[7] Although undated, a reference was made to the loops and reverses, this implying that it was written after 1882.

[8] A coarse black tea that was sown up in raw kidskins and transported in blocks or bricks weighing between 2.7kg and 3.1kg, measuring approximately 20cm long by 10cms deep. The tea was generally made in a large iron cooking-pot full of boiling water into which a quantity of black tea was chopped from one end of the brick. Butter, parched barley meal and a little salt were usually added, after which the brew was served in a metal teapot.

was still keen to develop a trade route with Lhasa, but that was more to get a foot into the political camp rather than being of any commercial interest. Prestage was adamant that Tibet was not a viable market and declared it to be *'a stronghold of the most obstructive ecclesiastics in creation'*. He maintained that Peking was dominating Lhasa, and that their view had been made clear when they met the British advance over the Jelap Pass with armed resistance. In this he was correct, for China had been cementing its authority over Tibet for the past two hundred years and was in no mood to relinquish it to the Raj.

On the wider scale of things, the Government would have seen Prestage as little more than a convenient pawn in the geopolitical chess match being played between Britain and Tsarist Russia. Known as the 'Great Game', this titanic struggle for imperial dominance and influence for the plateau of High Asia had been played out in the shadows since the 1830s. Britain had now consolidated its rule in India, but was deeply suspicious that Russia was looking for a stepping-stone to launch an invasion on the Raj and its Empire. Information and intelligence was gathered by soldiers and agents, who generally adopted the disguise of explorers, cartographers, archaeologists and their like.

It was the perfect opportunity for self-publicists like Prestage to fill in the blank spaces on the map, and he presented his initial report from Darjeeling on the 14th August 1888. On 25th June 1889, he officially informed the British Resident of Nepal that the Directors of the DHR were serious about their intentions, and followed this up by two further submissions from London on the 2nd July 1889 and 14th August 1889. The Secretary to the Government of India advised Prestage in a letter dated 20th September 1889 that there was no objection to his making any exploration of Nepal, on the condition that it was sanctioned by the Darbar and that he followed the protocol of first consulting the British Resident.

The plan was to attract a trade route by the construction of a bridle track into the cultivated valley of the Tambur via Ilam and continue to the important market of Dhankota at the eastern end of the Kathmandu valley. Once established, a railway

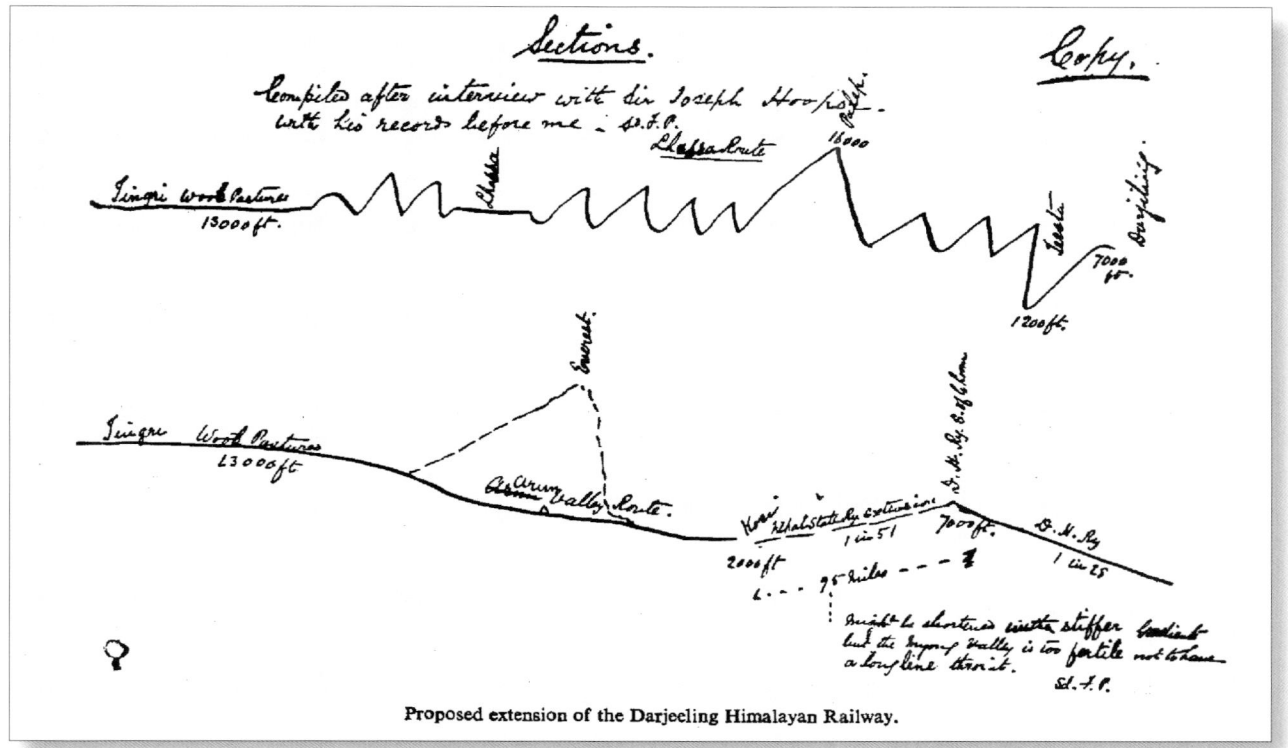

Proposed extension of the Darjeeling Himalayan Railway.

It was a daring and inspired idea to build a railway to Darjeeling, but to extend it from Ghum for 95 miles into Nepal was simply too audacious. Nevertheless, Prestage was adamant it was perfectly feasible, although his sketch to advance the cause shows his vision was not tempered by a deep understanding of the civil engineering issues it would raise, let alone the political consequences that would follow.

Collection: (The late) Fred Pinn

No.1B was the first of a class of 34 locomotives that were to become uniquely identified with the DHR. Ordered in 1888 and delivered in 1889, it survived in service until being withdrawn on 3rd April 1952.

Mitchell Library

No.1B was numbered 17 after being placed in service on the DHR, and is seen here on an early Up freight crossing the overbridge at Agony Point. The increased hauling power of these new locomotives was noticed at once, for they were capable of hauling 840 tons on the level and 50 tons on a 1 in 26 with a curve of 60ft radius, whereas the 'A' Class could manage 600 tons and 39 tons respectively.

Collection: David Churchill

track would be laid westwards along the ridge that extended from Ghum to Manibhanjan, the base of the Piontanka Tamarangor. This would descend by a gradient that averaged 1 in 51 to Tamakote, some 95 miles away, although Prestage advised this could be shortened to 82 miles if steeper grades were employed. The construction, maintenance and working of the railway would provide a substantial amount of work for the Nepalese, and it was envisaged that the extension would serve the fertile valleys of the Myong and Tambur rivers leading to Dhankota, the confluence of the Kosi and Arun rivers. This would place the railway on the direct trade route from the *Tingri Maiden*, regarded as the finest wool-producing provinces of central and western Tibet. Prestage calculated that the distance to Darjeeling via Tamakote would be 262 miles compared to the 770 tortuous miles via Lhasa, most of which crossed mountain passes.

He advocated that the benefits for Nepal would be numerous, stating that surplus food grains from Rangpur, Dinajpore and other districts of North Bengal could be quickly transported to the nearest markets in the Nepal Valley at cheap rates, particularly in times of famine or scarcity. No doubt reflecting on the successes he had witnessed around Darjeeling, he suggested that highly productive tea gardens could be planted along the route on most of the hill slopes between 3,000 and 5,000ft, and chil cultivated around the 6,000ft altitude. The Myong ridges were also abundant in cheer pine (the eastern chil), oak and other trees, which he claimed would give excellent charcoal for working the railway and drying tea in the Darjeeling district. Prestage estimated that the value of the land would increase more than a hundredfold, and assuming that only five miles on each side of the line were brought under cultivation, quoted a permanent increase of revenue to the State of Rs360,000 per annum.

There was also trade, which would not only enable Kathmandu to secure the Tibetan market, but was something still dear to the financial heart of the Raj. With this in mind, Prestage made sure that he asserted the gains for India and England, and these would come from the low cost of running the proposed railway, on account of the availability of ample fuel midway along the line. The tone of the submission cut to the chase when it was stated that subject to the stipulations of contract, the Darbar would be *'persuaded to grant, free of cost, the use of waste land upon which the line would be constructed, to permit the felling of useless timber en route within an area to be agreed, and also to allow the exclusive right to all timber grown on useless and denuded areas within an agreed distance from the railway'*.

The advantages accrued from this would be immense, and first-class timber for the construction and maintenance of the railway would be available at a moderate cost. Prestage felt that it would also pave the way for match-making and other such industries, whilst tea chests would no longer be imported from Japan; all this would tend to *'keep money in the country and stiffen exchange'*. Eager to attract investment, he contended that companies like Bradford and Saltaire in England would be able to obtain superior staple wood, which would give them a considerable advantage over continental manufacturers. The cost of transportation from the wool pastures of Tibet (13,000ft) to the proposed terminus of the railway (3,000ft) were calculated to be one-third of that by the Lhasa and Sikkim routes, and Calcutta in particular would benefit from the increase of valuable exports. A good profit was assured to all concerned, and to underpin his case he stated that the expansion of trade between Ghum station and Nepal had resulted in a 40% increase in traffic, and that it was *'cheering to note the perceptible increase of traffic on all roads leading to the frontier'*.

The proposals were intended to touch the same political nerves as the original submission for building the line to Darjeeling, and it was suggested that the Government of India would be saved the enormous cost of improving the *'unkind trade route via Lhasa'*. However, the Darbar may not have been overjoyed to learn that it would not be necessary to keep troops at the distant outpost at Gantong as the Government would be able to recruit Gurkha soldiers from Nepal, and it is doubted if they were any more impressed by his intention to *'draw the skilled intelligent labour required more particularly for working railways in the plains'*.

The reports had all the spin and flair of the flamboyant Chairman, but his assertions were falling on deaf ears with the Nepalese court. They saw things in a very different light, and despite his claim that *'the Nepalese people are most capable, intelligent and kindly and it would be a pleasure to be associated with them through this venture'*, it would take more than that to prise open the doors. His naivety in dealing with such matters was drawing him like a moth to a flame, and with it came the inevitable result. On 9th October 1889, the Resident advised Prestage that his proposal for the railway *'... was laid before the Darbar but was met with a distinct refusal to entertain even a preliminary survey'*. The Resident followed this up on 1st March 1890 with the information that he could not foresee any compromise *'... till some radical change in their 'Exclusive' policy is made'*. The final nail was hammered into the coffin on 4th November 1892 when the Secretary to the Government of Nepal informed Prestage of *'... the Darbar's inability to comply with your proposal for the construction of the Railway into this country'*.

It was a bitter blow, and one that must have left his standing with the DHR and its Directors terminally bruised. Indeed, there had been far more pressing demands on the Darjeeling line whilst he was promoting his vision of the Nepalese extension, and the motive power was in urgent need of improvement. An order had been made in 1888 with Messrs Sharp, Stewart to build four new engines, and these were to incorporate all the improvements that had been learned from the seven years of operating the railway. The new locomotives were listed by the manufacturer as the 'B' Class, and were accordingly numbered 1B to 4B for the official works photograph prior to their delivery in 1889. To bring the remaining stock in line, the railway now referred to the No.2 Class as the 'A' Class, and the four remaining No.1 Class side-tanks as the 'C' Class, as originally designated on the Sharp, Stewart drawings.

The Directors had also managed to tempt Sulyard Cary to return to the DHR as its General Manager and Chief Engineer in 1889, just as the Nepalese debacle was coming to a head. The reappointment of his brother-in-law was the last straw for Prestage; it had been ten tempestuous years since the first rails had been laid for his audacious tramway and it was now time to move on. Thacker's Directory listed him simply as a resident of Darjeeling in 1890, and after that no further entries were made.

Although it has not been substantiated, there is a belief that Prestage may have turned his interest to Africa, and in particular the railway being surveyed to cross Kenya and Uganda. It would certainly have appealed to his sense of pioneering and daring, particularly with the challenges faced with scaling the Rift Valley, and in the early days a number of personnel (and rolling stock) certainly migrated from India to work on the project. If he was involved, the report that Sir Guildford Molesworth

Of all the obstacles that the railway had to encounter, the Pagla Jhora (Mad Torrent) was certain to create the most trouble. If that was not bad enough, the railway was obliged to cross it twice, and a train bound for Darjeeling is seen here crossing the upper section. The caption beneath one copy of this photograph was dated June 1893 and read: 'When I visited Darjeeling, this bridge had been completely washed away by the tremendous volume of water which always rushes down this gorge after heavy rain. A footbridge had been constructed and a train was waiting on the other side of the break.'

Collection: Nick Rhodes

was asked to submit on the undertaking in 1891 would certainly have rubbed salt into his wounds. He had been an adversary of Prestage and the DHR from its earliest days, and his submission on the East African line stressed the serious lack of information that was necessary for planning a route and estimating the cost. It had been a problem that had haunted Prestage for over a decade, and it had to be said was contributory to

The transportation of goods formed a major part of the traffic in the early days of the railway. The principal commodities carried by trains bound for Darjeeling were building materials, coal, oil and food-grains, whilst those returning conveyed tea, timber, oranges and cardamoms. The location of this early freight train was unrecorded, although the vegetation and lay of the land suggests that it is between Sonada and Rangbhul.

Collection: Hugh Ashley Rainer

the position he was now in. There must also have been one or two red faces after reading the report submitted by Captain Macdonald and his Indian surveyors in 1892, for it advised that the descent of the Kikuyu Escarpment to the floor of the Rift Valley could be overcome by the construction of reverse sidings![9]

Whatever happened, Prestage spent his final days in India, for the ledger of his last Will and Testament shows there were outstanding accounts for the Great Eastern Hotel and The Pioneer in Calcutta, along with the Central Hotel in Simla. The latter teases the imagination, for it could not have escaped his attention that surveys had been made in 1884 and 1885 to construct a narrow-gauge hill railway from Kalka to Simla. Indeed, two further surveys were made in 1892 and 1893, and in 1894 four different schemes were proposed.[10] Two of the options suggested that the railway should be worked by adhesion and the other two by rack and pinion, and their respective merits were again discussed following yet another reconnaissance in 1895. Prestage was near Simla when he died at Kotghur on 18th October 1897, at the age of 67, but it was not until the following year that the contract was finally signed to authorise the Delhi-Ambala-Kalka Railway to construct an adhesion line to the hill station. As it is, one can only speculate whether it was his influence that the first locomotives delivered to Kalka were two DHR 'B' Class constructed by Sharp, Stewart and that the initial section of the

---

[9] An alternative route was subsequently used that avoided the need for reverses.

[10] Perhaps the most bizarre was the offer made by the Lartigue Construction Company to build the railway in 1893 on the condition that the land was given free and it received a subsidy for carrying the mail. The spectacle of the Indian Government being hauled by double-boilered locomotives on the monorail for its annual migration from Delhi to Simla would have indeed been one to treasure.

There was concern that the old wooden bridge over the Mahananda to the north of Siliguri would not support the weight of the No.2 Class locomotives, and four of the original lighter No.1 Class were kept for working trains over this section. It was clearly an unsatisfactory arrangement, and in 1894 the crossing was replaced by a seven span bridge supported by concrete pillars. Siliguri is believed to have taken its name from the Koch word for 'the stony place', rocks and boulders being often in evidence when the monsoon rains abated and the river bed dried out.

1896 DHR Guide

new railway was laid to the gauge of two feet.[11]

It was churlish that the death of Prestage did not appear to attract the attention of the Darjeeling Press, but the road that wound up the hill directly opposite the station to the Woodlands Hotel and the Auckland Road was named after him for many years. A brass commemorative plaque was also placed by his widow Eliza and their children at the Loreto Convent, where it can still be seen today. Cary was the executor of his last Will and Testament, and the report made in 1901 was mostly a ledger of accounts of rent and repairs on his four properties in Darjeeling (*'Dingle'*, *'Laurels'*, *'Ridge Cottage'* and *'The Yews'*). There was a fifth in Simla (name not recorded, but possibly *'Ellerslie Cottage'*), and this was sold to a Mrs Clayton, who for reasons best known to the good lady, also purchased his gun and rifle!

At the time of his death, Prestage's involvement with the DHR was confined to Rs70 paid by dividend at 7% for the half-year ended 31st December 1897 on its shares and Rs60 at 6% to 30th June 1898, whilst the value of 10 shares was listed at Rs209 each. The amount of Rs85 was outstanding for DHR postage, and Rs1,141 due *'In refund of advances made from time to time by Mr S. Cary'*. It had been a stormy relationship that had tested family loyalties and their friendship to the limit, but then they had been through a lot together.

Cary instigated a plan to upgrade the stations, and a particularly grand building was constructed for Darjeeling in 1891. The new stationmaster was Louis Mandelli, who had been working with the railway for two years as an assistant in the Traffic Audit section. He was a popular character in the town, and had an interesting family history that descended from the Maltese aristocracy. His grandfather Jerome had moved to Italy, and became such a great admirer of Garibaldi that he followed the Italian revolutionary to fight for the freedom of Uruguay in 1836. He left his son Louis (senior) in Milan, but by 1850 the political situation had become so dangerous that Louis retreated to India. It must have been a good move, for his fortunes advanced to the extent that he was responsible for managing a number of tea estates around Darjeeling, which was a perfect base to pursue his passion for collecting Himalayan birds. At least five species were to subsequently bear the suffix 'mandellii' in his honour

---

[11] The military advocated from the outset that the Simla line should be built to the gauge of 2ft 6ins, which the contractors finally conceded to in 1901 and accordingly had the wheels of the two locomotives widened.

The American railroad publicist Joseph Gladding Pangborn formed the World's Transportation Commission in 1894 to gather information about foreign systems for the Field Columbian Museum in Chicago. The party began its tour in Tunis with the intention of seeking trade for Americans interested in international markets, and over a period of two years travelled through India, Oceania, China, and Siberia. Quite what deals the Commission hoped to achieve in competition with the British Raj is not clear, but they certainly travelled on the DHR and their trolley is seen hitched to the rear of an Up train bound for Darjeeling. Note twin water towers.

The USA was in the midst of an economic depression when the grandly titled World's Transportation Commission set off. The party was headed by Joseph Pangborn, who is seen seated nearest the platform in this photograph of their trolley at Ghum. He was accompanied by a railway engineer, a graphic artist and the photographer William Henry Jackson.

Courtesy: Library of Congress World's Transportation Commission Photograph Collection
(Reproduction No. LC-D426-559 & LC-D426-566)

Sulyard Cary returned to the DHR in 1889 to become its General Manager and set out a programme to improve the infrastructure of the railway. The original terminus at Darjeeling had been unable to cope with the demands made with the growth in traffic, and a new station was high on his list of priorities. The building was completed in 1891, and looking in the direction of Siliguri, the immaculate paintwork suggests that the photograph was taken as the station was receiving its finishing touches. Two tracks terminated beneath the pleated roof at the far end, whilst a third ran the full length of the station under cover before continuing to the bazaar. The rake of four-wheeled stock is standing on an additional track laid outside the station to serve as a run-round loop and to also allow freight services to be run to the market without disrupting passenger trains.

Collection: (The late) Fred Pinn

No.17 was the first of the 'B' Class locomotives, and it is seen here taking water at the head of a Down train bound for Siliguri. The location was not recorded, although the adjacent rock face and the clothing worn by those on the road would suggest the train was on the higher altitudes between Ghum and Kurseong. The man wearing a topee is boarding a 1st Class carriage, and its more generous dimensions for passenger comfort are apparent when it is compared to the 2nd Class stock coupled behind.

Collection: David Churchill

and, after his death, his magnificent collection was purchased by Octavian Hume and later passed to the British Museum.

Perhaps the most ambitious civil engineering formation for Cary had been the design and layout of Loop No.2, which literally grasped the edge of a spur before chiselling into the side of the hill to gain height. The problems were not dissimilar to those experienced with the first loop, for the reinforcements to the deep cutting that passed under the bridge had not been robust enough to prevent earth movement from the embankment in bad weather. It appeared that sufficient thought had not been applied to catch-water drains from the upper slopes and drainage ditches at the base. The notion of filling in the central section of the cutting to form a solid embankment had already been mooted, and Cary adopted this plan without further delay. The sides were faced with stones to prevent any further soil creep, and a tunnel was formed through the base of the embankment to allow the train to gain height by the same route, with 'Loop No.2' being sculptured on the keystone above the entrance.

The bridge over the Mahananda near Siliguri was finally replaced in 1894, and this now permitted all the locomotives to cross. The remaining four 'C' Class side-tank engines were quickly disposed of to the North Western Railway to work the trains on their colliery line at Dandot. A move was also made to upgrade the track to 41¼ lbs/yard and rolled to a more suitable section. A technical report made in 1892 had noted the track as being *'flat-footed Indian State Railway standard of steel'* spiked to sleepers mostly of sal wood 4ft 6in x 8in x 4in (the dimensions originally specified by Cary during construction), with bearing plates being used under the outer rail of the sharp curves and double spiked. When viewed in section, this original rail was profiled with a rounded shoulder,

One of the earliest known photographs illustrating the mail being carried by the railway. The rear vehicle is a trolley of a more substantial construction than those solely for passenger service, and it can be seen that the post was transported in the large steel box bearing the royal cipher 'VR' and fixed to the mainframe for security. The date was recorded as 1885, although the 'A' Class locomotive at the far end of the train appears to have been fitted with a saddle tank and therefore suggests it was actually taken in 1886 or later.

Collection: (The late) Fred Pinn

which was found to wear rapidly on the sharp bends and contribute to the many derailments. Cary found this was affected considerably by speed, for when running easy, the wear was more pronounced on the moderate curves than on the sharpest. The inner rails on the curves were transferred to the outside as a temporary measure, whilst new track was commissioned with a broader shoulder and less rounded profile. The new rails were found to wear much better, whilst the old track was subsequently straightened in a rail-bending machine and relaid between Siliguri and Sukna, with the worn surface being placed outwards.

The investment in the railway had risen to Rs3,200,000 by 1895, which equated to Rs62,750 per mile (approx. £4,200). The cost still contrasted favourably with that of the Cart Road, which had set back the Government Rs90,000 (£6,000) per mile, but it had to be recognised most of the land had already been sculptured for its construction by the time the railway was laid. The estimates now being given for the construction of the hill railway from Kalka to Simla were the same as the road itself, although the final bill eventually came to three times the figure.

In March 1895, Gillanders Arbuthnot entered into correspondence with the Government of India Public Works Department over a stipulation in the original Agreement dated 8th April 1879. The Government had permitted the line to be laid on land provided free of charge, which in turn allowed the Secretary of State to terminate the contract and take over the line after an initial 25-year period, and subsequently reviewed at 10-yearly intervals. A revised Agreement was made that confirmed the date 4th May 1885 would now be taken as the date from which the time was calculated.

The railway was prospering, and the shareholders were delighted their investments were now returning 10–12%, and it was no wonder. It was taking 7 hours to travel the 51 miles from Siliguri to Darjeeling and the fare was Rs19; to gain some comparison, it took 16 hours to travel the 320 miles from Calcutta to Siliguri, including a ferry crossing of the Ganges, and the fare was Rs27! The increased power of the new locomotives allowed the passenger trains to be extended by three vehicles and the goods traffic was able to expand by hauling an additional two wagons. The receipts per mile from passengers were recorded as £327.00, and £539.80 from goods – way above any other Indian line except for the broad-gauge East Indian Railway.

The railway began to consider whether it needed a locomotive that was larger than the 'B' Class, and after having been in correspondence with the Locomotive Superintendent, Leslie Robertson prepared a paper on narrow-gauge railways for a submission to the Institution of Mechanical Engineers in London. Tindharia felt the weight of the locomotives would have to be increased to 18 tons, which was some 50% heavier than those originally built. It was also claimed that the traffic had now developed to such an extent that it would have been better if a wider gauge had been adopted, as it was difficult for an 18-ton engine to be worked on the 2ft gauge, although the Festiniog Railway in Wales might have disputed that particular point! An articulated engine that spread the axle loading might have been the only solution, although 'The Climber' had foundered on the drawing board and the Garratt had yet to make its debut. The mathematics of flange friction on the severe curves of the DHR might not yet have been understood, for experience was to show that longer trains were prone to derailment.

Further developments came in 1896, particularly in Kurseong, where the Clarendon Hotel had served as the station since the opening of the line. The convenience of the stop had no doubt been appreciated by the owner and its guests, but the railway needed to redress the situation and constructed a new station on the site it now occupies today. The trains continued to halt at the hotel, although the stop became somewhat demoted and eventually vanished some years later after the Clarendon closed for business. Other improvements were made at the time near Batasia by forming a siding, lengthening the passenger platform in Darjeeling, enlarging the goods shed, and laying sidings in the bazaar.

However, the annual report published for 1896/97 recorded there had been a slight reduction in traffic during the second half of that year. The 1st Class passengers had dropped from 2,676 to 2,562, 2nd Class from 6,018 to 5,533 and 3rd Class from 22,426 to 21,593, whilst the freight fell from 19,160 to 15,510 tons. The report continued to explain that the *'falling off with 1st and 2nd Class passengers being attributed to less tourists owing to a plague scare and a decrease in 3rd Class due to the famine'*.

It was nothing new to India that health and hunger had their class differences, but the question why was now being asked.

Chapter 4
Nature Takes Revenge

The endless cycle of devastation and regeneration had given much of India the ability to accept the reincarnation of its soul, but there was only so much it could take when it saw the fabulous wealth flaunted by the Maharajahs. The jewelled and the chosen were now jamming the gang planks of the P&O steamers to make their way to Britain, where preparations were under way to celebrate the Diamond Jubilee of Queen Victoria's reign. Four hundred million people, a quarter of the population of the planet, were to pay tribute, but as a foreigner the Empress was without caste and thus seen by Hindus as an untouchable. Her spiritual felony was compounded by the fact she was also a widow and had not committed *suttee*, whilst the thought of her bodyguards being referred to as *Beefeaters* did nothing to appease the concern of a good Hindu!

It was a blatant demonstration of the class and caste differences that haunted India, particularly with the famine and plague now brought on by the drought. Although they were a scourge of the plains and only touched Darjeeling in a commercial sense, the hill station was not to remain immune from the forces of nature for long, for a particularly vicious earthquake shook Bengal, Assam and Bihar at 5 o'clock in the evening of Saturday, 12th June 1897.

The tremors ran into the mountains and were felt for three minutes in Darjeeling, followed by fifteen minutes of a distinct rumbling sound. It was reported that a peculiar stillness and oppressive atmosphere then descended, after which the residents gathered themselves together and saw that nearly every house in the town had been wrecked in one way or another. Most of the citizens had been unharmed as they were not in their homes at the time, and they were able to see that many of the tea estates were also badly damaged. There were four further shocks during the night between 23.00 and 4.00, followed by more at 9.00, 12 noon and 17.00, but they were all comparatively light and caused no further destruction.

Being made of wood, the station building absorbed most of the impact and was relatively unscathed, and indeed most of the railway somehow escaped damage. The walls of several houses in Kurseong were cracked, large trees came crashing down, and initial reports came through that the station at Tindharia had fallen down the hillside. This was later found to be an exaggeration, although it had been considerably damaged. Large fissures appeared in the earth at Siliguri and water was seen bubbling up between the cracks. The Down 'Mail' from Darjeeling was running when the quake occurred, and by the time it arrived at Siliguri, all traffic had stopped on the metre gauge. There was no alternative but for the train to return through the night with its anxious passengers to Darjeeling, each nursing their fears of further tremors. Two days later the following account was despatched by a local correspondent:

> *'There is a feeling of suppressed excitement still in Darjeeling. Telegrams and rumours are flying fast, and we, not knowing the worst, are imagining all possible ills. Crowds of people have rushed down to the plains, and many have had to return, as they found they could get no farther than Siliguri for four or five days at least.'*

It appeared nobody was really sure what was going on,

An Up train arriving at Kurseong station towards the end of the 19th century. Although the 'B' Class cannot be identified, the rod passing through the saddle tank to operate the blower dates its construction to after 1893. The three tracks tapered to a single line, which in later years was relaid to form five sidings and a turntable on the left-hand side of the photograph. Note Banerjee's General Stores behind the train and the absence of buildings on the hillside.

for *The Englishman* reported on June 16th:

'Where ignorance is bliss, it is folly to be wise, and this may emphatically be affirmed of the Darjiling-Himalayan Railway [sic], which was assured on Saturday night (12th June) by telegram that its line was intact. It was subsequently stated, however, that the Cart Road at Sukna was 'riven with chasms'. This can only be an inflated way of saying that the road is covered in cracks, but if there is any accuracy in the statement the railway should be looked to.'

However, an article written in Darjeeling on June 26th was published to advise:

'I have never travelled up the DHR so quickly, and we got in just after 7pm. I now hear the 'Pagla Jhora', that piece of line that seems to defy all engineering skill, has gone again and will take some days to repair.'

The official celebrations for Queen Victoria's Jubilee were due to be held in Darjeeling on 22nd June, but it was barely ten days following the earthquake and the town was not really in the mood. Bonfires were lit on Observatory Hill, Senchal, Phalut and Sundakapu, but very little of the flames were seen, whilst rain spoiled the solitary attempt at illumination and the proposed gun salute was not fired for fear of bringing down the houses damaged by the 1897 earthquake. A further tremor the following evening at 19.30 sent a wave of panic across the town, but it did no damage other than to widen a few cracks. The correspondent for *The Englishman* observed that:

'Those with experience of earthquakes say this succession of slight shocks is our safeguard, or otherwise there would probably have been another severe shaking. The idea, at any rate, is consoling!'

The rumblings occurred again the following month and continued to remind the town that it was not all over. In a typically stoic manner, *The Friend of India* reported on the 14th July:

'We don't feel the tremblings while about during the day, except when sitting, yet they are stronger than usual. It is in the evening, when rolling in an easy chair, reading after dinner, and when lying in bed, that they are most felt. The chair and the book held up quiver every now and again distinctly. We are told that this is always the after-effect, and though the association imparted is far from pleasant, we are growing used to the phenomenon, and shall perhaps miss it when it ceases. Major King Hall is kindly trying to brighten us up by marching the troops through the station to the cheery music of the bugles and band now and again, and it is a pleasant sound and a pleasanter sight to see three or four hundred rosy-cheeked Tommies swinging along as if they didn't care for no blooming earthquake. The authorities of the Darjeeling Railway and Dooars Railway were very energetic in pushing their troubles aside, and succeeded in passing the mails over their lines almost at once, and resumed traffic in a few days, but those on the North Bengal Railway were not so prompt, and waited some days for orders.'

The Press adopted a more fractious tone with the report on 4th August that:

'... the train now arrives at 5.23pm and departs at 7.15am, both inconvenient hours for the new arrivals and for writing and posting letters.'

But events were to take a sombre turn two weeks later when the High Court sanctioned a hanging to take place following a murder near Tindharia. The assassin and victim were both local Muslims employed by the DHR in the workshop, and it was reported that the latter had been doing all he could for a long time to get the murderer into trouble, and thus precipitated the crime.

The newspaper reports during September continued to reflect the correspondents' irritation, who wrote that the only drawback to encouraging the return of visitors to Darjeeling after the earthquakes was the heavy charge made by the DHR for passage and freight. It was claimed that public bodies were up in arms against the rates and were about to lobby the Government, which it advised was supposed to have a greater control over the line than any other in the matter. The timing of this was guaranteed to attract the eye of the Lt Governor, who had arrived in Darjeeling with his private secretary and associates on the evening mail train. Despite the correspondents' promise of action, nothing more appeared to have been said, and the subsequent reports focused on a seemingly endless programme of attending races, cricket matches and dances. Saturday 9th October was regarded as the end of the holiday period, and the departing trains were reported as full to overflowing. The Lt Governor and his party remained until 13th November, and their

An unidentified No.2 Class leads a Down train to Siliguri. The two covered goods wagons were for transporting the baggage, whilst the livery of the first carriage designates it was for 1st class passengers and the remainder 2nd class.

Collection: Nick Rhodes

visit was marked by switching on the new electric streetlights,[1] along with the opening of the Pasteur Filter and the steam laundry.

The Viceroy, Lord Elgin, took his family to the hill station in December, and the journey was delightfully chronicled in the diary kept by his daughter, Lady Elisabeth Bruce. She refers to her father as H.E. (His Excellency), her mother as Her E., and her brother Christian as C., whilst Mr H. Babbington Smith (her father's private secretary) comes out as Mr. B.S. The story picks up after travelling through the night on the metre gauge to Siliguri and having breakfast on the station:

> *'From the platform we saw the hills in the distance, covered with clouds, but we hoped that was only heat rising from the plains. Their E.s had a little saloon, which was most comfortable; altogether the little toy train was all one could wish for. C and I had a carriage to ourselves, and until the first station he read a book and I watched the hills coming nearer and the views were often very pretty. Twice the line crossed a stream, and there were many fields of ripe corn and others of grass and mustard flower, which looked so well against the dark trees and blue hills. And the woods were real jungle where elephants or tigers might like to live; the names of the trees I cannot tell you, but they were quite different to those on the Simla hills and were often covered with orchid plants, ferns and creepers.*
>
> *Mr B.S. came to us at the foot of the hills and said he was going to sit in the open carriage, at which Her E. suggested that we should go too. And certainly I never saw more lovely views as we went higher and higher round the hills, the line creeping back like a black serpent, with the jungle stretching over the plains below, where one saw the rivers winding as it were into the sky. Half way up it began to rain and grew very cold; and after luncheon we went into Their E.s' carriage, for the mist closed round us and it still rained. At Ghoom when I got out to get my jacket it felt as if it was freezing hard, and we were glad to get out to walk up to the hotel to get warm.'*

The report that appeared in *The Friend of India* displayed a delicate touch:

> *'The dull and monotonous life of early winter was broken in upon in a very pleasant manner last Saturday, and we were afforded a little mild but agreeable excitement. The Earl and Countess of Elgin, the Ladies Bruce and suite, attended by Mr Greer, the Deputy Commissioner, arrived by special train under charge of Mr Airy* [correctly, Mr Cary], *the Manager, from Siliguri, late in the evening. It was bitter, raw, and cold, while a drizzling rain, which promised to turn into snow, added to the intensity of the weather. Notwithstanding this drawback and the darkness which was*

---

[1] The hydro-electric power station had been built earlier in the year by Messrs Kilburn & Co. of Calcutta. Situated at the foot of the Sidrapong spur, it was the first of its kind in India.

A contemporary photograph of Darjeeling covered in the winter snows. It rarely interrupted the railway service, although the first time that a snowplough was used on an Indian railway occurred in 1882 when snow drifted into the cutting near Ghum.

just setting in, there was a large gathering to welcome their Excellencies at the Railway station, which was fully decorated with flowers, ferns, and flags for the occasion. On alighting, the Viceroy was received by Mr. Nolan, the Commissioner of the Division, who was in full political uniform, and after a few words to him, His Excellency proceeded at once on foot by the back entrance, close to the station, to Woodlands Hotel.'

Their stay in Darjeeling was filled with visits to various monasteries, a convent, the water filtration unit and Ghoom rock. The only reference to the earthquake damage was a mention of the stone cross on the church swaying four feet backwards and forwards. Her E. was overcome by a sickness, but her spirits appear to have lifted with a display of jewellery belonging to the Ranee of Sikkim and the dresses worn during some entertainment provided by local dancers.

The party set out for their return on Thursday 9th December, with Her E. and Lady E.B. taking a gravity trolley. H.E. preferred the relative comfort of his carriage, but was persuaded to join his wife and daughter at Kurseong, where he: '... *got in after luncheon and we went on until sunset; he and I grew very sleepy and woke up feeling afraid we should fall out'.* They eventually reached Siliguri and the metre gauge, which they found: '... *so large after the tiny carriages we had been in all day'.*

The drought and famine continued throughout the next year, but Darjeeling had recovered from the earthquake and felt sufficiently divorced from the troubles that beset life on the plains. Indeed, the correspondent for *The Englishman* languidly reported on 14th July that:

'Socially "your own Hill Station" feels like a poor orphan: we are so uninteresting, that possibly no one will take the trouble to read about us. But we comfort ourselves in the knowledge of having arrived at our lowest depths. The trains have ceased carrying away our friends and affinities.'

It was only the railway that lifted the tedium for the following week:

'Our plucky little train arrives with more praiseworthy punctuality. Every day at 10

minutes before two we hear the cheery little whistle; and most of us are deep in our "Daily" by 3 o'clock – a great improvement upon old methods.'

Even the monsoon was unable to kick in with its customary fury, although it did manage to give some grief further down the line as the same correspondent wrote on 4th August:

'In spite of the four inches on the night preceding Wednesday, and again four inches on that preceding Friday, there have been no slips within municipal bounds. Near Mahanuddy, however, 14 inches were registered on Wednesday morning, which resulted in a big slip just above Gyabari. Passengers having to be transferred had to walk over a mile, which is weary work in slush and mud and pouring rain; particularly when there are infants or young children of the party! On Friday matters were so bad that the train did not arrive until 8.15. We felt uncomfortably prehistoric without our daily "Englishman", and thought with much sympathy of our forefars [forefathers] in pre-railway days. The authorities, however, worked with such laudable energy that on Saturday, the engine's friendly whistle was heard at five o'clock.

Another slip at Toong, however, again delayed arrival till 6.30 on Sunday. The line is clear now to all intents and purposes; but the ill fated little engine which brought up our English mail on Tuesday, the 2nd, burst a cylinder, and pluckily driven up with only one cylinder, arrived at six punctually. The much tired railway authorities have had their vicissitudes lately.

Nevertheless, and in spite of the very favourable season, Darjiling [sic] is very empty, and casting yearning eyes towards the middle of next week, when we hope to be outcasted no longer. The Darjiling-Himalayan Railway even feels the effect of the dull season, for it reports a falling-off in receipts during the first half of July of Rs7,400, as against the same period in 1897.'

The report of the 16th August suggested an air of self-pity, which only served to highlight the differences between the gentle life in the hills and the struggle for survival on the plains:

'... time has slipped by without leaving a mark. Regular trains and no subsidences are depriving this present month of August of the usual excitements. The weather has been monotonously soaking, gently drizzling, universally "sloppy". The trains neither carry away nor add to stagnant Society, which means an undisguisedly bored look at the Rink.'

There was certainly no disguising the fact that the British residents had created an artificial India, but it was understandable. The sub-continent was (and can still be) an intimidating place, and for Victorian Darjeeling it was best kept at arm's length. Half-timbered houses had been constructed and bestowed with names that reminded their owners of home ... 'Richmond Villa', 'Woodland', 'Craigmount' and 'Castelton', which with their disciplined gardens and manicured rose bushes gave a sense of security and springtime in Surrey. It was true that life could be conducted on a far grander scale than in the UK, and with an entourage of servants and staff to bow and respond to every whim, it was perfectly possible to play the part of rulers in style. The air of imperialism blossomed under the tropical sun, and conserving the hierarchy of social convention was a valiant denial of what they saw as an alien culture suffering from an alarming array of diseases and worshipping an excessive variety of gods.

Running the railway and the tea estates was strictly the province of the men, and whilst they were busy with the business of building the Empire, there was little else for their families to do but seek ways of coping with the boredom. There was an insatiable quest for amusements, and gathering in each other's houses to idly gossip about anything that had happened to anyone else was a means of filling the endless days. Afternoon musical parties, dog shows, and *tableaux vivants* were all part of the social scene and duly reported in the newspapers for others to wonder and pick over. And so it was that the Flower Ball held by the Maharani of Kush Behar at the Amusement Club in Darjeeling was reported by *The Englishman*:

'... among the dresses most admired we may mention Mrs Palmer as a Sun-flower, Mrs Percy Lyon as a Daffodil (which was particularly well done) and Mrs Coupland as a Bank of Roses. Mrs McPherson's buttercups looked charming and were very becoming to the wearer; Miss Pugh as a Daffodil was fresh and pretty; Mrs Shuldham Shaw as Violets, Mrs Arbuthnot as Daisies (a splendid bouquet of orchids complementing her costume) Miss Ordham as Red Poppies....'

In late Victorian times, the parasols, ponies, and a brass band at Chowrasta were an escape from the harsh realities of India. A Buddhist chorten known as the 'Chaitya' can be seen on the summit of Observatory Hill in the distance, having been moved from its site behind the pavilion to allow for the road to be broadened. The flattened area of the ridge where the original monastery once stood has become considerably overgrown.

It cannot be denied that life for many English ladies had indeed become a matter of ornamentation, but the mood for reporting such fripperies was turned on its head the following day as the news came in that Darjeeling had been devastated by a cyclone.

Gathering in the Bay of Bengal, it came without warning on Saturday the 23rd September 1899. Twenty-eight inches of rain fell ceaselessly during thirty-eight hours, and it was during the Sunday night that the land began to tear itself apart. Houses and villas came crashing down the mountainside as the cold, wet, slithering mud engulfed and dragged everything in its wake to the valleys below. Mothers and *ayahs* grabbed their children in the shivering nightmare to find sanctuary as the men and their servants endeavoured to rescue others buried in the devastation. Water pipes were severed and electric cables wrenched apart, plunging the town into total darkness as the wind howled and shrieked over the constant muffled, roar of land slipping and echoing across the valleys.

John Stagg had been laid up with an illness for ten days in the damp furnace that was Calcutta, and decided that Darjeeling offered a much better climate to convalesce. He was a passenger on the last train to get through from Siliguri, and whilst recovering from the ordeal at the sanatorium, was visited by a correspondent and committed the journey to paper for his friends:[2]

---

[2] He later corrected a few slight errors that he felt had crept into his narrative regarding the events between Tung and Ghum, and these have been accommodated as part of the original account.

'I left Calcutta on Saturday, the day preceding the great storm in the Darjiling district. All went well until the train reached Sara Ghat. The rain then began to fall in torrents, and the result was that we arrived at Silliguri the next morning one and a half hours late. Still we, that is to say, the passengers, had no reason to anticipate the difficult and dangerous journey that lay ahead of us. It continued to rain heavily, but we reached Kurseong without adventure.

The Railway authorities had reason to believe that our journey from this station to Darjiling would not be so uneventful, and wisely sent a number of coolies on with the train with a view to the clearing away of any obstructions that might possibly impede our progress. Mr Barnard, the Acting Manager of the railway, also came along with us, and as it turned out, it was lucky for us that he did. We had a clear run to Toong; and although the rain continued to fall, we hoped that we would reach Darjiling without difficulty. In this we were sadly disappointed.

Between Toong and Sonada we were arrested by an immense slip of rocks and earth, which completely covered the line. Mr Barnard at once perceived it would take days to blast the rocks and clear the line, so we awaited the approach of the down train for the purpose of transhipment; the waiting could not have been more than half an hour. The down Darjiling mail train arrived and the passengers changed places in the pouring rain. I need hardly tell you that our bedding and clothes were wet through long before the transfer was complete.

Off we started again and got safely through Sonada. Shortly after passing that station, however, we came to a large slip, which had submerged the line just after the down mail had passed. Had the down mail been struck by the slip, nothing could have prevented the train being hurled down the steep khud or the passengers, every one of them, from being killed. Mr Barnard and the coolies were soon at work on the slip, but, as it was a formidable one, assistance was sent for to Ghoom and Sonada. It took three and a half hours to clear a passage for the train, and even then we had to move on very cautiously as the branches of fallen trees brushed the carriages on either side.

Night had now set in. It was pitch dark. The wind was blowing a hurricane, the rain simply poured down on us, and the weather was bitterly cold. As it was quite impossible to see what was ahead of the driver, a flashlight was affixed to the engine, but the rain and the wind soon extinguished it. There were no lights in the carriages, and the train, in harmony with the night, was in utter darkness. After careful consideration, Mr Barnard decided to make a dash for Ghoom station, and it is as well that he did, for I am convinced that had the decision been to remain on the line where we then stood, the train and its passengers would now be thousands of feet down the mountain's side.

We reached Ghoom at 7.35pm, six and a half hours late. It was evident that the people on the Ghoom platform never expected to see the train come in. They had heard that we had gone over the khud, and they had no reason whatever to disbelieve it, considering the terrific storm that was raging and which had already worked great havoc in and about Ghoom. I can assure you that I and two other gentlemen who travelled in the same carriage with me never expected to reach Ghoom in safety, for we could distinctly feel the mountain vibrating as the train dashed along. It was really a very anxious time. We expected to meet with slips or chasms at any moment, and we hardly cared to think what might be the result of such an adventure.

On arriving at Ghoom we were told that the line between that station and Darjiling was entirely blocked, and that we [would] be obliged to remain at Ghoom for the night. This was unpleasant, as there were eight ladies and four children, besides a number of male passengers in the train, and there was not sufficient accommodation at Ghoom station for half the number. However, we had to make the best of the situation. The Railway authorities with the assistance of gentlemen passengers prepared the rooms, and did all they could to make us comfortable for the night's accommodation. ... Fires were lit in the ladies' and gentlemen's waiting rooms, and one of the godowns made comfortable, which proved quite sufficient accommodation for the distressed passengers ... By way of beds we annexed the cushions out of the railway carriages.

We had no provisions with us, and we were cold and hungry. At our suggestion, the

'A' Class No.12 on the climb from Darjeeling and Ghum with a train of four-wheeled coaches bound for Siliguri. With an average gradient of 1 in 20 (steepening to 1 in 16 on one curve), it was very demanding for the crews to operate and became the most severely damaged section when the cyclone struck on 23rd September 1899. Note the brakesman working the external levers on the first two coaches.

Hugh Rayner

stationmaster despatched coolies to the Sergeants' Mess at Jalapahar for provisions. The coolies left about eight o'clock, but did not return till midnight owing to the dangerous state of the roads. The liberality of the sergeants was far beyond our expectations. They sent us a most ample supply of bread, American beef in tins, condensed milk, essence of chicken and two bottles of brandy. We felt extremely grateful to the senders and were anxious to pay for the supplies so promptly and generously sent to us, but the Railway authorities would not hear of it and undertook to settle the bill. ... The majority of us, tired out with the day's journey and discomforts, were comfortably settled down for the night or asleep by time the refreshments arrived. One fellow-passenger very kindly came round to the passengers who had retired, to inform us the refreshments had arrived, and hot coffee and tea were ready in the booking office. The rain was coming down in torrents, and the night was so bitterly chilly and we were fairly comfortable, that the majority of us decided to wait until morning before partaking of the refreshments so generously provided by the Sergeant's Mess. In the early morning I can assure you we did full justice to the refreshments.

The train by which we had arrived remained in the station all night, and when I awoke the next morning I could not help noticing that the carriages were buried in slush and mud to such an extent that the wheels were not visible. The morning broke bright and fair and the sun shone out in all its warmth and glory, as if oblivious to the great disaster which had wrecked life and property the preceding night. There was great difficulty in obtaining ponies, dandies or coolies at Ghoom, but, to cut a long story short, all of us managed to reach Darjiling during the day, and there learned for the first time the dreadful effects of the storm through which we had passed.

It is only fair to the Railway authorities to state Mr Bernard was most indefatigable in his endeavours to get our train safely through to Ghoom, and I am fully convinced it is due to his skill and exertions we reached Ghoom in safety. Credit should also be given to the stationmaster of Darjiling who, anticipating landslips and difficulties, accompanied the down train from Darjiling to the place of transhipment, and returned on the up train. He rendered valuable assistance all the time. The driver of the train also deserves some acknowledgement from the directors of the railway in bringing his train safely to Ghoom. The stationmaster at Ghoom from the time of our arrival on Sunday evening until the last passenger had left the station on the following Monday morning, did his level best to make us all comfortable as his resources

Monsoon Disaster 1899

Twenty-eight inches of rain in thirty-eight hours

Above: John Stagg had been travelling on the last train that attempted the climb to Darjeeling as the 1899 cyclone hit with unmitigated force. After encountering numerous hazards and landslips, the passengers were forced to spend the night in the station at Ghum, having conscripted cushions from the carriages to make temporary beds. This contemporary photograph shows the extent of the devastation, with the road and railway completely washed away on the final stretch to the hill station.

Collection: (The late) Fred Pinn

These two photographs show the devastation near Darjeeling. It seemed inconceivable that the trains would be running again within a month, but the DHR was never one to give in to the forces of Nature.

Collection: Hugh Rayner

Situated at the blind end of a valley, the Pagla Jhora was a constant source of anxiety for the DHR. It caught the monsoon rains like a funnel, and its vulnerability can be seen in this early photograph of the lower section, where the water would tear down the mountainside with devastating force, dragging the road and railway in its wake.

Collection: Nick Rhodes

Blasting boulders from an avalanche strewn across the line. The worker standing with the pole in the centre foreground is drilling a hole for an explosive charge.

Nigel Plackett

would allow, and rendered every assistance he could.'

The rain finally stopped around 4.30 on the Monday morning, and as the dawn broke, the full extent of the damage began to unfold. There had been massive destruction as far as the eye could see, with raw earth revealing where forests had once grown and tea estates flourished, and a tangled mass of rubble that had been part of Darjeeling was slithering down the valley.

The stories of rescue were heroic, tragic, comic and incomprehensible. The ladies of the Raj rose to the ordeal magnificently by rolling up the sleeves of their Flower Ball costumes and getting stuck in straight away, standing no nonsense from anybody. It was found that many of those who had perished were natives, their shacks having stood no chance in the torrent. Faithful bearers were found having sacrificed their lives in the attempt to save their masters, along with *ayahs* who had perished with their arms still wrapped around children clutching their dollies. Channels were dug to divert the water from the hospital and colleges, and a Sister from the Diocesan School tucked up her gown and led the boys in her charge through the storm, none of them having a stitch of clothing on until being given the teacher's nightgowns and petticoats to wear as they passed through the Mall. But it was an obstinate display of caste compliance when nearly a hundred *bustiwallahs* in one of the tea gardens could not come to terms with helping to rescue other natives buried in the slurry, nor to carry away their dead children.

The Deputy Commissioner coordinated the salvage operation with the police and the British regiments from Jalapahar and Lebong, and it fell to him to organise a system of tariffs that would be fair to the coolies and not unreasonable to the employers. Five rupees a day was the going rate, but it was noted that this was five times the rate of the British soldiers, who had distinguished themselves working round the clock to rescue the injured and recover the dead.

The Railway published a statement that the line between Sonada and Darjeeling would be blocked for at least two months. The damage to the lower section appeared to be confined to landslides across the line and fallen telegraph wires, but both the lower and upper Pagla Jhoras had been carried away and there were severe slips from Kurseong to Darjeeling. The Locomotive Superintendent at Tindharia issued the statement on Wednesday the 26th:

'I now beg to state that the line is clear from Kurseong to the Lower Pagla, Bridges 25½ and 24½ mile will be clear by 10.00am tomorrow. Lower Pagla will be ready by Thursday, and the slips at 13½ and 14½ miles will be cleared by tomorrow, so the lower Section from Siliguri to Kurseong will be clear right through on Thursday 28th instant. The passengers booked at Sealdah yesterday have been transhipped today from Gyabaree to Giddapahar and thence by rail to Kurseong. Same yesterday. With the exception of one message from Mr Barnard at Darjiling I have had no communication with Upper Section since Sunday. We are just now for the first time getting into communication with Darjeeling.'

News was beginning to filter out from Darjeeling to inform the anxious parents, husbands, relatives and friends streaming into the newspaper offices in Calcutta. One correspondent submitted a series of graphic reports that recorded a unique insight into the devastation suffered by the railway. They have been included in full, and the first came from Tindharia on the Thursday the 27th:

'On arriving at the first railway bridge I found it completely swept away, and was obliged to walk across on a log of wood. One false step would have meant destruction. The railway lines were suspended in the air, all the ground that was once under them being swept completely away.' So wrote the newspaper correspondent as he grappled his way to Darjeeling on 29th September.

'It was known in Calcutta yesterday that the Darjiling-Himalayan Railway [sic] had been seriously breached in many places and that the repairs would take months to complete, but not withstanding this many ladies and gentlemen assembled on the Sealdah platform yesterday afternoon inspired by the hope that by some mysterious means they would be taken to Darjiling, there to satisfy themselves beyond all doubt that their loved ones were safe. But it was not to be. The Darjiling-Himalayan Railway authorities had telegraphed to stop all booking over their lines, and stopped it was, and many of the ladies and gentlemen I have alluded to, returned to their homes keenly disappointed. The furthest the Eastern Bengal State Railway would book passengers was to Siliguri, and no hope was held out that passengers booking to that station would be able to proceed further.

But there were a few of us imbued with the idea that we would be able to reach Darjiling somehow — though we had not the remotest idea how we were going to do it — so we booked seats to Siliguri and trusted to our luck to see us 7,500 feet up the Himalayas. Nothing but the Darjiling disaster was spoken of in the train, and the parents who travelled with me were determined, even if their children were safe, to remove them from Darjiling without a moment's unnecessary delay. They argued that Darjiling was not secure, and that their little ones would be ever so much safer on the plains.

We arrived at Siliguri early this morning and were told that we would have to stop there. As there seemed no immediate hope of proceeding further up the line, I went on a tour of inspection around Siliguri. Dr Mansfield, who was extremely obliging, explained to me that the greatest damage done at Siliguri was to the plague camp, which had been practically destroyed. The storm was most felt there about 3 o'clock on Sunday morning, when winds assumed a cyclonic form, and the station was deluged with rain. Returning to the platform, I noticed a Darjiling railway train being formed, and in answer to a question I was told that it was only going to Rungtong, a few miles up the line. I decided to go to Rungtong, and as tickets were not being sold, I got into the train without one. Later on the Railway authorities agreed to sell five tickets, and those five tickets were paid for long before the booking clerk had time to issue them. Subsequently tickets were sold to all-comers and off we started.

Between the Rungtong and Chunabatti stations occurs the first great slip, and this completely blocks the line for upwards of two hundred yards. We got out of the train here and walked across the slip, which was muddy, slushy and not a little dangerous. This slip, like many others further up the line, has played great havoc with the mountain's side, which has the appearance of being torn asunder, and up-rooted trees and huge boulders are strewn about in all directions. It is a pretty, but withal a weird sight. After negotiating this slip, we sat down on our luggage and waited for further developments. In about an hour's time a relief train picked us up and took us on to this station. We passed many small slips en route, and although these blocked the line when they first fell, the debris has been cleared away. In half an hour's time we hope to start for Kurseong, but whether we get there remains to be seen. We are told that the slips at Pugla Jhora block the line for a considerable distance and that the Pugla Jhora bridge is not safe. No particular damage, so far as I can ascertain, has been done at Tindharia.'

A second bulletin was sent from Kurseong the following day that referred to troubles with a van collected at Gayabari *after* negotiating the Pagla Jhora. However, this station is before the notorious torrent, and it is suggested that the van was actually coupled to the train at Mahanadi. The correspondent was not the first, and certainly not the last, to have become confused with the sequence of stations, loops and reverse sidings:

'I arrived here yesterday afternoon after an adventurous and interesting trip. Between Tindharia and this place I counted over fifteen slips, some great, some small. The worst slip of the lot was at Pugla Jhora. ... It is this Pugla Jhora that has proved a curse to the Darjiling-Himalayan Railway. It is everlastingly giving trouble, and it glories in it. Hence the natives have aptly named it Pugla Jhora [sic]. It does not know its own mind for two days alike, and is the terror of the Railway Engineers. I am told that the question will one day arise whether it would not be better and far cheaper in the long run to alter the alignment of the railway so as to give the Pugla Jhora a wide berth. The expense would be enormous and the task a formidable one.

Darjeeling Bazaar, from where a report in 1890 recorded that: 'It takes two to make a bargain' has no honour here; it never takes less than twenty, and all feel bound to shout, push, struggle and gesticulate. The crowd numbers many thousands and those jolly Hill-men appear to be the most good-natured people in the world ... every man carries a knife that would disembowel an elephant, but no one quarrels. Every woman is loaded with silver and gold jewellery, but no one is ever robbed. Lepcha lads play shuttlecock with the soles of their feet, which they turn upwards in the nimblest of fashion. Then come some stalls for tea, which is boiled up with molasses, a gruesome compound. Liquor is sold in the bazaar, mostly cheap fiery English spirit. In front of every shop is a board 'English soldiers cannot be supplied'.

On arriving at this Jhora we found, much to the credit of the Railway authorities, that the work of clearing the slip had just sufficiently progressed to enable the train to pass without any undue danger, but the bridge a quarter of a mile further ahead was still unsafe, at least for an engine to pass over. We got out of the train here and walked for about half a mile. The empty carriages in the meantime were carefully shunted across the damaged bridge and another engine took them in tow on the other side. We passed numerous slips but were not seriously inconvenienced till we reached Gyabari. Here an extra van was attached to our train, and that precious van caused us a considerable amount of delay, inconvenience and trouble. We had hardly gone a mile when it became derailed. It took half an hour or more to get it back on the rails again. Again we started, and again the van jumped off the line, and the work of replacing it had to be gone over again. We made a start, but had not gone two hundred yards when the van was off again. This settled its fate. Aided by the passengers, the offending van was removed from the line altogether, and we left it alone in its glory and came on to Kurseong without it. It was quite enough to be compelled to put

Arnold the Hero......

An extremely rare 15ct gold medal awarded to Frederick William Arnold (1874–1945) for his gallantry in risking his own life to save others at Pekoe Tip during the cyclone disaster. It is one of only twenty-five that were struck by J. Boseck & Co, watchmakers and jewellers of Calcutta & Darjeeling, and presented by the Lt Governor to members of the rescue parties on 4th November 1899 at the Town Hall. FWA returned to the UK on 9th April 1901.

A contemporary photograph of a team of women flattening the surface of the Hill Cart Road in Darjeeling with a heavy roller. It was a reflection of the times that on the reverse was the comment: 'Do not fancy these maids and matrons feel themselves ill used when they are pulling this heavy road-roller and the men are lounging at ease beside the way. They are frankly glad to have the chance, for they are about five times as strong in back and limbs as you would suppose, and generation after generation, they have become accustomed to the heaviest labour'.

Collection: Nick Rhodes

up with the antics of the Pugla Jhora, without having to tolerate a road van that would insist on making a road for itself.'

Undaunted, the correspondent continued to Darjeeling on the 29th:

'I left Kurseong on foot early yesterday morning, and was assured by those that had attempted the journey and had failed to accomplish it, that the betting was 500 to 1 that I would never reach my destination alive. This was very comforting information, but I had to go. If I did not reach Darjiling alive, I was perfectly certain that I would never reach it dead. So I started with two Bhutia coolies, who served the double purpose of carrying my luggage and acting as guides. They insisted on being paid four rupees each in advance and a respectable amount of bukshish at the end of the journey.

I have been round the world twice. I have roughed it in Australia, and I have roughed it in Africa and other parts of the world, but I can conscientiously tell you that I have never dreamed that there was a road so difficult and dangerous as the one that connects Kurseong with Darjiling at the present moment.

After leaving Kurseong I found tremendous slips on all sides. On arriving at the first railway bridge I found it completely swept away, and was obliged to walk across on a log of wood. One false step would have meant destruction. The railway lines were suspended in the air, all the ground that was once under them being swept completely away. A little further on the line was hopelessly wrecked, and the ends of rails were extended over the precipice. After this, for the distance of a mile or so, the road was, all things considered, fairly good. I then came to a regular avalanche of boulders, which covered the line for several hundred feet. Blasting operations were here in full swing. Climbing over this obstruction I got on to a patch of fairly good road, but the heat was excessive, quite as bad as it is in Calcutta. The constant climbing over obstacles, no doubt, made me feel more warm than I otherwise would have done. It took me one hour and three-quarters to reach Toong, which is distant about four miles from Kurseong, and between those two stations I counted eight large slips and two bridges entirely swept away.

I sat down at Toong station and took fifteen minutes' rest, well knowing that by far the worst and most dangerous part of the journey was to come. Within a few hundred yards of Toong there is a slip that completely covers the line for some distance, and a short way further on the railway bridge is washed away; beyond this the line is submerged 50ft deep

Looking towards Ghum, a temporary ropeway has been strung across the chasm where the road and railway previously ran. A train of freight wagons with provisions for the stranded hill station is being unloaded on the far side, whilst a passenger train further up the hill waits for passengers to be strapped to a chair suspended beneath the cables and transported across the breach.

Collection: (The late) Fred Pinn

for about 200 yards and gangs of coolies are at work clearing away the obstruction. A mile from this another bridge has disappeared, and I had to walk over a log of wood. A little further on another bridge is missing, and I had to act the part of Blondin once more. From this point to Chuttackpur siding I had to scramble over fourteen slips. Just a short distance from the last-mentioned station another bridge is missing and the lines are twisted into shapes that would defy an ordinary artist to represent. Beyond this the line is deeply covered for about 200ft. Then came four slips and a disappearance of the line for several hundred feet. Beyond this a huge avalanche of boulders which has torn the line from the mountain's side, and a short distance ahead a huge revetment, which must have cost a good deal to build, has been utterly demolished. The line will have to be resurveyed and rebuilt at this and many other points.

Following this there are two large slips, two bridges and other expensive revetments washed away. From this revetment to the Sonada Brewery siding there are five huge slips and, mind you, I am only counting the slips that obstruct the railway line. I could have encountered minor slips by the hundred, but I was much too exhausted for that.

On arriving at the Sonada Brewery siding I sat down utterly wearied, hoping that some one would bring me a pint of beer, but as nobody came I resumed my weary march, fully conscious that I had not accomplished half my journey yet and that a good deal worse was yet to come. I should tell you that the entire route from Kurseong to Darjiling is infested with myriads of leeches. Feeling utterly exhausted at one place I innocently sat down on the grass, and in a few seconds I had a leech busily engaged at my neck and one on each leg. It is impossible to pull them off, so I was obliged in the words of the music hall song, to 'grin and bear it' till the leeches condescended to take their departure. I shall never forget those leeches, and I still wonder why they were ever created.

After leaving the Brewery I had to make my way over five slips, two absent bridges, three more slips and another bridge that was not. Then I came to another costly revetment that had been washed away, and in honour to the fantastic shape of the lines I took a photograph of them, conditions being favourable, for I carried a camera all the way but had been unable to use it, owing to the fog, up to this time.

A few miles further on is Sonada station, and here I sat down and finished a loaf of bread, a ham and tongue patti and a bottle of pilsener beer, all of which I had brought with me. I can assure you that there was not a crumb left for the benefit of the crows. ... At Sonada I obtained a pony at a fabulous price and started off for Darjiling, leaving my luggage and the coolie who carried it to take care of themselves. The roads were so bad that, in spite of all I could do, it was dark long before I reached Ghoom, and I had to accomplish the journey to Darjiling along a very dangerous road in absolute darkness. I was within an ace of losing my life on several occasions, but after the most weary journey I have ever known, or ever hope to know again, I arrived at Darjiling at 8pm and found quarters at Boscolo's hotel. Owing to the frightful state of the roads my coolies had to halt in the jungle for the night, and only came in this morning. But here I am in Darjiling.'

The Empress of India telegraphed her Viceroy on hearing of the catastrophe, and asked to be kept fully briefed and to express her sympathy for the bereaved European and native families. The Viceroy in turn telegraphed the Lieutenant General of Bengal to express their joint anxieties, and requested that Mr Nolan, the Commissioner in Darjeeling, furnished daily reports. The Secretary of the Darjeeling Association announced that a relief fund had been opened for natives rendered homeless, and was followed by a request that the resources set aside for race meetings were made over to help establish similar support for the Europeans.

Gillanders Arbuthnot made an announcement that it was now possible for ponies and dandies to get down from Ghoom to within a mile of Sonada, and from Tung to Kurseong. The four miles between was still impassable for the ponies, although it was suggested that empty dandies could be carried over the remaining slips. There must have been some spirited clearance work, for a notice was subsequently issued on 30th September to state that ponies were now able to get through, although it was not published until three days later.

A wave of panic to leave Darjeeling followed the rumour that the breakdown of the water supply would

The railway was under no illusions that its heroic efforts to resume services after the devastation of the cyclone would soon be forgotten and that it would become the target of fun, as can be seen with this delightful contemporary postcard.

Collection: Nick Rhodes

bring with it typhoid, diphtheria and all manner of frightful diseases. Prices of what was left in the bazaar rocketed, with rice doubling to Rs1 for six *seers* and *bhuta* (the staple food) escalating from Rs1-4 to Rs3-4 per *maund*. The prices for oil and charcoal also doubled overnight, which prompted Mr Nolan to arrange for a supply of charcoal from the government supplies to be made available for the natives at a nominal charge.

Sulyard Cary, the DHR General Manager, arrived in Darjeeling on the 2nd October, and his previous experience on the East Bengal Railway on protective works and flood repairs was to prove invaluable. It would be a Herculean task, but he was confident to announce that the railway would be open again to Tung within the next couple of days, and by straining every nerve, he anticipated that trains would be reaching Ghoom in two or three weeks' time. The grim task of searching for bodies was stopped, and Darjeeling came to terms that the whole 4,000 feet of mountainside, that had slipped from Observatory Hill, had been consecrated to the rivers below.

On the same day in Calcutta, a grand fanfare was accompanying the train carrying His Honour, the Lt. Governor, from Sealdah station at 15.57. It was a world away from the anguish and torment in Darjeeling, to where he was bound. The party was due to reach Kurseong the following morning at 9.00 and proceed by road to the beleaguered hill station, arriving by 14.00. A hundred and fifty coolies had been ordered to attend the party, but the Press doubted if so many could be obtained, even at Rs10 a head. The coolies had been having a field day, charging Rs5 a head for carrying a package to Darjeeling, and correspondingly Rs40 for a dandy carried by eight of them. This charge made the price of food in the bazaars even higher, and there was going to be no let-out with that until the railway was running again.

Over Rs16,000 had been collected by the relief fund within the first week, and the first assistance was directed to building temporary accommodation for natives who had lost their homes. The open space adjacent to the botanical gardens was ideal, and the cryptomeria trees that had been uprooted nearby were used to form the framework, with bamboo *chittais* making waterproof roofs and walls. The building was constructed as double barracks, the ridgepole forming

The earthquake in June 1897 and the cyclone in September 1899 left an unprecedented trail of devastation, but true to form, the railway soon had the service back in operation. An Up freight pauses for the camera at the turn of the 19th century, whilst the photographers' gravity trolley waits at the bottom right-hand corner. The reverse sidings are one of the symbolic features of the climb between Rangtong and Gayabari, but recent encroachments have rendered them more difficult to capture on film.

the dividing wall, and was able to accommodate 152 people. Each family lived in one of the 38ft-square compartments, and each was fitted with its own door, whilst carpenters began knocking together wooden *chungs*, a sort of palette to sleep on above the sodden ground. A further barrack with 32 compartments was to be constructed nearby, and two police constables were put on watch to ensure the posts were not uprooted and made into firewood. Nevertheless, spirits were high in the temporary community, as the demand for labour had enabled coolies to command much higher wages than ever before!

The managers of the tea gardens were playing cards much closer to their chests, conscious that the value of the properties would be affected by adverse news. Company Agents were sent up from Calcutta to make special reports on the situation, and there was concern that the breakdown of communications with the DHR would prevent tea supplies from reaching the Calcutta market. It was possible that it could work in the favour of the plantation owners, for holding back the tea could bring about higher prices at the end of the season and help towards recovering some of the tremendous losses.

Gillanders Arbuthnot received a telegram from the General Manager dated 4th October to advise it was indeed the intention to run trains through to Tung, and from there the public were to make their own arrangements to continue to Darjeeling by pony truck. The Press reported that the railway deserved the highest praise, for within ten days of the disaster it had cleared the obstructions and re-erected two bridges on the section to Tung, allowing forty passengers to travel on the first down train to Siliguri. The remaining section to Sonada and the wholesale destruction between Ghum and Darjeeling was going to take a lot longer to clear. It was reported that thousands of coolies were said to be repairing the Cart Road for the railway, and that large numbers had been brought in direct from Nepal by the railway authorities. *'Their European supervisors are to be seen at frequent intervals,'* the Press proclaimed, adding that *'... Mr Barnard should be complimented on having got the repairs so well and so rapidly in hand and now, with the concentrated efforts of him and Mr Carey, we ought soon to be able to depart from Ghoom in our dauntless little railway.'*

The fickle affection between the Press and the DHR had been well rehearsed since opening, but there was no doubt that the railway was back in favour for the time being. True to journalistic form, the front page was the province of disaster and scandal, with praise being interred to the inside, but *The Englishman* ran the report on Thursday, 12th October stating that:

'Nothing could better illustrate the recuperative power of the Darjiling-Himalayan Railway, the skill of the engineering staff, and their magnificent power of immediately grasping with and overcoming difficulties, than the notice which was issued yesterday, announcing that through communication by train from Siliguri to the 39th mile (Chuttackpur) would be opened on and from Wednesday.

That such splendid arrangements should be made within 17 days of these destructive landslips, reflects the greatest possible credit upon Mr Sulyard Cary, the manager, Mr Barnard, the ubiquitous and capable Engineer, and upon all their staff. That in addition to the enormous extra work entailed upon them at this time, they have been able to arrange not only for the repair of the line, but have also undertaken the most useful work of arranging for the transport right through, coolies, dandies and all, stamps them as benefactors as well as competent organisers. Then everything is laid down so accurately and definitely. We are informed exactly what we wish to know, how far the railway will carry us, how far the line is not available, and how we are to get across this intervening space. Surely this should quiet much of the unnecessary alarm that has been worrying those who have friends in Darjiling.

Only a little over a fortnight since the line seemed to the lay mind utterly unrepairable. Now, we have only to arrange our own journey over to Ghoom, and this is quite easily accomplished. There the railway people taken us in charge, and land us, with only a matter of a trainless four and an eighth miles right down to Siliguri. After all, there has been little disorganisation of traffic, and now there will be less. Even the $4^1/_8$ miles hiatus will yield to gentle treatment, and there is already a talk of the line being opened from Ghoom into Darjiling. The suggestion is made that a temporary station for Darjiling should be erected on the Ghoom side of the yawning chasm, which breaks off the road and railway about half a mile from the present Darjiling Railway Station. When the line is cleared that length, we shall really have nothing of which to complain. Yes, even now there are a few who

A postcard of the main street in Kurseong dated circa 1900. Although Darjeeling was the original headquarters of the line, its location would have been ideally placed in Kurseong as it was approximately halfway between the two termini. In 1910 it was decided to transfer here, although it took a number of years before the railway community was fully established.

Collection: Nick Rhodes

would or do complain. On the contrary all are marvelling at the miraculous way in which the repairs have been so successfully and so expeditiously carried out.'

But the DHR knew that the fine words in print would only wrap vegetables from the bazaar the following day, and it would not be long before the railway would be criticised for not investing sufficient funds on the comforts of its passengers. The railway was in a no-win situation.

The weather remained equally capricious over the following weeks, but the clearing-up operation continued and the Superintendent of the Government Geological Survey of India arrived to inspect the dangerous buildings. It was evident that many would have to be abandoned, and the debates ran long into the night on the means to render the remainder safe. As to this day, much of the town depended on visitors for its livelihood, and the Government was adamant that no compromises would be allowed that would place other people's lives at risk. Extensive revetments were going to be necessary as safeguards, and the proprietors were going to face heavy expenses.

It was equally essential that the conventions of daily life quickly returned, and it was only here, amongst the mud and devastation, the Amusement Club could play to a packed house with *'Lulu, the Lily of Lebong'* and *'The Baron, The Butcha and The Bap'*. It must have been a curious sight to see the imperious dowagers of the Victorian Raj picking their way over the massive earth slips and debris, determined to see *'Baron Bounder Bill, roué, reprobate and ruffian'*, and *'Captain La-Di-Da Fitz-Fop of the Onety-oneth Slashers'*. And what could have been more reassuring than to read that the *'... tight fitting black velvet bodice and puffed white muslin sleeves, little caps surmounting each pretty head, made a charming toilette for the ladies'* – it was a sign that life was returning to normal.

There was a new season and a new Century to prepare for, and the spirit was positive that the town would recover to accommodate next year's migration escaping from the heat. Indeed, the hill station was becoming an escape from India itself.

Chapter 5

Investment and Improvement

The new century was rung in with the claim that the Empire had never been greater, leading one newspaper to report that it: *'Stretched round the globe, has one heart, one head, one language, one policy'*.

But the dawn of the century was soon to be marked by the end of an era, for at the age of 81, the Empress died in January 1901. Her son Edward VII was proclaimed the new Emperor of India on 1st January 1903 in a curious spectacle of British pomp and Hindu circumstance enacted on the Great Plains near Delhi. It created the unfortunate appearance of an oompah-Empire, during which the Viceroy Lord Curzon read out the statement that there would be a remission of interest on British loans for those states suffering from famine. This was followed by a pageant of fantasy and wealth, with a procession of a hundred potentates and princes of Indian States each taking their messages of greetings to the dais.

It was feared the new Emperor was becoming a loose cannon on the Ship of State, for the splendour of the presentation was a complete reversal of the austerity portrayed by the late Queen, who had never been seen in anything but black for the past forty years since the death of her beloved Prince Albert. It had little to do with the rest of India, trapped inside the belief of its own tradition and history, and it is no surprise to learn that seeds of unrest were already fermenting across the vast plains. The administration of the Raj was firmly in the control of British civil servants, who had stamped their vision of social justice and education as the only means of progress. However, they had not been in sufficient numbers to run such a huge territory, and educated Indians were actively sought who empathised with British principles. In truth it created a new elite, and one that conveniently fought against what it saw as out dated prejudices and superstition. The spread of English as the official language had given unprecedented access to Western knowledge, and a new professional emerged who was meticulously middle class, and at the same time was very much aware of his national identity as an Indian.

Anxious that a repetition of the 1857 mutiny should not occur, the retired civil servant Allen Octavian Hume had encouraged the formation of a discussion forum that would act as a safety valve for Indian opinion. So was formed the Indian National Congress in 1885, and this began life as a loose structure of influential men in provincial politics. It had to be said that it was somewhat top-heavy with Brahmin Hindus and lawyers, but all were loyal to the Raj and saw their role as focusing on issues of status and professional equality rather than radical social and political change. A number of limited reforms were advocated, but it became apparent that it could not remain divorced from the passion of social and economic issues inflamed by the religious differences in the regions. By the turn of the century the concerns had polarised the delegates into the Moderates and the Extremists, and it was the latter who had persuaded the Congress to adopt self-government as a political aim.

Trade with the Empire had certainly given India a new status in the world economy, and the DHR played an important part in the prosperity and development of Darjeeling, for along with the rice, flour, oil and coal, it brought the most prized of all commodities: tourists. The census taken in 1881 had recorded a population of Darjeeling as 7,018, which had doubled in size

Darjeeling Station at the turn of the century with 'B' Class No.21 departing at the head of a Down train for Siliguri. The railway was patched up after the devastating cyclone of 1899, and the large stack of sleepers was no doubt part of the repair programme. Built in 1892 and delivered in 1893, the locomotive subsequently became ISR 779 and was named 'Mountaineer' (in more recent times 'Himalayan Bird').

to 14,145 by 1891 and 16,924 by 1901. The figures for Kurseong had shown the population of 4,033 in 1881 actually fell to 3,522 ten years later, but by 1901 had climbed back to 4,469. Dividends for the DHR shareholders continued to rise to 11-14% by the turn of the century, and in 1905 the returns were showing that 29,000 passengers were carried and that the freight had increased to 31,570 tons. There was little doubt that the railway was really proving its capabilities to the community, and in an act of Raj bravado, it joined with the Maharajadhiraj of Burdwan in helping to establish a golf course on the abandoned ruins of a military cantonment at Senchal, close to Tiger Hill.

There was great excitement when it was announced that the Emperor's son, the Prince of Wales, was to use the railway to visit Darjeeling, and a special train was prepared for the event. Locomotive No.29, which had arrived from Britain only the previous year, was adorned with the Prince of Wales' feathers liveried on the saddle tank and a quartet of flags from the Empire flew ahead of the chimney, whilst the rerailing crowbar looked as though it had been freshly planed and polished. Two covered wagons and a string of immaculate carriages were assembled for the train, with the 1st Class four-wheeler No.63 designated and furnished out for its honoured guest. Alas, the visit did not materialise, but it did make for a splendid photograph.

The problem was political, for Bengal was about to go through a disastrous period of partition at the time

Delivered to India in 1904, No.29 was the first of the 'B' Class to be constructed by the North British Locomotive Company. Its wheels had barely turned in service when it was prepared to haul the special train for the Prince of Wales' visit to Darjeeling. With the armorial crest of feathers applied to the sides of the saddle tank and the flags of the Empire mounted ahead of the chimney, it looked magnificent at the head of an equally pristine rake of carriages and baggage wagons. Unfortunately it was all in vain and the visit never took place, for the growing problems caused by the Viceroy dividing Bengal in two had diverted the attention of the Prince.

Glynne Gladstone MSS

of the Royal visit. The Viceroy had reasoned that the racial, historical and cultural differences within Bengal were too complex for it to be managed as an entity and it should be divided in two. What was intended and what resulted were totally different, for the split polarised East Bengal into a Muslim majority, with the West being occupied by Hindus. It was the failure of the Raj to understand the importance of these very factors that made it a civic nightmare, and the Prince of Wales was decidedly unimpressed. He reflected that Britain appeared to be treating the Indians as beaten aliens in their own country, and they were rightly becoming very much aware of this.

The Prince of Wales might not have been going to Darjeeling, but there was still no other railway in the world that could attract a more eclectic roll call of travellers. The visit made by Alistair Crowley was no exception, for as a skilled mountaineer he was making a bid to be the first to climb Kanchenjunga, although his notoriety came from being a magician, a Satanist and revelling in his reputation as being the 'wickedest man in the world'. Leaving Sealdah in 1905, he recalled:

'The next day I left for Darjeeling. It is certainly one of the most impressive experiences that a railway can afford. One begins by jogging dully across the acrid plains of Bengal and then at Sara Ghat one finds oneself suddenly on the bank of the Ganges. I had seen the river before, higher up, and it is not particularly exciting, but here it flowed gigantically across a vast desolation. The time was sunset, the turbid water glowed with angry reds and oranges. There was an evil coppery sheen upon its waveless turmoil. Its breadth possessed a horror of its own; it was like a river of hell. Far away it reached to the right and left. There was nothing to break the horizon. It gave the desolate effect of ocean, but the boundlessness of the open sea suggests liberty. This river had told of barrenness and bitter bondage. The windless Ganges stank of putrefaction. It was not even the stench of rotting vegetation. It seemed as if it were the earth itself which was decaying. A more fantastic and more frightful sight I have never seen. We crossed this tartarean river in a steamer and the actual breadth may be estimated from the fact that dinner is served on board. It was a bad dinner, too; it completed the hellishness of the scene.

One lands. The eternal funeral march of the train is resumed. The heat of the night is stifling. ... One tosses in blind torment. There is no question of seeking relief; one has an instinct that nothing will do any good ... Then suddenly comes dawn. The slow train stutters and stops. One is still an insect on the infernal plain, but there is a touch of coolness in the air, which is not wholly the chill of death. The sticky sweat on one's body begins to evaporate and one's spirit to revive. There is a call to Chota Hazri. One steps out of the carriage ... a phantom of hope created by courage from the chaos of nightmare ... there stands the mass of Kanchenjunga, faint rose, faint blue, clear white, in the dawn.

On reaching the foot of the hills, one transfers to a toy railway, which climbs the six thousand-odd feet to Darjeeling by means of complicated curves and even loops. One ascends rapidly; the view constantly changes; one begins to appreciate the geology of the country as a whole. In the foreground the tropical vegetation is superbly thick and rich. One is so relieved by the change to cool shade and a suggestion of moisture that it comes as a shock to remember that this is the Terai, one of the most deadly fever districts in the world. By lunchtime the character of the vegetation is already markedly altered. The heavy tangle of the low country begins to give place to mountain sprightliness, but also the view tends to disappear altogether. One enters the region of almost eternal mist. The day is warm; and yet one is chilled to the bone. One is glad to come out on to an exposed ridge at Ghum and find the train begins to go down hill. It was the sign of the nearness of Darjeeling. I got off the train.

With unfeigned satisfaction, I observed immediately that the current legends about the amazing powers of the coolies were true. The principal item of my baggage was a full-sized wardrobe trunk, but its contents were not mostly air, as usual with the American variety of this device. It contained comparatively few clothes; boots, axes, rifles, revolvers, scientific instruments and books made up the tale. I do not know how much it weighed, because the baggage clerk at Calcutta had asked me to bribe him with a rupee to declare it below the free allowance; but I should have been very sorry to have to do more than set it up on end unaided. A young girl coolie took it on her back, as I might have done a rucksack, and carried it at a good steady pace up the steep narrow paths

Six native tea pluckers nervously pose for a delightful photograph in Darjeeling bazaar at the turn of the century. The sign between the roofs in the background reads 'Municipal Building A', whilst the top of the Hindu temple can be seen in the background.

to the Woodlands Hotel. I no longer disbelieved the story that a woman had once carried a full-sized upright piano all the way to Darjeeling from Siliguri on the plains.'

Crowley had been travelling to Darjeeling in the same year that the station at Ghum was upgraded with an extension to the building, an additional platform, a loop siding, a new engine shed and an extra godown for freight. The military also decided that it was time to open up the question of the DHR transporting its personnel who were being sent on relief to the barracks at Lebong, but the negotiating became somewhat protracted and acrimonious. Prestage had used the ability of the Railway to convey troops to the sanatoria quickly and efficiently as a powerful selling point in the early days, to gain support for the construction of the line, and the authorities decided it was now time to call in its card. There entered a long and politely bitter exchange of principle, with the military advancing they would expect a reduction in charges by guaranteeing full trains of twelve men in the standard load of eleven 3rd Class trolleys, with additional freight wagons for their luggage. The DHR refused to comply, stating the 3rd Class trolleys held 16 men and that it could not make the trains any longer because of the reverses and crossing sidings. However, the terms it did offer were calculated to show a 33% reduction over the standard 3rd Class fare on the mail train, but the military responded with proposals that it intended to march the men to Darjeeling and acquire camping grounds at Sonada and Tindharia.

Sulyard Cary retired as General Manager, and the Directors appointed George Belben Cresswell to the position in March 1906. Born on 26th June 1870,

George Belben Cresswell. Amongst his many achievements during his ten years as General Manager of the DHR, he was responsible for introducing the first generation of bogie carriages, the transfer of the headquarters from Darjeeling to Kurseong, the articulated Garratt locomotive, and the building of the two extension lines to Kishenganj and up the Teesta Valley.

The DHRS Archive

he was educated at Kings College in London and subsequently articled to the London, Brighton & South Coast Railway. He was trained as Pupil and Assistant in the Engineering Offices, and after moving on to the London & North Western Railway for six months, sailed to India in 1891. There followed a series of appointments with surveying and constructing the Bengal Dooars and the Assam-Bengal Railways until 1901, when he obtained a year's leave for a trip around the world. Returning to India, he finally became the General Manager and Engineer-in-Chief to the Bengal Dooars line, from which he resigned in 1904 to become the Deputy Manager of the DHR.

He came to the Himalayan line at a time when there had been little apparent improvement with the travelling conditions for its passengers, the railway having somehow survived through their benevolence and affection for a toy train, as Colonel Hume of the Royal Engineers recorded:

'The sun was well up when we reached the Junction, where we proceeded to change into the tiny mountain train, which had undertaken to carry us above the clouds. The squat engine, with its burly driver, a full size too large for his cab, and the low line of cars, some miniature coaches, others mere glorified trollies, gained little dignity by their proximity to the powerful locomotive and the roomy saloon carriages, from which we descended.

But the transfer of mails and baggage is rapidly effected, the toy trucks receiving their burden with perfect equanimity, we are hustled into our places, and the sturdy Lilliput puffs noisily out of the Station, as though to proclaim to all the world that His Majesty's mails, an hour behind their time, are at last in efficient hands. For the first hour we are accompanied by a wide cart-road, on which we meet many picturesque groups of native wayfarers, journeying to the market town. A knot of chattering, laughing women, a crowd of coolies, or a string of laden bullock carts, all displaying the same indifference to the flight of Time, so strange to Western eyes.

A long viaduct and massive iron bridge, spanning a few trickling channels in a sandy hollow far below reminded us that even in untutored Nature, appearances may sometimes be delusive. In the spring-time, when the snows are melting on the hills above, these harmless channels will unite in one great roaring flood, testing to the uttermost the stability and power of those overbearing buttresses. From the open cars we can see the dark mass of the wooded slope, behind which lie the great mountains; steadily ascending we draw nearer and nearer, and finally plunging into the depth of the dark forest. The tangled jungle creeps up on either hand, the rattling of the train is drowned in the appalling silence of the woods, and the hand of nature is already laid upon our hearts.... What does it reck of this wonderful railway?

The incidents of the journey are full of interest; the wooden stations and their strange names and adjoining clusters of rickety huts, the numerous devices of the snake-like ascent, the wonderful loop in which the track makes a complete circle, crossing itself by a bridge forty feet nearer the clouds – all seem unreal and toy-like against the background of the huge mountains.'

But the Company realised that if something wasn't done soon, the toy would soon become a joke. Cresswell's feet were barely under the desk when he began applying his experience to the underlying problems of the railway. The speeding up of the 'Mail' service was his first priority, after which he turned his attention to a number of designs for bogie coaches. The first carriage was placed on the rails before the year had ended, and a complete set was ready the following year. After a period of experimentation, they entered revenue-earning service on the 'Mail' and passengers were finally offered a new standard of comfort, whilst further improvements were made in 1908 when the coaches were fitted with electric lighting supplied by accumulator batteries.

The Government began considering its option of taking over the line in 1908, but it ultimately decided to continue with the existing arrangements. There was, however, continued concern over the high rates being charged for passengers and freight. It insisted these should be adjusted as a condition of continued private ownership, which testified to the concerns originally expressed by Lord Luard before the assent was given for the construction of the line. The DHR had been allowed to charge such fares owing to its much higher costs of operation and maintenance than a more conventional line, and it was not until a Mr G.W. Christison challenged the freight charges that they were finally checked. He had been running a long crusade with the blight on tea caused by red spiders and the potential disaster of deforestation in the Darjeeling area, and now turned his attention to the railway. He collected the comparable charges from mountain railways in Europe, United States and Asia before presenting his case, and after a long and acrimonious battle, the passenger fares and goods charges were reduced, with the transport of coal dropping 33%, rice by 25% and tea 10%.

Cresswell continued with his program of improvements by upgrading the track and cutting out nearly seventy crossings the railway made over the Cart Road. He also made the proposal of introducing a loop at Batasia to ease the gradient, which would have removed most of the crossings between Ghum and Darjeeling, but it was going to take a further ten years and his retirement before the work on that commenced. The Directors were approached by a number of interested parties for a revision in services or concessions to the fares, and it was agreed to allow Lady Minto's Nursing Association the privilege of travelling at the next higher Class for the next lower fare if they were in uniform and on duty. The Company was wary of opening the floodgates to everybody who could claim altruistic intentions, but it was sound business when the General Manager was authorised to make the offer in May 1909 to the Post Master General of Bengal:

'... to run out a train at night over the safe part of the line between Siliguri and Rangtong with the mails, which will be carried by runners from that point to Kurseong by the short-cut for a fee of 500 rupees a month for a period of twelve months only'.

The growth in traffic continued, and for the year 1909–10 the line advised that 174,000 passengers and 47,000 tons of goods were carried, the financial returns giving the DHR the opportunity to consider a number of projects that would extend its interests. The Directors were asked in March to consider plans for alteration and additions to the workshop at Tindharia, and announcements were made during September stating that the Company was formulating proposals for three extensions to be built and would be seeking the necessary sanctions from the Railway Board. It is interesting to note that none of the plans had been mentioned during the previous year when the Government was deciding whether to exercise its option and take over the line.

The intention was to lay a branch from a junction to the north of Siliguri that would run 70 miles across the plains to Kishenganj, which would open up and serve several tea gardens and jute plantations. A second extension would be constructed from Siliguri for 29 miles along the Teesta valley, where the fortunes were a little less obvious but could ultimately lead into Sikkim. The third line was to run for $4\frac{1}{2}$ miles from the bazaar in Darjeeling and follow the spur round to the barracks at Lebong. It was never built, but an agreement was subsequently reached with the Army for transporting troops as both parties had seen where their best interests lay.

It was inevitable that Darjeeling would be compared to Simla, which out of all the other Indian hill stations was its rival as the jewel in the Himalayan crown; it was equally certain that the relative merits of the two railways that served the towns would come under scrutiny. Both towns had cart roads constructed to link

The first bogie carriage on the DHR was built by Tindharia and placed on the line in 1906, with a complete set appearing the following year. Measuring 26ft 6in over the couplings, the new carriages were an instant success and were fitted out in a number of guises, including the open observation and closed saloons seen here. The condition of the Cart Road is interesting and shows the superiority of the train as a means of transport before the private motor car began to dominate the scene.

Collection: Nick Rhodes

Although the running number is not quite discernible, the locomotive is clearly one of the early 'B' Class that came from Sharp, Stewart. Seen here in its original form, it waits at a roadside halt with an Up train comprising a closed four-wheeled van and the splendid first generation of bogie coaches.

Collection: Hugh Rayner

An unidentified 'B' Class being refuelled in the yard at Kurseong, circa 1910. Building work on the new offices designed by George Cresswell had already begun in the vicinity of the station, and the transfer of the headquarters from Darjeeling was completed by 1914.

Collection: David Churchill

One of the few surviving photographs of the original Tindharia station. The similarity in its design to Sukna and Ghum can be seen, although the upper sections were subsequently lowered after the building was found to have been constructed on poor foundations and suffered considerable destruction by earth tremors in 1938.

Collection: Eddie Lambert

them with the plains before the railways were built, but work on the line to Simla did not begin until 1901, and there was plenty of experience to draw on from the DHR. Simla had been the summer residence for the British Government since 1863, when the Viceroy, Sir John Lawrence, had decided that the bureaucracy would function better in the more agreeable climate. Darjeeling was a lot closer, but the monsoons were too disruptive, and as a consequence the entire entourage would migrate the 1,170 miles from Calcutta every six months. When it came to building the railway, it was decided to cut a completely new furrow from Kalka and climb the 5,000 feet of the western Himalayas by a route that crossed 869 bridges and bored through 102 tunnels. It was a magnificent feat of engineering, and one should never underestimate the superlatives used for this railway.

The Press was not slow to lampoon the DHR, and over the years it would come to mock the line for remaining immune to its critics and charging high fares for a poor service, whilst praising the attitude of the Simla line with its response to change and improvement. However the DHR was obliged to challenge a unique range of hazards and conditions that ravaged the line like no other, and it was not in reality a fair comparison. By 1904 the expenditure for the line to Simla had staggered to Rs275,000 per mile, which had forced it to be taken over by the State, whereas the DHR had cost Rs60,000 per mile and was making a healthy profit for its shareholders.

The year 1909 had not drawn to an end when the railway learned that the Darjeeling municipality was proposing to establish a ropeway for the removal of night soil (sewerage) and refuse. The General Manager was able to arrange for the DHR to receive at least three months' notice of the termination of an agreement that had previously been made for the railway to carry the purification of Darjeeling for dumping at Batasia. The service had become locally known as the 'stink express', although it is not clear if the name was ascribed to the speed of the train or the haste of the people getting out of its path! Either way, it was an inglorious end to a busy year.

The following year opened with the railway submitting an application to the Government of Bengal to make a preliminary survey for a new extension from Ghum. It was to run for 10 miles along the Cuichona spur towards the Nepalese frontier and terminate at a point near Hoom, but as with previous ambitions in this direction, nothing further developed. Cresswell turned his attention to moving the headquarters of the railway from Darjeeling to Kurseong, and put his mind to designing the General Offices and accommodation for the staff. Many of the buildings were constructed in concrete, and although it took quite a few years for all the staff to transfer, Thacker's Business Directory for Bengal first recorded Kurseong as the new headquarters in 1914. Cresswell also submitted estimates to the Directors for re-ballasting the track, but their response stated they had been given to understand that it was not absolutely necessary to spend as much as was mentioned, and the matter was referred back to ask how much of the work was really essential. However, the Inspector's report for the year ending 31st March 1909 was received shortly afterwards, and in the July the Directors recorded:

'... that in compliance with his remarks, more ballast now nearly all at site, will be put on the road shortly and that 3 new-types of rerailing ramps had been fixed and 6 more ordered'.

Darjeeling had been working hard to become a fashionable hill station and the railway was now able to offer a comfortable service with its new bogie coaches. However there was still the matter of providing transport from the station to the hotels, which usually meant that the men took ponies, with the women and children riding in rickshaws or dandies, followed by female porters carrying the luggage on their backs. The dandy was in the style of a sedan chair carried by four men on their shoulders, and the advice given in the Darjeeling guide warned that they *'.... swing off with their fares up and down hill at a jog-trot, looking extremely well pleased if the occupants show the slightest sign of nervousness'*. Mark Twain visited the town in 1897 and wryly recalled *'.... at the railway station in Darjeeling you find plenty of cab-substitutes – open coffins, in which you sit, and then borne on men's shoulders up the steep roads into town'*. The Directors decided to approve the plans for Tindharia to build its own rickshaws for Rs250—300 a piece and let them to coolies at Darjeeling station for Rs250 a year, which was to be paid monthly and on the condition that they all wore uniforms.

The monsoon rains caused their usual damage to the line, the most acute being a 120ft section that subsided about twenty feet during the night of 26th July at mile 11¾, just before Rangtong. A 50ft length also subsided by approximately 2ft at mile 10, close to the approach to the first loop, and the track was temporarily packed up with sleepers to allow the trains to cautiously pass. The following day it sunk a further 8ft and the permanent way had to be slewed three times before a stable trackbed was found. The repairs were completed within 24 hours and the service

The railway had certainly been trying for years to find a form of motive power that could haul much bigger loads than the 'B' Class and cope with the constantly changing grades and superelevation of the track. The answer seemed to have come with the Garratt seen here on the Beyer Peacock test track at Gorton, but once in service, it was found there were many teething troubles to sort out before its viability could be properly assessed.

Manchester Museum of Science & Industry

resumed, a testament to what could be achieved with the right spirit.

A curious report appeared in the *Indian Railway Gazette* during the same year that reminded its readers of:

> '*A fact that had almost been forgotten: that the line was constructed by the Decauville Company of Paris, a firm which claims that its founder built the first light railway the world ever saw.*'

The French Company was indeed making a decided push for business in India at the time and had just opened an office in Calcutta, but there was no evidence to support its claims with the line to Darjeeling apart from the broad conception of light railway construction. The Government later suffered great losses after purchasing a line Decauville had indeed built up in the North West Frontier, and any further pretensions to their success in India quietly fizzled out. The DHR was content to ignore the report and declare that for 1910 a dividend of 8% would be paid to its shareholders, with a carry-over of Rs170,981.

The Directors received a petition in January 1911 from residents in Darjeeling to introduce an '*intermediate Class*' of travel, but the issue had been raised and discussed on previous occasions with the Board being of the opinion that it was undesirable. The railway had its attentions on higher matters of State, for King Edward VII had died in 1910 and was succeeded by George V. There would be a lavish Coronation Durbar in India and the Directors did not want to be caught on the hop with a chance of a visit to the hills. His Imperial Highness, the Crown Prince of Germany, confirmed his intention to visit Darjeeling and special instructions were issued to be observed for working the 'up' train on 7th February, with the return three days later. It was agreed that a special saloon at a cost of Rs3,500 should be constructed for such purposes,

A Sharp, Stewart 'B' Class with the Up Mail at Ghum in 1913. The siding with the four-wheeled stock was later removed and the station canopy extended to the edge of the through track. The early monogram for the railway can just be made out on the door panel of the 1st Class carriage.

Collection: Nick Rhodes

but the proposal for an additional charge of Rs1,000 for special fittings in anticipation of a visit to Darjeeling in cold weather by the new King-Emperor need not be incurred as *'it is considered most improbable His Majesty would be able to go to Darjeeling during the limited time at his disposal'*.

In reality his mind was focused on reuniting Bengal since witnessing the disastrous attempts during his 1905 visit as Prince of Wales, and he was actively supporting the transfer of the capital from Calcutta to Delhi. It was a shrewd move, for it took matters away from the rapacious business community, and any smarting of Bengali pride was overcome by the reunification.

The 1911 Durbar was more extravagant than ever, and it was the first time that a British monarch was to be crowned as Emperor. It was also a blatant demonstration, to the perceived chaos of India, where the seat of power was firmly sited. Thirty-six railway junctions were laid around the new capital to cater for the celebrations, with the esteemed guests being accommodated in forty thousand tents fitted out with drawing rooms, bedchambers and studies. It was a competition of splendour, with King George and Queen Mary striving to maintain some measured dignity in fear of the Maharajahs' diamonds outshining their example.

But no amount of jewellery could mask a shifting of the balance of power in India. The All-India Muslim League had been formed in 1906, following concerns that the Indian National Congress was predominantly Hindu. In 1907 the British Labour politician Keir Hardie had accused the United Kingdom of running India *'like the Czar runs Russia'*, which may well have prompted the late King-Emperor to have talked of *'prudently extending'* democracy a year later. In an assassination attempt, two bombs had been thrown at the Viceroy in September 1909, and many Indians were now seeing their land as the means to subsidise the British economy with cheap raw materials whilst becoming a market for its manufactured goods.

The real excitement for the railway in 1911 came with the appearance of a radically new and innovative locomotive, which quickly attracted the interest of the media. Built by Beyer Peacock at their Gorton works in Manchester, Great Britain, it was an articulated 0-4-4-0 to the design of Herbert William Garratt, and was grudgingly hailed by the railway Press as a distinct development. The manufacturer offered a second locomotive at a reduced price, but the minute book for the Company remarked in 1912 that the first had not yet proved itself as adaptable for work on the railway as the 'B' Class, and it was not long before they were considering selling it off to anybody who would buy it.

In March, the Directors consented to a maximum investment of Rs3,500 for a small guidebook to be produced for the railway. A contract was agreed in July with Messrs MacNeill & Co. to supply tickets at 1 rupee 8 annas per thousand, and in October the Directors confirmed the action of the General Manager by contributing Rs150 towards building a school at Tindharia. The spiritual requirements of the settlement were not forgotten either, for a further Rs150 were sanctioned two years later towards a harmonium for the Chaplain, the Reverend Arthur Waite.

But it was the volume of traffic on the Hill Cart Road that was now causing some anxiety, to the extent that on the 29th June 1912 the DHR sought the guidance of the police. There had been no provision made for preventing carts carrying long timber from colliding with passing trains on the *terai* section between Siliguri and Sukna, and the Company now saw this as a problem. It was coincidentally considering proposals to purchase the Ruikingpong Timber Compartments 6 & 7 of the Teesta Forestry Division, where it could fell the *sal* for sleepers and arrange its own delivery. An extension line was also up for debate from Darjeeling station to the Cutchery (the court rooms and offices for public business) that were close to the Government House, but the Bengal Secretariat decided this was not required.

Whatever the problems, the DHR always had the one card up its sleeve that no other could play, and that was the panorama of the Himalaya. There was great excitement in 1913 when the railway was used to carry a reconnaissance party and equipment for a survey of the unexplored Tibetan passes. This secluded and enigmatic land kept a close grip on its frontiers and, in theory, it was protected by the ruling Manchu Qing dynasty of China. The 'Great Game' was still in play,

The Dalai Lama and his supporters in Darjeeling.

One of the three 'B' Class locomotives ordered from the North British Locomotive Co. in 1913 stands for a works photograph alongside one of the fifteen 2-6+6-0 Mallet compounds built for the 3ft 6in-gauge South African Railways. Two more 'B' Class were to be built by NBR in 1916, but such were the commitments with supplying the War Department, the work was cancelled and an order for three engines placed with Baldwin in the USA.

Mitchell Library

Taken circa 1914, there can be little doubt of the photograph being Tindharia works, but it is not so clear as to which one. The layout of the track in relation to the orientation of the buildings and hillside suggests this is the back of the original workshop adjacent to the locomotive shed. Note the foundry casting boxes and also the wheels from the early 'B' Class which are not fitted with balances on the flycranks.

The DHRS Archive

This pre-1914 photograph shows the spur on which the new Tindharia workshop was to be built to accommodate the extra workload with the opening of the two extension lines. It would enable the railway to become as self-sufficient as possible, and indeed it constructed three of its own locomotives, albeit with spare parts left over from a cancelled order and earlier machines.

with Britain suspicious that Russia was courting the 13th Dalai Lama, and any such alliance would have been seen as posing a threat to the security of the Raj.

Tibet had recently strayed across the Sikkimese frontier, and the British Government saw it essential to know about the goings-on in Lhasa. It had previously sanctioned the dispatch of a top-secret mission in 1903 led by Colonel Francis Younghusband to sort the matter out, but they were sent packing as the enlightened Master had made it clear he had no intention of receiving them. The mission tried again with the back up of 3,000 troops, but it was a disaster, encountering an ambush on the way that resulted in a horrific Tibetan massacre near the village of Tuna. The task force continued on its bloodstained way to the capital, only to find the Potala Palace half-deserted. The surrounding area was little more than a malodorous tip, although one soldier found a sausage machine made in Birmingham and two bottles of Bulldog stout on a market stall in the *Barkhor*! The British assured all concerned that it would leave as soon as a treaty was signed that would settle relations between them and Tibet, but it sounded like a veiled threat as the agreement included granting the Raj the right to establish trade missions and forbade the Dalai Lama to make cessions to foreign powers.

Despite a further treaty in 1906 that recognised the supremacy the Manchus had over Tibet, Peking became angered by what it saw as an incursion into territory it regarded as its own, and dispatched an invasion force in 1910 to seize Lhasa. A number of boy Dalai Lamas had died under mysterious circumstances since the Chinese had imposed a military presence in Tibet in 1720, and the memory of this sent the current spiritual leader fleeing for his life. David MacDonald had been an interpreter with the ill-fated Younghusband mission, and was now able to patch things up by helping the Dalai Lama escape and take up residence in Darjeeling for 18 months. The move brought a Chinese linguist by the name of Yang Feng and a gang of accomplices travelling by train from Calcutta under assumed names, and in the guise of monks sought permission from the Dalai Lama to enter Tibetan monasteries. Their brief was his assassination, which would have rapidly advanced his next incarnation to one chosen by the Chinese. Despite a well-orchestrated plot, they were arrested and the DHR was commissioned to take them under police escort by train from Darjeeling to Siliguri and on to Calcutta for deportation.

The Manchu Qing dynasty in China was overthrown the following year and a Republic proclaimed, ushering in a period of instability that enabled Tibet to expel the warlords in 1913 and declare independence. A convention was held in Simla to resolve the matter, but the refusal of China to ratify the terms remains a matter for dispute to this day. However, the Dalai Lama returned to Lhasa, and the subsequent research of the Tibetan mountain passes for the Everest expedition was made possible only by the British having now gained his cautious confidence as an ally.

It was certainly a more auspicious time for the residents of Darjeeling. The British engineer Samuel Durrell and his Irish wife Louisa had their first son Lawrence whilst living at the hill station in 1912, and his brother Gerald was born 13 years later in Jamshedpur. Both boys were to become internationally acclaimed in their careers, with Lawrence being recognised as one of the great authors of the 20th century, and Gerald as a zoologist, writer and broadcaster.

The stars must have been in an equally favourable position for the Hartley family on Guy Fawkes night the following year. Ernest had not been alone with his dreams when he travelled from his native Yorkshire to India in 1905 at the age of 22 in search of a career and adventure. He became a junior partner with the brokerage firm of Piggott Chapman & Co. of Calcutta, and spent his leisure time racing horses and acting with the dramatic society. It was here that he met his future wife, Gertrude Yackjee, who had been born in Darjeeling in 1888 and was said to owe her striking good looks to her Irish and Armenian descendants. Their first child was tragically stillborn, and Gertrude was adamant she would return to the tranquillity of Darjeeling and take every precaution with her second pregnancy. She gave birth to their daughter during the evening of 5th November 1913, and recalled that during her confinement she had been told that if she looked upon something beautiful, her child would have a similar countenance. Such was her spiritual belief that she would gaze wistfully on the awesome beauty of Kanchenjunga every morning, and in time her daughter was to become the legendary actress Vivien Leigh.

It was an equally promising year for the railway, as the Darjeeling Himalayan Railway Extensions Company received the authorisation in January to build the branch lines to Kishenganj and up the Teesta Valley. The Government agreed to provide the land free of cost, and granted aid that contributed 5% on the invested capital. It was evident that the workshops at the back of Tindharia locomotive sheds would not have the capacity to cope with the increase in workload these branches would bring and that a new site would have to be found. The Cart Road hereabouts scales the southern face of Selim Hill by ascending a series of ridges, along which a community of houses, railway sheds and station had grown. It was decided to locate the new workshop at the end of the ridge below the settlement, around which the railway climbed and doubled back on itself through a cutting to gain height. It was certainly a commanding position, and the new works was to have all the facilities to allow the railway to become completely self-supporting. Two B&M two-cylinder vertical steam engines were installed to drive the LDM-40 kilowatt generators, which in turn supplied the power for a foundry, the erecting and fitting shops, and the associated buildings for woodwork and coach-building.

An announcement was made in the May that the railway had commissioned a detailed survey for a branch line on the Kishenganj extension, running from Naksalbari to Mirik by way of the Balsun Valley. It prompted the Darjeeling branch of the Indian Tea Association to seek an assurance from the railway that it would not offer inducements to the tea-garden coolies to leave and assist with the construction of the extension lines. The DHR happily promised the labour would not be interfered with, and although it abandoned its plans for the line to Mirik, the first section of the branch across the plains from Kishenganj to Islampur was laid by June the following year.

The expansion of the system came at a time when Britain was faced with serious difficulties, for it was now beginning to lose its self-confidence in being a global power. Competing countries were developing appetites for their own colonies and empires, and none was causing more concern than Germany. The causes of the Great War are beyond the scope of this book, but suffice to say that as Europe was inevitably being drawn into conflict, India adopted a policy of papering over the cracks that had been appearing with regard to its administration. It was done partly in fear of the consequences of a defeated Raj, and partly in the belief that a unified declaration of support would provide the evidence that India deserved the right to self-government. Supplies of manpower could always be relied on, as could the exports of cotton, jute, rice and tea, but India had no heavy industry to speak of. For that it was dependent on the UK, and its demands were put on hold as the priority was now to help forces on the Western Front. The DHR had been fortunate in that the construction of the two extension lines had been well under way by the time the restrictions were imposed, but even then some of the material to build the bridges was delayed.

The line to Darjeeling was now carrying 250,000 passengers, 60,000 tons of freight and paying dividends of 15–16%, but despite the healthy state of finances, the Company dragged its heels with any investment in the hydroelectric schemes developing in the area. The schools led the way by having fully established their own generating plants, but the railway showed little interest in providing electric lighting for its stations. To improve matters, it was decided to adapt a small four-wheeled van to house a 6hp petrol engine coupled directly to a dynamo with a capacity of 54 amperes at 65 volts, and this would be connected to cables fixed to the carriage roofs of the down 'Mail' and connected

The wooden bungalow constructed for the Locomotive Superintendent at Tindharia. It was raised on stilts to dissuade some of the wildlife from taking up residence, and had French windows that opened to a long veranda. It was remembered with great affection, but was eventually replaced in 1946 by a concrete building designed by Gordon Craig. In 2005 it was occupied by the Assistant Mechanical Engineer.

Betty Shaw

to cables fixed to the carriage roofs. It was not an unmitigated success, for the power was disconnected on arrival at each station and the power switched to a platform socket. This gave some hope in lighting the way for those who had been waiting in the gloom of an unlit station, but not much for the passengers pitched into darkness on the train. A contemporary report was led to declare that:

'The travelling public which contributes to the exceptional dividends declared each year, should enable it to expend the necessary capital, and indeed have a right to expect that several stations on this line should be adequately lit up.'

Nevertheless, the coming of the railway had reduced the journey from Calcutta to Darjeeling from two weeks to two days, and the only real problem was the ferry crossing of the Ganges. The broad-gauge trains of the Eastern Bengal Railway would depart from the Sealdah station in Calcutta at 15.37 and run the 116 miles north to the landing stage at the terminus of Damookdeah Ghat, where a flat-bottomed paddle steamer waited for the mile-wide crossing. However, the *'Osprey'*, and later the *'Porpoise'*, was obliged to ferry the passengers to any one of a number of ghats on the opposite side, owing to the mood swings of the river with its course. Such was the impermanence of India that the banks of the Ganges were forever shifting position and changing in depth, and a series of landings were constructed from which the metre-gauge could connect and run the remaining 210 miles to Siliguri. The river would often shrink in the dry season to the point that temporary rails were laid over the silt, although the abundance of crocodiles did little to settle the minds of the more nervously disposed!

The service was transformed with the opening of the Hardinge Bridge across the Ganges in 1915, its fifteen spans having been built in England and painted in different colours before shipment to facilitate its final assembly. It paved the way for a new era of travel to Darjeeling, and the Eastern Bengal Railway service from Sealdah to Siliguri was regarded as the fastest train in India. Built at the Kanchrapara workshops at a cost of Rs245,000, the nine-coach 'Darjeeling Mail' measured some 650 feet in length and weighed 361 tons. Comfort was now the key word, as the following contemporary report illustrates:

'The comfort of the passengers has been the primary consideration as evinced by the numerous devices which, though small in themselves but when taken collectively, contribute not a little to our creature comforts. The bathroom, on the Down train especially, will be appreciated as in addition to the usual shower-bath, it is provided with a spray-bath from jets along its walls. The electric fans are also now placed over the heads of diners instead of the centre of the table, thereby adding to the pleasures of the meal. Another convenience is the electric cigar lighter, which will save the loss of temper and keep the atmosphere from turning 'blue', a condition which did not prevail prior to the introduction of this patent device. The train is lit throughout by electricity, its lavatories are provided with paper towels (in rolls), while the basins are fitted with receptacles for containing liquid soap. The guard's and luggage vans, and the dining saloon are furnished with fire-extinguishers, while an alarm communication is attached to each compartment.'

However, a change to the metre gauge was still required at Santahar, and it would take a further eleven years before the broad gauge finally steamed into Siliguri.

The railway network was still expanding and developing across the sub-continent, but as part of the Empire, India found itself touched in a number of ways by the theatre of war being raged in Europe. It was estimated that 1.2 million Indians were recruited for the war effort, and many were sent to battlefields on the other side of the world. This could not have helped quell the spreading feeling that India should be allowed to take control of its own affairs and not have to fight the causes of others. Indeed, a local folk song lamented the departure by the Darjeeling train of the hundreds of recruits from the Gurkha Recruiting Depot at Takdah:

Indeed, how you have entranced me!
Riding this train I go far away from you
Farther I go, more intense my love grows for you.

The DHR was also honouring its responsibility for transporting many of the British troops located at Calcutta, Dum Dum, Dinapore and beyond to the cantonments, the temporary quarters set up by the British Raj as training camps for manoeuvres during the summer months. The principal sites were at Jalapahar and Katapahur, situated on a ridge some 800ft above the town of Darjeeling, and a report in the *Railway Magazine* reflected that it offered: *'some consolation for very natural and bitter disappointment at being*

Whilst the construction of the line to Kishenganj was relatively straightforward, the Teesta Valley extension was a formidable undertaking that required extensive civil engineering. Such a challenge is seen here at Milepost 22, where a supporting embankment had to be built to enable the railway to negotiate a 100ft curve round a bluff of quartz and rock that was too hard to tunnel.

The DHRS Archive

sent to Calcutta instead of the Continent'!

The cantonments were usually closed down for the winter months, and bullock carts would be brought in to haul the soldiers' kit to the station, where a chartered train would be waiting to transport them back to the plains. The journey on the DHR was always seen as a highlight by the troops, who were regarded with curiosity by the locals and, having received their pay only the day before, as a ready source of income by the traders at Kurseong, .

The new two-foot-gauge branches to Kishenganj and the Teesta Valley were open and running by 1915, the latter being the more challenging to construct. As Assistant Engineer, George Batterbury had taken the responsibility for surveying and building the line and, in recognition of his excellent work, the Directors awarded him a Rs50 increase in pay to Rs400 a month. George Cresswell, the General Manager and Chief Engineer of the Extensions, was praised by the Press for driving the enterprise forward, and the correspondent felt that Kalimpong would outstrip Darjeeling as a trading centre in thirty years.

He attended a spirited meeting of the Tea Planters' Association in Darjeeling, where it was agreed to submit a resolution to the Viceroy demanding that the broad gauge be extended from the Hardinge Bridge to Siliguri and to abandon the proposals to double the metre-gauged track. The building works on the final section of the DHR up the Teesta valley also commanded the interest of *The Englishman* on 11th September, when it noted that at:

'Gel Jhora, where it crosses the cart road near Teesta bridge, was supported by the railway with walls 20ft thick to carry the girders in connection with the new line. The boulders that were hurled down in this torrent actually ground away one of the pier heads entirely yet notwithstanding these drawbacks, the railway authorities have proved themselves quite equal to the occasion and have rebuilt the wall in three weeks; have spanned the chasm and will run the first through train from Siliguri to Teesta bridge on 1st October next. This speaks well for the assistant engineer of the line in whose hand the work was entrusted.'

It was an encouraging start, and surveys were made two years later to continue the line up the Teesta Valley to Gangtok, the capital of Sikkim, although the scheme eventually came to nothing.

The Kishenganj extension was an instant success, for there was now a huge demand for the export of jute to Britain for the manufacture of sacks, which were vital for the trench warfare being fought in northern France. With the supplement of the rebate from the Government, it gave the net earnings for the DHR Extension Company a balance of Rs129,527, but there had been so many railways opened in India of late that it was barely regarded as news. The completion of the extensions and their success attracted little coverage the Calcutta Press, which appeared to regard the DHR like its own wayward child and could scold or ignore it as a mother may choose.

The author of the *Darjeeling District Gazetteer*, L.S. O'Malley, had previously warned his readers: *'not to jump to the conclusion that the DHR is a wonderful engineering feat. Mr Prestage, we are asked to remember, only laid rails along a cart road and the thing was done'*. This was too much for the Calcutta Press to bear, and it came back with its claws inside a velvet glove by publishing a major article in *The Englishman* in 1915 to remind the readers of the railway's virtues:

'Now, this is all very well; but it will not do. Our Hill railway is much more than some iron roads bolted down to some sleepers laid on a cart-road. In trying to dampen our enthusiasm, Mr O'Malley is merely following the pestilential line of self-deprecation normal in Darjeeling. By too the same process of thought the Snows themselves are only a crumple on the earth covered with a layer of small crystals of hydrogen oxide. The wonder of the railroad is made up in part of the excellent grading of the anterior cart road, in part to the choice of suitable curves, but in still greater part of the skill and devotion spent year after year in keeping it in working order at all. With torrential rains, land-slides and hill-streams like the ill-omened Pagla Jhora, a large part of the credit of the railroad lies not in the original building but in the keeping of it in running order. Mr O'Malley remarks in general condescension that there are no tunnels on the route. That is so. But is that a reproach? The late shareholders and the present owner of the Kalka-Simla Railway would have been much better pleased than they are today if that railway could say it had no tunnels. There is such a condition as being too imaginative in planning a hill railroad. It may look effective to dive into a mountain and emerge on another valley a couple of miles away. But it is not always good business; and the late Mr Franklin Prestage was first and last a good business man.'

Whatever was said, the railway could not close its eyes to the problems brewing with the Hill Cart Road. The public had begun to agitate for the free use of motor cars, whilst the agreement with the Secretary of State had made it clear that the road was only to be kept open for cart and animal traffic. The Agents called on the Government Inspector of Railways for support in November 1915, but there seemed to be some reluctance with a response. A submission was made to the offices of the Government of Bengal three months later, for the railway felt it had to protect itself from the responsibility of any accident and was pressing for the official line on advice with the attitude it should adopt.

It seemed to be a confusing time for the official records, for *Thacker's Business Directory* in 1915 recorded that The Grand Hotel in Kurseong was under the management of the DHR, although no such entry appeared before or after that date. Equally perplexing was the Cresswell Institute in Kurseong, which Dozey mentioned in 1916 when writing *The Concise History of the Darjeeling District* but warranted no mention in Thacker's until its solitary entry in 1936! The President was named as B.C. Craggs, who had been the Assistant and later District Traffic Superintendent with the DHR from 1920 to 1935.

The Garratt was also proving troublesome, and the Company was in urgent need of new engines. In July 1915 it was decided to return to the tried and tested formula of the saddle tanks, and two new 'B' Class locomotives were ordered. The London Agents were authorised to decide whether to purchase them immediately or to wait for the chance of prices improving, but when the order was eventually placed with the North British Locomotive Company on 24th November, it was found that the manufacturer was already committed to contracts with the war effort and there would be a delay of ten months with the delivery of the engines. The order was cancelled and subsequently placed with the Baldwin Locomotive Works in America, who agreed to construct three engines identical to the 'B' Class. They were delivered in 1917, and although the manufacturer could not claim that it was actually one of their locomotives

Although the words may seem a little tortured in translation, there was no doubting the sentiment with the song 'Noble Leader' composed by Hari Dass Mukerjee, a clerk in the General Manager's office, in honour of the departure of George Cresswell.

*'Come brothers with love and respect
Garland our master with chaplet
Parting short will quickly end
His craven return our hurts will mend'*

The DHRS Archive

that had hauled Mallory and Irvine to Darjeeling on their first expedition to climb Everest in 1921, an element of dissimulation may have crept in with some of their contemporary advertisements. The North British records show that an entry was made on 6th July 1920 against the order revoked in 1916, stating that *'part of the materials were taken by O.G.& Co.'*[1] Tindharia began to construct the first of its own three locomotives in 1919, and although many of the specifications suggest they were rebuilds made from earlier machines, it appears they were a marriage with parts from the cancelled order.

The financial returns for the DHR remained steady through the period Britain was fighting the war, during which time the Indian Railway Board invited expressions of opinion on the relative advantages of private and State management of all the railways. It prompted several replies from the various Chambers of Commerce and other mercantile and public bodies, which seemed as good a time as any for some shots to be fired in the direction of the DHR. The *Indian Railway Gazette* reflected:

'We cannot believe that the pronouncement of the Darjeeling Planters' Association was intended to be taken seriously. This sapient body has declared in favour of State management, but its verdict is deprived of all value by the fact that it has been inspired by resentment against the DHR. For years past, the planters have complained, probably with good reason, of the heavy freights levied by the DHR and have urged from time to time that it should be purchased and taken over by the Government. These being the known facts, the Darjeeling Planters' survey of the comparative merits of State and Company management of railways may be discussed as more amusing than instructive!'

George Cresswell was granted medical leave following the completion of the Teesta Valley line, and retired to Tasmania after resigning from his appointment as General Manager. He left behind a remarkable legacy of innovation and improvement, which was certainly recognised by the Press:

'In wishing him farewell, we would like to say a few words about what he has done for

---

[1] Ogilvy Gillanders & Co. was the British office of the DHR Agent Gillanders Arbuthnot.

the district and the railway. As a municipal Commissioner his advice and opinions were always willingly given and greatly appreciated, and he has been most popular in the district with everyone, while he proved a considerable master to his subordinates in the railway. He has always been a very hard and indefatigable worker, and his watchword was progress. As improvements and expansions necessitate expenditure and a temporary curtailment of dividends, we fear he cannot be a persona grata with the Directors of the railway company, who are anxious to secure large profits. There is no work we have watched with greater interest than that of the railway, for on it depends the progress of our district.'

The article continued to list his achievements, although there was little doubt the Press was in the mood to scold the Directors. George Batterbury was placed in charge of the extension lines on 7th February 1916 and made Assistant Engineer in Charge, whilst Robert Bawn Addis was appointed as the new General Manager and Engineer-in-Chief on 1st June.

Robert Addis had been the Executive Engineer of the North Western Railway at Karachi, and his services had been 'lent' to the DHR for the past year. Born in Khushalgarh in the Punjab on 30th October 1874, he was sent at the age of 14 to England for five years' education at St. Peter's School in York. From there he obtained three years' scientific training at the Royal Indian Engineering College at Coopers Hill[2] before serving a year's practical course on the Lancashire, Derbyshire & East Coast Railway under R. Elliott Cooper and A.K. Smith. He returned to India and in 1897 he obtained the position of being the Assistant Engineer on the Vizianagram-Raipur Railway survey, and subsequently held similar positions with the Kohat-Bannu Railway survey and a division of the Khandwa-Aleola-Basim Railway survey. He graduated to becoming the Assistant Manager of the East Coast State Railway and the Assistant Engineer of the construction of the Kushalgarh-Kohat-Thal Railway, and his civil engineering skills were recognised by the Institute of Civil Engineers in granting him an Associate Membership in 1901.

His feet were barely under the desk at Kurseong when the Directors agreed on 10th June 1916 that an order should be placed for 100 tons of rails from either the Tata Iron & Steel Company or England *'... whatever the new Manager found best'*. The year closed with the sad news of the passing away on 16th October of George Mingay Garrard, who had for many years been the Consulting Engineer in Britain for the railway and the designer of the wondrous double-engine *'The Climber'*. His responsibilities for the railway were shared in later years with Mr Bernard, who had been the Resident Engineer on the DHR from its earliest days until 1912. On 1st January 1919 the Directors appointed Messrs Wolfe, Barry and Blake of London in their place and on the same terms, which amounted to $2^{1}/_{2}$% of the shipping value of material inspected and travelling expenses.

In 1917 the passenger statistics distilled down to reveal that 7,226 were carried by the railway in 1st Class, 29,103 in 2nd Class and 203,367 in the 3rd. The freight returns for the year showed that 59,740 tons were carried, the principal commodities being 17,804 tons of edible grains (flour, rice, etc), 5,354 tons of tea, 3,824 tons of potatoes and 1,634 tons of salt. Sugar accounted for 894 tons, but the 915 tons of metals transported were low owing to the effects of the war in Europe. It appeared the figures for the transportation of goods had reached a plateau, and indeed they were to remain fairly constant over the following ten years. It caused the Directors to scratch their heads at their Board meeting on 9th June regarding an extension of the Teesta Valley line as far as Rungpo on the Indian-Sikkim frontier, but they decided against it and the project came to nothing.

However, it was not known to what extent the figures for the freight may have been undermined by a major scam that came to a head in February 1918, when the trial of the Railway Gang Case opened in Darjeeling. The DHR had become increasingly concerned with the loss of goods consigned to the railway at Siliguri, resulting in a number of large claims being made for compensation. Assisted by the police and officers from the CID, the Traffic Inspector engaged undercover agents to keep watch on the movements of those working in the transhipment sidings, and after gaining the confidence of some of the accused, they were able to establish that a number of ways had been used to redirect goods to other members of the conspiracy further up the line. Card labels with seals attached to the wagons had been tampered with, whilst tally registers were altered and invoices removed, all of which enabled the stolen goods to be sold off to scurrilous traders. The case had originally involved

---

[2] The college was situated three miles from Egham in Surrey (UK) and could accommodate 150 students. It was founded in 1871 to meet the growing need for qualified civil engineers to serve in India, and the course of study embraced the theory of construction, mathematics, mechanics, the elementary principles of architecture, drawing, surveying, physical science, Hindustani and accounts.

There was nothing unusual about a derailment on the DHR, but it could always be guaranteed to attract a crowd. No.29 (the first of the 'B' Class constructed by NBR) has come to grief with an Up freight to Darjeeling in 1915, comprising newly-delivered stock built by the Metropolitan Carriage & Wagon Works. Like the Garratt, the freight wagons had not originally been fitted with the semi-circular dumb buffer that prevented interlocking on the tight curves, and may have been contributory to the predicament.

The DHRS Archive

40 people, but by the time the police completed the charge sheet, the number had been reduced to 18, although two absconded before the trial opened. *The Englishman* reported that the police had provided a list of 199 prosecution witnesses, of which it was said the court had examined the testimonies of about 110. The trial lasted for a month, during which time the Special Magistrate, Mr A.T. Banerjee, and an entourage of lawyers visited the goods yards at Siliguri, Riyang and a number of other localities associated with the case. Two of the accused were eventually discharged, but the remainder were committed to the Sessions as the Magistrate felt he could not pass adequate sentences on them.

The war in Europe finally came to an end in 1918, and Britain was keen to acknowledge the debt it owed to the Maharajahs for their contribution by agreeing to create an assembly that would represent their interests. There were over 660 of these Princely States, ranging from the 82,000 square miles of Hyderabad that supported a population of 14 million, to the three-tenths of a square mile of Kathiawar where fewer than 200 scratched a living. The Maharajahs ruled over 40% of India, and their rights were protected by treaties of alliance to the Crown represented by the British Resident. The new assembly became the Chamber of Princes, but it appeared the Empire was pre-occupied with its own survival as the sub-text was to bring the States closer in line with the Raj. It created exactly the reverse, for not only did it reveal the diverse political opinions of the States, but it also gave them the opportunity to open a debate that would require their relationship with the British to be explicitly defined.

Britain continued to run the Raj after the war as if nothing had happened, but for Indians it had brought politics into sharp focus. It proved to be the watershed for the Empire, for the war effort had imposed a huge strain on India's economy and raw materials. Rising prices and a shortage of essential goods were sparking discontent, and from that grew a feeling of resentment

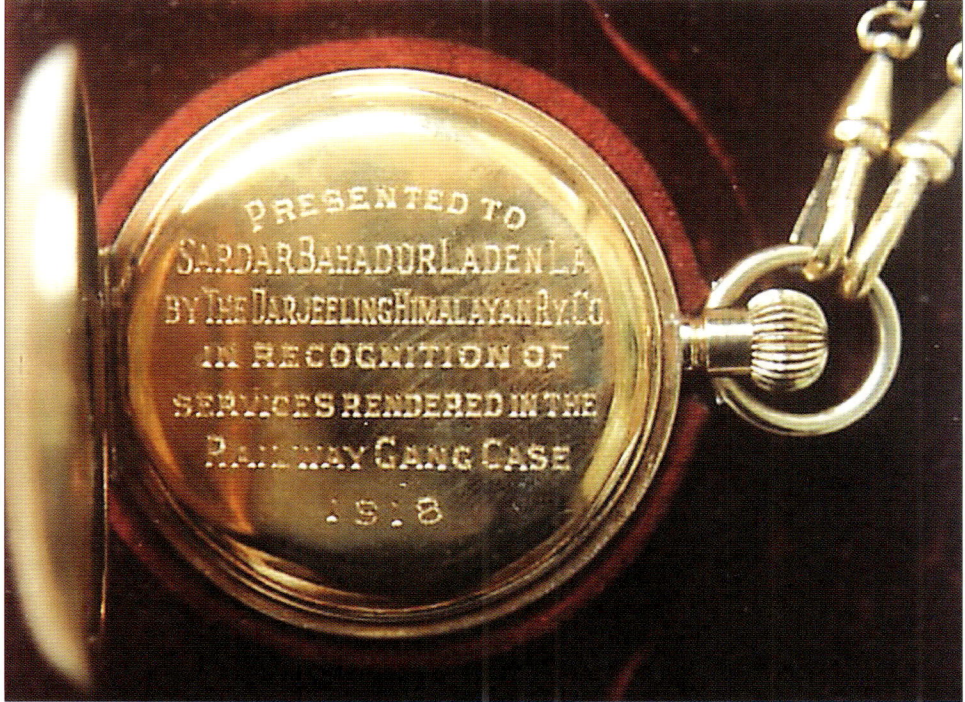

The Omega pocket watch presented to Sardar Bahadur Laden La in 1918 by the DHR in recognition of his services in solving the Railway Gang Case.

Nick Rhodes

and the founding of new political parties. Indian troops had fought as equals alongside Britain and her allies to defend the right and freedom of all nations to each determine their own future. But this was now seen as a contradiction for India, and it was asking why it could not also become self-governing.

The returning soldiers had seen Britain for the first time and they had not been impressed, for it was far from the image and portrayal of the throne and the vast Empire. Many were disillusioned with the Imperial Raj and its superior airs, plus the manner in which business was conducted in India was seen as a hollow sentiment, which served only to fuel the feeling of resentment against the British rule. The conditions in Europe had been unimaginable and the Indian cavalry fought with magnificent pride, but it had been a war with machines and not men, with armoured tanks spitting shells and biplanes dropping bombs and gas. Faced with an alien climate, the casualties were huge, and the Brighton Pavilion on the south coast of England was converted into an emergency hospital as it was felt the Mogul influences of its onion domes and minarets would make the wounded feel at home! The war may have been a noble calling for the Hindu warriors, but it perversely became impossible for them to die with honour on the battlefield. All the trees had been cut down for firewood to alleviate the freezing conditions of the waterlogged trenches, and that meant there was nothing to use as fuel for their sacred funeral pyres.

The war had also brought Britain in conflict with the Sultan of Turkey, whom many Indian Muslims saw as their *khalifa*, the spiritual head. This provoked further demonstrations, and an alliance was made with the leader of the Hindu Extremists, who had founded the Home Rule League in 1916. A Royal Proclamation was passed in 1917 that promised a gradual transition towards self-government on the lines that were pursued in Australia and Canada, but the subsequent collapse of Turkey only brought more unrest in its wake.

The DHR was not able to renew any track until peace had been declared, by which time it had decided to

---

Overpage: *Once the teething problems of the Garratt were sorted out, the DHR had a machine that was capable of hauling much heavier trains than the 'B' Class. This perversely created a new set of problems, for it was found that a long trailing load was prone to derailment on the more severe curves, whilst the reverse sidings would require considerable civil engineering to extend the over-run at each end. The locomotive is seen here on the Chunbatti loop, although most of its work in latter years appears to have been on the Kishenganj line where its capabilities could be used to better advantage. Note the sander standing on the buffer beam, the brakesman between the freight wagons, and the 'B' Class following in pursuit on the extreme right-hand side.*

By 1914 only two of the 'A' Class survived, and No.11 is seen struggling with an excessively long load over the Kalijhora Bridge on the Teesta Valley line. It was being used to test the repair after storm damage had torn away the approaches to the bridge and the protection embankments alongside the river. Note repair work on the railway still under way in the foreground and road bridge to the left.

The DHRS Archive

use 50lbs/yd rails and take the opportunity of sorting out the problems with the section between Ghum and Darjeeling. The final descent to the hill station was still taking the train down a gradient of 1 in 20, which actually steepened to 1 in 16 at one point on a curve, and presented the locomotive crews with long-standing problems. It was the returning trains that had the most difficulty, not only with adhesion but with the engine running in reverse and having the added complication of maintaining the water level over the crown of the firebox. It was not unusual to find the train stalled on this section and a load being divided before the summit was reached. It was agreed to adopt the proposal made by Cresswell ten years earlier to reprofile the line into a double loop round the natural outcrop at Batasia, which eased the descent to 1 in 22½ and the ruling gradient to 1 in 30. The loop added a further 0.7 miles to the journey and was opened for service on 10th March 1919.

The work at Batasia cost Rs125,000, and by now the investment in the railway had climbed beyond Rs4,600,000. Further demands were being made for improvements and the railway intended to remove eight of the remaining ten road crossings immediately after the construction of the loop. However, the work was deferred following a petition to the Governor regarding eighteen other crossings near Sonada. This was the most congested section of the Hill Cart Road and improvement work was urgently needed along with the bottleneck at Ghum, where the highways from Nepal and the Teesta Valley met.

There appeared to be no shortage of unsolicited advice for the DHR. Lord Ronaldshay, the Governor of Bengal, stated on his departure from Darjeeling that the residents wished for the widening of the railway track-bed so as to do away with the level crossings, which they regarded as a source of danger to wheeled traffic and the public generally. He went on to claim they wanted *'the replacement of the barn-like structure'*, which for years has served as a passenger station, by a building that was in keeping with the architectural design of the neighbourhood, along with the removal of the goods shed and the line that served it. An agreement was made to implement these suggestions, and money was set aside from the Mutual Improvement Fund, which belonged equally to the Government and the DHR. The improvement of the road crossings fell to the Government and was completed in due course, but the railway had already considered the plans and estimates to rebuild the upper terminus in the March of 1919 and postponed the decision, claiming to have already exhausted its funds.

In fact, the railway managed to hold on to its wooden station for a further twenty-six years, although an earthquake was to later inflict a certain amount of damage to the brick-built offices. Indeed, it seemed as though earth tremors were part of daily life at times, for geologically speaking, the Himalaya is a young mountain range and still growing.[3] In his biography, Dr Frederick Barnardo recalled he was travelling on the DHR in late July 1920 when the train drew to an abrupt halt between Mahanandi and Kurseong. After a short pause, it began to reverse back down the hillside for half a mile, but before the driver could explain his action to the passengers, two violent tremors shook the mountain and tore the section of track they had been passing over down the valley. The driver was a tall Sikh who knew his railway intimately, and had noticed that the small stones rolling down the mountain indicated the earth was vibrating and that an earthquake would soon follow. His quick thinking and evasive action prevented a major tragedy, and after the passengers safely negotiated the massive landslide, they spontaneously made a collection that totalled over Rs2,000. His pay had been but Rs12 a month.

Whilst Darjeeling was trying to hold on to its railway, Britain had been rethinking its ways to hold on to its Empire. The 1917 proclamation was not intended to be a document for independence, nor any indication that Britain was relaxing its control, but it did pave the way for constitutional reform with the Government of India Act of 1919. The changes were seen mainly as the transfer of responsibilities within the provinces and not in central government, where Britain felt it was essential to retain control as part of the Imperial equation.

Following a report made by the Rowlatt Commission, legislation was introduced to combat the growing threat of terrorism, which authorised the trial of

---

Opposite: *The severity of the climb from Darjeeling to Ghum was a problem for returning trains from the earliest days of the railway. In 1909 George Cresswell designed a double loop to ease the gradient and avoid the necessity of the train crossing and recrossing the road so many times. It was to take another ten years before the work was completed and to a cost of Rs125,000. This early postcard shows two Up passenger trains with the first generation of bogie carriages.*

Collection: Pat Orr

---

[3] Tremors have been measured in nearby Nepal up to 15 times a day.

political cases without jury and the right of appeal. India saw the move as a direct slap in the face, particularly after the sacrifices made with fighting Britain's war in Europe, and a one-day *hartal* (strike) was called in all the major cities in protest. Feelings ran so high that it erupted into days of rioting, and on a piece of wasteland known as the *Jallianwala Bagh* in Amritsar, the holy city of the Sikhs, events were to take a turn that would lead India irrevocably to independence. Under the command of the fiery Irish Brigadier General Dyer, a British army contingent opened fire on the demonstrators, and 379 were killed and 1200 wounded in the massacre that followed.

It was a turning point in Indian history, for it undermined any moral code of conduct that Britain could continue to stay. A wave of political parties were spawned in the aftermath, from those that were inspired by the Bolshevik success in Russia with the doctrines of Lenin and Marx, to the right for self-determination as championed in America by President Woodrow Wilson.

The mainstream of nationalism continued to be represented by the Indian National Congress and the Muslim League, and the former now had Mohandas Karamchand Gandhi as its new leader.

The tortuous curves and constantly changing superelevation of the track may have caused considerable flexing with the frames and chassis of the first bogie carriages. The second generation of passenger stock introduced was of a somewhat heavier design, as can be seen with the Up Mail as it storms past the site of a recent landslip.

Gwen Cattermull

A fine-looking train with a handsome rake of bogie stock running into Darjeeling. Note the heads of the brakesmen between the carriages and the sidings behind the train, since abandoned but still evident beneath the undergrowth.

Nick Rhodes

An Up Mixed bound for Darjeeling taking water at Tung at the head of three covered four-wheeled freight wagons and three first-generation bogie carriages.

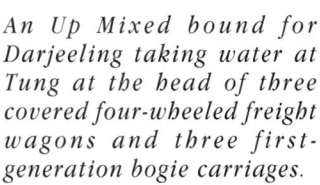

Climbing from Darjeeling to Ghum, this rake of second generation bogie stock shows the elegant designs and panelling well. The third carriage is saloon No.11, which featured an open observation balcony. It was later used as an inspection vehicle by the General Manager, bearing the name 'Himalayan Princess' and renumbered 124.

Nigel Plackett

An unidentified 'B' Class hauling a rake of second-generation stock through the terai forest, the first bogie passenger vehicle being a short-wheelbase composite for 3rd Class passengers and the guard. Note the safety valves on the locomotive are fitted transversely to the boiler and that the sanders have only a short platform to stand on, their support being maintained by the grab handles attached to the base of the headlight.

Chapter 6

Summits of Achievement

The soaring popularity of the railway was undeniable, but then it did have a virtual monopoly for providing the transport to Darjeeling. However, the First World War had given a tremendous impetus to the development of the internal combustion engine, and as the dust began to settle in Europe, new opportunities were presented for the public to own motor vehicles. The railway may have grown used to the annual challenge of the monsoon, but it was soon going to face a greater threat to the comfortable position it had become accustomed to.

The timetable was designed to make connections with the metre gauge from Calcutta, whilst taking the greatest opportunity of running in daylight. There were indeed some spirited workings, for the 7.00 departure from Siliguri in the early 1920s was scheduled to take but 3 hours 19 minutes to reach Kurseong, where a thirty-minute break was afforded for breakfast. There were two Down trains from Darjeeling, the 9.38 departure arriving at Siliguri by 15.33 and the 14.10 departure appearing at 20.00.

Since opening its doors as the grandest and most fashionable hotel in Darjeeling, the 'Mount Everest' had been trying every which way to secure favourable terms for its guests from the railway. The General Manager of the hotel, Mr A. Stephen, insisted on a rebate for the luggage and freight the railway transported, and free 1st Class passes for himself and the architect Mr Wilkinson. The DHR was unmoved on the matter, which prompted the hotel to look at alternative means of transport for its guests. It was decided to purchase a bus, and from the early 1920s it operated a motor service that would meet passengers on their arrival at Siliguri station at 6.00, and in three and a half hours have them sipping tea in the lounge in Darjeeling. Travellers considering the return journey could take the down train from Darjeeling at 14.10, whilst his motor would wait at the hotel until 15.30 and it would then take but three hours to descend to Siliguri, arriving one and a half hours before the train, with the free carriage of luggage and servants as an inducement.

This was challenged by Robert Addis, the General Manager of the DHR, who called for quotations from England for the supply of *'line motors'* to accelerate the train service. He anticipated such a vehicle could clip at least 90 minutes off the time the conventional train took by arriving in Darjeeling at 11.00, whilst passengers could leave the hill station at 16.00 and still catch the main-line connection at Siliguri. As it was, only one railcar finally appeared, and even then the timings had to be stretched for it to arrive at 11.30 and depart by 15.00. The accommodation was certainly comfortable, but it made little impact on the traffic as it was limited to carrying only nine passengers and was soon out of service.

To make matters worse, the railway was providing revenue for the maintenance of the Hill Cart Road whilst the competing bus service was causing its wear and tear. The Directors lodged a formal protest on 21st October 1921 to the Bengal Government, which resulted in a supplemental agreement being made on 14th August 1922 to the previous contracts between the Secretary of State and the DHR. Distilled down, the original agreement had stipulated that half the share of the excess profits made by the railway were to be used for the upkeep of the road. The amendment now set out that this half-share was to be divided equally between the Secretary of State and the DHR. The Government was to expend its share exclusively on or towards the improvement of the alignment of the Hill Cart Road on which the railway was located, whilst the Company was to use the money towards such improvements of the railway and undertakings of the Company as calculated to directly or indirectly improve the road. It did not fully resolve the matter in the eyes of the railway, but it was not long before it was considering taking over the service from Mr Stephen. However, after monitoring the number of journeys undertaken, the unanimous decision was taken by the Directors on 26th May 1923 that: '... *the competition was not serious and never likely to be*'.

The same could not have been said for the Prince of Wales, whose arrival in India in November 1921 was greeted by Congress declaring a *hartal* in the form of a national day of fasting and prayer. It soon flared into a series of violent demonstrations in Bombay, during which over fifty lost their lives in clashes between supporters of the boycott and those waving the flag. The rest of the visit was met by a series of strikes, and the future King Edward VIII found himself being led in isolated splendour through deserted streets, the magnificent entourage passing by with hardly a soul taking notice. The Government was incensed and felt that the situation with Gandhi and Congress was getting out of control. It reasserted its authority with a wave of mass arrests in the wake of the visit, and over 30,000 *'non co-operators'* were imprisoned. The young aristocrat, Louis Mountbatten, was accompanying the Prince, and his opinion of the demonstrations showed that he held little sense of empathy with the nationalists. Fate was to take a turn when he was obliged to meet the same movement twenty-five years later when, as Viceroy, his task was to facilitate the transfer of power for independence.

Darjeeling saw the protests as little more than annoyances of the plains, rather like the mosquitoes, for the eyes of the town had been turned to the materials and supplies arriving by the DHR for the expedition to conquer Everest. Known to the Tibetans as Chomolungma (Goddess Mother of the World), the British had named the mountain after George Everest, the 19th-century British Surveyor General of India, and the struggle to climb to its summit was seen as the ultimate challenge in the days of the Edwardian Empire. The mountains embraced the spirit of mystery and pioneering adventure, and the unfolding drama of the peach-and-grey might of Kanchenjunga was in full view from the train window, whilst the highest point on Earth could be seen from Tiger Hill, just above the station at Ghum.

One can imagine the soaring expectations of the British at home, still reeling from the devastation of four years, fighting in Europe, as the party set off from Darjeeling in their thick Norfolk jackets and asbestos-lined boots to climb to the top of the world. Led by Colonel Howard Bury, they reached the base camp at Tingri Dzong, with the porters and mules carrying such essentials as wind-up gramophones and '... *an imposing heap of yak-dung to serve as fuel on the Tibetan plateau'*. Mallory succeeded in reaching a height of 23,000ft and discovered the North Col, an ice-saddle that would allow a practical route to the summit, but the conditions forced the party to return to Darjeeling.

A second attempt was made the following year and led by Brigadier General H.C. Bruce, an eminent climber with some 30 years experience and a fluent knowledge of the local language. This time the equipment was transported by the Teesta Valley line to Kalimpong Road, where the group loaded their mules for an approach to Everest via the Jelap Pass. Mallory and his party succeeded in climbing to 27,235ft, but were overcome as they were approaching the North Col by an avalanche that claimed the lives of seven porters, and forced the party to return to base.

Captain J. Noel, a fellow of the Royal Geographical Society, recounted in his book that for the final attempt in 1924:

> '*Darjeeling station was crowded out with enormous packing cases containing developing tanks, drying apparatus, washing wheels, a motor generator for developing their own steady supply of current, chemicals, etc.*'

All this belonged to the photographic technician Pereira, who survived the expedition to tell the tale. He was not on the final push for the summit that Mallory made with Irvine, when both climbers disappeared into the silence at 28,230ft on this most awesome of mountains. The Tibetans had begged them not to break the soil nor loosen the rocks, for that they claimed had allowed the devils to escape during their first venture.

This attraction of the unreachable was undeniable for the British and their visitors, but for the folk that lived along the necklace of shanties to Ghum, the train had become a practical means of transport, and for the first time it was possible to travel from Kurseong to Darjeeling for work and return home at the weekend. The railway soon became woven into local songs and verse, and the children who travelled to school by train

BALDWIN
ASCENT OF MT. EVEREST.

The British Expedition to attempt the ascent of the world's highest mountain peak is operating from its permanent base—Tingri Dzong—within forty miles of Everest. To reach the present headquarters, the Expedition's materials and supplies were conveyed over the Darjeeling-Himalayan Railway, on which are operated a number of specially designed Baldwin Locomotives.

The locomotives referred to were built to the individual specifications of the Railway Company, and were constructed to stand the severest strains. They are operated over a road having a 2-foot gauge; 3-1/2 per cent. gradient and curves of 60 ft. radius. They are equipped with copper fire-boxes, copper stay bolts, brass tubes and Walschaerts valve motion. Soft coal is used for fuel.

Our nearest representatives are always at the command of any railway to give any desired information regarding new power, the forwarding of duplicate and repair parts for locomotive maintenance, and to arrange for the forwarding of needed supplies from our Works to any part of the world.

Baldwin Locomotives known the world over.

LONDON:
R. P. C. Sanderson, Manager,
34, Victoria Street, S.W.1.

CALCUTTA:
F. T. Slayton, Manager.
Temple Chambers, Old Post Office St.

THE BALDWIN LOCOMOTIVE WORKS,
PHILADELPHIA, U.S.A.,
Cable Address: " Baldwin, Philadelphia."

LOCOMOTIVES

The number of 'specially designed Baldwin Locomotives' was actually three and they were built to the plans drawn by Sharp, Stewart & Co., but the temptation to gain publicity from the pioneering climbs made by Mallory and Irwine on Everest was too much to resist. It did not claim that it was a Baldwin engine that actually hauled their train, and whilst it may have appeared a little unseemly to British eyes in India to make such a spin, to America it would have been seen more as a wasted opportunity.

could be heard singing the nursery rhyme *'Darjeeling Sano Rail'* (The small rail of Darjeeling):

> *'The small train of Darjeeling is now ready to depart*
> *Listen, O brother, the whistle of the guard has blown*
> *And lo, the green flag he has shown,*
> *It chugs on now with its bogies smart*
> *Chug ... chug ... chug.'*

The *'Darjeeling Darpan'* (*'Darjeeling Mirror'*) even offered an explanation of how the locomotive worked, although the scanning does suffer somewhat with translation from the original Nepali.

> *'With water on a side the fire on the other rages in turmoils,*
> *And thus the water confined boils,*
> *By the mass of steam the engine suffocates*
> *And to propel it, this steam motivates.'*

The DHR had indeed become a local train in all senses, and unlike the road transport, it was never seen as an intrusion into life, however intimate its terms became with the houses. It also remained as the means to break free from the drama of the sun, and there was all manner of helpful guidance on offer for passengers transferring from the main line to the train:

> *'At Siliguri the traveller is only allowed 40 minutes in which to partake of chota hazree (a light breakfast), and to book his bedding. The following procedure should therefore be adopted: As quickly as possible a seat on the left of a carriage in the toy-train should be acquired and the light luggage booked (for only handbags and wraps are allowed in the compartment on this line) before the refreshment room is entered. After disposal of this meal if there is still a few minutes to spare, and the morning air be clear, a fairly good view of the snowy range, which is 96 miles away, may be had from the south end of the platform.'*

The reason for recommending the left-hand side of the carriage suggested that it:

> *'... prevents giddiness from which not a few suffer, due to the ever shifting scenes of the hillside which are forced on the vision when seated to the right of the carriage.'*

This was something of a paradox when the spectacular views were a profound selling point! It didn't stop there for the brave, as the hints continued:

> *'... binoculars and cameras should always be handy or else much of the beauty of the panoramic views will be lost, especially on the hill section'.*

Siliguri Station in the early 1920s. Although the double canopy across the station and the building behind the carriages were still in situ in 2005, most of the trees had gone and the area was dominated by buildings and sprawling shacks.

The fortunes of Kurseong certainly took a positive turn when the railway began to relocate its headquarters in 1910. The town grew rapidly, and established a reputation for education in the area that was second only to Darjeeling. Looking uphill along the bazaar, the comparison with the illustration on page 110 shows the changes that had been made.

Betty Shaw

Counsel was also on hand for travellers on the Down train, timed to arrive at 20.00, which gave:

'... a full hour in which to change into lighter garments as well as dine before stepping into the East Bengal Railway coach'.

However, if the family was with you, the recommendation was to take the earlier train that left Darjeeling at 9.38am, which gave *'... five hours in which to feed and attend to children'*!

Lord Ronaldshay wrote of his journey that:

'One steps into a railway carriage which might easily be mistaken for a toy, and the whimsical idea seizes hold of one that one has stumbled accidentally into Lilliput. With a noisy fuss out of all proportion to its size the engine gives a jerk – and starts. The buildings of Siliguri, iron-roofed sheds, railway workshops of brick, stacks of timber, and here and there a one-storied bungalow resting in mid-air upon an understructure of substantial piles, straggle along on either side of the miniature track until they are brought to an abrupt standstill by the broad bed of the Mahanadi river. As one puffs along at something over ten miles an hour, the amorphous shapes in front of one take on clearer definition, and before long stand out as giant tree-clad spurs of the outer Himalaya.

As one climbs higher, one passes into a clearer air, and looking down upon the plains from which one has come one perceives them soft and indistinct through an atmosphere saturated with moisture. One such glimpse is sufficient to explain the why and wherefore of many things – of mosquitoes and malaria, of prickly heat and irritability of temper, of certain plainly marked characteristics of the people inhabiting these soggy plains which may be summed up compendiously as inertia.'

However such observations of life on the plains may have appeared, his previous comment as the Governor of Bengal that the station at Darjeeling was a *'barn-like structure'* had certainly bruised the Directors. They clearly had no desire to be summed up *'compendiously as inert'* and were prompted to consider a revised plan in May 1921 to rebuild the station. The estimated costs amounted to Rs157,629 and it was agreed the idea could be developed if Rs100,000 were recoverable from the Mutual Improvement Fund. The idea began to fade from their minds, but they were pleased to announce that 72 road crossings were to be taken out during the working season of October 1922 – May 1923, of which 44 were actually removed.

The railway had also been looking at ways to update its locomotive fleet and in 1921 Hunslet of Leeds (UK) prepared drawings (drawing No.13221) for a superheated 0-6-0 locomotive. The design bore many similarities to the 'B' Class, having the same 5ft 6in wheelbase and the water carried in saddle and well tanks, but the capacity was increased from 380 to 590 gallons. In full working order it would have tipped the scales at 22 tons and was calculated to have a tractive effort of 10,532lbs at 80% boiler pressure. The machine did not progress from the drawing board, and neither did the boiler fitted with a Belpair firebox from Robert Stephenson & Co. (drawing No.15745) following an enquiry made on 8th March 1922, but it showed that the railway was now casting its net wider than its dependence on the North British Locomotive Company.

The question of Darjeeling station would not go away, and the Directors were sent reeling when a new set of estimates for Rs424,019 was produced for an improved building. They were pacified by an alternative scheme for Rs170,000, on the condition the General Manager was satisfied it would also secure the Rs100,000 from the Improvement Fund. The details of the estimate were honed to Rs169,237 for the Board to consider at their meeting in June, but the plan went no further. Robert Addis was on leave when he tendered his resignation on 7th August 1922, after which he moved to Rangoon to become the Deputy Chief Engineer of the Burma Railway.

Robert Kirby, the Deputy Locomotive Engineer at Tindharia, had been standing in for the General Manager whilst he was on leave, but the resignation now left the post vacant. The Directors asked Kirby to retain the position for the next two years, and in time he was to become one of the longest serving employees on the railway. Born on 26th September 1883 in Darjeeling to Scottish and Burmese parents, he was educated at boarding school before travelling to Scotland at the age of 18 to attend the Paisley Technical College. His apprenticeship was served with Messrs Fishers Ltd, on Admiralty contract work, where he worked through all branches of the shop and drawing office until 1905, after which he went to sea as a Fourth Engineer to gain practical experience in the running and upkeep of marine machinery. By 1906 he had joined the Caledonian Railway as a 'learner' and worked through various jobs including a period at Polmadie Running Sheds. Two years later he became attracted by the prospect of India and was covenanted out to Messrs John King & Co. Ltd, the engineers, ship and bridge builders based in Howrah, Calcutta. He became their Chief Designer and Estimator and was responsible for the design of varied river craft including steamers up to 145ft long. It was in January 1916 that he joined the DHR, where he spent the rest of his professional working life, first as the Assistant Locomotive Superintendent before being promoted to Deputy.

In his capacity as General Manager, he looked at ways of generating additional income for the railway, and in 1923 came to an agreement with the Forest Department to construct a branch line from Sukna for the collection of felled timber. The track extended for a mile into the forest, being laid and maintained by the DHR in consideration of the earnings that could be made transporting the wood. The forest lay in the Kurseong Division, and the shortage of labour to assist with the hauling of the timber to the railhead was overcome by employing the mechanical system of 'skidding'. The skidder was a 70ft-high pole with a pulley attached at the top, and this was held in a near-vertical position by steel hawsers. A cable was run from a portable steam engine over the pulley and secured to felled logs, which could be anything up to a thousand feet away. By pulling against the obtuse angle of the skidder, the timber could be hauled to a small American semi-portable sawmill, where it was cut into the required sizes and loaded on flat wagons the DHR had specially built for the purpose by Stableford & Co. of Coalville.

The greatest revenue producer was the *sal* that had been cut into 32ft lengths, the maximum that could be transported to the sale depot in Siliguri. The smaller timber was used for making ploughs, rice-pounders and their like, whilst all the other pieces were sawn into $1/2$-inch planking for tea chests and the branches used as fuel. The softwoods, being susceptible to

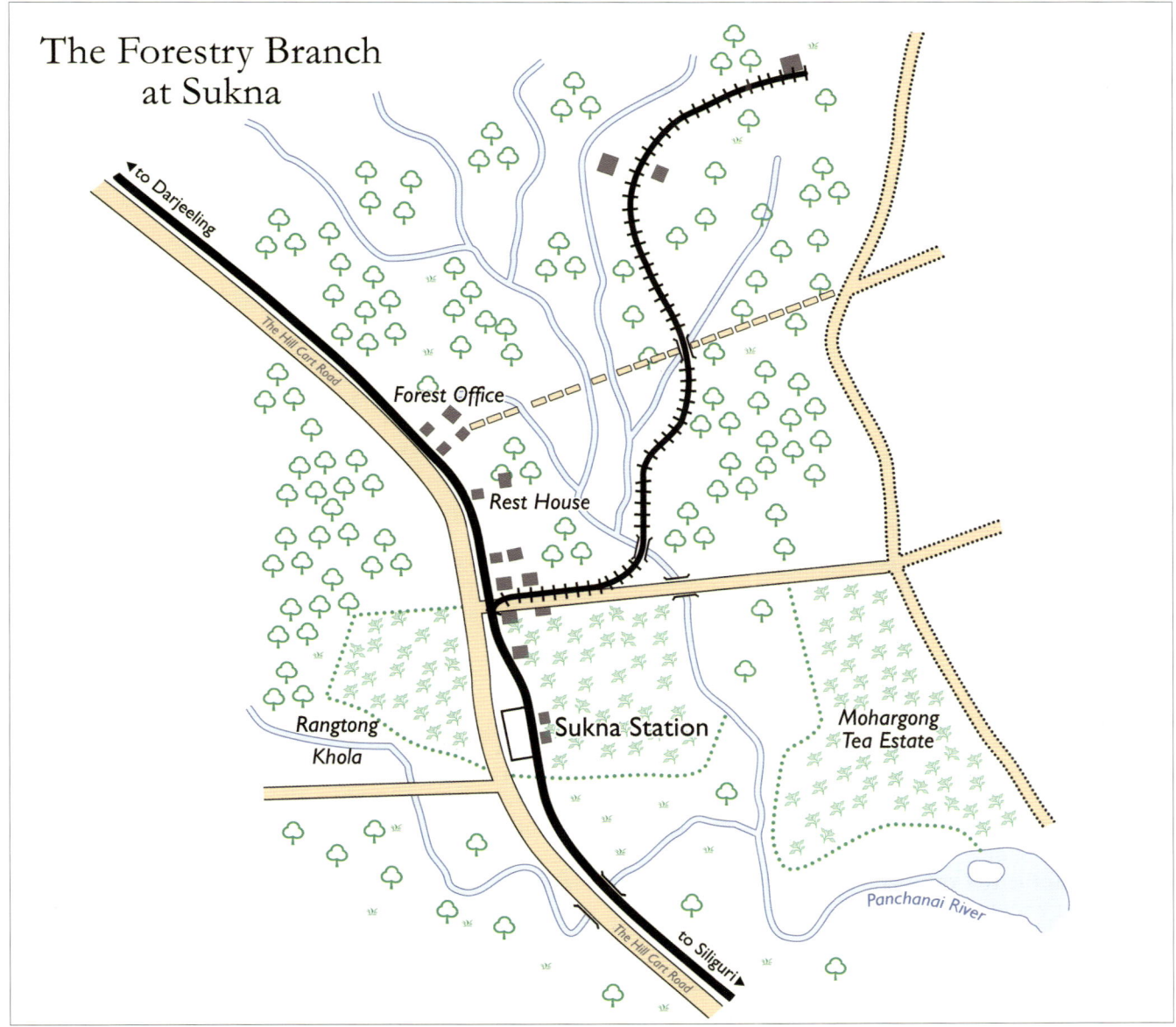

The Forestry Branch at Sukna

damage by insects and rot, were sawn up as soon as they were felled during the cooler months (October to March), whilst the hardwood was simply skidded into a large stockpile alongside the railway. Restocking of the forest would take place between April and May, leaving the skidder crew to load the *sal* logs and saw up the remaining timber during the rains.

It was a profitable business for all concerned, and a similar undertaking was set up at Tung, which had been previously been regarded as unworkable owing to its inaccessibility. There were two working circles for felling, the division being the old military road that ran at a height of 7,000ft. The logs were dragged to the road by an American steam logging-engine, which was mounted on a sledge and could haul itself to new positions. The logs were taken by bullock cart to a sawmill, which was, as with many things Himalayan, said to be the most elevated in the world. The work could be undertaken only between November and May, before the rains set in, and most of the labourers were porters who had been on the uppermost camps on the Everest Expedition. One-third of the timber here was hardwood and used for building and furniture; the remainder, being softwoods, was all converted into planking for tea chests. The sawn timber was transported down to the DHR by a 3,500ft-long aerial ropeway operated by gravity, which at any one time would have eight descending carriers each with a load of 160lbs, and eight returning empty.

Both logging operations were a sound enterprise, but

The Forestry Branch

The forestry branch ran straight through an avenue of sal trees for approximately 400 yards, after which it turned sharply to the left to cross a stream and meander through the reserve for a further mile.

At over 7,000ft above sea level, the Tung sawmill was said to be the highest in the world, and was operated by Tibetan porters used on the expeditions to Everest. The semi-portable sawmills came from America, and the cut timber was transported by gravity on an aerial ropeway to a siding on the DHR.

The vertical-boiler steam engine hauling the cable over the skidder to load logs on one of the DHR flat wagons. The machine was one of many built in England and readily obtainable in Calcutta at a cost of Rs20,000; it was estimated that mechanisation would bring an annual saving of Rs2,500 to a 40-acre site.

Below: *A train of sawn timber being taken on the Stableford flat wagons to the sale depot in Siliguri. There was a saving of between 1 and 1.5 annas per cu.ft if the sal was transported by rail instead of buffalo cart, and the ability to handle large-diameter logs in 32ft lengths gave an enhanced value to the timber of 8–12 annas per cu.ft.*

Courtesy: Jill Cartwright

Robert Kirby had to focus his mind on the competition of the motor service, which had refused to go away. The Directors began to keep a close eye on who was using the Hill Cart Road and for what purpose, and from May 1924 the monthly statistics were gathered for road journeys in both directions. The figures were read out at each Board meeting, the differences reflecting the seasons and the weather, but with the maximum travelling up to Darjeeling by bus being 55 in May and 74 for the return service to Siliguri in October, there appeared to be no cause for anxiety ... yet.

The reasons behind his resignation from the post as General Manager in July 1924 are not recorded and have been left to speculation, but Robert Kirby must have been regarded as a valued man for he became the Locomotive, Carriage and Wagon Superintendent in October. It was a key position on the railway, and with it came the responsibility for the upkeep of all the mechanical equipment and rolling stock, including the locomotives. With 700 men working directly under him, he took control of a programme to modernise the stock, and was awarded an Associate Membership of the Institution of Mechanical Engineers. His nomination had been supported by F.R. Bagley, who had become the Consulting Engineer for the line, and his former manager Robert Addis.

Colonel H.A. Cameron, the Agent of the East Bengal Railway, was appointed as the new General Manager, and introduced a number of initiatives for 1925 to help address the critics. It must be said these were not in short supply, and the Press had already been firing warning shots across the tracks, stating that it was in the railway's own interests to provide an efficient and up-to-date service at as low a rate as possible. It had long been felt that the charges made by the Company were unreasonably high, and it had achieved only this by maintaining its monopoly of the transport services to Darjeeling. If action was not taken now, it was feared the railway would find it increasingly difficult to show a favourable balance when compiling its annual accounts. The admonition continued to state the summer resort was losing some of its popularity, and laid the blame at the doors of the railway and its unsatisfactory means of communication.

An announcement was made regarding a number of alterations the DHR was seeking to the Memorandum of the Company, the most alarming prospect being to run its own motor services from Siliguri to Darjeeling. It was no doubt casting its eyes over the other districts it served, and although the suggestion went no further, it gave an insight into the direction in which the management was looking. It also sought the authority to construct and maintain a number of aerial ropeways, which had for some time been a cherished scheme with the planters in the Darjeeling area to convey the tea to Siliguri. A survey was already in progress to build a ropeway on the Teesta Valley extension from Rilli to Kalimpong to relieve the freight from being transported on the backs of coolies up seven tortuous miles of dirt track, but it would be a further five years before this was operational.

More proposals were made, which included expanding the business of the foundry and electrical workshops into general engineers. The Company was attracted to the thought of becoming a colliery proprietor, and although it was not stated exactly where the enterprise was to be developed, coal had indeed been noted poking through the undergrowth of the forest near the hillside at Rangtong. It had also seen the light in providing its own catering department for the needs of its passengers, who had until then been the victim of local traders whose sole objective was to relieve the passengers of as much money as possible. Perhaps the most welcome of all the ideas was the interest the Company showed in the welfare of its employees by the establishment and support of certain institutions and funds for their mutual benefit.

The Directors could not overlook the growing need for additional motive power, for two of the 'B' Class engines had worked themselves into the ground by the beginning of 1925 and were temporarily classed as unserviceable. The proposal to purchase two more locomotives from the North British Locomotive Co. for Rs70,000 was approved in February, the payment being spread over 5 years, and it was agreed to the Agents ordering a further two in June. However, the Directors' minutes are in conflict with the North British records, which show that only three engines were ordered in 1925 and the fourth was not placed until May 1927, by which time the locomotive fleet of the DHR and the two extension railways totalled 34 engines.

The railway was the largest single employer in the area, but there was no denying that tea was the undisputed king. However, the success of the industry was dependent on the railway, for it was the only realistic means of efficiently transporting the dried crop to the auction houses on the plains. Once plucked, the leaves first had to be withered by being spread out in thin layers on wire shelves to enable air to pass over them for approximately 20 hours in a dry atmosphere. From this followed the rolling process, which bruised the leaves and broke up the cells to bring the sap to the surface. Fermentation was the next stage, which involved the leaves being spread on a

The ultimate design of the 'B' Class for the DHR was represented by the three machines built in 1925 (£2,163.00 each) and the final locomotive in 1927 (£2,350.00). Seen shortly after delivery, No.47 was the third of the 1925 order, and in time was renumbered by IR as 800; it is now preserved at Lucknow Main Station (Charbagh). Note the brass number plate attached to chimney and the small platform Tindharia fitted for the sanders to stand on, with grab rails for support extending beneath the front headlamp.

Gwen Cattermull

The first generation of bogie carriages introduced in 1909 were an immediate success, and after twenty years of service they were rebuilt at Tindharia workshops with more substantial bodywork and distinctive panelling. Seen here on the 'Down' train waiting for the Darjeeling-bound service to pull into Batasia siding, the carriages were retained in this form until a second rebuilding in the 1940s to a lighter contemporary design. Note the super-elevation of the track in the foreground.

Collection: Hugh Rayner

wooden framework and covered in wet cloths. With the temperature maintained at 80°F (27°C), it would take 5 hours for the leaves to assume a copper tint and be ready for drying. Placed on wire trays, hot air would be passed over the leaves to render them dry and brittle, by which time they would have turned black and be ready for sifting into grades and qualities.

Tea picked on a Monday would be usually be ready for packing two days later in the wooden chests, which had been delivered by the DHR packed flat and assembled by the carpenters on the estate.[1] The chests were lined in lead or aluminium as the leaves were very susceptible to moisture, and each would hold an average of 100lbs of tea. The weight varied according to which of the ten grades of tea had been classified and indeed the month it had been picked. Ponies would transport two chests at a time, or coolies one strapped to their back, and climb the steep terraces of the gardens to the railway station, where they were loaded into the tea wagons which Tindharia had built for the purpose. Six chests were quantified as a *brake*, and each wagon could hold 18 *brakes* (108 chests).

Most of the leaf plucking was done by native women, collecting between 30 and 40 lbs a day, which would yield a quarter of its weight as tea. They could earn up to 12 annas a day, whereas a male coolie in the sheds would command only 5 annas a day, a woman 4 annas, adolescents 3 annas and child labour a pitiful 2 annas. The matter of caste drew a veil that few could really comprehend, for irrespective of his actual belief the white *sahib* was regarded as a Christian, and as such had no caste. Although the estate managers regarded themselves as the elite in the district, their spiritual probity rendered them untouchable by the natives. The coolies working in the gardens would have their provisions for the day tied in a cloth and hung on the side of the large wicker baskets carried on their backs. This food would have to be removed before the manager could make any inspection of the plucked leaves for fear of it being contaminated by his shadow, whilst it would have been unforgivable for him to have entered any native-occupied property on the estate.

Perversely, the manager was often asked by the *Panchayat* to arbitrate over disputes. Comprised of five elders from the community, they would debate the local issues and dispense their own form of rough justice to the native population.[2] Workers were also generally in the debt of their managers, having borrowed money to attend the innumerable family weddings and funerals that came with the caste. The bazaar was often the only place where the coolies from the plantations could meet each other, and on the occasion that love blossomed, the manager of one garden would send a *chit* to his opposite number and transfer the debt. The managers were fiercely protective of their workers, and would often be seen chaperoning them to the cinemas of Darjeeling and personally escorting them back to the estate.

The managers certainly saw themselves as the aristocrats who ran the district, with the Planters' Club

A native porter with a chest of tea from the Bloomfield Tea Estate, eight miles from Darjeeling. (It subsequently became the Orange Valley Tea Estate and is now under the management of the Longview Tea Company Ltd of Calcutta.)

DHR 1921 Guide

---

[1] A former tea planter advised the tea chests on his estate also came from the Andaman Islands, the one-time penal colony in the Bay of Bengal.

[2] The system was later replaced by elected Works Committees, following Independence and the Communist Party spreading its influence in West Bengal, but the process became complex and encumbered by political dogma.

Gandhi leading a party of supporters alongside the DHR in 1925. It was not recorded whether the Mahatma walked all the way to Darjeeling.

in Darjeeling becoming *the* place to meet and hold court. Its self-importance was evident by referring to itself simply as 'The Club' on its letterheads, and it was the exclusive watering hole for the planters, the Indian Civil Service, British Army Officers and of course the Railway. There was an unwritten precedence for the order in which alcohol was consumed, with beer being drunk from 11.00 to midday, followed by gin and soda in the afternoon; whisky never was touched until sunset! Beer had been a favourite tipple with the British in the early days of the Raj, the IPA (India Pale Ale) being specially brewed in the UK with a high alcohol and hop content in order to withstand the heat and rolling of the ship on its passage to the sub-continent. Although whisky had since become the most popular drink, especially amongst the men, it was the gin and soda that somehow epitomised the image of the Empire.

Malaria was rampant in the *terai* and across the *Dooars* (the plains close to the mountains), and many soldiers were sent on medical leave to Darjeeling for treatment and recuperation. The disease was treated with quinine, but the pleasures of the bar were frequently responsible for dulling the memory to take the prescription, to the point that the Civil Surgeon was obliged to devise an alternative strategy. To accompany the gin, the Club made its own soda water, into which it was agreed the doctor could mix the quinine and so guarantee some progress towards recovery. A visiting distributor commented favourably on the taste, which the Club referred to as their 'tonic water', the name by which it is now universally known.

It was certainly a comfortable life for the ruling castes and classes, but it presented a dilemma for the Rajahs and Maharajahs of India, who found themselves torn between clinging to old certainties and reaching out for a new future. The Princes saw themselves as the guardians of cultural identity, but this related only to their own State, for there was no Indian identity as a whole. The truth was that India had never been united, and it was paradoxically the Raj that unwittingly created a national consciousness by imposing British lifestyles and economics. These were often adopted by the Maharajahs to court the approval of the Empire, and their sons were encouraged to attend public schools in the United Kingdom. The price paid was seen on their return, for having gained a taste for fast cars and film stars, and with the next game of polo or cricket uppermost in their minds, they could barely raise an amused eyebrow over what they now saw as a comedy of tradition and belief.

India's ears were retreating from the imported prejudices of the British, who were becoming ever more preoccupied with creating their own caste system with such matters as the Order of Precedence. India was still firmly Victorian in principle, for recognising a change in attitude and approach would

Looking towards the station at Kurseong in the late 1920s, the use of the motor car for private transport is evident. An Up mixed train of five freight wagons with a solitary bogie coach and four-wheeler in tow works its way towards the town. The end of the locomotive shed roof can be seen in the bottom right-hand corner, whilst the passenger station lies between the roofs of the buildings seen beyond the curve.

Gwen Cattermull

be to recognise the change in India itself, and that was too much of a threat to the life style. Porcelain tea sets, silver cutlery and Bromo toilet paper[3] had long been amongst the measures by which standards were maintained, and having the correct accent was of course an eternal truth. However, it was now becoming terribly important to adhere to a strict protocol of seating people at the dinner table according to the status awarded to their employment. Unforgivable social indiscretions could be committed if one was to stray from the established order, and the publication of the list was eagerly sought to ensure there was always s*omebody* to look down on within their own community. Many of those who held governing positions had graduated in Classics at university and saw their role in a similar vein to those in the former Empires of Rome and Greece. The British Raj had become the province of the upper middle classes, and was firmly set on a tangent from the realities of life for the Indian native.

It was no wonder Gandhi had been promoting a programme of open non-cooperation with the British Government. He advocated that the political action was to be non-violent and saw the way to independence could be achieved through what many regarded as a curious pastiche of progressive and obsolete principles. His championing of the rights of the untouchables was revolutionary, although it put him in conflict with the Brahmin priests, whilst his encouragement for economic development through handicrafts was seen as little more than archaic. But the former lawyer knew exactly what nerves to touch, for in his homespun cotton shawl he was able to identify with the hearts of the awakened masses, causing many to wryly reflect on the comment Lutyens once made that '... *it was time for every man to do his dhoti'!*[4]

---

[3] It has been suggested that the name Bromo was adapted from Bronco for the Indian market, the hard 'c' presenting difficulty with pronunciation for some.

[4] Edwin Landseer Lutyens had been appointed the architect to design New Delhi as the capital of the British Raj. It took twenty years to complete, and the project is said to have employed 3,500 masons and 30,000 workers.

The movement was consolidating its strength, and the campaign of non-cooperation was met with a series of summary trials and imprisonment. It lit the touchpaper for civil disobedience, during which Chittarajan Das, who had become one of the most prestigious leaders of the Indian National Congress, was imprisoned for six months following the abortive visit of the Prince of Wales. He had been part of the committee that was appointed by Congress to enquire into the Amritsar massacre, and had forsaken a successful career at the Bar to devote himself entirely to politics. He became an advocate of *swaraj* (self-rule), and was subsequently elected as the first Mayor of Calcutta, but the demands of office were paid for with his health. Das travelled to Darjeeling in 1925 to rest and recuperate, where he was out of sight and out of mind of the riots.

He received a visit from Gandhi, who had been invited to visit the tea plantation of Mr Scarth, the Chairman of the Darjeeling branch of the European Association. The Press reported on 8th June that Gandhi was leading a rather quiet life in the hill town, having addressed a large crowd in the bazaar on the matter of temperance and a ladies' conference in the Hindi Public Hall on spinning and *khadi*.[5] Gandhi travelled back to Jalpaiguri by train on 10th June, and was due to speak in Nawabgunge the following day. However, the 'Darjeeling Mail' was running late and was not going to make the necessary connection with the 'Dacca Mail'. Gandhi responded willingly to the idea of hiring a special train on the spot, and a locomotive was duly summoned and coupled to a solitary coach with a guard's van for a cost of Rs1,140. It enabled him to reach Goalundo in time for the ferry to Nawabgunge,

---

[5] The fabric produced by hand-spinning local cotton.

The waiting room and office at Tung was on the opposite side of the road to the railway. The side of the valley dropped steeply beyond the stone wall, and with its fretted eaves, wooden balustrades and potted plants, the station was a most attractive stop for travel-weary passengers escaping the torrid heat of the plains.

Pat Orr

Disaster Strikes Again
1927

The annual damage caused by the monsoon was almost as predictable as the rain itself, but its severity in 1927 was more than usual. Many factors contributed to the undercutting of the slopes, but the deforestation of the complex and unstable geological formations made it significantly worse. . . . .

. . . . It had made the bare surface vulnerable to thermal expansion and contraction, which caused vertical cracks to form and disintegrate into falling blocks of rock. However, there was always a ready supply of labour and spectators to ensure that the railway service was resumed as soon as possible.

Pat Orr

The illustration above and the two below appeared in the weekly edition of The Times of India. Under the heading of 'Darjeeling Railway Washaway', the broken white line showed its readers where the track and road formerly ran.

The Railway was the only realistic means of getting to Darjeeling until the 1920s, when road transport began to challenge the monopoly. Both were vulnerable to the ravages brought on by the monsoon rains, and the Up Mail is seen here passing a recently cleared slip on 25th August 1927 at 12.30pm.

Collection: Pat Orr

although his critics were not slow to comment on how expensive his modesty could sometimes be. Das remained in Darjeeling, but suffered a fatal heart attack on 16th June, and his body was taken the following morning by the DHR on the Down 'Mail' to Siliguri. The last rites were to be in Calcutta, and 200,000 were waiting at Sealdah station in disbelief of the news of their leader.

The broad-gauge extension of the Eastern Bengal Railway finally reached Siliguri in 1926 and was formally opened on 1st October with great ceremony by Sir Hugh Stephenson, the acting Governor of Bengal. The new line enabled passengers from Calcutta to arrive without a break of gauge, and in the exchange of speeches the Governor spoke of the public now being able to travel to the hills in comfort and of the benefits Darjeeling would gain. He stated that the new travelling arrangements could create a boom with amenities and amusements, as passengers were now able to leave Calcutta after office hours and be in Darjeeling in time for a late breakfast the following day. No mention was made in his speech about the DHR, but the fact he travelled from Darjeeling by car did not go unnoticed.

This was seen as a new threat to the railway, for in addition to the bus service, the private motor car was now making an appearance on the Hill Cart Road and a further set of statistics were accumulated each month for the Directors to ponder over. In May 1926 they noted that 97 journeys were made in all by car and 378 by bus; by May 1927 these figures were 83 by car and 536 by bus. The fury of the monsoon rains brought heavy landslides in August, *The Times of India* reporting that it was *'the worst washaway in the history of the railway'*. There was some journalistic licence with the claim, although the severity was such that 300ft of the hillside was torn away and disrupted all traffic until a new course could be cut. There was an alternative route for the private transport and the figures remained constant until the end of the year, after which they suddenly shot up to 2,411 journeys and the bus service attracting 1,309 passengers.

The railway still held its monopoly with the

transportation of troops, as recalled in the memoirs of Vernon Wells, a schoolmaster travelling with the King's Shropshire Light Infantry to Ghum for a six-month summer break at Jalapahar. With regiments in India being on the move, it was essential that the children received some continuity with their education, and teaching staff would usually be recruited to the unit from the Corps of Army Schoolmasters. After arriving at Siliguri, they found:

'The carriages were like small taxicabs seating only three passengers on each side, and the baggage trucks seemed not much larger than packing cases. It was a big job transferring the baggage in cases almost as large as the trucks, and it took the troops almost all the morning to get this done. We made up a very long train and had two little engines in front to pull and another one behind to push. At first we rattled along in fine style, but as the gradients grew more severe, the boys sitting on the front of the engine were kept busy throwing sand on to the rails so that the wheels could get a better grip. Occasionally we stopped to take on more fuel, which was wood, and more water. In one place, in order to gain height, at a difficult spot the track described a complete tight circle crossing itself by a bridge. Our train was so long that as we crossed the bridge the foremost sand boy was able to sprinkle some sand on to the last carriages as they passed beneath him. We ploughed our way up climbing more than seven thousand feet to reach Ghoom at about eight o'clock that evening. At Ghoom we disembarked and had to walk up narrow winding paths to the barracks at Jalapahar.'

There were approximately fifty children of all ages in the school, and all were accommodated in the one room, with infants sitting at the front and successive rows increasing in age to the back where the teenagers sat. The schoolmaster's daughter recalled that it was a great relief for the children to be in such an equitable climate, for it had been so hot on the plains that they had to sprinkle sugar around the *punkah-wallahs* pulling the fans to attract white ants and stop them falling asleep! There was little chance of that happening in Jalapahar when the monsoon hit the mountains, although her father playing *'For those in peril on the sea'* with his concertina to pacify the children unaccustomed to the ferocity of the rain pounding on the tin roof did seem a little misplaced halfway up the Himalaya!

Colonel Cameron resigned as General Manager on 25th January 1927 on account of his poor health and returned to England. Mr Bagley covered the interim period, after which Reginald Nicholls was appointed to the post on 31st March 1928. Like Robert Addis, he was an ex-North Western Railway man, where he began his career in 1911 as a probationary Assistant Traffic Superintendent. He served with the NWR Volunteer Rifles, and had been made an Officer of the Military Division of the Order of the British Empire on 3rd June 1919 in recognition of valuable services rendered in connection with military operations in Mesopotamia. Many railway traffic staff in India had indeed been seconded from the military, particularly with the government-owned lines, and the Railway Volunteers were a reserve force similar to the Territorial Army. The NWR had the facility to transport troops quickly from Delhi to the North West Frontier in times of need, and at such times the reserves were able to step in at short notice to protect the lines from insurgence. By 1925 Reginald Nicholls had become the District Traffic Superintendent (survey) at Lahore, and moved to Darjeeling three years later with his wife Violet to take over the post as General Manager.

It must have been a confusing time to join the DHR, for the Directors appeared to be in a state of flux over its future. They had already made a formal submission to the Railway Board for the line to operate its own motor service from Siliguri to Darjeeling, but to the relief of many, they found the matter was falling on deaf ears. By the end of 1928 the number of car journeys had climbed by a further thousand, whilst the bus had doubled its figure to 2,953 passengers, and it was not long before the third dimension of road traffic arrived in the form of the lorry to add to their anxieties.

Political matters were also smouldering on the plains, where the demands were about to take a dramatic turn. Sir John Simon had been appointed to review the working of the constitution, but Congress was incensed that no Indian had been appointed as a member of the commission. With the support of Gandhi, the young lawyer Jawaharlal Nehru had been elected President of Congress, and the members were now seeking Dominion status for India. When the Viceroy suggested the same, Winston Churchill called the idea *'not only fantastic in itself but criminally mischievous in its effects'* and thought it advisable that *'the sober and resolute forces of the British Empire'* should stand against the granting of self-government to India. However, Nehru suggested few would be motivated to make sacrifices and go to jail with the battle cry for a *'Dominion'*; the inspiration he felt the movement needed had a far better ring to it ... *'Independence'!*

Climbing hard through the outskirts of Darjeeling, the train passes Dupuis, the Austin agent who supplied car gearboxes with reduced gear ratios to cope with the demands of motoring in such a mountainous terrain.

Gandhi stepped in with a compromise, and Congress agreed it would opt for full independence if freedom had not been granted under Dominion status by the end of 1929. Britain's attentions were diverted by an economic crisis back home, and despite the efforts of the Secretary of State, William Wedgwood Benn, the offer came too late. It orchestrated a new campaign of civil disobedience, and Gandhi, having his finger on the pulse of India, marched two hundred miles to the coastal town of Dandi to break the government monopoly with the right to mine salt. He picked up a handful from the sea pans, a symbolic act that took him to the heart of the poorest of the population. Five thousand similar protests were staged on the same day, and millions rose to the call and boycotted British products, leading to a wave of further arrests and imprisonment.

However grand such gestures were, the Indian equation for independence was extremely complex. The possibility of becoming self-governing was driving in the wedge between Hindu and Muslim interests, which only served to prove to the British that they were still necessary to India. Any shift in power had to embrace not only the religious differences, but also the diversity in cultural and ethnic issues, whilst the position of the Princely States in a federal structure was far from clear.

Instead of becoming dull and decadent as feared by the Press, Darjeeling was now aspiring once again to being a fashionable resort, with a new generation finding it the perfect escape from the gruelling heat of Calcutta. By the year ending 31st March 1930, the records show that with 258,000 passengers, the annual figure for the railway had remained fairly constant over the previous 15 years, and the freight had grown steadily to 80,000 tons. Despite the fears of the Company, it was the journey by the train itself, particularly in the open coaches, which was seen as an essential ingredient of the Darjeeling experience, for many saw it as sacrilegious to hurry in such wondrous scenery.

But there was no escape from the reality of the mounting political tensions on the plains. There were generations of British who had been born in the sub-continent and who regarded India as their home, and any reform was seen as a threat to their privileged position. The messages coming from London illustrated either a lack of understanding or a denial of the situation. In 1931, Winston Churchill broadcast a speech proclaiming: *'Things are going from bad to worse. Great mismanagement and weaknesses are causing unrest and distress to three hundred million primitive people whose well-being is in our care.'* It was a clear statement that primitive ideals were still being held, and made worse by them being couched in terms that were clearly offensive to many Indians. It was equally transparent there was a conflict of principles, for however altruistic the rhetoric, the *raison d'être* of the Raj was still trade. Fears were fuelled that an economic recession would follow if the door was closed to Indian goods and markets, with Churchill making claims that the sub-continent would descend into barbarism and pave the way for rival European powers (Germany) to assume control.

The writing was also on the wall for the privileged position held by the railway, and it had to formally record that it would absolve itself from any insurance liability by users of the road, for it was clearly never engineered with the motor vehicle in mind. As a consequence, a system of permits for road traffic had to be introduced in order to warn drivers of the presence of all trains and other traffic in each section before proceeding. The practice continued until the end of the Second World War, and motorists were required to register their journey with the stationmaster of each section of the line, where they were obliged to wait for all cars coming from the opposite direction to pass before being allowed to proceed.

The first car to be imported to India had come in 1902, and the earliest to appear in the Darjeeling district was said to have been owned by a 'coolie catcher' named Saboulle. He plied his dishonourable trade by retrieving missing workers from the tea plantations in return for bounties, and it was no doubt a shamelessly lucrative business. The petrol for his machine was sent up from Calcutta at a cost of Rs10 a gallon, whilst at their most profitable time of year, a labouring family of three would received but Rs14 a month. But of all the wondrous vehicles brought to India, including the five Rolls-Royces shipped from London by the Maharajah of Alwar for use as dustbin lorries on his estate, it was the humble Austin 7 that proved to be the most popular in Darjeeling. Maybe it was their nimbleness in negotiating the narrow roads that made them so attractive, and most were fitted with the 'mountain gearbox' supplied by Dupuis, who ran a workshop near Westpoint. The reduced gear ratios certainly gave hope in coping with the gradients and Dupuis made the extravagant claim that he drove one of his cars to an altitude of 10,000ft, although quite where there was such a motorable track was never explained!

There was much talk and correspondence in the Indian Press at the time of integrating rail and road services across the land, despite the mutual suspicions the interested parties had of being in competition with each other. The Government of India appointed a committee in 1932 to investigate the matter with the DHR and consider a report for the coordination of the service. The committee comprised L.H. Kirkness from the Railway Board and K.G. Mitchell as the Government road engineer, and they made themselves available for all the concerned parties to testify their case.

Gillanders Arbuthnot & Company, as the Agent for the railway, submitted that the existence of the DHR was now threatened by road competition; the earnings from passenger traffic had decreased from Rs475,000 in 1926–27 to Rs237,000 in 1931–32, and the receipts from freight traffic were commensurate with these figures. Mr Kerr, the Chief Engineer of the Roads and Buildings for the Government of Bengal, stated they regarded the fortunes of the railway as crucial, for part of its net profits went to financing the maintenance of the Hill Cart Road. This amounted to nearly Rs100,000 per annum, and he went on to advise that if the railway was forced into closure by road competition, the Government would be liable for the entire cost of repair and upkeep, which would soon spiral as all the traffic would be focused on the road.

The Government eventually placed restrictions to limit the laden weight and the number of lorries and buses plying for hire, but the road traffic was still able to charge 25% less than the railway. The DHR announced that from 1st July 1934 the fares for 1st Class would be reduced by 50% and 2nd Class by 30% to attract a return of traffic, and made its feelings known that it still intended to run its own road service to overcome the competition. However, the Indian Railway Board turned down the proposal on the grounds that it was not in accord with the Act of Legislature.

The year had barely started when on the 15th January there was a serious earthquake along the fault lines in the neighbouring State of Bihar. It measured 8.3 on the Richter scale and shook all of north-east India, causing serious structural damage in the whole of the Darjeeling area. The tremors began at 14.30 and lasted about five minutes, with reports coming in stating that oscillations had gathered strength to the point it was impossible to stand, and that masonry was crashing down. The cantonments at Lebong and Jalapahar were damaged, as was the Planters' Club, St Joseph's College, St Paul's School and Queen's Hill School. The effects were mostly felt along the ridge and many of the

Government House was damaged beyond repair by the earthquake that hit the Darjeeling area during the afternoon of 15th January 1934. Like many other buildings in the town, it had to be razed to the ground before rebuilding work could be undertaken.

Pat Orr

The monsoons have caused so many changes to the land on the lower sections of the railway that it can hamper a positive identification of unrecorded locations. It is thought that the two gentlemen wearing topees are stretching their legs near Pagla Jhora as an Up Mixed train for Darjeeling takes water.

By permission of the British Library (472/8 109)

shops were in ruins, the reporter for *The Statesman* noting that the chemist shops were '... *cacophonous cabins of jangling and breaking bottles*'. The London correspondent reported the tremors had ousted President Roosevelt's proposals from taking pride of place in the morning papers, whilst the news that the seismologist at the West Bromwich Observatory had '... *actually rung his earthquake bell*' must have been a great comfort!

The damage in Darjeeling was mainly confined to the buildings made of brick and stone, for their rigid structures gave no resilience to the tremors and were shaken to the ground, whilst those constructed in wood suffered little if any damage. It appears to have caused problems to the masonry of the offices and accommodation of the railway station, for the height was reduced and the remaining sections of the windows bricked in. The grace of the building was further diminished by the roof being replaced with one of a more squat design and fashioned in corrugated iron. The major problem on the line was at Batasia, for the loop had been severely breached and the Company was obliged to make arrangements for the transhipment of passengers and goods for some time.

It was estimated the repair work in Darjeeling would amount to Rs13 *lakh*, and at the request of the Governor of Bengal, the Viceroy sent Rs20,000 for the immediate relief of those who had suffered. The Deputy Commissioner for the town, Mr L.G. Pinnell, announced at a meeting in the Capitol cinema that the town '... *would be made good in time for the season and ... not by plastering over defects but by honest work to sound standards which would ensure Darjeeling would be as good, and in many ways better after the earthquake than before*'. Rumours were flying that the rents for visitors would be increased to recoup the costs, but W.J. Kydd, the Secretary of the Darjeeling Progress Association, deflated these by stating the residents were: '... *determined to make the town more attractive than previously and prices more moderate*'. The hill station took the matter in its stride, and within two months of the earthquake the ruins of Government House had been removed and Darjeeling had cleaned itself up in preparation for a busy season. Spirits were high, and with the promise of a visit by the Governor, the Press was confident there would be '... *a minimum of cardiac commotion*'.

The damage did not deter the annual meeting of the Railway Electrical Engineers being held in Darjeeling three months later. The main topic for discussion was the electrification of railway carriages and stations, but quite what they made of the DHR and its 4-wheeled wagon for lighting up the stations can only be imagined! The Signal Engineers Committee of the Indian Railway Conference Association also met there four days later, and again one is left to speculate if their knowledge was enhanced by the caprices of the journey, although that could be churlish when blessed with Kanchenjunga on the doorstep.

Sonada was unscathed by the earthquake, although the tea factory nearby at Bagri collapsed, and the

The Up Mail is seen approaching the halt that was established at the bottom of Essex Road for the senior management in Kurseong. The road can be seen rising between the trees in the distance, and at first sight the houses would not have looked out of place in the English countryside.

Pat Orr

'Sherston' was the accommodation for the Company's accountant and his family, and is seen here at the time Geoff Plackett held the post.

Nigel Plackett

'Beau Site' was the second of the houses ascending Essex Road and was occupied by George Batterbury, the Resident Engineer, and his family for many years until 1942.

Pat Orr

Below: *Symbolically set at the top of Essex Road, 'Elysia' was for the General Manager and his family. Photographed here in 1945 by James Shaw, his wife Betty can be seen standing to the right under the trellis with Kay Easton, whose husband was a senior Director from the DHR Agent Gillanders Arbuthnot.*

Betty Shaw

Opened in 1909 for Europeans only, the Kurseong Amusement Club in time opened its doors to native residents. It became known as the Mahatab Club (in respect of the Mahatab of Burdwan) and was the most popular meeting place in town for employees of the railway and friends. In 1961 it became the Kurseong station for All India Radio, broadcasting mainly for the Nepali-speaking community.

Betty Shaw

damage in Siliguri was mainly confined to cracks appearing in the Hill Cart Road, with water spurting out and depositing mounds of sand. The Teesta Valley line suffered more with six boulder slips between Sevoke and Gielle Khola, and one particularly heavy settlement near the gorge was such that it severed the telegraphic communication. The mail had to be taken by car and the Press feared that the trains might never run again, but as ever, the railway rose to the occasion and the service was back in operation by the following Tuesday. No mention was made of damage occurring to any other buildings along the three lines, and the Directors decided in June that no action should be taken to insure any of the major stations. One can only surmise that as these structures had proved to be capable of standing up to the forces of Nature so far, the railway seemed quite content to rely on providence, or that another tremor would not follow in the foreseeable future.

There certainly had not been any damage to the brick-built houses constructed in Kurseong for the senior executives of the railway in 1917. Nestling on successive levels of Essex Road on the northern side of town, they rose majestically up the hillside from St Paul's Church to the Accountant's residence at *'Sherston'*, followed by *'Beau Site'* (Resident Engineer), *'Pinecote'* (Assistant Traffic Superintendent) and *'Alcard'* (Personal Assistant to the GM) later named *'Valley View'*, with *'Elysia'* symbolically at the top for the General Manager. There was no denying that the names set the tone for entering the houses, conveying the illusion that India could be left behind and life revert to the pleasantries of a middle-class English country residence.

'Elysia' was indeed a grand building, with tennis courts, garages and two superb gardens laid out on different levels. It was perfect for entertaining visitors, which did not wholly suit the rather retired nature of Reginald Nicolls but delighted his wife Violet. Faultlessly attired, she assumed the role of being First Lady of the Hills with consummate ease, and regarded her own 'tennis teas' as quite the highlight of the social calendar. The house had a guest suite in addition to its eighteen rooms, and had the coveted luxury of five bathrooms equipped with water closets, a comfort indeed when most houses had to rely on the feared 'Welsh Hat'.[6] Norman Davison, who served with the RAF some ten years later and was billeted at *'Elysia'* with Geoffrey Plackett and his family, recalled in the letters he sent home that it was:

> *'... Tudor style with beams stretching across and giving the appearance of a long life and well-matured history. The fireplace of plain glazed brick and very wide and spacious, and*

---

[6] Many had to wrestle with their dignity when sat upon this inglorious arrangement, for it had been fashioned in tin to a shape that resembled an inverted form of the headdress. However, the hapless coolie whose caste had dictated his role in life was to empty the receptacle, would not have blinked an eyelid.

the mantelpiece of dark oak to match the lower half of the walls ... all the bedroom furniture being of dark Jacobean ... the front lounge furniture light and modern toning superbly with the lovely light wallpaper and containing all you need from a cocktail bar with which I am well acquainted!'

The railway also owned *'The Pelican'*, a smaller property on the Hill Cart Road that had been built directly opposite the lower end of Essex Road and approached by steps descending the valley. In later years it was simply referred to as *'The Little House'*, and it provided temporary accommodation with the privacy of a self-contained residence for visiting railway personnel and other guests.

With the headquarters of the railway being in Kurseong and the Locomotive Department in Tindharia, it was only right and proper for there to be clubs for the senior officials. The Kurseong Amusement Club had been established in 1909 and was situated about half a mile down the Pankhabari Road, whilst Tindharia had a smaller version inside the railway station itself. Both were furnished with excellent billiards tables, a small library and a bar, and Kurseong had the additional benefit of outside tennis courts. The club was a much-favoured meeting place during the day with many of the wives, who could feel quite alone once the children had been packed off to boarding school. Long afternoons of well-bred boredom could be whiled away by exchanging trivia and playing bridge, the stakes being set at 5 annas in one room for the ladies, and 10 annas for the gentlemen in the other, although it was possible to graduate to the higher wager by invitation. The monthly tea dance was also eagerly awaited, for a waltz to Victor Sylvester halfway up the flanks of the Himalayas was reassurance that life was indeed normal and that the English newspapers and magazines would soon arrive.

Down in the *terai*, the age-old problem of controlling tigers that terrorised the villages had become a sport that was readily adopted by the Raj. It had become a favoured outdoor pursuit for a number of the senior railway staff, who would recruit a local *shikari* (native guide and expert in game) to take the train to Siliguri and buy a goat. The pugmarks of a tiger would often be found close to a river where the animals drank, and the unfortunate goat would be secured to an adjacent tree to act as the bait. The tiger would attack at night, after which the hunter would be contacted the following morning and told to make haste on the down train to the *terai*. Meanwhile, a tree house would be constructed for the hunter to spend the following night in comfort and wait for the sound of an approaching tiger. With a torch strapped to his rifle, he would flash the light on to momentarily startle the animal before it was shot. The natives were entitled to the flesh, and the hierarchical order of the offal was determined by the village headsman, although a strict guard had to be maintained as the whiskers were highly prized in

'Half-Term. As we wished to travel'. So this delightful photograph at Ghum was entitled, and in the school tradition of referring only to their surnames, the back row were listed as Fraser, Griffiths, Sen, A.K.H., Mrs Fraser – middle row Trimmins, Thornton, Miss Rowlands, Mondel, Carter, Smith – front row Wilson, Nag and Simpson.

Collection: Hugh Rayner

Bruce Ellis, the DHR Assistant Traffic Superintendent, with his daughter Gwen on the banks of the Teesta. The bridge and the small bazaar on the right-hand bank of the river can be seen in the distance.

Gwen Cattermull

Below: *Almost timeless, this delightful photograph was taken in 1937 with Keith Roberts firmly in control whilst the picnic special to 'Woodcot' for the boys of St Joseph's School, North Point, waits in Batasia siding. Note the small steel plate pegged to the rear buffer beam to allow the fireman easy access to the firebox when running in reverse.*

Courtesy: Kenny Coutts

folk medicine. There was also the added benefit of the victor having a floor covering for the taking, as indeed one rather imperious old lady recalled during the research for this book that '… *if you needed a rug you went out and shot one!*', in which case the skin would be cleaned with saltpetre and sent to the taxidermist in Siliguri to be prepared.

Preoccupied with its own problems of unemployment and encroaching fascism, Britain passed the Government of India Act in 1935 to give the provinces self-rule with their own administration. With the exception of defence and finance, it made ministers responsible to their elective assemblies and broadened the vote from 6½ million to 35 million, including 6 million women and 3 million whose caste decreed them as untouchable. The foundations for the formation of a federation were also set out, on paper at least, but the Congress was not impressed with allowing the Maharajahs to govern on the same level as the provinces. But the changes were not progressing fast enough for some, as on 8th May an attempt was made by a terrorist movement on the life of Sir John Anderson, the Governor of Bengal, at the Lebong racecourse. The first elections were held two years later and Congress formed governments in seven of the eleven provinces, with an eighth following a year later. It brought a chorus of disapproval from many of the British residents, but the train for independence was now steaming ahead, and many felt like nervous passengers waiting on the platform with their coats somehow caught in the doors.

A Mixed train passes through Kurseong with a train bound for Siliguri, the first wagon reportedly transporting a car. Although private road vehicles were still something of a rarity at the time, the Directors of the railway were becoming increasingly concerned with the growth in their numbers and implemented control points to monitor and regulate the situation carefully.

Collection: Sushil Dikshit

The annual report for the railway for the year ending 1935 revealed there had been some falling off with passenger traffic. The returns for freight had shown an increase, but much of that was due to transporting the materials for repairs to the damage caused by the earthquake. The report illustrated a net profit of Rs320,165 had been achieved, and when added to the accounts brought forward from the previous year, it gave a figure of Rs491,353. An interim payment of Rs109,375 had been made on the preference shares, which left Rs381,978 as the net revenue available. A final dividend had been paid at 2.5% on the preference shares and 2% on the ordinary shares and after transferring Rs70,000 to the contingency reserve, a balance of Rs167,603 was finally carried forward.

The Company decided that retrenchments were necessary to keep the finances buoyant, and began by offering a 10% cut in salaries. Everybody reluctantly accepted the inevitable, but it was still not sufficient to remedy matters and some of the staff did not have their contracts renewed. One of the most senior losses was Bruce Ellis, who had been with the railway since 1925. He had trained at Bromley on the old London, Brighton & South Coast Railway before sailing to India in 1922 to become an Assistant Traffic Manager on the Eastern Bengal Railway. The intensity of the Calcutta heat caused his wife to become very ill during the birth of their daughter Gwen in 1924, and on medical advice he sought similar employment with the DHR in the more agreeable climate of Kurseong. The family moved into *'Pinecote'*, and it was not long before their young daughter was dispatched to boarding school in Darjeeling, the ornament of prosperity during the Raj and a matter in which she had no say. Bruce Ellis contracted cerebral malaria in 1930 whilst sorting out a major slippage on the Teesta Valley line, but the prescription of quinine succeeded only in making his teeth fall out! The railway physician, Dr Mukajee, recommended a more drastic treatment of spinal injections, but the side effect unfortunately acted against his spirit and changed his personality. He eventually found employment on the South India Railway, but the parting of this well-respected family was felt throughout the DHR community.

In 1936 the railway was running three through trains a day in each direction, departing Siliguri at 6.50, 7.15 and 10.05, with Down trains leaving Darjeeling at 10.20, 13.35 and 15.00. The fastest train of the day was timed at $5\frac{1}{4}$ hours for the journey, and this was supplemented by two local services that ran from Tindharia and Kurseong. The timetables also reveal there were two troop trains from Darjeeling at 11.30 and 16.10, but curiously there was no mention of any Up service for the military being provided.

The success of the ropeway from Rilli to Kalimpong on the Teesta Valley line inspired the construction of a similar system to carry the freight from the DHR goods shed in the Darjeeling bazaar to Bijanbari (approx 2,500ft above sea level). This settlement was about three-quarters of a mile from Pul Bazaar, and being at a higher level, made it more suitable as the base. Both were developing as centres for trade from eastern Nepal and western Sikkim, and with a large forest nearby and adjacent tea gardens, the potential for expanding the traffic was considerable.

The idea had been conceived by Mr N.C. Goenka in 1929 and the British Engineering Ropeway Company had entrusted the survey and design to their engineers,

Three of the senior railway staff were present for this photograph to celebrate the opening of the Darjeeling Ropeway Company in 1939. Reginald Nicolls (General Manager) is seated first on left, with Robert Kirby (Locomotive Superintendent) standing in the centre with Geoff Plackett (Chief Auditor) standing on his right. Mr N.C. Goenka, who conceived the idea of a ropeway, is seated third from right and Mr A.J. Elkins, a Director from Gillanders Arbuthnot, is standing second from left.

Collection: Nick Rhodes (The handbook issued by the Darjeeling Ropeway Company)

Messrs Hudson & Redwood, after successfully completing the system to Kalimpong. It was to be built on the same Berco Monocable design[7] of one endless cable, but it had taken some time to allay the fears raised through local objections and the scheme was not formerly sanctioned until July 1936. The Company was formed three months later on 16th October with an authorised capital of Rs500,000 divided into 50,000 shares.

The DHR showed a keen interest in the scheme from the start; Messrs Nicolls and Kirby (Locomotive Superintendent) were appointed as two of the Directors. It was agreed that the railway would be the Working Agents subject to the general direction and control of Goenka & Co. as the Managing Agents. The DHR was entitled to retain the position for 20 years as long as the portion of the goods shed at Darjeeling was used by the ropeway, the arrangement being terminable by giving 2 years' notice. The railway would receive a remuneration of Rs400, which included rent for the space in the goods shed for the first two years, and thereafter a rent of Rs30 per month. The remuneration was to be increased to Rs600 if the ropeway made a net profit of at least 15% and Rs750 with 20% or more.

The figures for the road traffic were now being recorded to show the percentage in relation to the total travelling to Darjeeling, and it did not make for comfortable reading. Private car users were measured against the passengers travelling in the upper-class carriages, and in December 1936 it was found that 51.71% were now using the road, which escalated to 73.6% by December 1937. Those travelling by bus were compared to passengers riding in the lower-class compartments, and the returns for the same period illustrated the figure rising from 10.86% to 17.61%.

The geological instability of the area was also causing the railway concern, and in particular the spur around which the Batasia Loop had been laid. Although no records have been traced of its construction, there is clear photographic evidence that a reverse siding was cut into the hillside on the Darjeeling side of the loop around this time. It was thought that it had been constructed to overcome the severe breach caused by the 1934 earthquake, particularly as trains needed to get through to Darjeeling with the building materials for the damaged sites. It has also been suggested by a former employee of the railway that it was a contingency measure following evidence of further slippage on the westerly side brought on by the monsoon rains. The track from the top of the reverse followed the base of the upper hillside and connected with the existing line close to Batasia siding, and thus avoided the entire loop. A short spate of earth tremors

---

[7] Berco was the acronym for the British Engineering Ropeway Company.

was felt in Darjeeling in March 1938, but Batasia remained undamaged and the loop continued to be used in favour of the reverse siding. The destruction at Tindharia was more severe, and the Memoirs of the Geological Survey of India published in 1939 recorded that the station had been built on poor foundations and that a fissure over 300 yards long was noted beneath the station yard.

The railway may have been having problems but business in Darjeeling had been doing very well, with *The Statesman* reporting in October 1937 that there was scarcely a hotel with any vacancies and that it had been '*... a most successful season. So much to do that it is almost incredible news that 22 people found time to play cricket!*' The retiring Governor of Bengal, Sir John Anderson, left Darjeeling for the last time on 8th November, and having just laid the foundation stone on the new Coronation Bridge that crossed the Teesta river at Sevoke, lauded the importance of new roads in the area at his farewell speech. He departed for Siliguri by car, and left the railway scratching its head as what to do next. Freight traffic was also being attracted to the road, and it is doubted if the railway could have survived the competition without the imposed restrictions, as its effects can be seen:

	Traffic by Rail		Traffic by Road	
Years	Passengers	Goods (Tons)	Passengers	Goods (Tons)
1909–1910	174,000	47,000	-	-
1919–1920	263,000	62,000	-	-
1929–1930	258,000	80,000	48,000	880
1934–1935	240,000	76,000	56,000	7,600
1939–1940	213,000	65,000	73,000	15,500

The Darjeeling Ropeway Company was finally opened for traffic on 7th January 1939 after overcoming a number of difficulties with its construction, primarily due to there being no proper roads to transport the materials over the steep hills and across the rivers. Five drums of cable, each weighing over two tons, had to be taken by Bhutia coolies to Chungtong. The first reel tottered over the top of the ridge through the excitement and overconfidence of the coolies; it was only stopped by crashing into trees, although it was claimed the cause was the propitiatory offerings made had been deficient by one chicken! To be on the safe side, a sizeable goat was subsequently offered by the workers to ensure the ropeway would work properly.

The opening ceremony was performed by Mr A.S. Larkin, the Deputy Commissioner, and after the usual speeches and congratulations, he pressed a button to start the ropeway and the first carrier arrived with a bouquet of roses in a silver bowl for his wife. Goenka & Co. announced that it was to organise a *Mela* at the other end in Bijanbari a week later, the fair promoting the cause of the new transportation and attracting local trade.

The ropeway was 180yds short of 5 miles in length, with two intermediate stations at Singtom and Chungtong. The longest span was $7/8$ mile (4680ft), a record for India, and at the time was only thought to have been exceeded anywhere else in the world by $1/8$ of a mile '*somewhere in Brazil*'. The ropeway was run in two sections and powered by two 24HP Tangye diesel engines, one being sited at Darjeeling and the other at Singtom, and with the carriers travelling at $4 1/4$ mph, it took just over one hour to complete the journey. Each carrier was capable of carrying three *maunds*, or if coupled together four *maunds* and up to 12ft in length, and as such the ropeway was capable of transporting 100 *maunds* an hour in each direction.

The maximum rate charged was 5 annas per *maund*, with the basic essentials of salt, oil and rice being transported at a lower cost. The freight brought up the valley comprised potatoes, vegetables, poultry, ghee, cardamoms and forest produce. Darjeeling returned the favours with cloth, yarn, sugar, salt, kerosene and metals. The ropeway ran directly into the freight shed of the railway, the final 600ft crossing a particularly congested area of the town protected by a bridge of six spans, the first of its type in India.

But for all the prosperity the ropeway brought to Darjeeling the DHR was losing money, and for the first time Gillanders had to consider whether to continue running trains or simply close the railway down. The Agents were acutely aware that if it was to survive, something clearly had to be done to modernise the railway service, and indeed modernise the management of its operation. They wanted to find new people with fresh ideas and thinking to take the lead, although they appreciated that could upset one or two of the long-term staff who were waiting to step into the shoes of those leaving. However, it would have been a greater risk if they had not made the changes, for that would only have allowed the old practices to continue under a different name and put the whole future of the railway into jeopardy.

Two senior appointments were made at the end of March 1939, the first being with Geoffrey Pilkington Plackett taking over from Reginald Nicolls. Born on 29th May 1905, he completed his secondary education at Wrekin College before graduating at Cambridge as a Bachelor of Arts in 1926. He was appointed as an officer of the Auxiliary Force with the Bombay, Baroda and Central India Railway Regiment in 1927, and became auditor for the railway in 1932. His transfer to the DHR came in 1936, where he was appointed to the post of Chief Auditor, and held the position until promotion to become a much respected and admired General Manager.

The second change was the recruitment of James Shaw to take over from Robert Kirby as the Locomotive, Carriage & Wagon Superintendent; he had been with the railway for 23 years. At the age of 56, he did not yet regard himself as a candidate for retirement and it was with some reluctance that he left. He took up residence with his young wife Joan in the large white house he had built just beyond Tindharia, where the railway enters the valley to Pagla Jhora, and there they lived until he died ten years later.

James Shaw (known on the railway as Jimmy but to his family as James) came as a breath of fresh air to the staid atmosphere of Tindharia. Born on 7th May 1901 in Paisley, near Glasgow, his student education was completed after taking evening classes in engineering, machine drawing and mathematics at Paisley Technical College. By a curious coincidence, this was the same college that his predecessor Robert Kirby had been sent to from the other side of the world! Shaw served his apprenticeship in the machine and fitting shops of Messrs Fullerton, Hodgart & Barclay and Vulcan Engineering, where he specialised in the manufacture of steam engines, winding machinery and hydraulic pumps. He became a marine engineer with the British India Steam Navigation Company, and in 1931 obtained a 1st Class Board of Trade Certificate of Competency in Glasgow. In 1935 he was appointed as the superintending engineer with the Indian Molasses Company and the Indian Water Transport Company, where he was responsible for the operation and maintenance of barges and the paddle steamer fleet, and from where he moved to the DHR appointment.

The Directors spelt it out quite bluntly; the railway *'was in a shambles',* and it now had to face its greatest challenge. Indeed, Geoff Plackett and James Shaw were to take the railway into its most innovative and demanding period, for no sooner had they started to devise a modernisation plan when the mood was darkened by the drama unfolding in Europe, threatening India itself.

A rarely recorded view of Darjeeling station looking in the direction of Siliguri, the photographer having stood astride the track leading to the bazaar. The Jubilee Restaurant reflected the same spirit of design as the station opposite and the locomotive shed seen in the middle distance.

Collection: Sushil Dikshit

Chapter 7

War and Attrition

If the First World War had touched India indirectly, then there was no doubt of the impact that the second global conflict could make. The Congress governments formed in 1938 resigned, as none of its representatives had been consulted when the Viceroy declared that India would enter the war. It was felt the offence was compounded by the future of India not being made clear in the objectives, and the situation became untenable as Indians were now being asked to fight for liberties in Europe that they did not enjoy at home.

Preoccupied with the affairs of war, Britain suspended all negotiations regarding independence, which was not helped by an internal battle that had been brewing over the future distribution of power and control in a federal India. Congress was predominantly Hindu, and although it had gone to considerable lengths to secure their demands, most regarded the Muslim League as the main body that addressed their specific interests. Deftly guided under the leadership of Mohammed Ali Jinnah, the League saw new possibilities in the wake of the resignations made by the Congress governments, and in 1940 avowed its goal was the formation of a separate homeland for the Muslims. Jinnah advocated the idea of two nations that were historically and culturally different, but quite how the provinces were to be separated was going to be another matter.

The build-up of armed forces may have been seen as defending British interests, but for many it was regarded as provoking the Japanese, and this accelerated the momentum for India to gain its independence. British troops had long been kept as a defence against Russian and Afghan advances on the North West Frontier, and the recent severing of the Mediterranean supply route for the British forces fighting in Egypt had highlighted the strategic importance of India. Vast quantities of materials had been transported by rail to the ports of western India, but now the north-eastern area itself was being seen as vulnerable to the Japanese Army encroaching on Malaya, and in particular Burma.

Communications in the north-east were reliant on the broad-gauge line from Calcutta to Siliguri and the metre gauge that branched from Parbatipur to Tinsukia in north-eastern Assam, which included crossing the swiftly flowing Brahmaputra by a small wagon ferry. There were also two broad-gauge branches that ran eastwards to Goalundo and Sirajganj, but again the river had to be crossed by ferry to meet the metre gauge from Chittagong. This line continued north-east to the junction at Lumding, and was close to the front with the Japanese army occupying Manipur and Nagaland. It soon became apparent that the defence of the area would need the support of motor transport, but the lack of usable roads made the railway the only means of conveying the vehicles to key positions. The 'Motor Vehicle Run' became crucially important traffic, and a road ramp was built at Siliguri station to allow the lorries to be driven straight off the wagons.

The demands for more trained staff could not be realised within India and had to be met by the British Army, with the Royal Engineers sending troops as a railway operating company. They received their initial training at Longmoor and Derby in England, and although they were not told at the time where they were going, the fact they were issued with ex-Boer War pith helmets allowed them to make a shrewd guess! The challenge was to galvanise the native railwaymen into action, for Indian operating methods were at

A superb study of native passengers boarding a 1st/2nd Class composite carriage whilst the locomotive crew attend to No.36. The elegant panels and ornate fittings made this second generation of bogie carriages appear somewhat heavy and they were soon to be replaced by the lightweight stock introduced by James Shaw.

their best conducted at a relaxed pace. Although this afforded maximum safety with often-illiterate staff and suited the temperament and climate perfectly, it certainly did not fit in with the pressures now faced by the threat of a Japanese invasion. It had been drummed into the native staff during peacetime that the 'Darjeeling Mail' was the most important service and should never be delayed. No amount of persuasion could shift them from this belief to give priority to the troop trains, which were ignominiously shunted onto a loop or siding to let the mighty 'Mail' pass.

The Japanese victories in south-east Asia catalysed Britain in sending Sir Stafford Cripps, the Leader of the House of Commons, to negotiate Indian co-operation with the war. The carrot was to be a self-governing Indian Union at the end of the hostilities, although Britain wanted to retain control of the defence policy. Congress rejected the proposal, and Gandhi launched a 'Quit India' campaign to halt all war production and immediately force the British out. Over 60,000 were arrested, including Gandhi, who had become a considerable thorn in the side of the Raj and was disparagingly referred to by some as the 'Nutcracker'. There was no time for delicacies, for the spectre of famine was sweeping across eastern India and Japanese advances were placing food supplies for the troops in jeopardy. For all its idiosyncrasies, the DHR was in a strategic position and the railway was mined at key points, in order that it could be permanently damaged in the event of a Japanese invasion.

Despite the political protests, over two million Indians volunteered to join the Army,[1] for independence seemed inevitable under the Raj and a lot more uncertain at the mercy of the Axis powers. America also

---

[1] At the outbreak of the War, the Indian Army had 189,000 regular soldiers; by the end of the hostilities, it had grown to more than two million and became the largest volunteer army in the history of the world. The numbers were gradually reduced after Partition and divided into the separate armies for India and Pakistan.

played a decisive hand, and made it known to Britain that it saw the relinquishment of Imperial control as a condition of their entry into the war, although any benevolence for Indian affairs was mostly motivated by frustration in not having been able to develop its own commercial interests.

But the war had frustrated commercial interests worldwide, and nowhere was it felt more painfully than in Europe with the advance of Hitler's army. Production was turned to the benefit of the occupying forces and workers were hastily displaced to avoid the wrath of Nazi doctrinal purges. Prior to the invasion of Czechoslovakia, Bata had become the largest shoe manufacturer in the world and had a vast network of outlets that spread across many countries. Dr Eugene Straussler was a company physician, and in 1939 was transferred with his family to a branch factory in Singapore. His wife, Martha, and two sons were amongst the families subsequently evacuated to India by the British Army before the Japanese attack on Pearl Harbour. Dr Straussler stayed behind to support the defence of Singapore, and lost his life when he boarded a boat packed with refugees caught in the line of fire by enemy aircraft. Martha took her sons to Darjeeling in 1942 and supported them by working as the manageress of the Bata shoe shop, next door to Keventer's restaurant.[2] The boys attended Mount Hermon School, and in 1945 their mother married Kenneth Stoppard, a major in the British Army who had helped with the evacuation. The family moved to England in 1946, where the youngest son Tom completed his education before becoming the internationally acclaimed author and playwright.

The drafting of British and American forces to the north-east brought a change of fortune for the DHR, with traffic peaking as thousands of battle-weary troops were sent to the cantonments at Ghum and Darjeeling. Families would also open their houses to those sent on recovery leave and offered a much needed respite from the cauterising heat of the plains, the steaming swamps of the Ganges and Brahmaputra, and the fetid jungles of Burma. There was an unprecedented rush of traffic, and James Shaw turned his attention to designing new sets of rolling stock to help cope with the demand.

As Locomotive Superintendent, he had already been looking at ways of modernising the DHR, and in July

---

[2] Mr Pliva, who owned the Windamere Hotel and ran the restaurant and confectionery shop in Commercial Road (now Glenary's Bakery in Nehru Road), was also a native of Czechoslovakia.

Track inspection. James Shaw (centre) and George Batterbury (right and wearing a tie) talk to an engineer crouched on the track, whilst Geoffrey Plackett (on far left wearing white topee) is in discussion with the Assistant Resident Engineer. Note the American station wagon belonging to the railway parked alongside the inspection trolley.

Betty Shaw

1940 the Directors had agreed to sanction an order for a diesel locomotive from Walford Transport Ltd of Calcutta. It was to have a streamlined body that would create a new image for the DHR, but it was to take two years of development and testing before it was ready to be despatched to Siliguri. The trials were undertaken on the Howrah-Amta line in Calcutta, a suburban affair that ran across the flood plain of the Hooghly and where the diesel was perfectly at ease demonstrating its maximum speed of 37 miles per hour. However, the climb to Darjeeling was a completely different matter, and the locomotive was returned to Walfords for the gearing to be reduced before any serious assessment could be made.

Meanwhile, Tindharia began to produce a series of modern, lightweight coaches fitted with air-braking to connect with the Westinghouse system on its new diesel. The stock included four 1st Class buffet saloons with a bar at one end and a large, square observation window set in the bulkhead at the other. Comfortably furnished with ten upholstered armchairs, they became extremely popular with the troops on leave, particularly after James Shaw secured a supply of the virtually unattainable Teacher's whisky. A fifth saloon was built for the General Manager to complement the buffet coaches, its most distinguishing feature being a prominent rounded end in which a large panoramic window had been set. All five coaches were named after Himalayan peaks, the GM's vehicle bearing the title *'Everest'* in honour of its status.

The diesel eventually arrived at Siliguri, but to everybody's disappointment it was found that it had the power but not the weight to give it sufficient adhesion on the climb to Darjeeling and it was able to haul only two of the lightweight coaches. The mechanical drive allowed all five speeds to be used

The Walford diesel did not live up to its expectations, but it was a brave experiment with a pioneering locomotive. Geoff Plackett (in shirt sleeves and topee) and John Ager (Workshop Foreman wearing cap) discuss its progress as the crew takes a rest from its sonorous interior whilst on a test run. Note the DJ prefix of the number plate (for Darjeeling) on the support motor vehicle.

Betty Shaw

in both directions, but for some reason the body was designed only to face one way and as a consequence the locomotive had to be turned at the end of each journey. The engine was also found to be prone to overheating, whilst the low skirting and undercarriage made it difficult to manoeuvre the machine back on the track in the event of a derailment.

A heavy demand was also being placed on the railway for the transportation of wounded soldiers for convalescence. James Shaw designed a special ambulance train and four coaches were adapted to accommodate stretchers. However, Colonel Leroux from the Jalapahar cantonment was at a loss as to how the injured would cope with being thrown from side to side by the constantly changing curves and super-elevation of the line. To overcome the swaying, Shaw devised an innovative system of suspending the stretchers from cables attached to the ceiling, the principle being that as cradles they would hang vertically in the nature of a plumb line. Each carriage was fitted to carry eight stretchers, and doors were fitted into the bulkheads at each end to enable them to be carried on and off with minimal disturbance to the patients. A small compartment was also sectioned off at each end and furnished with conventional chairs and a table, where wounds would be dressed and the medical staff could relax.

The injured would generally arrive at Siliguri on the overnight 'Mail' from Calcutta, and the priority was for them to be taken to the ambulance train whilst the rest of the passengers had their breakfast at the station. Each carriage would be separated from the next to allow the stretchers to be carried into place through the end doors, and once loaded, the train would set off ahead of the main service. Most of the patients were taken to Ghum and transferred by road to the military hospital at Jalapahar, although some continued to Darjeeling for the cantonment at Lebong.

The coaches were painted white with large red crosses to symbolise their use, as was the four-wheeled covered van taken from stock to transport the baggage. The train was staffed by a Sister, an Orderly and a VAD nurse (Voluntary Aid Detachment), and Beryl McConville recalled the time she spent serving on the ambulance train after being sent to India in 1944. She had risen to the call from Lady Edwina Mountbatten for *'ladylike nurses'* to serve in Poona and set an example to the Indians reluctant to care for the troops. Interviewed in London, the distinction of her school was the only qualification that appeared to be necessary to satisfy the Board, and having just returned from a Swiss finishing academy, she was regarded as perfect for the cause! She found herself on a troopship bound for Bombay without further ado, and the only advice given to the nurses on their departure had been: *'Remember, girls, keep your suits brushed'*. Dressed in blue cotton, grey Lisle stockings, lace-up boots and fashionable white 'Pamela' hats, they felt the Board had anticipated their work was going to be little more than attending a series of cocktail parties.

There could be nothing further from the truth, for her feet had barely touched Indian soil when she was sent to the infamous Manipur Road, the only highway that crossed the mountains to Burma. It was here that she was to attend the sick in an emergency field hospital located deep in the jungles of Assam and perilously close to the Japanese advance. Six months had been the accepted maximum period of service in such conditions, but it would take two years before the posting to Darjeeling came through to recuperate and serve as a VAD nurse on the DHR. The pay for working on the train equated to £3.00 a week, and whilst her jungle fatigues were finally replaced by a khaki uniform, they did turn out to be the standard men's issue!

Petrol for private use was now rationed, which severely curtailed the use of motor vehicles on the Cart Road. This hit the social life of many tea-estate managers where it hurt, for the highlight of their week was to meet on a Saturday for some serious drinking on the Quarterdeck, the prominent semi-circular balcony at the Planters' Club. They were now dependent on the train for their return home, but this was scheduled to leave Darjeeling at 17.20 when matters were just warming up nicely. James Shaw was seen as *'... a decent sort of chap who fitted in with the planters' lifestyle admirably'* and it was decided that a special exception was to be made for him to join the Quarterdeck. United in friendship, he arranged for a 'special service' to get the members home, which usually steamed out of Darjeeling around nine o'clock at night. There was no paper trail left to record what came first, the new carriages fitted with a bar or the introduction of the 'Club Special', but it led to the suspicion that the idea of dressing one of the 'B' Class in a streamlined shell might have been conjured up on a returning train late one night!

The truth was that the failure of the Walford diesel had left the railway without any motive power to reflect the spirit of its new rolling stock, and Shaw set about designing an aluminium casing that would sit over locomotive No.28 and create the appearance of it being a modern machine. It certainly looked the part when it finally emerged from the workshop at Tindharia, and

In sickness and in health . . . .

The problem of conveying injured troops to Darjeeling for convalescence was solved by the Ambulance Train designed by James Shaw. It is seen here passing through Kurseong hauled by No.47, one of the four 'B' Class that carried the pale grey livery of the modernised passenger rolling stock.

Opposite: Once recuperated, there was nothing more welcome to travel in than the new 1st Class bar saloons, and two of these splendid coaches are seen here with the 'Streamliner' on a test run to Darjeeling. The locomotive certainly created the illusion of speed and efficiency, but in reality it was 'B' Class No.28 dressed in an aluminium casing and was no faster than the rest of the fleet.

Betty Shaw

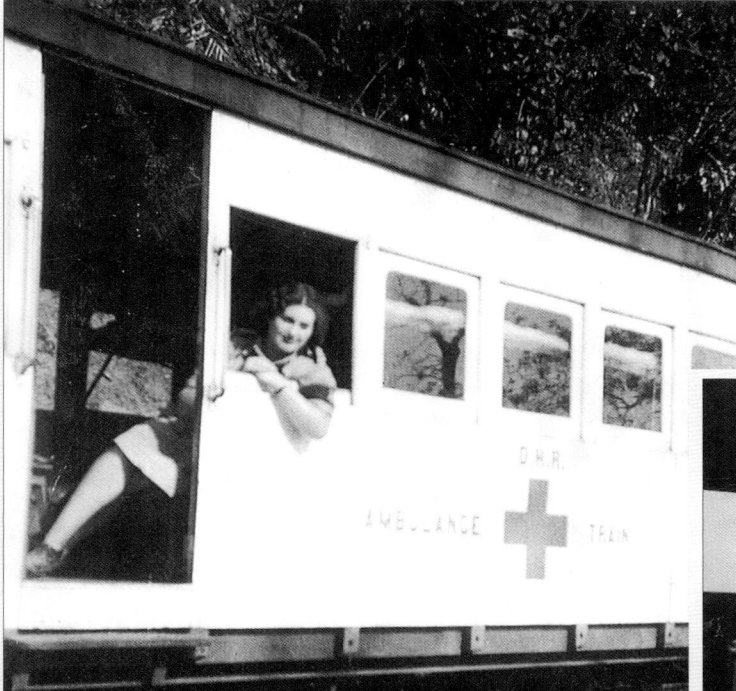

The Ambulance Train with Beryl McConville, who served on the train as a Voluntary Aid Detachment nurse. A top stretcher can be observed through the nearside windows and another is silhouetted through the open door on the far side. The coach pictured is No.43.

Beryl McConville

although it was never any faster than the rest of the fleet, it created the illusion that it *might* be. Indeed it bore a close resemblance to the three streamlined 'PC' Class 'Pacifics' supplied by Robert Stephenson & Hawthorn to the Iraqi State Railway in 1941, one of which had been illustrated in the October edition of the *Railway Magazine*.

The DHR named its revamped machine *'Jervis Bay'* in honour of the famous ship that was sunk in the Atlantic whilst defending a convoy on 5th November 1940, but the enthusiasm for the fabulous folly was not shared by the operating crews. The hinged panels at the front had to be wired open to accommodate the coolies manually sanding the rails, both of whom must have been deafened inside its cacophonous cladding and soaked to the skin when the rain funnelled in. It also took the skills of a gymnast to scale the smooth exterior and fill the water tanks, whilst the workshop was no more euphoric at having to strip the casing off when undertaking routine service and maintenance.

Barely three years passed before No.28 was taken back into Tindharia and returned to its former condition, leaving the stories of the 'Streamliner' as another of the DHR legends to tease the historians.

The winds of change were also blowing through Darjeeling itself. The servicemen saw Simla as being stuffy and somewhat haughty with it being the government retreat from Delhi; on the other hand, they regarded Calcutta as the city of *'ladies, legs and liquor'*, and its hill station was becoming very popular as a consequence. Inevitably the social graces of the Raj were starting to crumble, and such traditions as the Order of Precedence, which many clung to as an affirmation of their importance, began to look faintly ridiculous. The hierarchy had been that Tea spoke to Oil but not to Railways and Coal, and nobody spoke to Jute, but in Darjeeling the importance of the Railway was unique and it ranked with the highest. The endless round of social engagements, with cocktail parties, formal dinners and full-dress balls

No.49 pulls away from the top section of a reverse siding with a rake of second-generation coaches, their bowed chassis showing distinct signs of age. Note the pipe running along the base of the coal bunker on the locomotive, which is thought to have been part of an experiment to supply additional water from a tender.

Das Studio: collection David Churchill

The increase in traffic during the Second World War brought with it a demand for additional motive power. Geoffrey Plackett is seen here on an inspection of the Matheran Hill Railway, where it was claimed that the DHR was interested in their four articulated 0-6-0Ts. Note the initials MST on the freight wagons to denote the line was still referred to as the Matheran Steam Tramway.

Nigel Plackett

was rapidly becoming a thing of the past, as was the Knights-Errant. Sponsored by the bachelors and grass-widowers[3] of the district in return for the hospitality they had received, it had been an annual event staged at the Gymkhana Club with the Governor being the guest of honour. It was considered the high spot of the year, and had been a lavish affair for those dressed in full regalia of white tie and tails, knee breeches, red sash and buckled shoes, for they regarded themselves as being irresistible to the ladies. It had all been so reassuring, but now the future was no longer what it used to be.

James Shaw suggested that it was time for the Planters' Club to open its doors to all, for no native Indian had previously been allowed over its doorstep. Geoffrey Plackett seconded his submission, and made it quite clear that he would resign if the proposition was not passed. It was becoming increasingly absurd for the likes of Telu Khan[4] to be denied entry, and with most of Darjeeling relying on the Railway, the motion was passed to avoid a major embarrassment. Nevertheless, the move was resented by the committee, who felt *'as it was, so it shall ever be'*, and saw the Club as being for the exclusive entertainment of the colonial community. But that was now sounding like a fragile claim made by an insecure Raj, and as if to prove the point, one of the tea-estate managers laid a bet with a native female porter to prove she was stronger than the men. At the time it was not the accepted form for a gentleman to be seen carrying a bag or package around town,[5] and porters would wait for custom at the crossroads adjacent to Keventer's restaurant, which was just below the Club. The lady in question rose to the challenge in style and staggered round the dance floor with the grand piano strapped to her back!

It had been much more relaxed in Kurseong, for there had been no colour bar at the Club for years. It was also no stranger to some delightful characters, including the remarkable Bella Munday, who was noted for wearing the most extraordinary collection of hats and for her uncanny ability to tell fortunes. Members would regularly engage her in a consultation, although

---

[3] Married men with wives living on the plains or in the United Kingdom.

[4] A.W. (Telu) Khan was the Traffic Superintendent of the DHR.

[5] The custom continues to this day inside certain Gentlemen's Clubs in London.

The ferocity of the monsoon rains on 26th June 1942 totally destroyed loop No.2, and the decision was made to replace it with a reverse siding cut into the hillside. James Shaw is seen sitting on a section of rail washed away between the upper and lower levels of the loop, whilst teams of native workers cut a profile into the hillside for the new trackbed. It would take three months before the service could resume.

Courtesy: Nigel Plackett

some doubt was cast on her wisdom after she asked about a young couple who had recently married. The wife had been suffering from a sore throat and, after her doctor had noted that the irritation was caused by the uvula at the back of her mouth being too long, he recommended that a small section should be removed under local anaesthetic. Mrs Munday subsequently enquired about the lady's health, and when informed that her uvula had been snipped, proclaimed to everybody at the Club that it was such a shame, as the young couple had been so looking forward to having children!

Nothing would have daunted some of the members, one of whom was the formidable Mrs Mumford. She had lost a leg and an eye following an attack by *dacoits*[6] and felt perfectly secure in the knowledge that she could quickly remove the wooden limb and use it most effectively as a weapon! The Reverend Roband was another regular at the Club, and being very tall, very slim and wearing a dog-collar, would be immediately recognisable as he made his way down the Pankhabari Road *'just for a small sherry and a game of tennis'*. Never one to abdicate from his pastoral duties, he would engage in conversation at the drop of his Panama hat, particularly with the ladies. The story was told of the time when the road had recently been resurfaced and his discourse went on for so long with Vera Linberry Kerr that she had to be dug out of the tar, which had melted in the sun and welded to her rubber shoes. His sober manner lent himself to being great sport for some innocent flirtation by the ladies, to which he would be heard to say, *'You really do provoke irrelevant remarks to fall from my lips,'* although nobody could claim to know what they were.

The elegantly attired Mrs Linberry Kerr would often be seen making her way through the Club with the consequential walk of a well-upholstered royal, gracefully holding a cigarette in one hand and bowing profusely to everybody she met. She embarked on the enterprise of importing Magnolia ice cream from Calcutta and selling it from the *'Wood Hill'* hotel in Kurseong that was run by her sister Ida. It was brought up on the DHR packed in cases of ice and straw, but as often as not the train would be delayed and the frozen confection arrived half-melted. Despite the protests she made to James Shaw and her insistence that he improved the train service for her ice creams, the raspberry continued to ripple into the chocolate, and having set into bizarre shapes, she would sell these as *'deformities'* to members of the Club. However, the temperature certainly dropped one afternoon when a new guest mistakenly asked how much she charged for her *'abortions'*!

The monsoon of 1942 left the usual trail of destruction in its wake, and brought the Railway to a halt for three months. There was a major landslide on the 26th June that destroyed the lower section of the second loop between Rangtong and Chunbatti, washing a considerable amount of the earthworks into the valley. It had been the most complicated of the loops to construct, and with the lower part having been cut as a terrace into the exposed side of the spur, it was the most vulnerable to slippage. Geologically the ridge was part of the Siwalik system of soft sandstone and shales, and with little vegetation to abate the ferocity of the monsoon, the rain easily percolated through the coarse grains and decomposed the feldspar into a lubricant. There had also been concern for some time with the increase in traffic, for the thrashing exhaust from the locomotives in the confined space of the short tunnel had been affecting the lining. The decision was taken to cut a reverse siding into the hillside that led up to the loop and connect the track with the top section of the spiral just past the old tunnel. The Railway was closed down for the duration of the work and the opportunity was used to make further improvements by installing radio communications between all the stations.

The mercurial moods of the new diesel, the questionable benefits of having streamlined a 'B' Class, and the urgent need for additional motive power, took James Shaw to visit the redundant Jorhat State Railway in Assam. He proposed that the DHR should purchase four of its locomotives for use on the Kishenganj extension, but the directors decided not to proceed with his recommendation.[7] However, the Raipur Forest Tramway in the heartland of India had just closed its doors, and with it being another line managed by Gillanders Arbuthnot, it was a simple matter for its four 'B' Class tank engines to be transferred to the DHR between the June and August of 1943.

Two civilian passenger trains were now being run in both directions on the 'main line' from Siliguri to Darjeeling, but with 308,872 passengers being carried for the year, the loads were often such that they had to be split into four or five sections. The Kishenganj extension recorded 459,204 passengers for 1942–43, running one through train in each direction, supplemented by an early morning departure from

---

[6] A Hindi term for a robber belonging to an armed gang.

[7] The notes made by the late Harold Bowtell during a visit in 1944 intriguingly refers to the Matheran Hill Railway claiming that their four 0-6-0Ts had been sold to the DHR, although this was later denied by James Shaw.

Thrashing up the new reverse siding, the livery and post van immediately identifies the train as the Mail bound for Darjeeling.

Betty Shaw

'B' Class No.53 came to the DHR from the Raipur Forest Tramway in August 1943. It was being driven by Balchan Singh barely six months later when the brakes failed approximately one mile after descending the Batasia loop, the two sandmen losing their lives as the locomotive left the track.

Thakurganj at 5.50 and 6.00 to both termini, the trains returning at 20.15 and 20.35 respectively. The Teesta Valley carried no more than 35,988 during the same period and the service was limited to a single mixed train in each direction. From these figures, the number of passengers travelling to other railways via Siliguri amounted to 38,687, but only 1,551 used the connections at Kishenganj.

The numbers of passengers travelling to and from the principal stations were recorded as:

Station	Section	To	From	Total
Darjeeling	Main Line	63,147	101,984	165,131
Ghum	Main Line	41,436	50,061	91,497
Sonada	Main Line	11,062	16,703	27,765
Kurseong	Main Line	44,910	54,069	98,979
Gielle Khola	Teesta Valley	12,635	14,860	27,495
Riyang	Teesta Valley	2,321	3,539	5,860
Matigara	Kishenganj	28,351	36,295	64,464
Bagdogra	Kishenganj	24,003	27,613	51,616
Naksalbari	Kishenganj	53,656	55,725	109,381
Siliguri and Siliguri Road	Joint	101,207	95,693	196,900

Troop trains were run as required, and this stretched the Railway to the limit, for it was unable to handle all the traffic needed to bring the supplies to the increased population in Darjeeling. The military had no option but to bring in its own road transport, and additional help had to be solicited from local hauliers. This was not run on a strictly commercial and competitive basis, for the road continued to be regulated to no more than 60 taxis, 25 trucks and 15 buses, which caused a confused reading of the returns:

Years	Traffic by Rail		Traffic by Road	
	Passengers	Goods (tons)	Passengers	Goods (tons)
1940–41	206,000	57,000	81,000	16,500
1941–42	240,000	63,000	63,000	16,800
1942–43	309,000	63,000	27,000	5,900
1943–44	311,000	76,000	34,000	9,000

The freight returns for the Railway during 1942–43 showed that 2,769 tons of coal were carried to Darjeeling, along with 7,104 tons of rice, 1,007 tons of salt, 540 tons of sugar, 417 tons of grains and pulses other than rice, and 773 tons of provisions (including building materials, cement, iron etc). Imports up to Ghum included 1,167 tons of coal, 3,505 tons of rice, 513 tons of salt and 434 tons of provisions. The freight returning from Darjeeling moved 1,298 tons of tea and

The wheel-turning lathe at Tindharia in 1944. The workshop employed 381 men during the war years, and with the heavy demands stretching the railway to the limit, it was no surprise to find it had become a tinder box for political unrest.

Betty Shaw

The Down Mail at Ghum in December 1945 with No.25 in charge. Delivered from Sharp, Stewart & Co. in 1900, this locomotive was subsequently renumbered 782 by IR and in more recent times has carried the name 'Mountaineer'. Note the footbridge in the background and the washing being laid out to dry on the canopy above the roof of the carriage.

The Frank Thornton Jones Collection

1,080 tons of potatoes, with more passing through Ghum as 2,190 tons of tea, 1,529 tons of potatoes and 515 tons of timber were transported to the plains.

The Railway now had a stock of 39 working locomotives, and with over 2,000 staff it was the major employer in the area. The monthly salary for Geoffrey Plackett in his position as General Manager was Rs1,200 (his assistant Mr S.A. Smith receiving Rs525), followed by Rs1,125 for the Resident Engineer George Batterbury. The Assistant Traffic Superintendent Henry Cowley and Sauri Bose, the Auditor, both received Rs625 and James Shaw, as the Locomotive Superintendent, Rs 600; Dr S.K. Biswas, the Medical Officer at Kurseong, commanded but Rs90 a month. However, Henry Cowley was soon called away for military service, and Joe Martin was awarded temporary promotion to cover the post. He felt that his higher status warranted the purchase of a new car, but such was his pride with the vehicle that he would not take it out in rain. It has to be said that this somewhat limited its use in the hills and created a great deal of amusement in the Club, particularly when he would be seen fighting with his umbrella in the monsoon downpours.

The machine-shop at Tindharia was equipped with 17 lathes and all the equipment for drilling, planing, milling, shaping, slotting, grinding, shearing and punching, alongside the carpenters' shop which handled all the work on the carriage and freight stock. The works employed a staggering figure of 381 men to keep the Railway running, including a number of hillmen:

Skill	No.	Hill men
Fitters	115	78
Turners & Drillers	26	22
Blacksmiths & Strikers	37	33
Boilermakers & Riveters	91	88
Moulders	14	14
Carpenters	29	20
Tailors	6	6
Khalasis (cleaners)	42	37
Painters	21	19

Such was the demand for trains that an additional service from Siliguri to Darjeeling was implemented

John Ager, the Workshop Foreman and Chargeman, at Tindharia station with the streamlined locomotive. Named 'Jervis Bay', it was to give the railway a modern image after the failure of the Walford diesel, but the smooth cladding did not make it easy for the crew to access the water filler on top, and there was nowhere to accommodate the coolies needed to manually apply sand to the rails.

Betty Shaw

The Up Mail makes a splendid sight as it comes off the loop at Agony Point. Despite the problems the railway was experiencing during the war year, the locomotives and rolling stock were always kept in pristine condition.

Collection: Nick Rhodes

The Up Mail passes two locomotives waiting their turn of duty in the sidings at Kurseong. The aperture in the side of the electric headlamp on No.47 would normally have been covered by a glass panel that illuminated the running number. The first coach is the travelling post office and the letter box for late posting can be seen beneath the shielded electric light.

The Frank Thornton Jones Collection

in 1943 in the form of the 3 Up and 4 Down Mixed, along with two shuttles each way from Kurseong to Darjeeling if ordered. Tindharia worked flat out to maintain the stock in a serviceable condition, to the point that an additional 100 hands had been engaged to cope with the abnormal demands placed on the Railway by the war. The staff was now exhausted, and with the Radical Democratic Party stirring in the background, matters came to a head with a revolt lead by Sagina Mahato. Recently promoted to head brakesman, he was able to unite them over their poor housing conditions and called a strike in 1944 that closed down the whole of DHR. The flashpoint was said to have come from a small incident when it was alleged that the Carriage Foreman had been caught red-handed whilst forcefully spending a night with the wife of one of the workers. The affair sparked off a whole chain of events, and with it the demands for regulated hours, fair wages and decent living conditions.

The DHR authorities agreed to the terms, but the strategy was a little more devious than had met the eye. They came to an arrangement with a most unlikely organisation, the Communist Party of India (CPI), which had first attached itself to the complication of Indian politics in the early 1920s. Quite how such a dogma reconciled itself with the entrenched belief of caste had never been understood, but it was seen as sufficiently subversive for the Party to be outlawed by the Raj in 1934. However, with India being a land of survival, it continued as an underground movement until its recognition was finally negotiated as part of the Stafford Cripps mission in 1942, when a united front was formed against fascism and the Japanese.

Sagina Mahato became President of the left-wing Mazdoor Union, and as such the CPI was able to extend its influence with the workforce of the Railway. The DHR made him a Labour Welfare Officer, and with this title came a bungalow in Kurseong and new responsibilities. Instead of being able to attend to the labour problems of the DHR, the Communist Party now sent him all over India to talk to labourers of other industries. While doing so he lost his base on the DHR, and when he finally returned to Siliguri from his whirlwind tour, he found that he had been duped and the campaign was lost. The Railway workers rose against him since he could not improve their lot, and his body was found the next day on the railway tracks in the Sukna forest. Nevertheless, his legacy was to set a standard that became the benchmark for all Indian railway workers.

Geoffrey Plackett took his family back to England on leave at the end of 1944, and being aware of a deteriorating situation in India, reluctantly decided it was time to tender his resignation as General Manager. He had taken the Railway through some of the most demanding times in its history; it was a testament to his skills and loyalty that his staff kept in close contact with him until he passed away in 1968. James Shaw was asked to oversee the work in his place in February 1945 and was officially made the General Manager of the Railway on 1st January 1946. He was the last to hold this office with the Company, and his subsequent correspondence with Geoffrey Plackett not only applauded his friend's wisdom of remaining in the UK, but also revealed he would have welcomed such a move himself.

As Locomotive Superintendent, James Shaw had been living in the wooden bungalow at Tindharia. His wife Betty recalled it as a delightful residence built on stilts with French windows that opened to a long veranda, although its desirability was also shared by the snakes that lived beneath and the rats that multiplied profusely above. As Chairman of Gillanders Arbuthnot, Thomas Gladstone agreed that it was about time the building was replaced, and sent Gordon Craig to Tindharia to come up with a design. He was reputed to be the finest architect in Calcutta, and stayed with the Shaws for a week to agree on the plans and layout. With the Placketts now in the UK and 'Elysia' empty, James hastily returned one afternoon to announce they were moving up to Kurseong that night. It had just come to his notice that a smallpox epidemic was sweeping through Tindharia, and the railway workshop and surrounding area was to be placed under quarantine. A field hospital was set up under canvas in the charge of the DHR physician Dr Gupta, but it was to take months before life got back to normal, whilst the work on rebuilding the house, now the current residence of the AME at Tindharia, dragged on for years.

The DHR staff was granted a bonus to mark the end of the war, and the Directors agreed on 24th August 1945 that all officers, supervisory and office personnel were to receive one month's salary, whilst the operating staff and labourers were to be content with one week's pay. The demands made of the line had been overwhelming, and it had been impossible to keep up with the need for new locomotives and rolling stock. The Railway had never been built to the exacting standards of the broad gauge, but had still been expected to give an unconditional service against tremendous odds. It was quite simply worn out, and time was rapidly catching up with it in many ways.

Something had to be done, but nobody quite

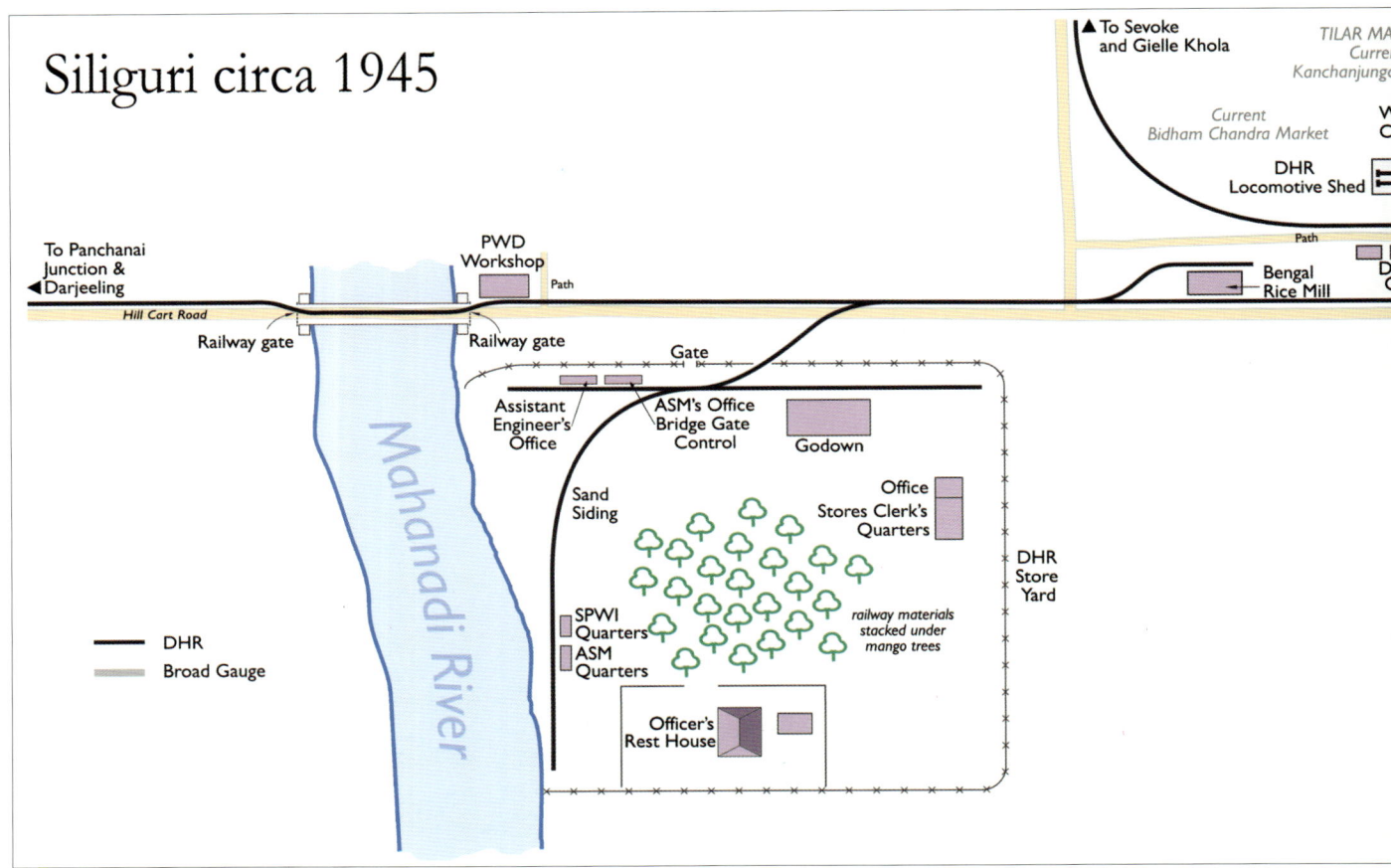

expected such a bold statement as the new station for Darjeeling, which was quite unlike anything seen before. The once-elegant wooden canopy had become an eyesore over the years, and the whole thing was in urgent need of rebuilding as it was near the point of collapse. Thomas Gladstone had been advocating this for some time, although with the gift of hindsight, the Railway could have hung on to its tottering structure for a while longer. It was already evident that independence would lead to some geographical surgery being required on India to appease the religious communities, but the Directors must have felt confident the DHR would remain a private company when India became self-governing. The investment in building the station made it clear that nobody at the time realised the effect that partition would have on the Railway.

As it was, the old brick-built offices were pulled down at the end of 1945, although the pleated wooden roof was retained as a temporary measure for the train service to continue. Banshidhar Dikshit recalled that in addition to his role as permanent-way inspector, he was given the task of supervising the dismantling of the old station and the construction of the new. He told the contractor that he should be present at the demolition of the stone chimneys, but this was ignored and the work was undertaken that evening. It resulted in two Bhutia workmen being killed, and the contractor was fined and made to pay compensation to the relatives after investigation by the police.

A radical art-deco design in concrete began to emerge inside the spidery scaffolding of bamboo poles, from which the local contractors felt the need to hang a shoe, a sweeper's broom and a basket. Such customs were a stark reminder of India, where superstition and the evil eye ran through the course of everyday life. The belief was that anybody contemplating the theft of the building materials would be beaten with the shoe, an act of unforgivable disgrace, and swept by the next most dishonourable item, a broom, into the basket for disposal to the nether world.

It had to be said that the spiritual insurance was turning out to be far from foolproof, for early in 1947 a section of the balanced cantilever roof over the island platform collapsed with five 15ft spans, killing one man and injuring another. The police impounded the drawings and prosecuted the contractor for removing the shuttering that supported the concrete before it had properly set, with damages

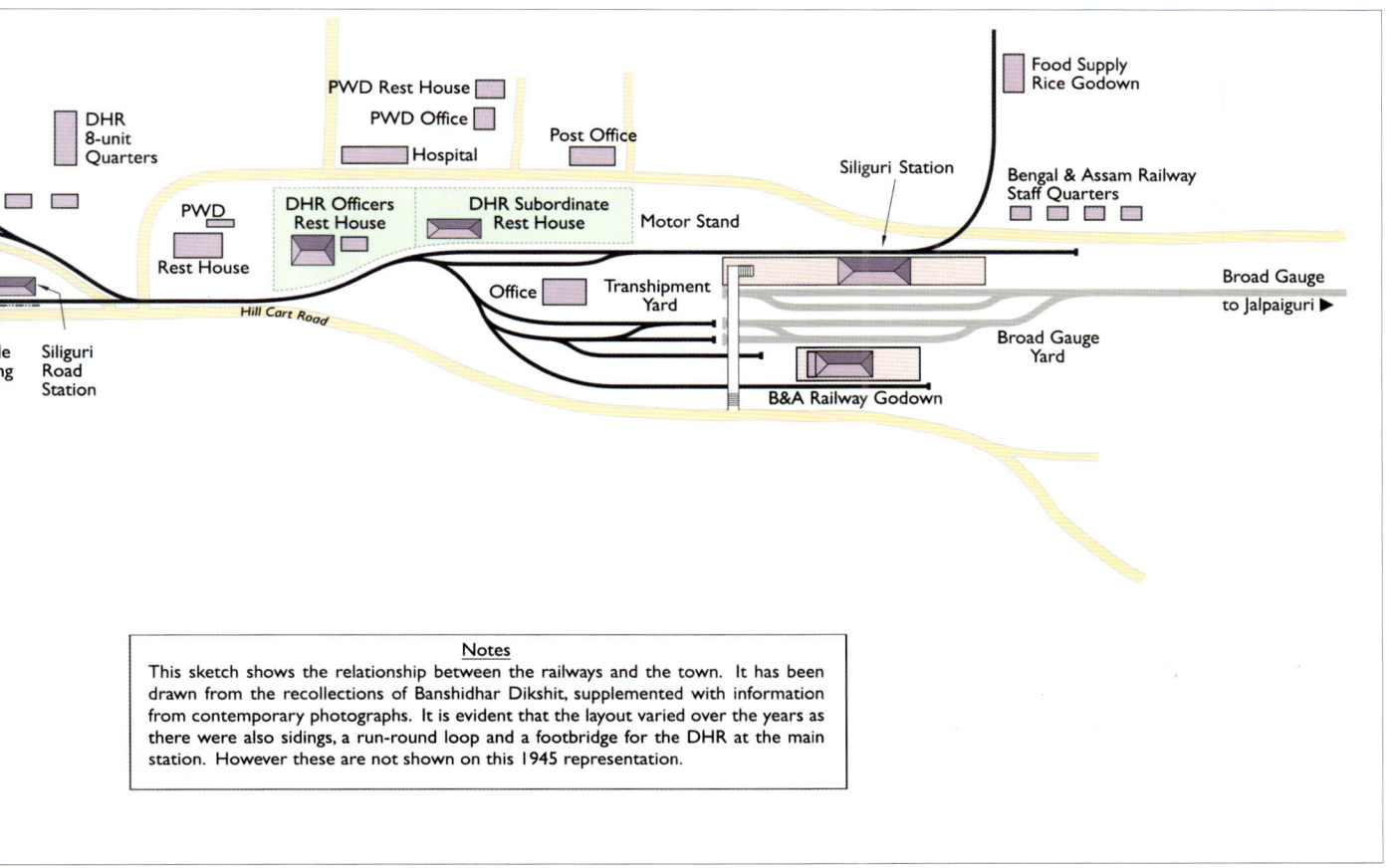

Notes
This sketch shows the relationship between the railways and the town. It has been drawn from the recollections of Banshidhar Dikshit, supplemented with information from contemporary photographs. It is evident that the layout varied over the years as there were also sidings, a run-round loop and a footbridge for the DHR at the main station. However these are not shown on this 1945 representation.

being paid to the relatives of the deceased workers. It triggered off a great deal of talk in the district, and James Shaw reported that the Gurkhas asked him to condemn the entrance to the building. The new station was beginning to look more like a modern cinema than a railway terminus, and however much at ease an 'Indian Odeon' may have appeared in a city suburb, it was another matter when it stood in the shadow of Kanchenjunga. However, influences of the style had already been seen with the facelift given to Keventer's restaurant, the semi-circular extension of the Planters' Club and the new dining room of the Windamere Hotel. Darjeeling Deco was becoming the fashion by reflecting the spirit of the future, and that was something India was nurturing with a passion.

The excitement was indeed running high, for the mutual suspicion between Congress and the Muslim League had locked them into a conflict over the control of an independent India. The British attempted to broker an interim government in which the two parties alternated, but Congress rejected the proposal as they regarded any obligation to share equally with the Muslim League as an affront. Violent riots broke out in Calcutta, which soon spread to other cities and provinces, and Gandhi went on a series of fasts in a vain attempt to stop the carnage.

Although the problems on the plains were not overtly touching the hills, they were certainly being influenced by the events. The CPI saw the cause of the Gurkhas as being ripe for agitation, and began to advocate that the Darjeeling district should be amalgamated with southern Sikkim and Nepal to become Gorkhastan. Riots began to spread into the hills, and with James Shaw being haunted by further problems with the Union and the natives becoming drunk with temper, the earnings for the Railway dropped rapidly. Shaw turned down enormous bribes from a local merchant called Mawari to secretly run his supplies of rice by train and store them to wait for a famine to develop, and it seemed as though the whole area was turning in on itself. K.S. Rumba, the new president of the Mazdoor Union, called for more strikes on the Railway, but their success foundered on account of the Employees Union, who did not agree to the disruption and would not support its actions. Shaw was fluent in a number of local dialects, and as such was usually able to pacify the leaders and prevent the Railway being sabotaged. He was also looking for alternative ways of keeping the workers at Tindharia busy.

Robert Shaw plays at 'Elysia' with one of the wooden models of the 'B' Class. His father, James, made over a hundred of these immensely popular toys for the children of the railway staff and tea planters.

Betty Shaw

The workshop, which had already turned its hands to making furniture for Geoffrey Plackett, was now fabricating dining-room tables, cabinets, inlaid tea trolleys and standard lamps for the senior staff. Many of these specialist jobs were given to Luru, a gentle giant of a man and a naturally talented engineer. He was devoted to James and helped him to make over a hundred wooden models of the 'B' Class, which became a much-treasured present for the young children of the staff and the tea planters. Dorothy Harley was a planter's wife, and so impressed James with the scones she made on an iron griddle that he instructed the workshop to begin casting copies in the forge and offer them for sale. They were perfect for *chapattis*, but none of the enterprises James introduced to Tindharia seemed more unlikely than the manufacture of coffins. The climate in Kurseong dictated that it was necessary for any deceased person to be buried as quickly as possible, but the only caskets available were rudimentary boxes that had been hastily put together. It was on the occasion of Pitty's funeral that James decided the railway workshop should begin to make something decent which could be kept in store and then be available for immediate use.

Pitty was the affectionate name of a very popular tea-planter from the *Dooars*, and there was great excitement at his funeral in Kurseong to make sure he was seen off in fine style. He was rather short in stature, but the only coffin available was one of such massive proportions that it could have accommodated him three times over. The cortège was a horse and cart, and as was the local custom, the coffin was to be carried into the church by workers from the plantation. It had been made from unseasoned wood, and was so heavy that it took twenty coolies to stagger up the aisle with it balanced on their shoulders and place it on the bier in front of the altar. Betty Shaw was seated in the front row between her husband James and Bert Sarstedt,[8] and at one point during the service found she had dropped her handkerchief. Reaching down to retrieve it, she glanced up and noticed there was no bottom to the casket, and hence no body inside. Stifling a fit of the giggles, she nudged James, who bent down and saw that both were indeed missing and that the Reverend Roband was conducting the service with clipped perfection to an empty box. Sliding out of the church by the side entrance, James quickly summoned the coolies together to retrieve the vacant coffin, but in the hushed reverence of the church, the sound of them scurrying down the aisle was not unlike an oncoming train. Praying that it was nothing more than a bad dream, the Reverend Roband launched into a spirited hymn as the casket was whisked outside to be reunited with poor Pitty, who was still laying in full view on the back of the cart. The service continued inside the church to the accompaniment of much hammering and banging outside, before the thundering herd returned him to the trestles for his soul to depart in propriety!

It was agreed that nobody would have seen the funny side more than Pitty, but it was also recognised that the listless feeling of uncertainty was becoming ever more pervasive. To add to this, it was not long before the General Manager was faced with more earth slips and mounting problems with the Union. Henry Cowley was demobbed at Deolah and returned to work on 10th June as the Traffic Superintendent, by which time the monsoons had already washed out the Pagla Jhora.

---

[8] Albert Sarstedt was the DHR Auditor, who lived with his wife Coral and three sons in Kurseong. The boys went on to have careers in popular music, Peter having a worldwide hit with his song *'Where do you go to, my lovely'*, Robert establishing himself as the 1960s singer Eden Kane, and Clive playing in his brother's band.

It was nothing new, and five days later a further ten inches of rain fell in just two hours at Kurseong. Telu Khan resigned from the Railway and a farewell tea was held for him on the 24th June in Sorabjee's restaurant at the railway station. He had risen to being the Deputy General Manager of the commercial operation of the DHR, and Martins Light Railways were making enquiries about his salary with the intention of offering him the position of Traffic Manager. His skills were later recognised in the wake of independence, for he was selected for the post of Commercial Secretary to the Pakistan High Commission based in Delhi.

The station restaurant was one of three on the DHR run by Sorabjee, the others being at Siliguri and Darjeeling. The first had been founded by Sorabjee Colah and Dinshaw Bamjee at Sialkot in the Punjab, and it had so impressed a British railway official that he offered them a contract in Bengal. The partnership of Dinshaw Sorabjee & Co. was then formed, and in 1885 they opened their first refreshment room on the East Bengal State Railway. By 1896 they were running similar establishments at over 30 stations, including Siliguri, Kurseong and Darjeeling on the DHR, and it was not long before further contracts were secured from the North-Western Railway. The agreement was terminated after Partition as the new government stipulated they must serve only Indian food. The Company was simply not geared for this type of catering, having imported all its china and cutlery and being used to serving Governors and the like.

It certainly appeared to be a time for people moving on to higher things, and no less so than on the 10th September 1946 when an Albanian nun by the name of Agnes Gonxha Bojaxhiu was travelling on the DHR. She had joined the Loreto novitiate in Darjeeling in 1929, and after having taken the vows of a nun in 1937 became known as Mother Teresa. Working in Calcutta at a time of food rationing, she had succumbed to tuberculosis and was returning to the Loreto Convent for rest and recovery. It was on the train that she received what she termed the *'call within a call'*, which was to give rise to the Missionaries of Charity, her lifetime of work for the poor and destitute in the slums of Calcutta.

On a more prosaic level, James Shaw tried to raise the spirits of his staff, as he recalled in a letter to Geoffrey Plackett in December 1946:

> *'Life here in Kurseong goes on the same as usual and the Club is very dull. The railway people appear to keep it going. I redesigned the main bar (near the Bridge room), erected a fine fireplace with a flue cut through the wall separating the Bar and Badminton Court, 'backed' up a tremendous large sideboard behind the bar and am now in the process of making a new bar (semi-circular) – put down new flooring – fitted new single doors in place of the dreadful half-doors which is a boon to the bridge players – fitted pelmets and curtains to cover the high-arch doorways – fitted new lighting to put some cheer in the place, but with all this we have a few members and it's difficult making ends meet. It must have been a tremendous leakage of bar receipts during the War. I think I told you in a previous letter that I sacked the Club babu*

Henry Cowley and Marjorie Ellis, the English nurse the Placketts engaged for their sons Nigel and Tony. Henry Cowley had been the Traffic Superintendent of the DHR since 1938, but in the period leading to the takeover by the Indian Government in 1948, he deputised as General Manager when James Shaw was on leave.

Courtesy: Nigel Plackett

and I took over as Chairman. So my attempt at doing the Club up to try and get members to take an interest is almost futile and I see in the future having a small Railway 'Institute' in Sorabjees.'

Newman's Indian Bradshaw railway timetable in October 1946 curiously included a 1st Class bus service with the DHR trains, departing Siliguri at 6.30 to arrive in Darjeeling at 10.00 and returning at 15.00 for Siliguri at 18.30. Former residents and those associated with the Railway have not recalled the DHR running its own buses, nor is there any reference in the minutes of the Directors' meetings, and the reference may well relate to a relief service as a temporary measure during the aftermath of the war.

James Shaw attended a round of meetings held in Delhi in November 1946 for General Managers to discuss the future of the Indian railways, and he returned to Kurseong with the warning that the DHR would probably be taken over by the Government. With the growing feeling of restlessness in the hills, he packed his station wagon with the essentials in order that his family could make a safe departure at short notice, and felt that Kishenganj on the plains would be a safer haven than Darjeeling. It did not come to that, but it certainly appeared for many that the Raj was now on a suicide mission, and the Railway staff began to turn on themselves. The frustrations and uncertainties can be seen in two letters written by Joe Martin, who had stood in for Henry Cowley whilst he had been away on military service. The first one was dated 20th May 1947:

'Life is certainly not as rosy as it used to be in the old days. Cowley took over from me on 10th June '46, but I was kept on to assist him at Kurseong until the end of the month. Then I decided to take a month's leave, which I felt I richly deserved, and finally took charge at Tindharia on the 1st August on Rs600 plus Rs50 travel allowance a month. Nothing was done about my designation till I passed some cryptic remarks in the Club one evening. Finally it was decided to call me Loco Officer. To be honest I felt fed up and thoroughly disheartened and almost packed in but for Eileen and the kids and the fact that jobs were scarce and that 'beggars could not be choosers'.

Siliguri Station in 1945. The broad-gauge East Bengal Railway and the Assam Bengal Railway were merged in 1942 to become the Bengal & Assam Railway; ex-EBR No.69 retained its old running number and is seen arriving at the head of a train from Calcutta. It was one of the L Class 4-6-0s originally built by North British in 1907 for the Oudh & Rohilkhand Railway in 1907 and transferred to the EBR in 1926. Partly obscured by the haze of steam from a nearby locomotive, the DHR waits on the far side for passengers changing trains for the bills.

Pat Orr

The crew prepare No.51 at Tindharia station and a little girl watches during the last days of the railway operating as an independent company. The locomotive came from the Raipur Forest Tramway in June 1943, where it had been running as No.B3. The roof and slats of the ventilator above the institute building on the right are looking a little suspect and were later boxed in with sheets of corrugated iron. The station was refurbished in 2001 and the decorative timberwork restored.

Betty Shaw

Below: *The official programme of trains issued by the DHR for schoolchildren returning home at the end of the 1948 term.*

Date	School/College	Pupils	Station	Train	Time
16.11.48	St Augustin's European School	19	Gielle Khola	42 Down mixed	14.30
17.11.48	Mount Herman	100	Darjeeling	Special	12.00
20.11.48	St Paul's School	80	Darjeeling	Special	12.00
21.11.48	St Paul's School	60	Darjeeling	Special	12.00
23.11.48	St Joseph's Convent	80	Gielle Khola	Special	11.45
24.11.48	Loreto Convent	100	Darjeeling	Special	12.00
24.11.48	Loreto Convent	30	Darjeeling	6 Down	8.25
25.11.48	St Joseph's College	95	Darjeeling	Special	12.00
26.11.48	St Joseph's College	95	Darjeeling	Special	12.00
28.11.48	Victoria School	60	Kurseong	Special	13.45
29.11.48	Victoria School	60	Kurseong	Special	13.45
30.11.48	St Helen's Convent	100	Kurseong	Special	13.45
3.12.48	Dow Hill School	65	Kurseong	Special	13.45
4.12.48	Dow Hill School	80	Kurseong	Special	13.45
5.12.48	Goethal's Memorial School	65	Kurseong	Special	13.45
6.12.48	Goethal's Memorial School	78	Kurseong	Special	13.45
7.12.48	St Helen's Convent	8	Kurseong	2 Down Mail	15.35
8.12.48	Goethal's Memorial School	22	Kurseong	2 Down Mail	15.35
10.12.48	Goethal's Memorial School	11	Kurseong	2 Down Mail	15.35
10.12.48	St Helen's Convent	6	Kurseong	2 Down Mail	15.35
10.12.48	St Andrew's Colonial Homes	50	Gielle Khola	Special	11.45
11.12.48	St Andrew's Colonial Homes	80	Gielle Khola	Special	11.45

Fate seemed to have been working against me with a vengeance, for not only had the loco department been ruined and everyone allowed to do just as they liked, but there were colossal oil and coal shortages to face and the office and discipline in general to put right. The task has been stupendous, but I am glad to say it is beginning to bear fruit at long last. But what makes me feel very bitter about things is that Holguette is being patted on the shoulder and is being made much of. The same time I resumed duty at Tindharia, he was given an increment of Rs100, which was a similar amount which the Agent had sanctioned me for additional responsibility, and also revised his agreement with an increment of Rs25 a year against Rs15 which had been sanctioned him when he first joined. Nothing is done for me however, and when I spoke to Jimmy about my t.a, he told me that he could do nothing about it. What surprises me though is the fact that the Agents have now agreed to give Holguette Rs100 a month as a fixed travel allowance for the duration of the monsoons, the excuse being that he will have to do all the outdoor work while Cowley is acting GM.

Suffice it to say, I feel the pinch and badly too. The hole of nearly Rs300 in my income and no fault of my own!!! Had things been going well for the Railway I couldn't really grouse, but with a drop of 9½ lakhs on my best endeavours and Rs60,000 above on April's figure for the current year, certainly helps to make some people see red – what!!! Cowley has budgeted for an income of Rs20 lakhs this year (having only made a bare 24 last year), but at the pace earnings are following, I doubt whether we will get through the first half of the present year. Added to this the staff are screaming for better terms and the workshop crowd very near went on strike a few days back with the last increments Jimmy had sanctioned them. He certainly has a headache to face when he comes out, because matters are being kept in abeyance until his return, and the agents have made it only too clear that they are not meddling. That is the position of the DHR today and will leave you to draw your own conclusions.'

The second letter was dated 18th November 1947:

'To be honest I have had a pretty tough time with staff problems ever since I came down to Tindharia, more so since Jimmy went away on leave. The demands of the Union are never ending and they seem to take a delight in setting up the illiterate staff all manner of impossible requests and love putting their Heads of Departments into embarrassing and unenviable positions. I am well near sick and tired of things in Tindharia and to add to our troubles, the Railway is not doing as well either. Our earnings are now down to half of '46 and to about 30% of what they were in '45. We have just got over a strike, which lasted about 36 hours, and which might have gone on indefinitely had not the Government of India stepped in and agreed to arbitrate. Jimmy is still on leave and makes out that he hasn't been able to secure a passage so far. The Government is taking over the Extensions from January as they are linking up Kishenganj with Siliguri. Due to the two Dominions not seeing eye to eye about many things, Gillanders are trying their best to force a decision on the main line at the same time, as they don't wish to hang on to a played out toy any longer. You will be surprised to hear that the Darjeeling station is still going up and has not been completed as yet, and that I am still waiting to get into my new house. Basu seems to be working backwards ever since he left Kurseong. I shall not forget to send you a photo of both buildings when they are completed.'

Despite the changing colours on the political map of Asia, the British tried to ensure that it was business as usual in Darjeeling, where commerce was still conducted without caste and life could remain as close to normal as was possible. The Rink and Capitol cinemas were as popular as ever, the former having been a venue for roller-skating until the superb arena was built at the Gymkhana Club, whilst the latter had the added distinction of being in front of a laboratory where a pockmarked man with one eye ran an illicit business supplying guinea pigs as children's pets! For a modest 4 annas you could obtain a seat on the front benches of either cinema and join in with the locals whistling or shouting at Randolph Scott chasing the villains or at Tarzan swinging through the jungle. Although there was no padding, the seats for 15 annas gave some assurance by being placed a little distance from the over-excitement of the front benches, whilst 1 rupee 4 annas bought a simple cushion and 2 rupees 8 annas provided the best money could buy. However, in winter the entire audience were obliged to bring their own hot-water bottles and wrap themselves in blankets to keep warm!

With hundreds of excited schoolchildren packed into the carriages, the locomotives hauling the 'Going Home Day' specials would often encounter difficulties on the steep climb between Darjeeling and Ghum. Coolie women could make good money carrying the school trunks on their backs up this section, for the added weight was liable to bring the train to a standstill.

Although somewhat smaller, the Plaza cinema in Kurseong had recently benefited from having two magnificent projectors installed, which delighted the audience as it could mean there were no breaks in the film to change the reels. They had been bought by the owner from a sale following a fire at a rather grand cinema in Calcutta, but it seemed that having to cope with two machines was more than his hapless projectionist could now cope with. It was recalled that he was prone to showing the reels out of sequence and confusing just about everybody with the story, although some felt the realism had gone too far at one showing when the monsoon caught the corrugated-iron roof and sent it clattering down the valley. It happened during a film featuring Myrna Lloyd and Tyrone Power, and there was more than a touch of irony that it was the Louis Bromfield classic entitled '*The Rains Came*'!

The racetrack at Lebong retained its attraction for those who wanted a flutter on the horses, and with there being few roads in the area, the ability to ride was a mark of one's credentials for working in the hills and tea estates. Lebong had grown around the military cantonment and was about five miles from Darjeeling, the village being in full view from the eastern side of the Mall. Horse racing was introduced on the parade ground in 1925 and held in May and October every year, which coincided with the arrival of tourists, as well as royalty, British officers and tea planters. It was claimed to be the highest, smallest and most crooked racecourse in the world, with its track being but a quarter of a mile long, and was the only one where the horses would run anticlockwise, due to the terrain. It was certainly a contender to be one of the highest, and it may have been the altitude that confined most of the horses to being the local *tats* (hill ponies) and not the thoroughbreds seen at the Calcutta races. This did not diminish the fervour and excitement, for the stands would be packed every Wednesday and Saturday during the season, with the locals and visitors sharing in the questionable wisdom of betting and the delight of racing in the Himalaya. The actress Felicity Kendal recalled a later time when one of her teachers at the Loreto Convent celebrated her 75th birthday by borrowing a horse from a jockey and galloping at full speed round the track. Standing barely four feet tall and dressed in her full nun's habit, Mother Marie Antoinette mounted the horse and rode with consummate skill. '*I used to race as a girl ...*', she told the astonished onlookers, '*... but I haven't lost it, have I?*'

The boarding schools were a tradition the British had established since the early days, when families were faced with the agonising decision whether to return the children to the UK for education. Situated in the hill stations, the schools not only had the most agreeable conditions but were also ideal for parents to visit on vacation. Special trains were laid on by the DHR to meet the children arriving on the broad gauge at Siliguri, and after making a dash to save their seats in the tiny compartments, they would head straight for Sorabjee's restaurant on the platform. But the excitement of the journey was almost too much to bear and, as they devoured the set breakfast of cereal, thick slices of bread and butter, hard-boiled eggs and tea, porters

A busy scene at Darjeeling in December 1945. Of particular note is the bamboo scaffolding surrounding the construction of the new station in the middle distance, the old pleated canopy roof being retained as a temporary measure until the work was completed.

The Frank Thornton Jones Collection

The wonderful Witch of Ghoom. Studio postcards and souvenir prints were sold in the area for many years, but it is rare to find an illustration of the somewhat mephitic lady alongside the train. Her hand is characteristically outstretched for rupees in exchange for fortune telling, or in this case a photograph taken by Mr Andrew Robertson in 1899.

Courtesy: David Churchill

loaded their tin trunks into the freight wagons.

School specials were indeed good business for the Railway, and Hazel Craig recalled in her delightful book 'Under the Old School Topee' the annual adventure of taking the train to watch the sunrise over Everest from Tiger Hill. Rising at two o'clock in the morning, the girls of Mount Hermon School would make their way in the dead of the night to the station for the train that had been laid on to take them to Ghum, from where:

> '... we continued our hike to Tiger Hill. The sun didn't always oblige, that is it certainly came up, but sometimes the mountains were shrouded in mist. But who cared? This was our most exciting outing, not to be missed. It was here that boyfriends and girlfriends could walk hand in hand in the gloaming under the eye of a benevolent teacher. And it was here that I actually walked hand in hand with a Parsee boy, a once-only performance for both of us. When morning had broken we would go to the tea stall at Ghoom station and drink hot, sweet tea out of earthen 'chatties' (pots) before boarding the toy train for the return to school. Today this is a tourist attraction for visitors to Darjeeling, but it surely can't be as much fun as it was for us all those years ago.'

The schools were usually open from the beginning of March to the end of November, and boys arriving for the first time recalled the feeling of leaving the known world as the train clawed its way up the mountain. It had been bad enough saying goodbye to family and friends in Calcutta, and the pangs of homesickness could be overwhelming as the train rattled through the night to Siliguri. Changing to carriages the size of those on the DHR only heightened the anxiety for a new boy, and after having somehow survived the enveloping forests of the *terai*, the sight of the older boys leaping off the train at the loops and zig-zags and scrambling up the hill was all that was needed to convince them that they were escaping. What terror possessed them to get back on the train higher up could not be imagined, but in nine months' time their fears would miraculously have transformed into the high jinks of the *'Going Home Day'* Specials.

It was good business for the DHR, as the programme issued for the schools in 1948 shows. All the schools travelled at 2nd Class, with the exception of those from St Andrew's Colonial Homes who were obliged to take 3rd Class down the Teesta Valley and resume 2nd Class on the East Bengal Railway. The Railway also advised all stationmasters to see that the trains were not unnecessarily detained, which was something of an understatement as they were only too pleased to see the rear lamp swaying round the next bend!

It was huge fun for the children and preparations had to be made, including the purchase of the Malacca canes that were deemed as essential items to wave and beat at anything that had the misfortune to pass by the train. A giant crest of the school would be attached to the front of the locomotive, the board being made from vast quantities of exercise-book paper and newspapers matted together with glue. Nailed to a wooden frame and decorated with poster paint that had taken a walk from the art room, the shield would be guarded by the senior boys until it was time to secure it to the front of the locomotive with rope. Honour had to be staunchly defended, and it could come to blows if parties from different schools were obliged to share the train, although this was usually resolved by hanging the banners either side of the locomotive. The EBR engine crews continued with the tradition by attaching the school shields to the front of their locomotives before arriving at Sealdah, and former students have recalled seeing them subsequently being used to make shacks in the vicinity of the station!

With bunting and streamers flying from the carriages, the noise from hundreds of liberated schoolchildren had to be heard to be believed as the train stormed out of the station. Eager to impress, the boys would send the girls' hats spinning through the windows before leaping off and catching them, for it was an easy matter to climb back on board as the locomotive pounded its way up the steep gradients to Ghum. Indeed, coolie women would often have to run alongside the line carrying the school trunks on their backs, for the added weight was liable to bring the train to a standstill.

'Going Home Day' was a favourite song with the children leaving Mount Hermon School, the first verse being sung to the tune of the *'Camptown Races'* and soaring above the noise of the train:

Going home day has come at last, do-da, do-da
Going home day has come at last, do-da-do-da-day
We travel all the night, we travel all the day
We spend our money on the DHR, do-da-do-da-day

The melody then ran seamlessly into that of *'Riding down to Bangor'*:

Down from old Mount Hermon on the small toy train
After nine months mugging, back to home again
Teachers are so rosy, children are the same
Everyone is happy waiting for the train.

Ghum, Sonada, Kurseong, all are left behind,
Though the journeys very long, I'm sure we do not mind
When we reach Sealdah, hail it with a shout
Pan, berri, cigarette, hop the beggars out!

Ghum station was a popular stop for the children, for it appeared to be the gathering place of those verging on the mad. Stories were passed around of the witch who used to assail travellers on the train for rupees in exchange for a fortune telling conducted from the charms of her wretched shack. Local postcards were sold of her and a verse recalled:

One hundred years of age is she
The Indian Witch of Ghoom,
She tells of love, of wedding bells,
Of wealth, and coming doom.

Sorabjee's refreshment room on Kurseong Station. Before Partition in 1947, the ever-popular caterers could also be found at Siliguri and Darjeeling, along with all the broad-gauge stations to Sealdah (Calcutta).

Gwen Cattermull

The Indian-Odeon architecture of the new station for Darjeeling was a radical departure from the style the town had been accustomed to and certainly reflected the spirit of modernity James Shaw had long felt would benefit the railway.

Betty Shaw

The DHR saw the first use of a snow plough on an Indian railway in 1882, although falls on the line are a comparative rarity. Shortly before being taken over by the Indian government, an Up freight bound for Darjeeling was caught on camera with a tractor clearing the Hill Cart Road in the distance.

Das Studios

There was little doubt she was of an advanced age and had a relaxed attitude to personal hygiene, it being recorded that there was no truth in the report that she used Pears' soap! The doughty old crone wrapped herself in any odd piece of cloth that she found, the layers never being removed but simply adding to her bulk. Whatever gifts the witch possessed, there were no misgivings about the fortune she made, for it amounted to Rs10,000 by the time she died!

Nobody knew if Tom Tom Mary was a descendant of hers, but genetic transference had not been kind to the present victim of the children. It is said her name had come from being jilted by a British 'Tommy', which had possessed her to wear a soldier's tin helmet and no doubt howl at the moon. She would stack up to seven hats on her head and shriek abuse at the children leaning from the carriages, who had great sport in trying to knock them off with their canes.

More fun was guaranteed from the local Bhutia boys, for such was their malaise at having to bare all and sundry in the bitter cold when crouching to relieve themselves, they adapted their trousers to what became ingloriously known as *'ever-readies'*. This was achieved by the simple surgery of creating a slit in the rear seam, but whilst it certainly addressed their bodily needs, they appeared completely unaware of it being an endless source of amusement to the passing trains of school children watching them whilst they played marbles and other games that involved squatting!

The songs continued with the popular *'Riding Roads of Sunshine'* as the train squealed round the bends and slowly meandered downhill:

See the winding roadway on to Kurseong,
Purple is the sunset as we roll along,
See the plains before us, dark and far away
Calling us to hasten, going home today!

The stop at Kurseong was generally timed to allow for a visit to Sorabjee's refreshment room on the station, or for the more daring a dash to Munro's chemist shop on the other side of the road. Here you could buy soft drinks with a marble in the neck of the bottle, or for the little darlings hell-bent on horror, time for a quick gawp at the gruesome two-headed lamb preserved in a large bottle of formaldehyde.

The schools of Kurseong could put up as spirited a departure as any in Darjeeling. Shrieking with excitement as they ran downhill to the station, the boys and girls of the Victoria and Dow Hill Schools would reserve seats in the carriages of the waiting train with their luggage before looking for presents to take home from the bazaar. A hundred delicious Darjeeling oranges could be bought for one rupee, and if ordered in advance, would be packed in large conical baskets known as *gunny-bags* and delivered direct to the station. The excitement of Christmas would justify the purchase of holly and mistletoe from the local boys, but it was soon regretted as it was not the easiest of things to carry with suitcases and trunks in a crowded train. The girls were tempted by the bead necklaces and woven girdles peddled by Nepalese women on the platform, and there was always a ready market for the stink bombs and fireworks that would ensure a memorable exit as the railway officials dodged the water pistols and peashooters!

Pagla Jhora was eagerly awaited, where the monkeys became the favourite targets for torment by the children and their slingshots. However there was an enviable revenge with the animals chasing and pelting the train in return, which sent the children scurrying in mock surprise. The monkeys are still to be found guarding the outcrops between Gayabari and Mahanadi to this day, waiting for the final act of settling the score. Gayabari was also well known to the boys of the Victoria School for the shortcut from Gidapahar, which was found to be a useful escape route for those making an attempt at running away. However, it was equally familiar to the schoolmasters, who would wait here patiently for their charges and return them on the next train.

The reverse sidings offered more opportunities for mischief, with some former students recalling that they were able to jump from the carriages and run down the hillside to have a crafty fag before the train and their teachers reappeared. The Railway removed the steps from the carriages in an attempt to stop them jumping on and off and the hillmen from hitching a free ride at the reverses, but they were soon replaced after a 1st Class lady passenger put her foot on a step that was no longer there.

Darkness would creep into the forest as the school train passed Tindharia, and the singing would fade with a final verse as their fears came alive with the hauntings of the night:

Now we're riding homeward, through terai at night
On a silver highway, singing our delight,
Now the plains before us, now we swing and sway
Into Siliguri, going home today!

It was then time for the tales of the *churail*, a ghost who had taken the female form and fallen in love with

In its final days of the railway running as an independent Company, No.34 sidles past with a Down freight whilst a 1942 Vauxhall waits at a checkpoint for clearance to proceed on the Hill Cart Road. Renumbered 789 under the ISR system, the locomotive was one of four later sold to work in the coalfields of Assam.

Jill Cartwright

one of the locomotive drivers. The phantom used to wait for the train and travel with him, sometimes riding at the front of the locomotive and on other occasions sitting on the roof of the guard's carriage, depending on her mood. Her desire was to lead him to water, a useful situation considering the plight of the shortages, but there she would drown her victim. It was said that one should never look at her feet, which happened to be turned backwards, for that was sure to guarantee entrapment.

It was not just a question of avoiding the *churail*, for it was also believed that a number of *nats* (spiritual beings) lived in the trees and were best avoided on certain occasions, particularly after taking a bath. The demons were said to be always on the lookout to obtain possession of the human body and would willingly enter the soul when the pores of the skin were dilated. It was a useful excuse the schoolchildren offered to absolve them from such ablutions, although in retaliation, the adults travelling with the children reminded them that to secure immunity, they should also refrain from opening their mouths! Indeed, it was recalled that certain natives would snap their fingers at a person yawning, fearing their soul might take leave and be occupied by a *nat*, the noise frightening both to return from whence they came.

Even a change of trains at Siliguri was not a guarantee of a release from their anxieties, particularly following the newspaper reports that had appeared in *The Statesman* of a *'colossus'*, said to have been seen emerging from the jungle towards the Teesta river. An EBR engine driver on the 'Darjeeling Mail' claimed to have seen the 18ft-high two-legged being and had measured its footprints as 22in by 11in, which the Geological Survey actually took the trouble of examining. The primeval forests of Jalpaiguri were infamous for their legends of long-lost buried cities and secret avenues from the Himalaya, and nobody was prepared to completely dismiss the possibility of the 'Mail' being held up by the survivors of a lost race of giants!

But for all the air of innocence and convention that had become the hallmark of Darjeeling, the die had already been cast with the consequences of the war, and that would change the very fabric of life. It would not touch the hill station in any material way at first, but everybody knew that when Calcutta caught a cold, it was never long before Darjeeling began to sneeze. No entries were made in the records for the immediate post-war developments for the Railway, but James Shaw had said that plans had been discussed for the Railway to be replaced by a freight ropeway from Sukna up to the hill stations and a bus service to be run for passengers. The possibility of electrification may also have been considered, for the 1947 Gazetteer for Darjeeling advised that despite the powers not having been ascertained, it could be handled effectively with 3,000/5,000 kilowatts if such a proposition was deemed economic.

Nothing was to come of the proposal, nor of anything else, for the stage was now set for India to achieve its status of independence.

It was time for the Empire to lower its flag.

Chapter 8

The Restless Dream

Exhausted after the war, Britain was not inclined to protract the inevitable outcome of the debate regarding independence, and the last Viceroy, Lord Mountbatten, formally handed over control of India on 14th August 1947.

The final entry in the DHR Company books was made barely a month later on 19th September 1947, but a reading of the Directors' minutes gave the impression that it was business as usual. It was anything but that for the Nation, for new borders were being drawn across the land to accommodate the seemingly incompatible wishes of the Hindu and Muslim beliefs, and India was heading towards the greatest and most painful exodus in its history.

Gandhi tried every means at his disposal to oppose an enforced partition, firmly believing it was possible to establish a peaceful coexistence through a federation of village communities that acknowledged and respected each other's differences. He spent four months trekking across Bengal and Bihar trying to stop the massacres and began his fast *'unto death'* in September 1947 to bring an end to the violence. It only interrupted the carnage and he became the target for Hindu extremists, who felt drained by the suffering and disillusioned by the sermon. They saw the solution in mounting terrorist attacks, which led to his assassination on 30th January 1948, accused of giving too much away to the Muslim community.

Jawaharlal Nehru became the first Prime Minister of India and remained the unchallenged leader until his death in 1964. He had been Gandhi's choice in 1946, but their views had diverged over the matter of partition, which Nehru felt was the only solution that would allow the formation of a strong centralised state. Although the constitution formally gave most of the executive powers to the President, it was understood they were usually exercised on the advice of the Prime Minister and Cabinet, and could function only with their blessing.

The new Muslim homeland was an independent state called Pakistan, the acronym said to have been formed from the initials of the Punjab, Afghan Provinces, Kashmir and Sindh with the final letters of Baluchistan. As President of the Muslim League, Mohammed Jinnah became the Head of State, and with that came the positions of Governor General and President of the Constitutional Assembly. The three offices were distributed individually after his death in the following year, which unfortunately set the stage for further instability in the embryonic state. Never ones to miss an opportunity, the Communist Party of India had been agitating for the Gurkhas to also have their own homeland. They demanded that the district of Darjeeling should be formed with southern Sikkim and Nepal into Gorkhastan, but the cause was falling on deaf ears.

Partition caused a major redesigning of the railway systems in the north-east, for East Pakistan (which later became Bangladesh) absorbed a substantial part of the broad-gauge network. The new frontiers nearly severed Assam and the northern area of West Bengal from the rest of India, the only link being a corridor but 12 miles wide around Siliguri, and the only communication was dependent on the two-foot gauge DHR extension from Kishenganj.

In 1907, Siliguri had been described by O'Malley in the

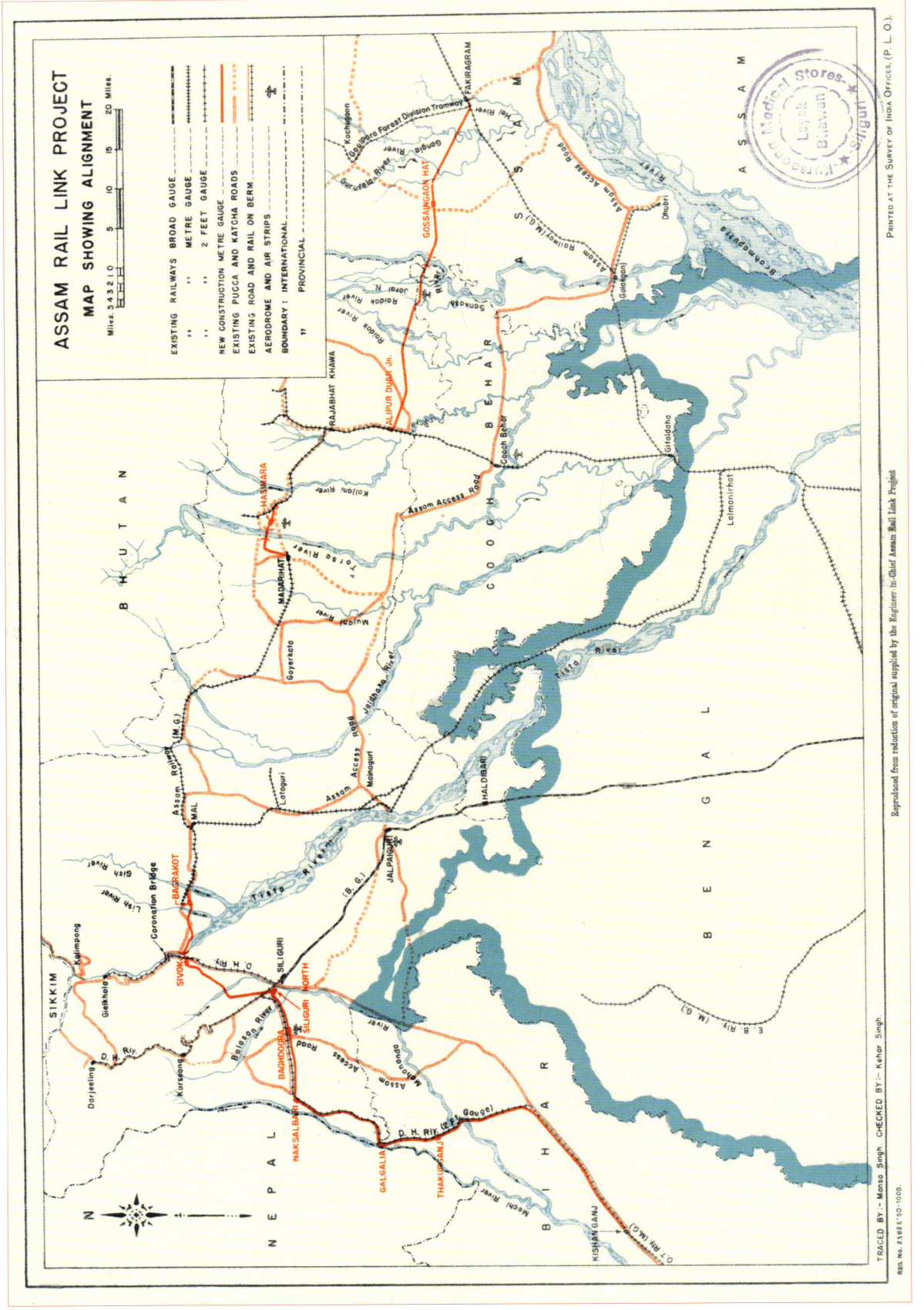

The map of the Assam Rail Link Project as produced in the official booklet. With the exception of the final approach to Siliguri, the first section of the new metre-gauge line from Kishenganj followed a similar route to the former DHR extension, although it was set back further from the roads to allow faster running. A completely new course was laid for the next stage from Siliguri to Sevoke to avoid the street and roadside running of the DHR Teesta Valley branch.

The DHR was purchased by the Indian Government on 20th October 1948 and became part of the North Eastern Railway on 14th April 1952. It was important that the line was given a new visual identity, and the locomotives and rolling stock were repainted in an unlined livery of red. The colour appears to have been subjected to a number of interpretations over the years that were accentuated by the effects of weathering, as can be seen on this Down train being hauled round the Batasia loop by No.32.

Das Studio

Bengal Gazetteer as *'a swampy malarious village with 784 souls'* (at the time Kurseong had a population of 4,469 and Darjeeling 16,924), although he recognised that the meeting of roads and railway had given it some local significance as being a focus for trade. Since then the town had grown from the nucleus of *godowns* and commercial establishments built by the wholesale traders in the Khalpara and Nayabazar areas close to the railway station. A bi-weekly market was established, and the community gained further eminence with it becoming the headquarters of the Deputy Magistrate. Business slowly expanded during the 1920s with the Railway transporting rice and timber, and sidings were laid to serve a Government sawmill and stores depots close to the left-hand bank of the Mahananda River.

The importance of the town rose during the Second World War as a distribution centre for the military, particularly as a centre for communications between the plains and the hills. It also became a convenient base to billet the battalions, and the town gained quite a local reputation for its nocturnal pleasures. However, matters came to a head when the District Commissioner received a somewhat extravagantly worded letter of complaint from the local prostitutes, claiming that they were *'overworked and underpaid'* and were to go on strike until all the outstanding bills had been paid from some particularly popular American quadroons!

On a more prosaic level, the town had five independent rice mills and three sawmills, whilst local merchants took the responsibility for distributing coal from the depots maintained by the two railway companies. It had also become the railhead for petrol and kerosene, and had the capacity to store 50,000 gallons of the fuels. Indeed it was a reflection of the times that the town now had six petrol pumps for public retail supply, whilst Darjeeling had but two, with one each in Ghum and Kurseong. The annual consumption during the War had been estimated at 250–300,000 gallons with rationing in force, whilst in peacetime 110,500 gallons had been sold for passenger vehicles, 140,000 gallons for goods and 102,000 gallons for private use.

Siliguri now held the key of the door to Assam, and the strategic pressures and commercial importance of the area demanded immediate attention. From this came the Assam Rail Link Project (ARLP), and its task was to develop a viable connection across an area of thick forests and jungle laced by torrential rivers gorging the foothills of the Himalayas. A four-point plan was devised, which would unite the metre-gauge network in the south:

(i) To Siliguri by completely replacing the whole DHR extension from Kishenganj (105kms/66 miles).

(ii) From Siliguri to Bagrakot (35kms/22 miles), by replacing part of the DHR Teesta Valley extension as far as Sevoke, before crossing the river to connect with Bagrakot, the terminus of the old metre-gauge Bengal Duars Railway that ran to Madarhirat. This new section alone would require over a hundred bridges.

A long freight comprising bogie and four-wheeled stock cautiously descends from Ghum towards Darjeeling in the early 1950s. The train is headed by an ex-Raipur Forest Tramway 'B' Class, which had recently been repainted in the red livery of the North Eastern Railway.

Das Studio

(iii) From Madarhirat to Hasimara (14kms/8½ miles), where the main challenge was bridging the mighty Torsa river, which until then had been regarded as impossible to span. This would provide a rail link to Hasimara, the terminus of the Bengal Duars line to Alipur Duar.

(iv) From Alipur Duar to Fakiragram (72kms/45 miles), which included a section that passed through the dense forests of Cooch Behar, previously only accessible by foot or elephant.

The new lines would unite the strands of the existing railways into one system, and thereby link Assam to the rest of the Indian network. The scheme was to be given the highest priority in order that work could begin as soon as possible on all four projects. Partition had brought too much dislocation for any of the neighbouring railways to take the work, and the project was obliged to start from scratch with no staff, no offices, no equipment and no stores. The ARLP came into being on 8th November 1947 and began with no more than a stenographer working in a small room at the Railway Board office in Delhi. Permission was obtained to transfer to the Koilaghat Office of the former Bengal-Assam Railway in Calcutta, which enabled officers drafted into the project to meet and formulate their plans.

As General Manager of the DHR, James Shaw felt that his days were now numbered and he longed to return to Britain to visit his family and old acquaintances. He also intended to assess the employment situation, but when he arrived at the end of 1947 he found food was on ration, a freezing climate, and men returning from war seeking work. He sailed back to India on 4th December, and with his ship docking at Bombay some nineteen days later, he eventually arrived in Kurseong on 27th December. His hands were tied, for the fate of the Railway and staff was being determined by the Government, however hard the Agents tried to fight on their behalf. His task was to keep the trains running as best he could, but in the words of his locomotive officer, it was *'a played out toy'*. Two days later he wrote to his old friend Geoffrey Plackett:

'Great changes have taken place since I went on leave and Government take over the extensions in October this year. On 1st February they start construction of a metre-gauge line from Kishenganj to the Duars (Bagrakot), bridging the Teesta at a point between Sevoke and the Coronation Bridge. The line from Bagrakot will be extended through to Assam. The reason for this construction is to have a line connecting Assam with Bihar, which does not pass through Pakistan. The B.A. Railway no longer exists from Calcutta to Siliguri. The line from Calcutta to Ranaghat is now the EIR and from Ranaghat to Hilli is the Pakistan Railway, and from Hilli to Siliguri is EIR run by Pakistan Railway under contract. At present we do not know what government plans are regarding the main line, but we will know definitely May this year when we are due one year's notice. There has been suggestion that we keep the main line and

operate the TV section for Government as the narrow gauge is remaining to Giellekhola.

The problem which is giving me a certain amount of concern is houses and office accommodation. As you are aware, the officers' bungalows, staff quarters and head office belong to the Extensions, and in October if Government say we want our houses etc; well, 'we've had it'. At the moment we are trying to get the people in charge of construction to take over the Club (which is closing down) as their office, and Woodhill Hotel as staff quarters, but the whole affair is most uncertain.'

Time and costs were against the ARLP building accommodation and stores in the field, and a main depot of ten sheds, each measuring 100 x 40ft, was rented in Siliguri from the Civil Supplies Department of the West Bengal Government. The Club at Kurseong, so beloved by the DHR staff and their families, was closed and hired as an office for the project, taking over most of the assets including the furniture and the billiard table. The main bar remained as a railway officers' club, and the DHR personnel were made associate members.

Nothing was going to stand in the way of the new metre-gauge line, for the orders to start construction were issued on 27th January 1948 and before the details of taking over the DHR had even been agreed. Surveying in the Indian plains was usually undertaken in the winter, the summers being either too hot for instruments to function accurately or too wet to allow movement along specific lines in the field. But time was already running out for the project, and aerial surveys had to be made to supplement those being hastily undertaken on the ground. The Deputy Commissioners of each district were ordered by the Provincial Governments to waive any formalities regarding the requisition of land, which not surprisingly led to some spirited exchanges with the tea planters. It was crucial to have their cooperation, for they held a great influence over life in the area and, as Engineer-in-Chief of the project, Karnail Singh arranged to meet them at a time and place of their convenience to discuss the issues.

There was still no news regarding the future for the remaining DHR staff, and the unsettled situation regarding their houses and staff quarters only served to exacerbate the matter. Tensions were at a height, and Gillanders asked James Shaw to attend a meeting in Calcutta. On 11th March, Joe Martin (the Locomotive Officer at Tindharia) wrote:

'You may be surprised to hear that Henry Cowley has been given his walking ticket. He was summoned down to Gillanders suddenly and was forced to submit his resignation immediately. They have allowed him nine months' leave but have told him to vacate his quarters by the end of the current month. This has been the result of a general uproar about the movement (imperceptible) of traffic into the district and Cowley's inability to handle tea dispatches on the Teesta Valley and stations in the terai. There's also been a lot of talk about preference being extended to the clearance of jute from the Kishenganj extensions and the attendant charges, which accompany such privileges. There were also rumours of Denis Holguette being implicated and talk of his services being dispensed with as soon as Jimmy Shaw returns with his family from Bombay at beginning of next week. The Agents have said nothing so far as to who will be selected to fill Cowley's place, but Bert Sarstedt is certainly making an all out effort to create impressions and to double up on his job. If he succeeds I have every intention of asking to be transferred over to Government along with the extensions in October, if they fail to give us notice in May about talking over the main line as well.

...The weather is fast warming up again and I am not looking forward to the GI's inspection early next week. I only hope we have a spot of rain to keep the dust down on the Teesta Valley and S.K. section, and Mr Banijee is coming, but why he is insisting on looking over the extensions when Government takes over in October is not clear, when only last year we went over all three sections with Mr Mubaya.'[1]

The Indian Government wanted to acquire the DHR Extensions Company, and a meeting was held on the Easter Sunday of 1948 between the Railway Board and Gillanders Arbuthnot. The Agent advised that the DHR and the Extensions Company had the same operating personnel and workshops, and as a consequence the Government would have to take over the Darjeeling line as well. The Articles of the Extension Company had clearly set out the manner of fixing a price, but the position had never been laid out for the DHR itself, and in order to resolve the problem it was suggested

---

[1] S.K. Banerjee was an Assistant Engineer with the Teesta section of the ARLP, but the position held by Mr Mubaya has not been established. M.F. Mobedjina was listed as the Assistant Engineer on the Kishenganj section.

James Shaw and the Maharajah of Burdwan at the Café de Paris in London

Betty Shaw

the Government paid the market price as quoted in *The Statesman*.

James Shaw returned to Kurseong and wrote to Geoffrey Plackett on 23rd April:

'Well Geoff, we've had it. Government is taking over the main line along with the extensions in October this year and, as indicated in my last letter, 'Master' may ask you to take me on as your assistant. The news regarding the main line has come as a sort of shock and the officers and senior subordinates are gravely concerned as to how they will fare. Government will be responsible for paying off under the Company's rules, the settlement due including gratuity of the staff who may not be offered or may not accept employment under Government.

You know Geoff, the officers' rules regarding leave furlough, and gratuity and we are in my opinion, bloody ill off, particularly in my case, the only European here and just back from leave after having just spent all my savings. I have put the case up to Gillanders hoping for last-minute changes to our agreement (which I'm afraid Government would view with considerable suspicion), but I visualise myself pleading to Gillanders for charity to the officers. So our sojourn in 'Elysia' is almost at an end. How sorry we are. Next month we hope to divide the 'spoils' – if any – Kurseong is absolutely dead, so we will live a very quiet life.'

Matters did not improve over the following months with arguments over the transfer of staff, the main trouble being the gratuity rules that were in fact more liberal than those applied to the State railways. Gillanders Arbuthnot issued three months' notice to all the staff on 20th July, whilst the officers were interviewed and recommendations sent to the Railway Board. Each officer was offered a job with the Government, but there was to be a substantial cut in the total emoluments. James Shaw was offered Rs1,150, with Rs550 for Bert Sarstedt (but in a lower gazetted service), Rs470 for Joe Martin and Bistu Basu, and Rs350 for Denis Holguette and Dr. Sen Gupta (both to be in a subordinate cadre). Gillanders were taken aback by the offers, for the demotions added insult to the injury, and they made their feelings known to the Board.

But it was to no avail, for Bert Sarstedt, Joe Martin and Dennis Holguette were offered about 60% of their previous salary and refused the offer. Gillanders eventually took on Bert Sarstedt themselves, whilst Joe Martin found work with MacNeill & Co. (Agents for the Rivers Steam Navigation Co.), and Denis Holguette secured employment with Kilburn & Co. (Agents for the India General Navigation and Railway Co.). James Shaw was incensed with his offer, for he had received Rs2,450 with the Company and was now being offered less than half '... *and I politely told them what to do with it!*'

The Government retained his services at his old salary until the end of the year in order that he could tie up any loose ends with the transfer '... *which meant going to the office occasionally and signing a few papers*'. Early in December he was given the opportunity to witness the construction of the new Assam Rail Link. Halting one night at Hasimara by the banks of the River Torsa, he was invited by the Engineer-in-Chief to listen in on a dispute with the tea planters over the construction of the bridge. The Managing Director of Davenport & Co. (Agents for the Hasimara Tea Co.) was also present and subsequently offered him the post of Chief Engineer to their tea gardens. Shaw wrote: *'There were good clubs, lots of Europeans and we were favourably impressed, so on my return I went to Calcutta and discussed terms and eventually took the job,'* but the spirit that had been his hallmark on the DHR had taken a severe beating and, on 23rd April 1950, he left India for the last time on a BOAC flight to London with his wife Betty and two sons.

He was tempted to move to the United States by an offer from Colonel Emmanuel, an American officer he had previously met in Kurseong. The relationship between the British and the Americans during the war had been somewhat acrimonious on the plains, the differences in battle skills, pay, uniforms, and food being ever-contentious issues. However, there was a much better rapport in the hills, and it was during the occasion that the Shaws were entertaining at *'Elysia'* that James met the Colonel and struck up a friendship. They shared a mutual interest in engineering and railway operation, and it was after the Colonel returned to the USA and took up a senior position with the Santa Fé Railroad that he offered James work. As it was, he decided that with a wife and two young children there had been enough upheaval to last the family a lifetime, and settled on returning to Paisley in his native Scotland.

The family bought a house in the Meikleriggs area, but as the winter winds whipped off the moors and chilled the looming granite buildings, it all seemed a far cry from the glories of Kurseong and *'Elysia'*. James opened a china shop in Sneddon, seeing that there was a market for bright modern crockery in the grey austerity of post-war Paisley. Two more business opportunities came with an ironmongers and a shop for household goods in Maryland, but when he met a friend from his seafaring days who promised to introduce him to Lloyds of London, the family packed their bags and moved south. Once there, he quickly rose to the position of becoming a senior surveyor, during which time he spent two years in Baghdad undertaking surveys for the construction of oil refineries and pipelines. He died in 1979, his spirited innovation and consummate skill in steering the Railway through its most difficult times defining him as one of the great legends of the DHR.

The Railway and its extensions were duly purchased by the Indian Government on 20th October 1948 and the Company went into liquidation. The total investment on the Railway and its two extension branches had amounted to Rs12,000,000 (approx. £900,000) by this time, which included a £150,000 security borrowed against its assets; £115,000 of this debenture was subsequently taken up in London. All the British employees had now gone, and the only member of the administrative staff who was retained was Bistu Basu; he had been the Resident Engineer since George Batterbury handed over in 1942, and his position was now to be redefined as Assistant Engineer-in-Charge.

'B' class No.42 at Tung with a Down passenger train, the engine being the first of the three built at Tindharia. The locomotive at the head of the Up service on the adjacent track would be taking water here.

Richard Booth

The opening of the new metre-gauge station of Siliguri North and the closure of the Teesta Valley extension in June 1950 relieved the DHR from the obligation of running passenger trains alongside the Hill Cart Road to Siliguri Town. The DHR track was diverted to run into the new terminus and the station was renamed Siliguri Junction. 'B' class No.33 (later ISR 788) prepares to leave with a well-loaded Up Mail. The two-foot-gauge track in the foreground was changed to serve the metre gauge when the DHR was extended to New Jalpaiguri and ultimately lifted when the station became a junction with the broad gauge.

John Clemmens

So the association of the Railway with Gillanders Arbuthnot ended and the baton was passed to the management of the Assam Rail Link Project. The change from two-foot to metre gauge on the Kishenganj extension was given top priority, for the only practical means of transporting the construction materials to the main storage depot in Siliguri was dependent on the old broad-gauge East Bengal Railway, and that now passed through East Pakistan. The all-India route would not only be longer, but would also involve transhipments from the broad-gauge at Sakrigali Ghat to a ferry on the Ganges that crossed to Manihari Ghat, after which there was the metre-gauge to Kishenganj and the DHR to Siliguri.

The conversion work at Kishenganj began on 13th April 1948, and at first progressed at a phenomenal rate, despite much of it being laid during the monsoon. The DHR tracks followed much of the road in tramway fashion, and this would clearly not be a suitable arrangement for the new arterial link to Assam. The metre gauge was therefore laid further back from the road to permit faster running, which necessitated the construction of new earthworks, embankments and bridges.

The timetable issued for 1st June was probably one of the final duties compiled by Denis Holguette in his capacity of Traffic Superintendent for the DHR, and it still reflected a similar service to the past years with one through passenger train running in each direction and departures from Thakurganj at 4.30 for Kishenganj and 5.20 for Siliguri. However, metre-gauge trains were already rolling into Thakurganj by 1st July, and Naksalbari was reached by the end of the month. This became the terminus for the DHR for the next year and was run as a joint station with the ARLP, for the work from here on was not going to be so straightforward.

The problem was the crossing of the Balasan River and the approach to be made to Siliguri. The fourteen-span bridge had been the longest on the DHR network, and the monsoon could turn its dried-up bed into a furious river that would tear at the piers and supports. A new bridge had to be constructed for the heavier metre-gauge trains, and after passing Matigara, a new route was surveyed for a direct access to Siliguri. The DHR branch had made its approach to the town by following what appeared to be two sides of a triangle, which avoided crossing the Panchanai River at a particularly difficult point. The metre gauge now being constructed was taken on a route that would follow the base of the triangle and lead directly to a new station to be called Siliguri North on the edge of the town.

A new course had to be found for the ARLP from here to Sevoke, for the DHR Teesta Valley extension strayed through the streets after leaving the original station in the centre of the town. A route was charted that would take the line from Siliguri North through the Sukna forest, and after 6½ miles reach a point where the Teesta could be crossed. The survey parties determined that an alignment could be made with a ruling gradient of 1 in 150, whilst the river could be bridged by a central span of 250ft with two 150ft spans on either side. However, working on this section was no easy matter, for reports started coming in of fighting tigers and herds of wild elephants during February and March of 1948. Armed guards were employed as protection, although nothing could match the evil reputation the area had for a particularly malignant strain of malaria and blackwater fever.

The construction of all four sections of the ARLP had been undertaken simultaneously, and it was a testament to the efforts of all concerned that the work had been completed by 9th December 1949. The last train from Naksalbari had run on the remaining spur of the two-foot-gauge Kishenganj extension during the previous day, but there was little ceremony as all the attention was now on Assam being once again connected to the rest of India by rail. The occasion was marked by the first metre-gauge passenger train from Kishenganj steaming into Siliguri North and a goods train running the full length of the new line to Fakiragram. The service for through passenger traffic began on 26th January 1950, by which time the cost for the 142-mile project was estimated to have been Rs88,971,204. It was a lifeline for Assam, for the State was dependent on the export of its tea for foreign exchange, and there was now the potential to exploit its small but vitally important oil reserves. History was to prove the new route was also strategically crucial for defence, for it conveyed a substantial part of the military traffic during the conflicts that were to come with East Pakistan and China.

The DHR did not initially connect with the metre gauge at Siliguri North, for it continued to amble alongside the Hill Cart Road and cut straight through the town to the original station. It was here that it connected with the remaining 40-mile spur of the broad gauge that once ran to Calcutta, but that had now been severed by partition. The Pakistani Eastern Bengal Railway[2] worked this section until January 1950, after which the Indian Government converted it to metre gauge and constructed a temporary pile bridge over the Mahananda River to connect it to Siliguri North and the new rail link to Assam.

The activity on the plains may have deflected attention from the political claims now being made in the hills, where the All India Gorkha League was turning up the heat by stating that the Darjeeling district, with Sikkim, Jalpaiguri and Cooch Behar, should be formed into the single state of Uttarkhand. However, there was little chance of a sympathetic hearing, for nobody else was in the mood to now consider severing Assam from the rest of India and passing over the control of any frontier shared with Nepal, Tibet, Bhutan and East Pakistan.

An early monsoon had been predicted for 1950, but there had been no warning signs that the rain that began to fall on the night of Saturday 10th June was the onset of a major disaster. The tea planters had welcomed it at first, for an unusually long dry spell had left the land parched and cracked, and the situation was becoming serious in a number of gardens. The evening train steamed into Darjeeling as usual, but it was only when the mail and newspapers failed to arrive the following day and the rain fell incessantly, that it was apparent there had been a breach. This was not an unusual occurrence for the DHR, but the intensity of the downpour was such that the hill slopes around the town were beginning to loosen. The news came on Sunday night that the water supply had ruptured, and was shortly followed by the town plunging into darkness as the electricity supply failed. The rain continued to fall relentlessly, and the only sound that could be heard above it was the rumbling of the sliding hillsides dragging houses down in slurries of mud. The entire police force was mobilised for the rescue operation and military aid was called in.

There was no respite with the weather the following day as Darjeeling examined the collapsed houses strewn across the road and valley. The cyclone finally retreated on the Tuesday, after which the full extent of the tragedy was seen as residents scrambled around

---

[2] The lines absorbed by East Pakistan became known by the former title Eastern Bengal Railway. This was changed to Pakistan Eastern Railway in May 1961, and following independence became Bangladesh Railway in December 1971.

Monsoon Destruction 1950

The damage to the upper sections of the Hill Cart Road brought on by the monsoon rains in June 1950 was such that trains did not steam into Darjeeling until early the following year.

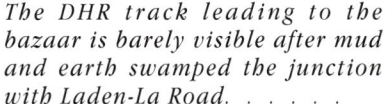

The DHR track leading to the bazaar is barely visible after mud and earth swamped the junction with Laden-La Road. . . . . .

. . . . . . whilst the foundations of the Hill Cart Road crumble away and residents pick their way over the devastation.

Das Studio

in the cloying drizzle. Forty-three inches of rain had fallen in the space of two days and the devastation was everywhere, whilst the feeling of melancholy was heightened by the muffled drums and mournful conches of the funeral possessions now moving through the bazaar. Destitute workers from the tea gardens struggled their way across the savaged land and began to arrive in the town in search of the relief centres being opened for those made homeless.

The tea planters had virtually run the area over the years, and it was to them that the new Deputy Commissioner turned for help with organising the recovery from the disaster. It was true that independence had bitten hard into the political life of the land, but it was still of little concern for many of the native Indians outside the major towns and cities. They had little awareness about who had ruled them in the first place, and whether it had been the Moguls, the Maharajas, or the managers of the tea estates, there had always been *someone* in charge who organised their lives and dispensed justice.

The Planters' Association rose to the occasion magnificently, and by the Thursday had arranged for relays of couriers to get the mail to Siliguri. The road and railway were so damaged that the train service was suspended until the beginning of the following year, and a temporary footpath was cut into the hillside to connect traffic with the old Military Road running close to the ridge of the mountains. Porters who had been used on Everest expeditions were now working as guides on the path, and ponies were proving invaluable in carrying stranded families back to the tea plantations. The Army assisted in restoring power and water to Darjeeling and began the onerous task of clearing the streets of landslides, collapsed buildings and fallen trees. Food supplies were now presenting a serious problem and severe rations had to be imposed. Clubside Motors, as the agent for 'Airways India', undertook a reconnaissance of the area, and according to the official estimates, the storm had killed 121, injured 63 and demolished over 175 houses. The Socialist Party headquarters in Darjeeling advised that 200 bodies had indeed been recovered from the debris and feared there were many more still buried, whilst conservative estimates were given that 400 acres of tea had been lost.

One of the planters recalled that a huge surge of mud enveloped the Club and caused such a rush of air that it blew poor Mrs Dampier-Childs straight out of her room! This tall and formidable lady had been very much in charge of the male-dominated society and, recovering from her shock, was relieved to find that a massive boulder casting its shadow over the Capitol cinema nearby had at least remained intact. Earth had slithered down the hill and engulfed the old wooden DHR freight shed, whilst on the other side of the road further faults were exposed with the concrete construction used when building the new station. Several sections of the line and the Hill Cart Road had vanished into the valleys below, particularly between Sonada and Tung, where over half a mile had been washed away. The havoc in Kurseong was just as devastating and the breakdown of water and power supplies added to the misery. There were four major, three medium and numerous minor slips across the section to Siliguri, but the clearance work was already under way and the uphill section to Mahanadi station was opened to road vehicles by the Thursday.

The electricity came back on in Darjeeling during the following Saturday, but the waterworks remained disrupted and arrangements were made for pipes and spare parts to be sent by air in order that the supply could be restored. The hanging clouds and poor visibility prevented further reconnaissance flights by the Army, and the only link with the outside world was dependent on the coolies tramping the mountain path for Rs100 a day. Group Captain Lal and Major Banerjee finally managed to undertake a successful reconnaissance flight in an Indian Air Force Dakota, to explore the possibility of dropping food, but it was still found to be impractical unless the weather was absolutely clear. Trucks were commissioned to meet the immediate need, for it had been estimated there was 99,000 *maunds* of rice held in stock in the Government-owned Civil Supplies depot at Siliguri that could be transported to Kurseong, after which it could be transferred to ponies and mules bound for Darjeeling.

Refugees from the outlying areas continued to arrive in Darjeeling, and it was reported on Tuesday 20th that 11,700 *maunds* of rice and 300 *maunds* of salt were being loaded on the train at Siliguri for Kurseong. However there were still major obstacles near Mahanadi station, but it was thought five wagons of food could be got through if arrangements were made for its transhipment. Supplies for Darjeeling continued to be taken on foot, and plans were drawn up for a temporary ropeway across the major breach at Sonada to enable a daily transfer of 2,000 *maunds*. The planters, under Mr J.C. Henderson, proposed to clear the old Military Road from Ghoom to Kurseong to enable jeeps and light cars to get through, but the military was in full agreement with the Civil Authorities that the top priority was to open the main Siliguri-Darjeeling route.

The first trains steamed into Tung a week later, from which point a chain of coolies carried the supplies on a footpath through the forest. Meetings were held with local engineers, and after finding a suitable engine in Tung and that cable was readily available at Rangbhul, it was agreed that a ropeway could be constructed with the assistance of tea-garden labour. However, it was clear that the final stretch of the Hill Cart Road from Ghum to Darjeeling was going to take much longer to repair, and the Deputy Commissioner asked the military if the old route via Jalapahar could be used. An army of volunteers, including many schoolboys, pitched in to get this former route open, and the Chief Commissioner held discussions with Dr B.C. Roy, the Chief Minister for West Bengal, to see if a new alignment could be found for the railway. Whole parts of the mountainside had collapsed and houses were hanging in the air over the damaged line, but it was agreed that the opening up of the old Military Road did not necessarily mean that a new railway track could be built alongside it. The original route was retained, although it would not be until the following year that the trains would finally run into Darjeeling.

The section of the Assam Rail Link that ran across the plains came off relatively unscathed, most of the damage on the Kishenganj section being confined to the bridge between Adhikari and Naksalbari and the Mahananda riverbank between Thakurganj and Taiabpur. The new metre-gauge line to Sevoke was also destroyed at the river crossing, where the Teesta had washed away the banks and left only the central section of the bridge standing. But it was in the valley where the storm had done its terminal damage, tearing down the earthworks and track of the DHR line and severing all communication with Kalimpong. The Chief Commissioner of Railways reported to a Press Conference at the end of June that he feared the two-foot-gauge line up the valley would have to be abandoned. It was quite simply going to be too expensive to make the alignments that would be necessary to rebuild it, for the new Nation now had new priorities.

The closing of the Teesta Valley branch made it no longer necessary to use the original town station as the lower passenger terminus for the Darjeeling line, for trains could now start from Siliguri North and the connection with the Assam Rail Link. As a consequence, the station was renamed Siliguri Junction, and a new track was laid that led the DHR away from the Hill Cart Road to a diamond crossing with the metre gauge. A locomotive shed and coaching depot was built just to the north of the station, which the approaching train passed by taking a long sweeping 'S' bend before drawing to a halt alongside its own platform. The old Siliguri station was retained as the southernmost goods terminus for the DHR, and trains of merchandise bound for the markets continued to work alongside the Hill Cart Road and avoid Siliguri Junction. This section became known as the freight bypass route, and one of the most important workings was the weekly market special to Tindharia carrying all the necessary commodities for the workshop staff.

The forty-two railway systems of India were consolidated into six zones on 14th April 1952, and the Darjeeling line was part of a package that merged the railways

The Joy Ride Railway was constructed near the station at New Delhi by the Corps of Engineers in 1953 as part of the 30-acre site to celebrate the centenary of railways in India. 'B' Class No.48 heads a train on its leisurely twenty-minute journey round two miles of the exhibition site.

H.C. Towers, courtesy of the Narrow Gauge Railway Society

The crew of No.48 refill the saddle tank from the stand pipe as passengers board the train at the Kanchenjunga station on the Joy Ride Railway in Delhi. The station was designed with clean angular lines that reflected a new generation of Indian architecture.

H.C. Towers, courtesy of the Narrow Gauge Railway Society

of Oudh, Tirhut and Assam to become the North Eastern Railway. The closing of the two extension lines from Siliguri enabled the Railway to look at its weary locomotive stock and sort out the quick from the dead. The Walford diesel had already been sent back to Calcutta, but it was the original 'B' Class No.17 that was the first of the steam engines to be withdrawn and three more followed in May, with all their vital parts being kept for spares.

Considering the trauma the country had suffered, there was little to celebrate in India after Independence, but for the masters new to their tasks, the centenary of the Railway system in 1953 could not have been more propitious. It was decided to stage an exhibition on a 30-acre triangular site close to New Delhi station, where sidings could be laid for easy transportation of rolling stock from all over the country. Murals depicting numerous forms of transport in India decorated the walls, and the centrepiece was the Indian Railways pavilion housing exhibits from the six new major railway zones. The displays ranged from the curiously titled *'Fluff to Feather'* model railway that illustrated the development of signalling in the Eastern Zone, to a collection of semi-precious stones found whilst boring tunnels on the Central Railway. But for many the star attraction was the splendid '00'-gauge working model of the DHR in the North Eastern section, and as a bonus there was an example of the full-sized line operating outside.

Over two miles of two-foot-gauge track had been laid by the Corps of Engineers around the area at the apex of the site, and in the course of a twenty-minute ride, the train took its passengers through a tunnel, across artificial hills and over a number of model bridges. It

A 'B' Class in the North Eastern Railway red livery scurries round tortuous bends with a Down train bound for Siliguri. The twin white lines at the base of the coal bunker and cab sides usually denoted that the locomotive was one of those designated for hauling the 'Mail'.

Below: 'B' Class No.32 climbing round the top loop of Batasia with a Down train in the early 1950s. Built in 1912 and delivered to the DHR the following year, this was the first of the Class that was built by the North British Locomotive Company at their Queens Park works in Glasgow.

Das Studio

was officially known as the *'Joy Ride Railway'* and the DHR prepared two of its locomotives for the event, along with the observation saloon *'Everest'*, a new closed coach, an open toast-rack bogie carriage and a handful of four-wheelers. The main service was operated by 'B' Class No.48, which Tindharia had attached to a tender that might well have been lying around the yard since the days of the streamlined *'Jervis Bay'*. It was assisted by a two-carriage train hauled by *'Baby Sivok'*, which had been fitted with a tiny saddle tank and coal bunker, along with the date plate of 1881 to record the opening of the DHR. Trains ran from a very modern brick-built station that bore the name Kanchenjunga, which was staffed by uniformed employees from the Railway and fully equipped with a platform lever frame and signal, watering facilities and the like. The exhibition was declared open on the 7th March, and Jawaharlal Nehru was the first of the honoured guests carried by the DHR train.

The celebrations could not hide the fact that there was a price tag attached to independence, for as India was promoting a constitutional programme of justice, liberty and equality, neighbouring China was marching into Tibet. The invaders were now communists and, intolerant of Buddhist beliefs, brought about an exodus of the defeated escaping persecution. Many crossed the mountains and passed through Darjeeling, Kalimpong and the Teesta Valley, and the Hill Cart Road and the Railway became a lifeline. It was crucial that they were maintained in good order, which delighted the European families living in Darjeeling, many of whom were still running well-established businesses. They knew no other life and were not inclined simply to pack up and leave, although it was evident that the paint was indeed beginning to peel from the boarding houses and the masonry to fall into disrepair.

The British Raj may have passed into the history books with indecent haste, but Darjeeling was not going to give up so easily. It was a gallant effort by a dying breed, although it was inevitable that deeper cracks would appear as the younger generations moved away to new challenges and opportunities. Those who remained tried to maintain some semblance of normality in an abnormal situation, and there was plenty of room inside the adversity for eccentric behaviour to flourish. If they thought everything about them was sinking into a state of decadence, then one could always rely on the Club to maintain its standards. Indeed, a valiant stand was made by having a Melton Mowbray pie flown from Fripos Restaurant in Calcutta to Bagdogra airport every week and brought up to Darjeeling by the Thursday morning train, conveniently arriving just in time for lunch.

Mrs Kelly was one of many delightful characters who added to the singularity of the town, and lived just below the road junction near Keventer's restaurant. She was well known for her jams and jellies and equally renowned for her capacity in consuming alcohol, to the point that on one occasion she had to be carried home from a party on piggy-back by a Bhutia porter. She unfortunately relieved herself whilst he was staggering up the hill, but instead of becoming embarrassed, shouted out to the onlookers *'Look dearies ... behold the lakes of Ireland!'*

Carl Smart was the undertaker, known to his friends as *'Carlie'* and to the less charitable as *'Kanwar'*, a local term that related to his unfortunate affliction of being cross-eyed. This was a source of great fascination for the children, who would eagerly watch him in the restaurant chasing the last pea on his plate believing there were still two. He always wore a cloth cap pulled over his eyes and a black-and-white band on his coat, and when meeting him in the street, would complain that business was very bad whilst looking the other person up and down as if gauging their size.

Colonel McLevie was remembered as a short, dark gentleman with a white moustache and a nut-brown bald head. A staunch churchgoer, he would occasionally read the lesson or take the collection, and was known to the children as *'Abide with me – hi-di-diddle-diddle-de'*, owing to the muttering he would make under his breath when the hymn was being sung. The story was passed around that his standing in the town tarnished somewhat after he was admitted to the Eden Hospital following a calamitous accident with a detached enema. Another colonel by the name of Mercer was regarded by many as the most eligible bachelor in town, and became known as *'Colonel Mercy'*. He could always be relied upon to come to the help of somebody in difficulty, and once even offered his truss as a form of first aid in an emergency to help an old lady in distress!

Tales were also told of the antics hoteliers would contrive to encourage custom, and when all else failed, the old beliefs of witches and ghosts were sure to come to the rescue. One very eccentric old lady by the name of Betty Brooks, known to the locals as *'Brooky'*, used to live in a large house called *'Durely Chine'* with her cat and a shaggy black-and-white dog named *Jumbo*. Poor *Jumbo* developed some disease of the mouth and gums, and after losing all his teeth, sadly had to be put down. *Brooky* became very depressed after this, and one day went to the bazaar and purchased a length of stout rope before going to Pliva's Restaurant (now Glenary's), where she ordered a *burra-peg* of rum and gave the bartender a small bottle to fill for her to take home. *Brooky* hanged herself that night from the staircase, a tragedy that sent shock waves across Darjeeling, but it was not long before rumours of her ghost began to abound. Residents in the *'Ivanhoe'* guest house, just above *Brooky's* place, complained that they could hear cries of *'pooss ... pooss'* late in the night, which they claimed was *Brooky's* ghost calling out to her cat. One night, the braver of the house guests decided to investigate these strange cries, and following the sound, were led to a rough pathway beside *Brooky's* house, where they found a small Nepalese boy crying out as loud as he could in a long wavering call. He had been employed by a rival guesthouse to scare off the residents of *'Ivanhoe'* so that the owner could get their custom!

Business was also becoming difficult for the DHR, and for the first time in its life it was losing money. The truth was that the revenue from the Kishenganj section had in effect been subsidising the main line to Darjeeling, and now the money was no longer there. Banshidhar Dikshit had been made the Permanent Way Inspector for the entire section from Siliguri to Darjeeling, and recalled that there were frequent derailments as the track began to break and the sleepers rot. A proposal was made to relay the track with 50lb rails on a five-year cycle, but when the points and crossings failed to arrive, he made twenty sets of 1 in $8^1/_2$ crossings[3] in his own blacksmith shop and Tindharia manufactured the tongue rails[4] to his drawings. The track was relaid between 1952 and 1956, by which time twenty sets of points finally arrived from Japan, but these were found not to fit. Mr Dikshit made a number of further changes that enabled ten sets to be laid in the yards and the remainder held in store.

A move was made to standardise the locomotive fleet in February 1954 by withdrawing No.9, the sole surviving 'A' Class saddle-tank in working condition, although the remains of No.11 were still to be found in Siliguri yard some fifty years later! There was no useful work for the Garratt since the closure of the two extension lines and it was scrapped in the following November; the fact that it had held on to life for so long disproves the assumption that it was an unsuccessful locomotive. By 1955 the numbers were down to 32 locomotives, which included the two 'Pacifics', although with their home line converted to metre gauge, there was some debate as to for what duties they could now be used.

Although the 'Pacifics' were excellent machines and in good working order, they were unsuitable for the climb to Darjeeling, and since 1950 had been restricted to shunting in and around the yards of Siliguri. They had been designed solely for use on the Kishenganj line, where the points leading to the run-round loops and sidings were all laid at a divergence of 1 in 12. The pivot of the two-wheeled Bissell truck under the cab was positioned to trail and not lead, and as such it had been the practice to turn the locomotives at the end of each run. It was decided to assess their suitability for the run to Sukna, but there was no turntable at the station and the locomotives were obliged to work tender-first for the return to Siliguri. It was found that the Bissell truck became prone to derailing when running in reverse on this section, which the Engineering Department sought to remedy by making the pivot on the centre pin solid. Unfortunately they had not consulted the Permanent Way Inspector and blamed the state of the track whenever the engines damaged the rails as they ran on to the run-round loops. The locomotives were worked up to Rangtong to see if they behaved any better, but it was found that the points at all the stations were set at 1 in $8^1/_2$ and could not cope with the now-lengthened rigid wheelbase of the 'Pacifics'. The only solution was to create a slack of $3/_4$in on the curved lead rail, which helped to a degree if the engines were driven very slowly over the points, but it was never really satisfactory. This left the empty carriage workings to Sukna as the only remaining duties they could perform, and they were often seen scratching around for some work to do.

In 1955 the Railway received an unexpected visit from Hollywood. Faced with competition from the new technology of television, the cinema industry fought back with big productions, and the wide-screen system developed by Cinerama caused a sensation. It had been launched in 1952 with a spectacular film, which was shot with a triple-lens camera and shown through three special 35mm projectors that lined up the images on a single wide screen. It was the brainchild of Fred Waller, a special-effects engineer and prodigious inventor who had set up his own production company in the wake of scepticism and a lack of investment from the major studio. A two-camera system had previously been attempted with filming the Atlanta fire sequence on *'Gone With The Wind'* in 1937, but this was dropped owing to the expense of fitting out cinemas with the specialist projection and sound equipment. However, the new Cinerama system caught the attention and imagination of the public, and the third production was a travelogue entitled *'Seven Wonders of the World'*.

---

[3] The measure relating to the angle by which the two rails branch at the 'V' in the points (the closer the ratio, the greater the divergence).

[4] The rail on the point that leads away from the main line.

The ZDM-1 diesel re-gauged from the Kalka-Simla Railway and sent for trial on the DHR in 1958 promised much, for it had been designed to work a gradient of 1 in 20 and negotiate curves of a 15-metre radius. However, it appears not to have coped well with the rapid changes in the super-elevation of the track, and it was soon passed on to work a children's railway in Delhi. Unfortunately it has not been possible to secure one of the rare photographs of the machine in operation on the DHR, but it was identical to NDM-1 502 seen here working on the Matheran Hill Railway.

(The late) Peter Bawcutt

The film was directed by Lowell Thomas, who had brought the young British officer T.E. Lawrence to international fame as a result of his news reports of the war in the Middle East in 1917. From the moment Lowell saw Cinerama demonstrated, he believed that it would give a unique and involving experience by showing sights from the mundane to the exotic in a most unusual way. He had thought that Cinerama would have been the ideal medium to tell the story of Lawrence of Arabia, but filming 'Seven Wonders of the World' appealed to his sense of adventure and would take his audience from the Pyramids of Egypt to the giant sequoia of Yosemite, stopping on the way to witness such diversities as Angkor Wat, man-eating crocodiles in Africa and a special benediction from Pope Pius XII.

If that was not exciting enough, the film crew spent ten days on the DHR filming a runaway-train sequence. One of the ex-Raipur Forest Tramway 'B' Class was painted in bright colours to show up better on the screen, and it was hoped that the film would bring some much-needed publicity. A story line was written which took an American tourist by the name of Drowsy Dan on the train to Darjeeling, and Indian Railways cooperated in every way it could, even to the point of holding up the scheduled service for hours to complete the filming. The journey was treated as high comedy, with the locomotive being fired by a domestic hand-shovel and the sand being strewn across the rails by two coolies called Moe and Joe. The train climbed against a backdrop of superb scenery until it ran into trouble when it met a baby elephant and its mother

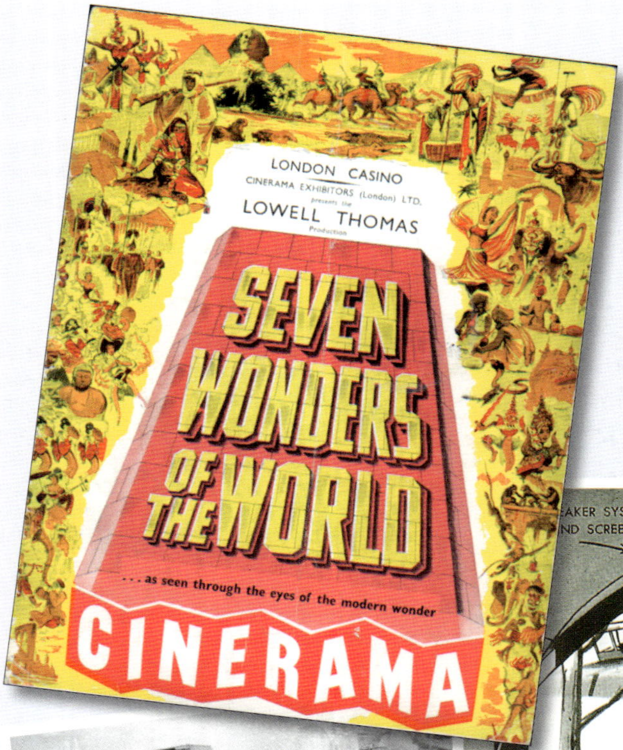

Hollywood comes to Darjeeling . . . .

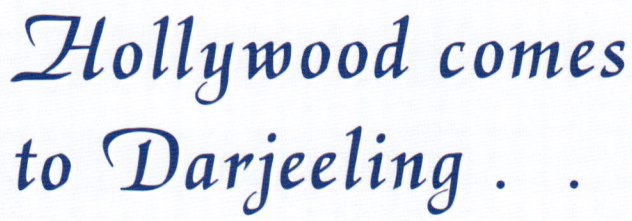

The DHR was used in the Cinerama programme to explain the triple-lens filming and projection system used by Lowell Thomas for the production of 'Seven Wonders of the World'.

Collection: David Churchill

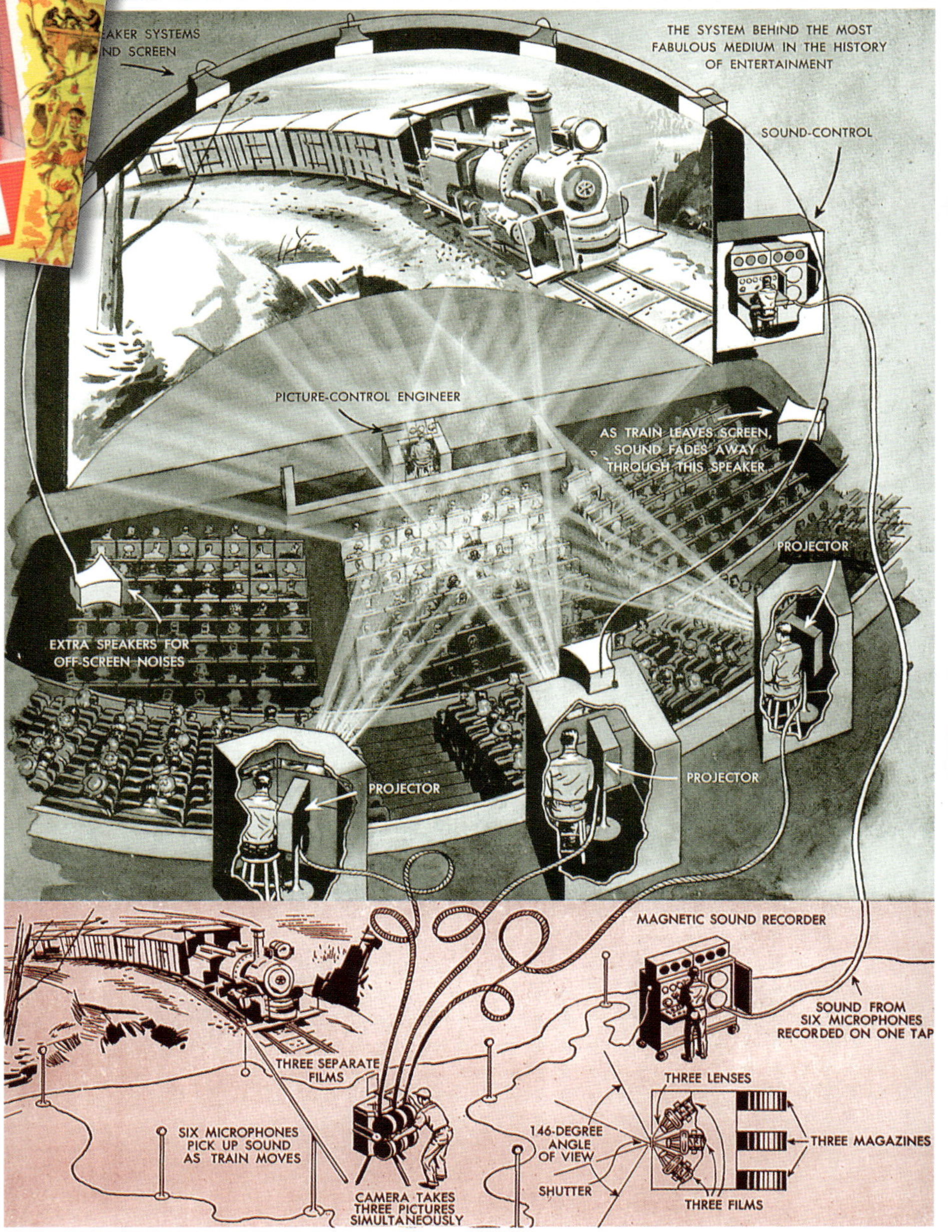

... in 'Cinerama'

With the triple-lens camera being set up on the right, Moe and Joe take up their positions as the two sanders at the front of the locomotive.

Although this sequence was filmed in the terai between Sukna and Rangtong, the story depicts the train having already climbed the loops and reverse sidings. A baby elephant and its mother are asleep on the track and the crew and passengers try to encourage them to move away.

The train has run backwards out of control as the astonished crew and passengers watch the young mahout Sabu leading the elephants away.

After racing back down the loops and reverse sidings, the engine crew catch up with their train as Drowsy Dan believes he has arrived at his destination.

asleep on the track. The crew and passengers tried to encourage the animals to move, but they took no notice until Sabu, a tiny elephant boy, arrived on the scene to take control. The astonished passengers watched as he led the elephants away, only to hear the sound of their train running backwards out of control. The film was speeded up as the train raced round the loops and bends, and created the impression of it being a roller-coaster. It had the audiences clinched in their seats until the train finally drew to a halt from the point where the journey had started, leaving Drowsy Dan waking up believing he has arrived in Darjeeling.[5]

Any excitement there had been in the hill station with the filming was short-lived, for in 1956 there was further Communist agitation and a series of strikes were called throughout the district. The troubles focused on two rival factions fighting for supremacy, and the police unfortunately shot six workers in one particular vicious dispute on a plantation. The managers took the bodies to Darjeeling hospital for identification, where it was noted that it had been the first time that Nepalese had shot each other. To make matters worse, there was also a feeling that India had grown less united than it had been at the time of independence. Part of the problem lay with the demand for boundaries between the states to be redefined on linguistic lines, for in the case of Bihar it had divided West Bengal in two along the Siliguri corridor. Such a reorganisation would have led to an increase in local power, and that would not sit comfortably with the view held by Nehru for control being held at the centre. There were also fears of creating minority groups speaking a different tongue but, despite the arguments, most of the state frontiers were redrawn in 1957 and the Siliguri corridor became part of West Bengal.

The town of Siliguri was expanding fast, and to open up employment opportunities, the Directorate of Industries set up a centre for training in carpentry and the manufacture of timber-related products. New roads were built to accommodate the growth of traffic, and the town soon became the largest transport and commercial centre in north-east India. The Hill Cart Road had become a main highway, although the DHR was still allowed to plod inconveniently along its side with wagons of freight. The old road-and-rail bridge that crossed the Mahananda was replaced by a new structure in reinforced concrete, which obliged the train to run in the centre before returning to the right-hand side in front of the shops, causing ever-increasing congestion and an operational headache.

The railway grouping was refined into nine zones on 15th January 1958, and the DHR became part of the newly-created Northeast Frontier Railway that had been formed mainly for strategic reasons. The NFR administration decided to see if the service to Darjeeling could be improved with the introduction of diesel locomotives, particularly having witnessed the success of the eight B+B machines specially designed by Arnold Jung of Jungenthal (Germany) in 1955 for other Indian hill railways. Nos.700–704 had

---

[5] James Shaw greatly disapproved of the film, feeling it belittled his beloved railway, and flatly refused to see it. However, his wife Betty did see it.

With the conversion of the Kishenganj extension to metre gauge, No.808 was relegated to the indignity of empty carriage working from Siliguri Junction on 12th October 1962. The sad condition of the 'Pacific' does not diminish the grace it would have lent to hauling a passenger train in its more glorious days.

John Clemmens

Workings on the extension to the bazaar in Darjeeling did not often attract the interest of the photographer, but a Down freight was caught on camera weaving across the road in October 1962, having just rounded the first corner after leaving the bazaar.

John Clemmens

been supplied to the 2ft 6in-gauge Kalka-Simla Railway (ZDM-1 Class) and Nos.501–503 for the 2ft-gauge Matheran Hill Railway (NDM-1 Class). The two classes were identical except for gauge, and the design was in effect two locomotives closely coupled, each having its own engine with a Voith hydraulic transmission system, and carrying the cab structure between them on a three-point mounting.

No.704 was sent from Kalka to be re-gauged to 2ft and taken to Siliguri for a trial on the DHR, but it appears that it soon ran into troubles. The clearances on the line were certainly more restricted than on the other hill railways, and although the story may be apocryphal, it is said to have collided with the canopy of Darjeeling station. This was measured in 2005, and whilst it must be accepted that the height of the trackbed may have altered over the years, it appears that the cab would certainly have run into one side of the roof on the bay platform but cleared it alongside the main line. The former Permanent Way Inspector was of the opinion that the articulation of the diesel did not cope well with the changes of super-elevation of the track, added to which the climate may have affected the automatic sanding equipment and there was no provision for it to be applied by hand. Whatever problems it did encounter, it was not long before the diesel was secured to a transporter wagon and passed on to Delhi to work a children's railway at Pragati Maidan.

The passenger service under the first year of NFR control featured two trains operating the full journey in each direction. The fastest was the 1D that departed Siliguri at 6.10 after connecting with the incoming *North Bank Express* on the metre gauge from Sakrigali Ghat. The arrival in Darjeeling was timed at 12.00 noon, after which 2D would be the returning train at 13.25 to reach Siliguri at 18.50 for the 20.45 departure of the *North Bank Express*. The 3D Mixed was timed for passengers arriving at Siliguri on the *Avadh Tirhut Mail* and would leave at 12.30. Although it was termed as 'mixed', 3D did indeed carry the mail and as a consequence, the carriages and accompanying freight wagons used for this service were soon repainted from NER red to the NFR blue in order to match the livery of the metre-gauge train. The DHR train was scheduled to be in Darjeeling at 18.50 and return the following morning as the 4D Mixed at 8.50, arriving in Siliguri by 15.10 for the 16.00 departure of the *Avadh Tirhut Mail*. The two through services were supplemented

No.53 at Kurseong on the front cover of La Vie du Rail *in 1957. Although the colour of the livery could be affected by the climate, the difference in tone when compared to No.39 (below) was probably more due to the printer's ink. Note the names of the crew painted on the side of the coal chute.*

Courtesy: La Vie du Rail

A superb study of an immaculate No.39 in NE livery at the head of a Down train waiting to depart Darjeeling. The locomotive was the first of the three Baldwins to be built and was delivered to the DHR in 1917. Even the fire-irons carried beneath the re-railing beam look polished, and the condition of the machine is a testament to what can be achieved with some care and attention.

Das Studio

With the soaring peaks of Kanchenjunga, the third highest mountain on Earth, dominating the razor-backed skyline of the Himalaya, an Up train nudges round the top loop at Batasia. The town of Darjeeling can be seen in the middle distance, and the red NE livery of the locomotive and the NFR blue of the carriages identifies the date of this photograph as circa 1960. Note the wicker coal basket on the cab roof and the brakesmen between the four-wheeled freight wagon and bogie coaches.

Das Studio

Descending from Ghum with the Up Mail to Darjeeling in 1960, 'B' Class No.790 looks smart in her red livery hauling four carriages and a matching four-wheeled covered wagon in the recently applied NFR blue.

Das Studio

The second of the Baldwin-built trio No.793 (44913/1917) climbs across the bridge on the top section of the Batasia loop with a Down Mail in 1960, the crest of the Himalaya being seen in the distance.

Das Studio

by the early morning mixed train from Kurseong for schoolchildren and local workers, which left at 7.00 and would stop at all the halts and stations. This was due to steam into Darjeeling at 9.30, where it would wait until 17.10 to provide the return 10D service that was timed to sidle into Kurseong at 19.45.

If the growth of Siliguri was to be sustained, then something had to be done about its dependency on the metre-gauge line for transport. Partition had set back the rail link with Calcutta to the pre-1915 situation, and it was again necessary to cross the Ganges by ferry, followed by a transfer to the broad gauge. There was also concern about the strategic vulnerability of the area, and although Kanchenjunga and the Himalayan crests had always given a sense of impenetrable security, the differences between the people on the plains and those in the hills were becoming more evident.

Darjeeling was standing on a watershed of cultures and religions, and a serious wake-up call came in 1959 when the 14th Dalai Lama escaped from Chinese persecution and arrived at Siliguri by train. He was welcomed by 7,000 Tibetans to the accompaniment of his native music wailing from the loudspeakers on the station, but his exodus was a symptom of the profound differences that had developed between Nehru and Zhou En Lai. These festered into a simmering dispute along the Indian border until the situation flared into heavy fighting, making the Chinese mount a full-sized surprise attack in October 1962 with Nehru suffering a humiliating defeat. The Chinese had amassed artillery on the Nathu La barely thirty miles away from Darjeeling, and there was a fear that it would lead to an invasion of Northern Sikkim. An atmosphere of panic spread through Darjeeling, and many fled the town following the rumour that the Chinese could land paratroops in Siliguri and sever the area from the rest of India. Indeed, there was further alarm in August 1965 following an attack by Pakistan near Lahore. Although the fighting was confined in the west, there was panic in Darjeeling after India refused to comply with the Chinese ultimatum that it must dismantle the defences it had since installed at the Nathu La. The United Nations subsequently sponsored a ceasefire, and the hostilities ended on 22nd September.

The world had already witnessed the deterioration of relationships in 1962 between democracy and communism with the building of the Berlin Wall during the previous year, and the tension was now being taken to the edge with the Cuban missile crisis. America stood firm, and bolstered by its success when the Soviets retreated on 28th October, it confidently offered its support to Nehru. China decided to halt its advances on 21st November, having the whole of the Assam plains at its mercy with the capture of Bomdila, a key defence and administration position in the Northeast Frontier Agency. Beijing felt the objective had been achieved by establishing its domination over the democratic model India was pursuing, and was content that its upstart of a neighbour had been taught a lesson. Although China withdrew its forces from much of the territory, some of the strategically important border regions were retained, which kept the whole area on the alert and Darjeeling aware of its new importance to the defence of India.

The war with China had caught India on the hop and had shown it was tactically weak on its north-east frontier. There was no doubt that the Assam Rail Link had met the immediate needs of the area, but it was only a single-track railway and was vulnerable to the annual ravages of the monsoon. The problem was that the line ran too close to the foothills of the mountains, and as such caught the full force of the swollen rivers gorged by the deluge of rain. Bridges and railway embankments were relentlessly torn away, causing havoc with commerce and in particular the tea industry on which so much of the economy depended. Just about everything that was needed to keep the business running was dependent on being transported by rail or river, and it was not only the trains that were disrupted. The loading points for the river steamers were forever changing, with the surging water cutting new courses into the Brahmaputra and clogging up others with the deposited silt, added to which the boats were obliged to pass through East Pakistan before reaching their destination.

The powerful Indian Tea Association had been highlighting the problems to the government since the mid-1950s, and had stressed the urgent need for an alternative line that was free from the devastation of flooding. It was an unfortunate coincidence that the rains came at the same time as tea production reached its peak, and the hygroscopic nature of the dried

The elegance of Darjeeling Station in 1960. Its classic architectural lines reflected the Modernistic spirit of the 1940s, but this was compromised by the construction of an ugly rectangular rest house astride the flat roof in 1983.

Das Studio

leaves created its own set of difficulties with storage. There were simply not enough wagons to meet the seasonal demand, and those that were available often leaked, whilst the stations rarely had adequate covered accommodation for the tea waiting to be loaded.

An alternative alignment had been surveyed between Mal Junction and Bunnaguri during the second Five-Year Plan, but it had come to nothing and a rail link with Assam without a break of gauge was now crucial. It was decided to extend the broad-gauge network from Calcutta through the Siliguri corridor, convert the metre-gauge section to Jalpaiguri back to 5ft 6in for the second time, and continue with another new line through Falakata to Koch Bihar and into Assam. A new station was built in the Siliguri corridor three miles to the south-east of the town, and there was no real surprise with the news that it was to be called New Siliguri and that the NFR was printing the name on its tickets. However, when it was found that the station was lying just inside the administrative border of Jalpaiguri, the district authorities took the case to court to insist that it bore the name of their town, although it was confusingly some 25 miles away.

It was an easy matter to lead the remaining section of the metre-gauge from Siliguri Town into New Jalpaiguri station and build a set of platforms close to those for the broad-gauge. The DHR also had to make the connection, and a new route was formed that ran close to the metre-gauge from Siliguri Junction to Siliguri Town, the tracks coming together to share the crossing of the Mahananda river. It was a welcome move, for it allowed the freight bypass route alongside the Hill Cart Road to be abandoned as it was getting tangled up with the road traffic and causing no end of problems. It was a relatively straightforward matter to continue the tracks for the five kilometres from Siliguri Town to New Jalpaiguri. Freight trains were running into the new transhipment sidings with the broad and metre gauges in 1962 and the passenger service was inaugurated in April 1964.

It is said that B.C. Ganguli, the General Manager of the Northeast Frontier Railway, modelled the layout of New Jalpaiguri station on American practice, with extensive marshalling and transhipment yards to facilitate the change of freight between the three gauges. Approaching from Calcutta, the Up and Down lines of the new broad-gauge crossed the Mahananda river by separate bridges before taking a ninety-degree turn to pass under a road bridge serving the new railway hospital. The transhipment yards opened out to the left and broad-gauge marshalling yards to the right, flanked by numerous railway offices. The two main broad-gauge lines continued into the passenger station, one branching into a loop and served by the side of an island platform designated as number 1, the remaining two running each side of a second island platform numbered 2 and 3. The DHR approached the station from the opposite direction and terminated on the opposite side of platform 1, which was somewhat confusingly referred to as platform 4. A short broad-gauge spur was let into the platform at the far end and became known as the 'Saloon Siding', for it was to accommodate the inspection vehicle. The two-foot gauge was provided with a long loop in the station that was served by platform 5, whilst the first of the metre-gauge tracks ran into platform 6 on the opposite side. The last island platform was numbered 7 and 8 and served a further two metre-gauge lines.

The changing fortunes of the new station over the ensuing years have been reflected by the expansion and subsequent reduction in the number of platforms. Two further 5ft 6in lines were laid each side of a new island platform on the broad-gauge side, the nearest being numbered 4 and the other known simply as line 8. As a consequence, the platform numbers for the two-foot and metre gauges were all increased by 1, with those serving the DHR becoming platforms 5 and 6. A subsequent exercise took place in the early 1990s to reverse the numbering sequence of the broad-gauge platforms in order to overcome the confusion and fall in line with the rest. As will be seen later, the conversion of the metre gauge to a single 5ft 6in line from NJP to Siliguri Junction in 2004 resulted in all the metre gauge platforms being torn up and the DHR track diverted to cross the new broad gauge and approach a long island platform adjacent to the booking hall.

It was hoped the new junction would boost freight traffic for the DHR, which had been in steady decline since independence. Restrictions that had previously controlled the number and weight of vehicles using the Hill Cart Road had been removed, and the Railway now faced direct competition from private hauliers. There had also been complaints that the Darjeeling tea gardens only had licences for plying to their nearest DHR station, and this was not only adding to the cost of sending the chests to Calcutta, but to the transportation of stores that were essential to run the estates. A report had recommended that permits should be issued to use the road and bypass the rail, and this was to include the gardens in the Teesta Valley that were obliged to divert to Jor Bungalow when the river flooded.

There had been a huge number of second-hand Jeeps left by the American Army after the War, and their

Although the DHR was taken over by NFR in 1958, No.777 still retained her iron-red livery of the North Eastern Railway in April 1964. Seen here under the canopy of the goods shed at Kurseong, it was the second of the 'B' Class to be built and at the time the oldest working on the line. The locomotive was taken to the National Rail Museum in Delhi on 20th November 1974 and repainted in the original green livery (not as seen in 2005). Note the young lad about to do a somersault on the left.

(The late) Peter Bawcutt

four-wheel drive had made them eminently suitable vehicles for the Hill Cart Road. The obligation for the DHR to subsidise the maintenance of the road also no longer applied, which was just as well as it was now making a loss every year. Indeed, most of its business was coming from the passenger traffic, and for the year ending 31st March 1964 it recorded that 102,100 passengers were carried. It was still able to transport 92,500 tons of freight that year, but it was taking almost twice as long for the train to get to Darjeeling as it did by road and costing nearly twice as much.

With Siliguri Junction no longer being the passenger terminus for the DHR, the track alongside the platform for the Up trains was relaid to metre gauge and plumbed with a gantry of overhead pipes to replenish water tanks in the carriages. The two-foot-gauge layout was redesigned with a passing loop and was set a little beyond the main platform area, obliging the train to run past the station buildings and halt beside a corrugated canopy. The locomotive sheds and carriage depot were removed at the same time and transferred to a site about a mile from New Jalpaiguri station and the inquisitive eyes of its residents. Two broad-gauge tracks were laid into the new DHR depot to deliver coal and transfer stock, behind which ran the curving embankment on which the old metre gauge from Siliguri Town had previously continued to Jalpaiguri and Haldibari.

The monsoon rains in June 1964 hit the Railway particularly badly at Gorabari, about a mile before the station at Sonada. They damaged the irrigation channel high above the track and caused a heavy landslide that tore down 320ft of the rail and road into the valley below. Darjeeling had already been running low on food and coal and the Deputy Commissioner was anxious to get the trains running again as soon as possible. The Public Works Department (PWD) saw the only solution was to build a ropeway across the breach, but the Assistant Engineer of Indian Railways in charge of the DHR section empowered the Permanent Way Inspector to assess the feasibility of cutting a temporary course for the track into the hillside. Such was the urgency that most of the necessary equipment was delivered to the lower side in two days, during which time the railway gang had formed a new trackbed. It took but a further two days to lay the rails, and with the speed on this section restricted to 5mph, the first train was able to get through. It took fifteen days for the goods trains to get all the food to Darjeeling, and after three months the trackbed had to be handed over to the PWD to be used as a road.

The train service was severed again as a consequence, and for a further three months the Railway was dependent on transhipment for all its traffic. Ms Padmaja Naidu was the Governor of West Bengal during this time and would use the Railway with her staff when the government moved from Calcutta to its summer seat in Darjeeling. Returning to the plains, she was carried on a chair by four men on their shoulders up and around Sonada station, over the top of the slip and back down to the road to resume her journey. The trackbed was returned to the Railway after six months, but the area continued to give problems over the next two years as the PWD had not undertaken the necessary protection works. Complaints were made to the Chief Engineer in Calcutta, and after an inspection of the damage being caused by loose boulders, the work was properly completed and has given no trouble since.

Like a gallant old trouper, the DHR could still pull in the crowds when the situation demanded, and it was not unusual to see the passenger service become so intense that the train had to be divided into five or six sections at Sukna. The records show that in 1965–66 the Railway carried 105,310 passengers and 120,470 in 1966–67, earning Rs341,380 and Rs304,222 respectively. The freight returns for the same periods were 58,546 and 51,145 tonnes, producing an income of Rs1,216,000 and Rs1,024,000, the balance in the books being accounted for by *'other coaching and miscellaneous items'*.

The nightmare of road competition was returning with a vengeance, and financially the Railway was hanging on to life by a thread. As a comparison, the transport charges for tea to Calcutta per *quintal* were:

	Railway	Road
From Darjeeling	Rs19.66	Rs9–12
From Ghum	Rs19.66	Rs9.50–12.50
From Kurseong	Rs16.95	Rs11–12.50
Transit time	4-6 days	3–4 days

The loss in revenue the Railway was showing reveals just how worrying the situation was:

Year	Earnings	Expenditure
1959 – 1960	Rs1,330,000	Rs5,301,000
1960 – 1961	Rs1,423,000	Rs4,186,000
1961 – 1962	Rs1,633,000	Rs4,199,000
1962 – 1963	Rs1,587,000	Rs5,853,000
1963 – 1964	Rs1,955,000	Rs6,032,000
1964 – 1965	Rs1,525,000	Rs8,472,000
1965 – 1966	Rs1,647,000	Rs7,194,000
1966 – 1967	Rs1,472,000	Rs5,718,000

But there were other factors to consider, for it was not only Darjeeling that geography and politics had cast into a strategic area. Partition had given Siliguri the key of the door to Assam, and the broad-gauge line that passed through New Jalpaiguri had shown just how importantly the corridor was now regarded.

It was essential to maintain some social stability in this increasingly volatile area, and for all its ancient glory, the DHR was part of that equation.

Chapter 9

The Pendulum of Politics

The roots of the social problems in Siliguri extended in many directions, but one major source of conflict came from the feudal practice of the *jotedar* (petty landlord) leasing ground to the *adhiar* (labourer) for cultivation. The *adhiar* would receive the use of a plough and be given seed and subsistence, often by means of a loan that had to be paid back with interest, and in return would receive half of the crop he had grown. The situation was made worse by the *adhiar* having no security of tenure and bearing the expense of tilling an exhausted soil, for the tea gardens still had their monopoly with the deliveries of fertiliser. It was a primitive and corrupt system that resulted in the yielded crop being one-third of the average for Bengal, and it was no surprise to find a long history of peasant militancy, including an uprising at Naksalbari on the Kishenganj extension in 1939.

The new Indian government passed the Land Acquisition Act soon after Independence, and the series of reforms that followed included the stipulation that nobody could hold more than 25 acres. This was immediately countermanded by the landowners dividing their excessive estates between the members of their not-inconsiderable families. There followed a second insurrection in Naxalbari[1] in 1959, which was ripe for the pickings of the Communist Party of India (CPI) who were ready to exploit any such unsettled situation for political advantage.

The Bengali leaders had previously fought against the loss of territories to East Pakistan brought about by partition, and they had since gathered strength despite the conflict of their religious beliefs and agrarian lifestyles. Wrangling over the Sino-Soviet question polarised loyalties into supporting either the line from Beijing or Moscow, the former giving rise to a Marxist splinter group referred to as the CPI(M). Further internal rivalries broke the membership into workers' revolutionary groups and their like, but their disagreements were soon settled in the wake of the 1967 elections in order that a United Front could be formed to gain control of West Bengal. A militant Naxalbari faction rejected what it saw as the appeasing attitude of the Central Committee in Calcutta, whose Deputy Chief Minister had originally been educated by nuns at the Loreto Convent in Darjeeling. The new Land Minister was sent to Siliguri to meet the local leaders on 17th May, where he was faced at the railway station by a large banner proclaiming:

> 'This movement can only succeed by the armed struggle and resistance of the working classes. Resistance is meaningless without guns – let the working class collect guns and be vanguards of the struggle.'

The touchpaper was lit a week later when it was heard that an attack was likely at Naxalbari Police Station. Twenty constables and two officers were despatched from Siliguri and met by a crowd rallying to the revolutionary call at Prasadjote, a tiny hamlet of shacks distinguished only by a tea stall and a railway ganger's hut by the level crossing. A second crowd appeared, and after refusing to retreat, the police were ordered to fire into the groups, killing many of the women and children who had been persuaded to stand at the front.

---

[1] The recognised spelling of Naksalbari at this time.

With a blistering sun casting deep shadows across the metre gauge, a 'B' Class backs down from the locomotive shed to the station at NJP in 1971. The frontier with East Pakistan (now Bangladesh) was barely over the horizon, and the influx of refugees that came from the civil war then being raged was to intensify the political complexities of Siliguri.

Michael Bishop

The police headquarters in Darjeeling was told by the Government to stay clear of the area, but the tension escalated and the guerrillas soon attracted a substantial peasant following. A murderous regime that became known as the Naxalites evolved, with the landlords and moneylenders being the first they selected for decapitation. The reprisals spread to those who left the movement for other causes, including the district leader of Siliguri, whose body was found near Naxalbari soon after he joined the CPI(M). Any international leader from Kosygin to Indira Gandhi was liable for their vengeance, and a reign of terror spread across the State that culminated in a declaration to New Delhi that the Assembly had been suspended, as the Constitution had collapsed. President's Rule was declared, which gave the Central Government the right to assume power, and the military moved in to enforce an unsettled peace that held the pressure against bitter animosities. Further wrangling saw the Marxist wing of the CPI finally coming through to govern West Bengal, and to this day they have adroitly maintained a communist organisation supported by a capitalist economy.

The DHR had to survive, for it employed nearly a thousand people. The Government could not afford to close the railway down and exacerbate matters by putting so many out of work in a key area that had become politically volatile. Indeed, it had established the Industrial Training Institute in Tung five years earlier to address such a problem, it being one of eighteen in West Bengal to develop the skills in a variety of trades from fitters, carpenters and blacksmiths to bookbinders, tailors and knitters. The training was to last between one and two years, and a new building had been constructed in Tung to accommodate 400 workers.

Ways were examined to upgrade the DHR service and make the line less uneconomic, and it was decided to run a series of trials with vacuum brakes fitted to the rolling stock to see if the running times could be improved. The theory was sound and had been well rehearsed on the main line, for vacuum braking had proved particularly suitable on protracted downhill sections as it could be progressively controlled.

New carriages were designed at Gorakhapur in 1967 and were delivered to the DHR fully equipped with vacuum piping and squat vertical cylinders attached to the underframe. Tindharia was not so sure about the fittings supplied for the locomotives, for it appeared that it was surplus equipment that came from the metre- or broad-gauge workshops. The DHR fitters were obliged to adapt it to the 'B' Class and assess its viability for full adoption, but there was considerable suspicion from the outset that it was part of a scheme to reduce the size of operating crews. It was seen as particularly affecting the men employed to work the brakes on the individual coaches, and taking away a man's job was adding fuel to the communist cause for agitation.

A number of the 'B' Class did finally emerge from the workshop with various alterations and bits attached, although none had *all* the modifications and *all* the equipment fitted that was necessary to actually make it work! What attempts were made were spectacularly unsuccessful, and three people were reported killed in one disastrous accident. It was found that the locomotives were unable to generate a sufficient supply of steam to create the vacuum without compromising their ability to haul the trains up the unrelenting gradients to Ghum. The idea was soon abandoned and the changelings were left running for a few years, looking even more like tinkers' carts until the articles of vacuum machinery were removed and consigned to the scrap heap.

It was thought that the monsoon during 1968 had been slightly more forgiving than usual until 3rd October, when the rain began to fall incessantly and swamped the eastern hills and *terai*. Two days later the rainfall was recorded as 499 millimetres, causing landslips that severed communication so severely that it was several days before the extent of the damage was known in Calcutta and Delhi. There were 944 landslides in all and the Hill Cart Road had been breached in 18 different places, with over 500ft of the road and rail at Gidarpahar being torn away. An aerial survey, undertaken by the General Manager of Northeast Frontier Railways, revealed that the damage extended to the broad- and metre-gauge lines on the plains, and it was reported that approximately 1,000 passengers bound for Calcutta were stranded at Siliguri and New Jalpaiguri, whilst in the hills there were a further 135 at Kurseong, 600 at Sonada and 2,500 at Darjeeling.

The passengers in two Down trains on the DHR had a narrow escape after the first ran into a large landslide shortly after passing the Salesian Siding. A further slip came down between the two trains, and as the news got through, Banshidhar Dikshit (the Permanent Way Inspector) contacted the Salesian College to see if the 300 passengers could be given shelter. The Fathers responded immediately, and shortly after evacuating the carriages, the four vehicles of the rear train were washed 200ft down into the valley and buried in the debris. Another locomotive was reported to have been swept down the hillside whilst passing a *jhora* above Chunbatti Station, with two of the crew losing their lives. The leaders of the hill tribes rounded up volunteers to help the railway staff clear a passage through the landslide, and two days later a minibus from Sepoydhura was able to get through to the stranded passengers and ferry them to Kurseong. A fleet of taxis was chartered, and over the following two days all were taken to Siliguri via the Old Military Road.

Unable to contact higher authorities, the DHR and local PWD engineers came to an agreement whereby the permanent-way gangs would help clear the way for

The carriages built at Gorakhapur in 1967 were equipped to work on vacuum brakes. Although it was never operational on the DHR, the vacuum cylinder (highlighted by arrow) can just be seen still in place on luggage wagon No.154 in 1980. Note the small ventilated door to accommodate dogs travelling on the train.

David Churchill

It appears that the trials with vacuum brakes were somewhat half-hearted as none of the locomotives was fitted with all the necessary equipment to make them work effectively. No.790 had more than most, and the vacuum reservoirs fitted to the cab roof and connecting hose on rear buffer beam can be seen still in place as it waits at Pagla Jhora for the Up train to pass in November 1970. Note the large sandboxes fitted to the saddle-tank in anticipation of the manual sanders/brakesmen no longer being needed.

Lawrence Marshall

Siliguri Junction in November 1970. 'B' Class No.790 waits on the left with a train bound for Darjeeling, which would run in this formation over the plains as far as Sukna, after which it would be reduced to four-carriage units for the climb. YP 2425 waits on the metre gauge under a gantry of pipes that had been installed to fill water tanks in the carriages.

Lawrence Marshall

cars and lorries and the road engineers would assist with the repair of the rail bridges. Army engineers were drafted in to assist, and it took a further five days before communication links could be restored between Kurseong and Siliguri on the Hill Cart Road. The death toll in the area was officially estimated on 12th October to be 667, although many locals had placed the figure much higher. The Teesta Bridge had been torn away by the swollen river, which had ripped through the 659 houses that made up the bazaar on the right-hand bank and rendered 543 families destitute.

Trains from New Jalpaiguri to Kurseong did not run until 5th April the following year, and Darjeeling had to wait until the summer before it saw trains arriving again. The service had barely got under way when an 'All India Railway Strike' was announced. Representations were made by the DHR staff to the local president of the Mazdoor Union not to participate, particularly as it would be welcomed by the Government when the Railway was making such a loss. The Union was not persuaded, and on the first morning of the strike, Banshidhar Dikshit found the station at New Jalpaiguri was closed. Walking to the locomotive shed, he found the crews had prepared the locomotives for work and they were in steam. His blacksmith was summoned and told to break the locks, after which the engine was hitched to the coaches and run into New Jalpaiguri. The stationmaster at Tung was contacted and told to expect a train, by which time a large number of railway staff and public had gathered and were blocking the track. Mr Dikshit telephoned for the assistance of the police, who arrived to disperse the crowd and if necessary use a baton charge. The train finally left unmolested and arrived in Tung without any further problem; the strike action failed and the service settled back to normal.

But it was difficult to claim that things were ever normal, and less than two years later a civil war broke out in East Pakistan, whose frontier was barely ten miles from New Jalpaiguri. Partition had created Pakistan as a geographically unique country, for it was divided in two by one thousand miles of foreign territory. The two wings were united by a religion, but were ethnically and economically very different. The east had over half the population but was only one-seventh of the total area. It was also the home of the Bengalis, and they would fight like their native tigers to retain their heritage and culture.

Spurred on by the lack of their representation in the central administration, the Awami League was formed to challenge the domination of West Pakistan. The grievances were fuelled by resentment over economic exploitation, and the League received an overwhelming majority in the first national elections held in 1970. The military felt threatened and planned to annul the election, which brought on a surge of Bengali nationalism, strikes and an all-out revolt in 1971. Guerrilla warfare drove the army into a deadlock situation, and the crisis came to a head when Indian armed forces crossed the border and came to the support of the League, driving the Pakistani troops out. New Delhi saw their action as restoring stability in a dangerous situation, but the view was not shared by West Pakistan, especially when the leaders of the Awami League announced the foundation of the new state of Bangladesh. Unable to defend themselves, the conflict brought with it a wave of refugees fleeing the violence, and for many the nearest sanctuary was New Jalpaiguri. With the exodus came the inevitable sprawl of shacks and shanties, the sinister security of the alleyways leading to nowhere but Siliguri and its own set of problems.

A shuttle service was operated between Siliguri Junction and New Jalpaiguri, but the timetable for the summer of 1971 showed there was only one train running the full journey to Darjeeling, and that now departed at 5.30. However, there was an afternoon service that left New Jalpaiguri at 13.10, which would terminate at Kurseong for the night and resume its journey to Darjeeling at 7.20 the following morning. This allowed for two Down trains to be run from Darjeeling, one leaving at 6.35 and the other at 13.05, whilst freight trains were run as and when necessary, which usually amounted at least to one on most days.

The reduced demands for motive power enabled four of the 'B' Class to be sold to the Assam Railways & Trading Company for work in the north-eastern coalfields at Tipong Pani. The locomotives were still in the olive-green livery of independent days, and had probably been out of use for some time when they were dispatched to Calorex (Calcutta) to be put in working order. The legacy of the Company being more used to equipping factories than locomotives was betrayed by the ungracious chimney stacks and industrial safety valves they fitted, whilst the new smokebox doors were little more than flat discs. The engines were not endowed with a great deal of care and attention at Tipong Pani, where they were subjected to further local modifications and butchery to keep them in running order. The colliery has become embroiled with the militant politics of Assam in recent years and information is sometimes difficult to obtain, but the last that has been learned is that one of the locomotives is kept in running condition and another is 'dead but complete', the other two having been reduced to a pile of spares.

As the Up Mail takes water at Sukna in 1971, the rolling stock in the sidings suggests there was still plenty of freight traffic. Locomotives would also be marshalled here to wait for the service from NJP to be divided into trains of three or four carriages for the climb to Ghum. The station was renovated following the inscription of the railway as a World Heritage Site by UNESCO in 2000, but despite its listing as a fixed asset, most of the sidings were lifted to make way for a Heritage Rail Park.

Michael Bishop

In 1968 four 'B' Class went to Margherita, the headquarters of North Eastern Coalfields in Assam. The engines were overhauled by Calorex of Calcutta, but it was a company more used to fitting out factories than locomotives and they did not bequeath any cosmetic favours to the Class. Ex-DHR No. 784 seen working a passenger special on 14th February 1992, the elegance of a time-honoured design having been compromised by a complication of pipework and discharge valves, the graceless chimney and smokebox door only compounding the trauma.

Lawrence Marshall

Situated close to the border with Myanmar (Burma), the locomotives were used to haul coal from the drift mines at Tipong Pani to the railhead at Lekhapani, the most easterly station on Indian Railways. By 2004 only ex-DHR No.789 was in service, seen here storming from the tunnel at the head of a rake of coal wagons.

John Clemmens

The transportation of British troops to the sanatoria was one of the reasons advocated by Franklin Prestage for the construction of the tramway in 1879. Ninety-five years later No.788 approaches Pagla Jhora in November 1974 with a Down train that has the first carriage designated 'Military Only', but now the passengers were Indian and their task was to protect and secure national frontiers.

Lawrence Marshall

The pendulum of politics seemed to be forever swaying in the path of the DHR, and it was once again pointing in the direction of Sikkim, which held centre stage between the largest democracy and the largest communist state in the world. The Chinese invasion in 1962 had shown the communists to be by far the superior force, and their unilateral decision to withdraw put to an end the policy of non-alignment and peaceful coexistence adopted by India. The 11th Chogyal of Sikkim had died during the same year, and had been succeeded by his son Palden Thondup, who was to become the last of the ruling dynasty. The new Chogyal married the American debutante Hope Cooke the following year, whose fragile claim to fame appears to have been the introduction of *crème de menthe* to Gangtok society. A referendum was held to measure the growing dissent against the monarchy and the reforms they were introducing, and this revealed that 97% of the electorate were calling for union with India. The Chogyal conceded and made a request in 1975 for India to take over the administration of the country, a move that China has refused to recognise to this day.

The route from Siliguri up the Teesta Valley became the umbilical cord for the new Indian state, and the Army rebuilt the road to secure its position. Its vulnerability lay with the mood swings of the river and the ability of any hostile action to easily sever communication. As a consequence, Darjeeling held the key of the only other door into Sikkim, by way of the route that drops in a series of precipitous bends to Naya Bazaar on the Rangeet River. There was also the steeply descending road that led from Jor Bungalow to the Teesta Bridge and Kalimpong, but either way there was sufficient political motivation to ensure the maintenance of the Hill Cart Road was upheld.

Constitutionally, India was a restless adolescent still

trying to cope with the diversity of traditions and cultures it inherited. The question of Kashmir had boiled over again since the death of Nehru in 1964, whilst the policy adopted by his daughter Indira Gandhi of maintaining a strong central government over economic and social life led to a conflict within Congress itself. A state of emergency was declared in 1975, and the entire country was placed under direct rule from Delhi.

The DHR managed to hold on to life throughout the emergency, but there was only one train running the full length of the line, which now left New Jalpaiguri at 8.30 for arrival at Darjeeling 16.25. The Down train left the hill station at 10.40, which enabled it to reach New Jalpaiguri just as the sun would be passing over the horizon at 18.05. The local stopping service for schoolchildren and workers continued to run from Kurseong at 7.00 and appear at Darjeeling by 9.40, making its return at 17.00 for its arrival in Kurseong at 19.45. The shuttle service from New Jalpaiguri to Siliguri ran in the evening, departing from the broad-gauge junction at 17.15 for its thirty-five-minute journey and returning at 21.10 for connections and overnight stabling.

The railway presented the Government with a dichotomy, for despite the losses involved it was, and still is, in its broad interests to sponsor the continued running of the line, as it retains public affection in a strategically important area. The vast majority of the people in the region speak Nepali, a legacy from the British encouragement of workers to the tea plantations over a century ago, and a feeling of antipathy had been brewing for a number of years. The State had made a substantial financial investment with Sikkim, but it was felt little had filtered through for Darjeeling. The average Indian of Nepalese origin saw this as discrimination by the West Bengal Government, who had even failed to recognise their language in the Constitution and offered work only to those who could speak Bengali (Nepali has since been included in the schedule of Indian languages).

The question of the status of Darjeeling was not new, and indeed had been simmering as far back as 1885 when it had been defined as a *'non-regulation district'*. This had been given its own political interpretation in 1907, when the leaders of the hill people had called for the administration of Darjeeling to be separated from the rest of Bengal. Similar demands were made over the next forty years, each notching up a degree of insistence until 1947, when it was stressed that an independent state of Gorkhastan should be formed from the Darjeeling district, southern Sikkim and Nepal. Two years later it was asserted that the state of Uttarkhand should be created from the Darjeeling district, Sikkim, Jalpaiguri and Cooch Behar, but neither of these proposals had cut any ice with the Indian government or the communist administration of Bengal. However, the problem would not go away, and in 1980 the Gorkha National Liberation Front (GNLF) was formed under the banner of the area being recognised as a self-governing state known as Gorkhaland.

The pre-eminence of Darjeeling had certainly been tarnishing, for it had at one time enjoyed plentiful supplies of drinking water and hydroelectricity,

The pensive-looking late Jawaharlal Nehru on the stamp of this special DHR cover was not inappropriate. His daughter Indira Gandhi had recently lost the National election, and by the end of the year she was expelled from Parliament and imprisoned in Tihar Jail. Such were the turns of fortune with Indian politics that she was returned to power as Prime Minister two years later!

The Up Mail passes under the green flags and a banner that reads 'Welcome to Gorkhaland' in 1985. The tension was rising for a self-governing state to be recognised, but the strategic implications for national security were too contentious.

Peter Jordan

but now found itself suffering from water shortages and power cuts. As a counterbalance, the fortunes of Siliguri had been rapidly increasing, and its key location had meant it was no longer seen as a poor relation to the hill station. In 1961 it was recorded that there was a workforce of 4,814 employed in 464 factories in Siliguri, the businesses ranging from flour and rice mills to those for the manufacture of furniture, aluminium utensils and umbrellas. Ten years later the population had grown to 97,462, and the town was attracting some of the most enterprising businesses in India. Colleges were established to study a range of disciplines from medicine to postgraduate diplomas in tea management, whilst its status as the centre for Himalayan Studies came as a severe blow to Darjeeling.

The 1981 monsoon kicked in with its customary fury and pulled down a section of the railway between Chunbatti and Tindharia. It was decided to cut a new reverse siding into the hillside and take the line to a higher level and a more stable bedrock. Trains were run from NJP to a point just before the slip, whereupon passengers were obliged to climb up the earthworks for the new reverse to a waiting train at the higher level. A through service was being run by the following spring, and the height of the new formation was such that the 'Up' trains to Darjeeling actually went downhill for a short section before the climb resumed. It was the same year that a Rs2.85 postage stamp was issued along with a special first-day cover, to celebrate the centenary of the railway's opening to Darjeeling. Nobody seemed to notice that it was a year late, but it was better than being forgotten and there was probably little mood for celebration.

There was not a great deal to rejoice about in 1983 when an unsightly concrete house was built on the roof of Darjeeling station, for it blatantly destroyed the architectural symmetry of the Modernistic design. It seemed to reflect a careless attitude, although the decision to lift the rails over the half-mile extension to the bazaar in 1984 was based on the economic fact that freight traffic had all but fizzled out. It seemed pointless keeping the rails laid in the road any longer, and the track was reduced to a 100-metre spur beyond the main station as an overrun.

A further culling took place at Ghum by lifting the points of the sidings to the goods depot and laying tarmacadam across the tracks that crossed the road to the freight shed. The following year saw the railway giving a second audition to one of the NDM-1 articulated diesel locomotives. It came from the Matheran Hill Railway but, alas, it fared no better than its predecessor from the Kalka–Simla line. Its credentials with articulation were in no doubt, but it appears that the changes in the super-elevation of the track caused the locomotive to derail beyond Sonada. It was also reported to have suffered from problems with combustion and overheating at the higher altitudes towards Ghum, although it was not apparent when the class worked to Simla which stands at 6,870ft above sea level. Reports also came through that the engine crews were wary over redundancies, with no manual sanders and coal-breakers being needed, but

The graffiti with the hammer and sickle may appear a little incongruous on the side of the goods shed as the Up Mail leaves Sonada in 1980, but the Communist Party had seen the claims by the Gurkhas as an ideal cause to gain control since the first days of Independence. Serious cracks were to appear in the relationship, and with the formation of the GNLF, the railway became a political conduit for the opposing sides.

David Churchill

By 1981 the demand to transport goods had diminished to an occasional train, such as the Down freight seen on the through line whilst an Up passenger waits on the passing siding. The last wagon is one of the four-wheeled water carriers then still in use, and a keen eye will note that the top section flares outwards. There were at least two such wagons with this feature, and without any obvious reason for the design, it is tempting to suggest they resemble the tender used at the IR Centenary in Delhi in 1953 and the modified rear section of the Garratt scrapped in 1954.

(The late) Norman Glover, now in the collection of Alan Wycherley

The service between Chunbatti and Tindharia was severed following the 1981 monsoons and the opportunity was used to form a new track-bed on more stable rock, necessitating the formation of a new reverse siding.

No.795 arrives with an Up train from NJP at the lower point close to the landslide on 2nd March 1982. The carriages were built at Gorakhapur in 1967-68 and originally fitted with ventilators; note the square patches on the carriage roofs covering the gaps left after their removal. . . . .

. . . . No.780 backs down to the connecting train waiting for the passengers on the upper section on 2nd March 1982. No.785 is at the far end and will return uphill running light.

Chris Pietruski

. . . . . . *Looking back downhill on 1st March 1982, it can be seen that the new formation was higher than the point at which it connected with the existing track, causing Up trains to run downhill for a short section.*

Chris Pietruski

In March 1982, a solitary four-wheeled van was all that comprised an Up freight as No.804 sidles through the station at Rangtong. The rounded profile between the base of the bunker and the coal chute, along with the splayed-out carrying-arm for the rerailing bar, indicates that the locomotive was originally built for the Raipur Forest Tramway.

Chris Pietruski

No.779 'Mountaineer' (since named 'Himalayan Bird') trundles across the plains in March 1984 with one of the more conventional straight-sided four-wheeled water carriers used for supplying outlying communities. Darjeeling has an annual rainfall of 2,759mm (UK 584mm), and whilst it may seem perverse there is a shortage, many hill communities are above the water table and fed by streams only active during the monsoon.

Lawrence Marshall

whatever it was the diesel was soon returned to the Matheran line.

The timetable for 1988 reflected a degree of optimism by returning to a daily service of two through trains running each way and a local service between Kurseong and Darjeeling. The two departures from New Jalpaiguri left at 7.15 and 9.00 and were scheduled to arrive at the upper terminus by 15.30 and 17.30. The downhill services were timed to leave at 8.25 and 10.00 in order to make connections at New Jalpaiguri by 16.20 and 17.45. The through trains were supplemented by early morning local service from Kurseong at 6.40 with the ambition of reaching Darjeeling by 9.45, the train returning at 17.00 and nosing its way through the bazaar at Kurseong by 20.05.

But the optimism was short-lived, for tempers were flaring in Darjeeling with the demands for an independent state being made yet again. The hostility broke out into two years of agitation, during which hundreds of people in the area were killed and thousands lost their homes. The train service came to a grinding halt, tourism collapsed and the Indian Army was drafted in to control the situation.

It became extremely tense, for the social stability of India had already been severely rocked in 1984 when the Sikh community in the Punjab had made their own demands for a separate State. Mrs Gandhi had ordered the Indian Army to storm the Golden Temple in Amritsar and flush out the armed radicals, but the desecration sparked off major riots and problems within the Army itself. In a clear act of reprisal, Indira Gandhi was assassinated by two of her own Sikh bodyguards, and her son Rajiv reluctantly took the baton and became Prime Minister. His administration failed to resolve the Sikh unrest, and with the Kashmir question continuing to haunt, the demands being made in Darjeeling had to be handled with consummate care. With this in mind covert support was given to the GNLF as it was seen to challenge the Marxist government in Calcutta, which many regarded as a thorn in the side of Congress.

An air of peace matured with assurances of reform and a redistribution of finances within West Bengal. The Darjeeling Gorkha Hill Council was formed and given autonomy from the State Government, and it was to be voted on through independent elections. Not everybody was satisfied, for a splinter group later evolved claiming the GNLF had compromised its ideals. It was also reported that the splinter group was backed by the Marxist wing of the CPI, who felt the support they once enjoyed had been drained by the GNLF. Some felt that progress in India had been slow in the years since independence, but as one resident was overheard to say: *'There is too much democracy ... there are too many vested interests, and that makes it too anarchic.'*

The national elections held in November 1989 underpinned the comment. Rajiv Gandhi was at the head of the largest single party to win, but there were not sufficient numbers to form a government in its own right. Five parties put together a National Front Government, but their views were too disparate and new elections were announced. The fortunes of the GNLF in Darjeeling were one of a number of political barometers many had been watching, including the Tamils in northern Sri Lanka, who had strong linguistic and cultural links with Tamil Nadu in southern India. Once again demands were made for a separate homeland; once again it spilled into guerrilla warfare, and once again it ended with the assassination of the Prime Minister. Narasimha Rao took over the leadership, and continued with the policy of dragging India kicking and screaming into the realities of world economics by floating the rupee against a number of hard currencies. This in turn attracted foreign investment and the expansion of the private sector, along with the trend to favour business acumen over religious merit.

The economic climate gave Indian Railways the opportunity to take another hard look at the DHR and decide just what it was going to do, for the line simply did not fit into the business plan. It had been taking a severe battering from the annual monsoons in recent times and hardly a year passed without sections of the permanent way being devastated, causing major disruptions to the service. The railway had become like some restless animal, forever changing its position to find a more comfortable way of fitting into the land and being accepted. Loop No.1 near Rangtong was washed out towards the end of 1991 by bad flooding and a landslip, which reduced the service to a shuttle running between New Jalpaiguri and Siliguri and a school train between Ghum and Darjeeling. The decision was made to take the spiral out and realign the track on a new profile, but it was not until the following spring that the work was completed.

With over 1.6 million staff, Indian Railways was one of the largest single employers in the world, transporting 10.5 million passengers daily over 38,000 miles of track to 7,100 stations. It had taken a policy decision in 1985 to replace all of its steam traction by 1996, and tenders were invited to purchase locomotives from a number of narrow-gauge systems, including three of the 'B' Class that Tindharia had deemed as condemned. The working engines on the DHR were given a reprieve until the year 2000 as there was nothing suitable to replace them, although it was noticeable that deficiencies were creeping into the standard of their maintenance. As it was, the sale received widespread condemnation and Indian Railways withdrew the offer. A ban was imposed on the scrapping of any further locomotives, and although this was a welcome move, it was all a bit too late. The DHR was unscathed by the exercise, but it continued to be handicapped by a lack of funds and exhausted motive power.

It was around this time that Indian Railways had a new generation of officers who were talking about a concept that it had never considered before ... railway tourism. The 'Palace on Wheels' began as a luxury steam-hauled train on the broad gauge, and was now earning a most respectable income. Departing from Delhi, it took its well-heeled passengers on a tour of palaces in Rajasthan, travelling in coaches formerly used by the Maharajahs. The nostalgia had since given way to the motive power becoming diesel and the original coaches replaced by replica rolling stock, but the inescapable fact was that its passengers were prepared to pay a premium price for a first-class service. The metre gauge had adopted a similar package with the 'Royal Orient' to Gujarat, and eyes were now turning to see if the problems of Darjeeling could also be changed by similar business opportunities.

A meeting was called in 1994 by residents and enthusiasts in the town to discuss a strategy that would enable Indian Railways to see a viable future for the DHR as a living museum. The steam engines were recognised as the pictorial signature of the railway, and it had to be said that their demise could affect the tourist industry on which the town was dependent. It led to the formation of the DHR Heritage Foundation by Sherab Tenduf, a director of the Windamere Hotel, Teddy Young, the Manager of the Tumsong Tea Garden, and Alfred Gottwaldt of the Berlin Museum of Transport and Technology. The Articles of the Foundation were signed on 30th

Hugging close to the hillside and following every fold in the land, the DHR is the very essence of a roadside tramway. Indian Railways had to face the challenge of maintaining a unique transport system that did not sit comfortably with its modernisation programme.

Peter Jordan

Below: *A line of condemned 'B' Class wait on the scrap line at the rear of Tindharia works. Indian Railways was looking to replace all steam-operated services over its lines by 1996 and three of the DHR locomotives were put up for sale. The offer was withdrawn in the wake of widespread protests, but little was being done to maintain the existing fleet to the high standard once associated with the railway.*

Peter Jordan

The demand for the Up Mail during the 1970s was such that it still needed dividing into sections for the climb beyond Sukna. Two trains are seen storming round the original Loop 1, which was later washed away during the monsoon rains of 1991. The track was subsequently relaid on a profile that avoided the construction of a new spiral.

Das Studio

Seen in the attractive green livery that it wore in 1990, No.806 drifts by with a crew working on the permanent way. Note the ancient symbol of the swastika on the GNLF poster, a common sight in India that is orientated in both clockwise and counter-clockwise directions. As seen here it relates to Ganesh (the elephant-headed father of Buddha, associated with the Sun), and when counter-clockwise is linked with the goddess Kali-Maya, mother of Buddha (associated with the Moon).

Nick Lera

Towards the end of 1997, Tindharia decided to repaint fifteen coaches and four baggage wagons in three bands of red and yellow to match the broad-gauge 'Rajdhani Express', but the livery lasted only twelve months before it was returned to the NFR blue. No.782 'Mountaineer' pauses in Mahanandi with an axle-box running hot in February 1998.

May, the objective being to ensure that the most interesting elements of the railway were not lost in the march of modernisation, and to achieve this it was necessary to establish a dialogue with Indian Railways. The enthusiasm led to the formation of a network of interested groups and individuals known as 'The Friends of the DHR'. Although somewhat amorphous in structure, it provided a forum for the considerable knowledge and expertise that had been gained worldwide with railway preservation and marketing.

Indian Railways was listening carefully, for it recognised the DHR had the makings of being a jewel in its crown and reaffirmed a commitment to its retention. Representatives from a number of interested Boards that included the Ministries of Railways and Tourism and the Chairman of the Darjeeling Gorkha Hill Council, came to Britain in June 1997 to gain first-hand experience of the success of preserved railways. Visits were made in November that year to the Welshpool and Llanfair Light Railway and of course the Ffestiniog, where Charles Spooner had discussed the Darjeeling line with his nephew Thomas prior to his appointment as a Sub-Assistant Engineer at Tindharia some 110 years earlier. The party returned to India with a clear understanding of the potential the DHR had, but it would need a substantial investment.

There also had to be a sense of political stability, but the creation of the new State of Uttarakhand, in northern Uttar Pradesh during 1996, was all that the pessimists needed to believe that India was now following the same path of disintegration as Yugoslavia and the Soviet Union. The optimists saw Indian unity consolidating over the past 50 years of independence, but it was being expressed in religious terms during the 1996 general election with the victory of the Bharatiya Janata Party. Despite the majority, the BJP was unable to form a government, and the matter could only be resolved by a coalition of 13 parties to be called the United Front. A further election in 1998 subsequently established the BJP in a commanding position, and a Hindu nationalist government was formed. The economic policies continued to attract foreign capital, and there was no shortage of overseas companies who were anxious to reap the rewards from the growing numbers of Indians with disposable income.

However justified the politics of Darjeeling were felt by the GNLF, it had to be recognised that it was creating nervousness within the international business community for such investments. Nevertheless, there were people overseas who were willing to devote their knowledge and enthusiasm to the railway, and raising awareness would help to focus support for its survival. The Darjeeling Himalayan Railway Society was formed in Great Britain by David Barrie, and with an enthusiastic committee, its success was immediate. Membership came not only from the UK and India, but Australia, Austria, Canada, China, France, Germany, Holland, Italy, Japan, New Zealand, Norway, Pakistan, Portugal, Switzerland, Thailand and the USA. The interest in Australia was so strong that it paved the way for the Darjeeling Himalayan Railway Supporters Association to be formed the following year for enthusiasts living in Oceania, South and South-east Asia, and similar areas, and it would not be long before a DHR Support Group would emerge in Siliguri itself.

Above: *The monsoon rains in 1998 tore at the Pagla Jhora with particular vengeance and closed down the railway for seven months. Cages of boulders were set into the hillside in an attempt to prevent further soil creep and damage, with the road being laid where the track once ran and a new course for the railway constructed on the outer edge.* Left: *Not a local execution squad but two workers manually breaking up the rock that destroyed the railway at Pagla Jhora!*

Peter Jordan

A meeting was held at the beginning of 1998 in New Delhi at the offices of UNESCO to discuss the feasibility of the DHR gaining recognition as a World Heritage Site, a move that would certainly make a significant difference to underpinning the security of the line. It stemmed from a suggestion made two years earlier by Dr Ronald Fitzgerald in discussion with Prem Sharma, the Divisional Railway Manager at Moradabad, and the idea had been gathering support from many quarters.

Having the responsibility for the operation and maintenance of the DHR, the administration of the Northeast Frontier Railway prepared the necessary formalities for the Government of India to make an official application. The Secretary of the Railway Board and the Director of the National Rail Museum in New Delhi subsequently attended a meeting to complete the submission in the required format for evaluation by UNESCO, highlighting the engineering genius, the aesthetic qualities, and the social and cultural significance of the railway. Dr Robert Lee, the Director of the Centre for Asian Studies at the University of Western Sydney in Australia, was nominated by the International Council on Monuments and Sites (ICOMOS) to undertake the study and make the recommendations.

The monsoon rains of 1998 were particularly vicious in the wake of the weather cycle of *'El Nino'*, and caused extensive damage to the Hill Cart Road, already weakened by too much heavy traffic. Large sections of the land around Upper and Lower Pagla Jhora were torn away and strewn down the mountainside, along with extensive destruction in the upper valleys beyond Kurseong. Boulders were swept away by the gorged rivers and violently scoured the land, undermining numerous bridges across the plains that stood in their way. The metre gauge between Siliguri Town and New Jalpaiguri subsided, and the decision was made to use the DHR girder bridge for taking the essential oil traffic and commuting passengers. A new bridge was subsequently built for the metre-gauge line and the old one was returned to the DHR, during which time the Hill Cart Road on the damaged mountain section was laid on the trackbed of the railway and a new profile cut deeper into the rock face for the train.

It was time to call in the 'big guns', for the future of the railway was going to be dependent on pulling together the interested parties to identify the problems and discuss short-, medium- and long-term solutions. This was the task the 4th Conference of the Heritage Foundation set itself in April 1999, and there was no shortage of support. The inaugural address was given by Mr V.K. Agarwal, the Chairman of the Indian Railways Board,[2] followed by the keynote address from Dr Robert Lee. Further presentations were made by senior personnel of Indian Railways on the viability of the DHR, conserving India's railway heritage, and tourism, but the real crunch came with the outline of the DHR infrastructure by Mr B.K. Agarwal, the Chief Engineer of the Northeast Frontier Railway, and the challenges of maintenance by Mr S. Dhasraty, the Additional Member (Mechanical Engineering) of the Railway Board.

There were hard facts to face, for the railway was earning less than 5 *lakh* rupees a year and costing 500 *lakh* rupees to run. The staffing levels were quite staggering considering that the service was one train a day in each direction for the full journey, supplemented by the early morning mixed from Kurseong to Darjeeling. There were 309 personnel engaged on civil engineering, 562 on mechanical, 66 in commercial and 51 on electrical work. The civil engineering itself was equally astonishing, for there were 556 bridges, of which 241 had a corbelled arch and 55 crossed waterways with a span that exceeded 10ft. Most were of original construction, and the estimated cost for their renovation was 200 *lakh*.

The track was also regarded with some caution, for the old 50lb rails were wearing out, particularly on the sharp curves, and 35% of the wooden sleepers were regarded as needing replacement. Road traffic had been responsible for damage to the track by hitting and mounting it in places, and at the same time crushing some of the sleeper ends, whilst natural erosion had caused a loss of ballast and a strain on the sleepers holding the gauge. It was estimated that 1,750 *lakh* rupees would be needed to replace the track with second-hand 60lb rail from the main line, although 50lb would have to be used on some of the sharper curves to prevent kinks forming. Check rails were also required over some 20kms of the curves, and the estimates included 20 *lakh* for this work. It

---

[2] The Railway Board, which reports to the Railway Minister, controls the administration and management of Indian railways. At the time of writing it consisted of a Chairman, a Financial Commissioner and three other members, which by virtue of their office are Secretaries to the Government of India. They are responsible for the principal functions of the system, i.e. Traffic, Civil Engineering, Mechanical Engineering and staff, and are referred to by title as Member (Traffic) etc. Each of the current nine railway zones is headed by a General Manager, supported by a Senior Deputy Manager and eleven Heads of Departments (Chief Engineer, Financial Advisor & Chief Accounts Officer, Chief Operating Superintendent, Chief Commercial Superintendent, Chief Mechanical Engineer, Chief Electrical Engineer, Chief Personnel Officer, Chief Signal and Telecommunications Engineer, Controller of Stores, Chief Medical Officer and Chief Security Officer).

For those denied the gentle pace of light railways long passed from the European scene, the battered charm of the DHR was irresistible. A mechanical breakdown with No.792 was being debated in the terai forest in April 1999, and with the railway appearing to be locked in a time warp, it was tempting to wish it could remain so. However, it was not an option for those trying to justify the costs and maintain a credible service for its survival.

was also calculated that 750 *lakh* rupees would fund the release of 52,000 secondhand broad- and metre-gauge sleepers, and toe walls could be constructed to protect the ends from road vehicles.

The Hill Cart Road had been built in 1861 for the bullockcart and certainly not constructed for the intensity of traffic now witnessed with heavy lorries and trucks. The foundations simply did not stand up to the continuous pounding and stresses caused by the excessive axle loads of modern motor traffic. The rain would beat on the weakened surface which would wash away the smaller particles and dissolve minerals in the bedrock, leaving the insoluble material to be blown as an abrasive dust. Winter would also freeze the rain that collected in the weakened crannies, and with the onset of the thaw, expand beneath the surface and cause further destruction. Seven bridges alone had needed replacing following the 1998 monsoon and another required major remodification, whilst new alignments were necessary at several locations along large lengths of the line. The cost of this work had amounted to 75 *lakh* rupees.

At the same time, the land had suffered from the universal complaint of it being regarded as a commodity belonging to the developer. The widespread deforestation that made way for the tea plantations and buildings had allowed the rains to pound the rock surface with no abatement, and as such it would tear much of the soil away. The sun would heat the exposed surface by day and cause it to expand, whilst by night it contracted with the cool air. The bedrock loosened with the stretching and compression, and as a consequence it broke into boulders, fragments of stone and dust.

An unofficial water stop for the passengers! No.792 pauses about a mile uphill from Chunbatti at the site of a natural spring, and nobody appears to be in any particular hurry.

The disruption to traffic had been severe, as could be seen from the statistics of closure:

Year	Days	Year	Days
1984	101	1992	109
1985	111	1993	6
1986	241	1994	35
1987	Closed due to political unrest	1995	192
1988		1996	97
1989	231	1997	36
1990	159	1998	254
1991	113		7th July–19th March

The charm of the rolling stock was undeniable, but it was also worn out. The operation of the 14 remaining steam locomotives was being compromised by poor-quality coal and water, and much of the latter was being siphoned off by locals for domestic use. The 44 coaches that remained were timber-bodied and ran on plain bearings; few could make the claim they were comfortable to ride in. The internal lighting was hardly electric sunshine, and with the train being dependent on hand screw and lever brakes, it gave little opportunity for a faster service. It was certainly rare to find such an authentic 19th-century railway operating in a modern public transport system, but could it survive without compromising those very qualities?

The consensus of opinion agreed that it was certainly possible, but it would require the skilled coordination of managing the environment and conserving the railway. By virtue of its nature and length, the DHR is not an easy site to manage, and a reforestation programme would have to be developed in tandem with the control of air pollution and rubbish. Short-term stabilisation of the slopes could be achieved with biodegradable matting sprayed with grass seed, but it would take 8 to 15 years for trees to establish their roots. The use of boulder-arrestors on the river courses above the Kalka-Simla Railway had shown these could be effective in controlling monsoon damage,

Care and Attention

and a joint policy with the Highways Authority would be needed to widen and regularly maintain the river culverts. Perhaps more controversially, the weight of the road traffic would need to be controlled; the old weighbridge at Sukna used to limit the road vehicles to 4 tons and ensure that no more than 15 lorries and 35 passenger buses operated at a given time, but now it was little more than a free-for-all and the price was being paid.

Conservation was going to be the litmus test, and that was not going to be made easy when a local community did not see the need for self-restraint as a natural virtue. Indian Railways certainly understood the importance, and made clear it would welcome the advice and guidance of experts from the international community on preserving its heritage.

The question also had to be addressed of preserving the fixed assets of the line, and research was required to determine what the buildings originally looked like. Much of this was voluntarily undertaken by Peter Tiller, an architect by profession who had a wealth of experience with refurbishing old buildings in the UK. He had also been involved with the original exhumation of Boston Lodge, the workshop of the Festiniog Railway that now had an international reputation for excellence. It was apparent that the stations on the DHR would require careful and expert restoration, and craftsmen capable of this sort of sympathetic work needed to be found or trained.

Peter Tiller presented his report in September 1999 and persuaded NFR to appoint a local architect, Shasheesh Prasad, to produce drawings and specifications for the refurbishment of the stations from Sukna to Ghum. Being interchange stations with the main line, the question of New Jalpaiguri and Siliguri was more complex, whilst some drastic structural surgery would be needed to return Darjeeling to its original post-1946 appearance. The unsightly rectangular rest home imposed on its structure in 1983 had compromised its elegance, but with this removed the railway would undoubtedly have a classic example of the Indo-Deco architecture now so universally appreciated. It was also evident that the whole concept of heritage had yet to be appreciated in certain quarters, for a concrete rest house had unbelievably just been built on the outer edge of Agony Point, surely one of the most symbolic fixed assets of the line!

It was fitting that as the 20th century drew to a close, the announcement was made on 2nd December that the DHR was officially recognised by UNESCO as a World Heritage Site. The Heritage Conference had shown what was diplomatically possible, but the challenge now was to make it scientifically certain.

The strategy was simple, but it was not going to be very easy.

Extending the Lines

An Introduction

Proof No. 2. Cipher: TONNENGEL

The Darjeeling Himalayan Railway Extensions Company Limited.

Incorporated under the Indian Companies Acts, 1882-1900.

CAPITAL - Rs. 50,00,000,

In 50,000 Shares of Rs. 100/- each.

Of which there is now offered for Subscription at Par, 43,750 Shares of Rs. 100 each,

PAYABLE AS FOLLOWS:—

Rs. 10/- on Application;   Rs. 20/- on Allotment;

and the balance as and when called up, but so that not more than a further Rs. 50/- per Share shall be called up before 1st July, 1913.

Directors.

E. H. BRAY, Esq., *Chairman* (Messrs. Gillanders, Arbuthnot & Co.);
THE HON. MR. NORMAN McLEOD (Messrs. McLeod & Co.);
R. G. D. THOMAS, Esq. (Messrs. J. Thomas & Co.);
W. K. DOWDING, Esq. (Messrs. Turner, Morrison & Co.);

AND

a Government Inspector of Railways appointed by the Government of India.

Bankers.
BANK OF BENGAL.

Solicitors.
Messrs. MORGAN & CO., Calcutta.

Auditors.
Messrs. E. W. S. RUSSELL and E. E. MEUGENS.

Managing Agents.
Messrs. GILLANDERS, ARBUTHNOT & CO., Calcutta.

Registered Office.
CLIVE BUILDINGS, CALCUTTA.

London Agents.
Messrs. OGILVY, GILLANDERS & CO., Sun Court, 67 Cornhill, London, E.C.

PROSPECTUS.

Purpose of Company. THIS COMPANY is formed to provide funds for the construction, under a contract with the Secretary of State for India, of the following railways on the 2 ft. gauge:—

(1) From a point on the Darjeeling Himalayan Railway, near Siliguri to Kissengunge, a distance of about 66 miles.

(2) From Siliguri Station, on the Eastern Bengal State Railway, to the Tista Bridge Bazaar in the Tista Valley, near Darjeeling, a distance of about 29 miles.

The annexed plan shows the intended alignment of the proposed Railways, which it is intended should serve as feeder lines to the Eastern Bengal State Railway, and generally to develop the trade of the country which they traverse.

Extending the Lines

An Introduction

By name and association, the Railway has always been linked to Darjeeling, but it will have been seen that the DHR also built and ran two additional lines from its terminus at Siliguri. Their histories are an integral part of the story, and should be reviewed before the final chapter considers the challenges the railway faced with World Heritage accreditation at the beginning of the 21st century.

The Railway first deliberated on the prospect of constructing the lines in 1909, when the growth in traffic had increased to the point that the Directors were able to consider a number of projects that would develop the interests of the Company. An announcement was subsequently, made that September, of the proposals being formulated for three extension lines; one was to run in a south-westerly direction across the plains to Kishenganj, the second would follow the valley of the river Teesta in the north-east towards Kalimpong, and the third wouuld trace the periphery of the spur from Darjeeling bazaar to the barracks at Lebong.

Although the plans for the military extension later foundered, the Directors sought sanctions from the Railway Board for the other two lines, and in 1911 estimated that the gross returns would be:

Kishenganj branch	320,000 rupees
Teesta Valley branch	232,000
Gross total	552,000
Less 50% working expenses	276,000
Net earnings	276,000
Dividend at 5% on 4,375,000	218,750
	57,250
Less half to Government	28,625
Surplus for the Company	28,625

The Darjeeling Himalayan Railway Extensions Company was first registered on 20th January 1913, and its construction authorised by the Railway Board in their telegram No.251 R.C. dated the 6th February 1913. The Board of Directors comprised E.H. Bray from Gillanders Arbuthnot as Chairman, the Hon. Norman McLeod, R.G. Thomas and W.K. Downing. Gillanders Arbuthnot & Co. was appointed as the Managing Agent with a capital requirement of Rs5,000,000, for which 43,750 shares of Rs100 each were made available by subscription. The prospectus made clear that the intentions of the extensions were to serve as feeder lines to the Eastern Bengal State Railway and to generally develop the trade of the country they traversed.

The principal contract between the Secretary of State and the Extensions Company was dated 25th April 1914, and set out the terms for the DHR working and maintaining the lines and the rolling stock. The main provisions included providing the land to be used in British territory free of cost, and permission to make use of any roads for the purposes of the extension railways as authorised by the Governments of Bengal, Bihar and Orissa. The Company would receive 50% of the gross earnings, and if a rebate was required, it would be given from the Eastern Bengal State Railway to make up 5% interest on the expenditure charged, as was the payment of interest out of capital at the rate of 4% during the construction of the lines on the money actually invested.

The agreement was modified on 4th April 1918 for the rebate to be a sum not exceeding in any year the net earnings of the EBR, exclusive of earnings derived from the carriage of revenue stores and traffic originating or terminating on the extensions. This, together with the net earnings of the Company, or with half the gross earnings after deducting half the sum of Rs15,000 payable on account of management and office expenses (whichever was the greater), was to make up an amount equal to interest for the year at a rate of 5% per annum on the actual expenditure charged in the capital account.

The creative ambiguity of this conundrum may have been an ingenious riddle designed to occupy the accountants during the long summer evenings, for it was simplified on 1st April 1931 to allow for the deduction of the actual expenditure incurred by the Extensions Company and for the DHR to receive 90% of the remaining gross earnings as its remuneration. However, this supplementary agreement reverted to the original terms of the principal contract should the Secretary of State be required to calculate the payment of a rebate or the Company the balance from a surplus profit.

The rates and fares for passengers and goods were to be agreed with the Company and the Secretary of State, subject to regular review. The classification of freight was to conform to the State railways of a similar gauge, provided that the maximum rates and fares for the Kishenganj branch were double, and the minima the same as those permissible on the EBR The rates and fares for the Teesta Valley line were similarly compared to the Western Extension of the Bengal Dooars Railway. It was also stipulated that the Company must reflect the same service level and favourable charges as the State railways for the conveyance of the mail, troops, police, high Government officials, Government stores, Government bullion and coin, and the persons in its charge. The final contract laid down that there would be three classes for passengers, and determined the charges for 1st Class would be at 36 pies per mile, 2nd Class at 24 pies and 3rd Class at 9 pies, with an additional 6 pies for luggage and parcels at 12 pies per maund. There were five classes of freight, the 5th Class attracting 5 pies per maund per mile, 4th at 4 pies, and 3rd, 2nd and 1st Classes at 3 pies. The concession was made to reduce the charge for transporting coal, edible grain and other low-price staple foods to 1 pie.

George Batterbury (left with topee) with his brothers Jack and Frank (centre). George joined the DHR in 1911 as an Assistant Permanent Way Inspector, after which he became involved with surveying the Teesta Valley Extension and developed a distinguished career as the Resident Engineer. Jack became an Inspector of Works for the railway in 1915 and was based at Ghum, whilst Frank was a Sub-Divisional Officer of the Engineering Branch at Siliguri until he lost his life during active service in 1916.

The DHRS Archive

George Batterbury outside his tent at Sevoke during the initial surveying of the Teesta Valley extension.

Pat Orr

The initial stretch of both extension lines crossed similar country after leaving Siliguri before the one crossed the cauterising plains of Bihar and the other burrowed deep into a capricious Himalayan valley. A mixed Up in 1945 is at the head of a train on this first section, but the photographer only recorded the details of his journey to Darjeeling and not of any visit to the two extensions. However, the Permanent Way Inspector working on the DHR at the time has identified the train is either at Sevoke in the Teesta Valley or possibly Bagdogra on the Kishenganj line. The large girders seen beyond the left-hand track were similar to those used for the construction of bridges on both lines.

The Frank Thornton Jones collection

It is interesting to note that under Clause 16 of the contract, the extension lines were to be worked either by electricity or steam, although there is no evidence that serious consideration was to be given to the former. The Secretary of State agreed to pay the costs of all the work at Kishenganj station that was for the sole purpose of effecting a junction between the new line and the EBR, whilst the DHR was to fund all the other work including buildings, etc. Clause 40 (i) stipulated that the two extension lines were to be ready and opened by 31st March 1916, with the penalty of forfeiting the project if this was not met.

The Government insisted on having the option of purchasing the railways at the end of 30 years from the date of being declared open for traffic and at subsequent 10-yearly intervals thereafter. The price that would be paid was set as 25 times the average net annual earnings (excluding payments on rebate) during the three years prior to the purchase and subject to a maximum of 120% and a minimum of 100% of the capital expenditure. These terms were modified in the 1918 agreement to 25 times the annual net earnings during the three years or 115% of the total capital expenditure, whichever was the greater. The Government also stipulated that it could exercise the option to purchase the lines at any time, subject to one year's notice, if it considered it desirable to alter the gauge, convert the branch into a through line of communication, or extend the branch and the Company was unable or unwilling to provide the necessary capital. Nobody could have foreseen the events that would follow some 35 years later, but these clauses were to prove invaluable for independent India to establish its essential links with Assam.

The General Manager of the DHR estimated the cost of construction and the first provision of rolling stock as Rs4,200,000. A detailed account had been made of the carts used on the roads to provide a basis for traffic predictions and was endorsed by Sir Bradford Leslie, the Chairman of the Southern Punjab Railway in a letter to the Directors:

'I am of the opinion that within a brief period after the Railways are opened for traffic the 5% rebate from the Eastern Bengal State Railway will be effective, and that in the ordinary course of events the earnings from the Railways will be such as to give a minimum net return of 5.75% upon the Capital of the Company, with gradually improving results, which are bound to follow when the advantages of the Railways have tended to develop trade generally. It is of undoubted advantage to the Extensions Company to be under the management and the control of those who have so successfully conducted the affairs of the Darjeeling Himalayan Railway Company. It is not to be expected that the Extensions Company will produce the returns which are now being realised by the Darjeeling Himalayan Railway Company, but the Extensions Company certainly starts with every element conductive to future success.'

The records do not show what motive power was to be used for constructing the lines, but the circumstantial evidence points to '*Baby Sivok*', an Orenstein and Koppel 0-4-0 well-tank. Gillanders Arbuthnot certainly obtained such a locomotive at the time the estimates were published in 1911, and its original design as a wood burner would have made it eminently suitable for working up the heavily forested Teesta Valley. Tindharia have advised the engine was originally known as '*Sivok*', the name no doubt being bequeathed by the gorge that the river and one of its new railways ran through.

The workshop also modified two of the 0-4-0 saddle tanks in 1913 to assist with the construction and running of the extensions. No.9 from the 'A' Class and No.22 from the 'B' Class both had their frames lengthened and a Bissell truck added to make the ride steadier, although it was not long after the opening of the branches that they were returned to their original form. The demand for additional motive power was such that the Company could no longer afford to tie up any of the 'B' Class on works trains, and searched for an additional locomotive that could be delivered at short notice. The light-railway engineering company of Robert Hudson had a works in Calcutta, and their records show that the 15 HP Hudswell Clarke 0-4-0 well-tank No.1055 was delivered direct to the DHR on 16th February 1914.

By the close of the 1913-14 year, the total capital outlay for the construction of the two extensions amounted to Rs2,292,311, which climbed to Rs3,987,838 by 31st March 1915. A new engine shed at Siliguri was sanctioned in June 1915 and constructed at a cost of Rs3,079 on land acquired by the Extensions Company. At the same time, the workshops at Tindharia were moved to a new site and enlarged to accommodate the increased workload that would be imposed by two extension lines of very different temperaments and character, as described in the following chapters.

The Engineer's bungalow at Kalijhora in 1915, built for the construction of the Teesta Valley extension. A 187ft-long siding was laid nearby to enable passing trains to cross, and although it was not always advertised in the timetable, a small halt was opened to serve a local settlement.

The DHRS Archive

Chapter 10

The Kishenganj Extension

The country which the Kishenganj extension crossed was iron-flat and fertile. The passenger traffic on the line was primarily local, and with the basic necessities of life being uppermost in the minds of those who laboured in the fields, little attention was ever paid to record the memories of those who travelled across its tracks. It was the longest, the most profitable, and the least-known line of the DHR.

The area was farmed primarily for jute, which had been cultivated for its strong fibre and used for the manufacture of ropes and sacks. The crop was to become one of the principal traffic commodities for the line, and much of it was destined to be transported by sea to Dundee in Scotland, which had become a centre for the production of sacks after the Crimean War terminated the supplies of Russian hemp. Jute was also found to be ideal for manufacturing the sandbags used in trench warfare, and at the time of the Great War there were eight million being sent every month through Calcutta to the War Office. Many Scots came to Bengal to manage the mills, where there were huge profits to be made, and the industry remained solely under British control until Independence in 1947.

At first sight the area remains as undistinguished to the casual traveller as the rest of the Indian plain, but the dust here has blown across a particularly traumatic history. The records are somewhat shy, but they can be dated back to 1540 when the Mughal Empire came to an abrupt halt after the Emperor Humayan was deposed by the Afghan soldier of fortune Sher Shah. Humayan lived in exile for the next 15 years until the Shah of Persia despatched Syed Khan Dastur[1] to lead an armed force and restore him to the Delhi throne. Following the successful purge, Khan Dastur was sent to resolve a problem of lawlessness in the district of Surajpur, an area that lay on the east bank of the Mahananda River and had fallen into Nepalese territory. It was under the control of Rana Sukhdeo, and had a fierce reputation for its uncivilised hordes of marauding bandits who freely plundered wayfarers and travellers along the outskirts of the district. Khan Dastur established his headquarters in what is now Kishenganj and drove the Nepalese back into the hills, after which he was conferred with the title Raja, was appointed as the Kanungo (Dictator of the Law), and granted the entire 729 square miles of territory free of revenue.

His descendants maintained their favour and privileges during the Mughal rule by keeping the Nepalese at bay and defending the land from numerous Bhutia advances, but there came a point when a family dispute arose over the rights of succession. The rents were collected by the Nawab Saif Khan during the feud, and claims were subsequently made for the money to be returned. Counter claims were made for revenue, which continued to the next generation and the point when the acrimony exploded into bitter fighting, imprisonment, kidnapping and suicide.

Changes began to occur when the East India Company took control under Lord Clive, and in the mid-18th century Lord Cornwallis granted a decennial settlement to Syed Fakhruddin Hossain, the ninth in line of descent, on the condition that substantial revenue was paid as military services would not be

---

[1] The term Syed referred to a lord, the designation in India of those who claim to be descendants of Mohammed.

Panchanai Junction in July 1914 with an impressively-long transportation of the 4th Wiltshire Regiment and its military band bound for Darjeeling. The band had sailed to India in advance of the main regiment, having been formed at Trowbridge from volunteers following the outbreak of war. Ernest Wootton was one of a number of lads who had joined up from the Warminster Town Band, and later recalled that they could not get the bass drum out of the carriage as the railway had lost the key! The carriages tantalisingly hide the Kishenganj extension veering away to the left, the first section of which had been open for only four months.

David Wootton.

needed of them! The Syed built his residence at Khagra, where one of his two sons Raja Syed Hossain resided, and on the eastern side founded a market known as Kutubgunge.

Syed Atta Hossain was the twelfth in succession, and was conferred with the title Nawab in 1887 on the occasion of Queen Victoria's Jubilee, the British having decided to make a distinction between Hindu (Raja) and Muslim (Nawab) noblemen. He founded the Mela at Khagra, a huge fair and agriculture exhibition designed to help improve and promote the conditions of the people. The community that grew around the market at Kutubgunge became known as Kishenganj, and trade grew to the point that a metre-gauge branch line was opened on 15th December 1892 from the south-western edge of the town to Barsoi Junction, where it connected with the main Eastern Bengal Railway system. The town had a population of 7,671 by 1901, and had become the administrative centre for the Kishenganj sub-division of Purnea,[2] with the Public Offices and Jail having been moved to a site adjacent to the railway station.

There were no major engineering difficulties envisaged with building the new DHR extension, for the route was not dictated by the contours of the land but the need to connect farming settlements with the markets, the centres of production, and the main railway network. Its course was somewhat dog-legged, running straight until a change of direction became necessary to find a village, bypass a forest or cross a river. Indeed, the line did not set out from Siliguri in the general direction of Kishenganj, for that would have entailed crossing the Panchanai River at a particularly difficult point. The less expensive option adopted was to share the same track as the Darjeeling line alongside the Hill Cart Road for three miles and cross the river by an already-existing bridge. The small station of Panchanai had been located just beyond this point since the earliest days of the DHR, and the Directors had already sanctioned a maximum of Rs7,244 for its replacement in December 1912. It made an ideal junction for the new extension to Kishenganj, and a watering point

---

[2] A British district of 5,878 square miles named after its principal town.

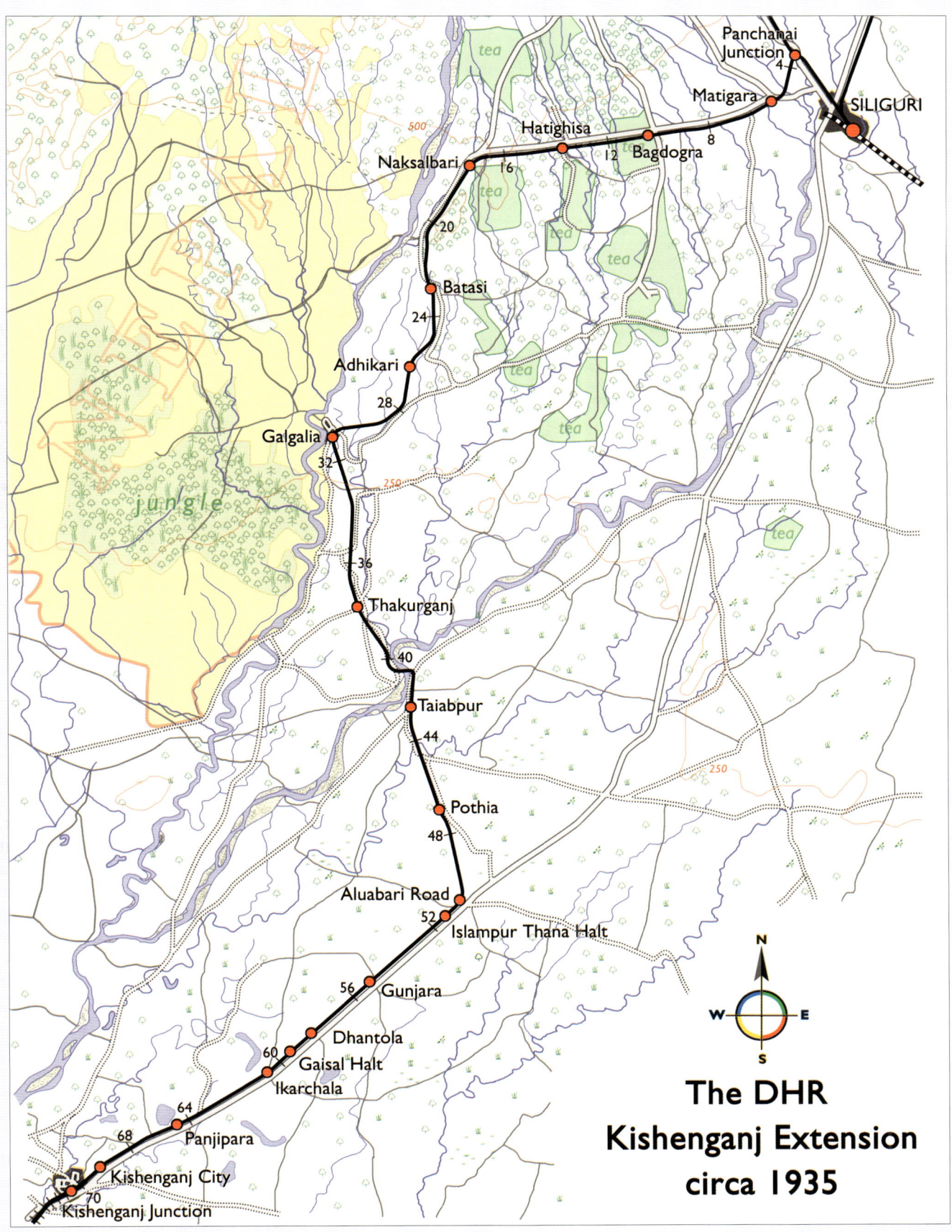

was placed alongside the track on the northern bank of the river. The working timetable later published by the DHR in 1940 refers to a triangle at Panchanai under the heading of 'Turntables'; Banshidhar Dikshit[3] has recalled there were indeed approaches from both directions of the main line, although the one that would have led from Sukna had been lifted by the time he began working for the railway.

Construction began simultaneously at both ends of the line and British standard section 40lb/yd steel rails were laid on *sal* sleepers ballasted with sand, although this was replaced with broken stone during the 1930s. The northern section was laid alongside a road and thus avoided the need to trespass into the tea gardens between Panchanai and Naksalbari, after which the line crossed the flood plains of the Mechi and the Mahananda. The rivers across this central area were somewhat somnolent until the monsoon rains turned them into full spate, and a number of low embankments were constructed to maintain a level gradient and keep the track above the surging water. The railway resumed, running alongside the road for the final stretch beyond Islampur, and this obviated the construction of any further earthworks for the last twenty miles to Kishenganj.

---

[3] DHR Permanent Way Inspector 1942–1972.

The first section of the new extension was opened at Panchanai Junction on 16th March 1914, with the Kishenganj branch curving away from the Darjeeling line at ninety degrees. Matigara was the first station along the way, and served a town that had grown to become one of the most important markets in northern Bengal. However, the Balasan River flowed just beyond, and until 1895 there was no bridge to cross its surging currents. Anybody intent on reaching the opposite bank would require the assistance of the coolies from the nearby tea gardens, conveniently assembled on the riverbank and waiting for custom. By joining hands to form a chain, they would wade into the river, although it was not unknown for the leader to end up half a mile downstream before a crossing had been made.

The Public Works Department finally erected a wooden bridge in 1896, but it lasted only five years before it was washed away. It was replaced by a much stronger construction also built in wood, and the Extension Company did not plan to undertake its replacement unless the traffic demanded it. The intention was to rely on a ferry service and provision was made for this with the estimates. In the end it was decided to build a stone bridge, and it took 14 spans to cross the river, each one being 40ft long. It was not long before the floodwater tore away at the pier-heads, which collapsed at both ends, and the delay with the repair

Illustrations of the Kishenganj extension are a great rarity, for to the eye of the traveller and photographer there were far more interesting panoramas to be captured on film in the mountains. A 'B' Class is seen with a short train of four-wheelers and a first generation bogie coach crossing the bridge over the Balasan River, the longest on the system with 14 spans.

The DHRS Archive

work meant that the section for the next 12 miles to Naksalbari was not opened until 1st February 1915.

The line was constructed with much greater speed from the Kishenganj end, with the 19 miles to Islampur having been laid by 15th June 1914 and the following 9 miles to Taiabpur opened on 1st November. The final link between Taiabpur and Naksalbari was made on 1st May 1915, and the 67-mile branch became the longest section of the entire DHR system. There were plans to extend the network further, and the Assistant Engineer, George Batterbury, was asked to map out a route and report on an extension of the branch into Nepal. The project was later abandoned as the Nepalese Government had not changed its stance since the attempt made by Prestage in 1889 and continued to fiercely protect its independence, not making strangers any the more welcome. The figures were also collected in 1916–17 to examine the feasibility of constructing a branch from Naksalbari to Mirik, which at 5,300 feet above sea level was seen as being ideal for development into a health resort. The DHR surveyed a course that ran via Panighatta and Namsu, but again nothing was to come of the project.

Two 4-6-2 'Pacific' locomotives (designated 'C' Class) were ordered from the North British Locomotive Company Ltd of Glasgow in 1913, and were designed specifically for drawing loads of up to 800 tons across the plains. They were delivered the following year and used primarily to haul freight, the 'B' Class being retained for the mixed passenger trains. The new passenger bogie stock was rarely used on the extension line, the open-sided trolleys being better suited for coping with the merciless sun that scorched the plains. It was not the natural terrain for the saddle-tanks, and double-heading or one engine working as a banker was occasionally necessary on the uphill section between Batasi and Naksalbari. However, the Garratt was found to be more at home working the extension than the climb to Darjeeling, and the long straight sections through the bamboo thickets suited its temperament just nicely. Elderly residents in Siliguri have also recalled seeing 'Jervis Bay' at work across the plains, and whilst the image of streamlining would have been of little consequence to the native farmer travelling to market with a bag of live chickens, there was no need for sanders to face the ordeal of sitting inside the cladding. The tender would also have given the locomotive an advantage over the other 'B' Class with its increased capacity to carry fuel across the long distances, and may well have helped to justify its cause for a short time.

It was an easy if somewhat mundane run for the locomotive crews, for the steepest gradient was only inclined at 1 in 100 and the sharpest curve profiled with a radius of 100ft. Panchanai Junction took its name from the river that flowed nearby, although one authoritative source has suggested that it may have been derived from pan (the betel nut), chai (tea) and ni (nothing) to signify there was little of any virtue to be found there! The station building was adjacent to the Darjeeling line, and at 418ft above sea level, it was three miles from Siliguri. Trains for Kishenganj curved away from here to the left and headed straight as a die in a south-westerly direction, slowly descending across two miles of open grassland and the tea gardens of the Chandmani estate. Rising on a low embankment to bridge a meandering tributary of the Mahananda, the train curved to cross the Siliguri-Naksalbari road at an angle before running into Matigara (389ft – 5½ miles). The name originated from 'the mud house', for those in the hills were built from stone or wood whilst here was the first that had been made from the alluvium of

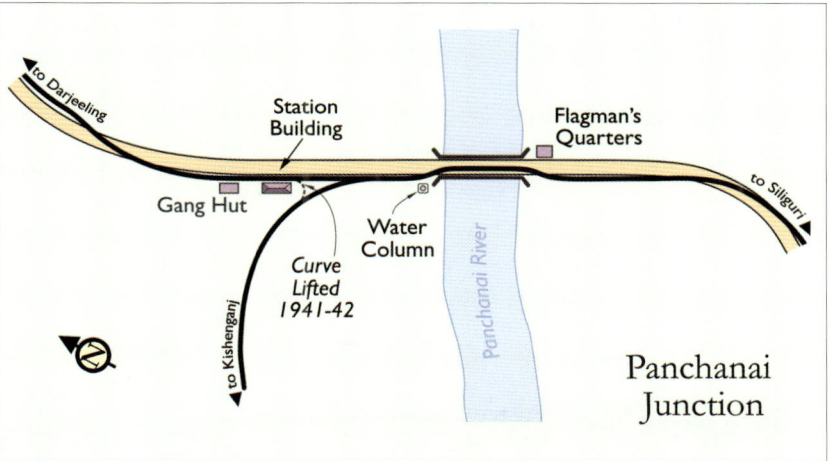

local rivers. The station was on the far side of the town and backed on to the Motibagan tea garden, close to the junction with the Pankhabari Road.

The railway did not stray from the southern side of the Naksalbari road for the next 12 miles, passing over the temperamental waters of the Balasan ('River of Golden Sand') and through the northern part of the Bainganbari tea gardens. The countryside opened out for the next four miles to fields of jute interrupted by scrub and bunched grassland, the train running on occasional embankments and crossing 11 bridges and culverts before steaming into Bagdogra (453ft – 10 miles). The town is known today principally for its

One of the two 'Pacifics' waits on the far bank of the Mahanandi River with a train of four-wheelers from Taiabpur and Kishenganj. The incident of the span being swept away has not been traced, but no doubt it was brought down by a surge of water caused by the monsoon rains. Circa 1915

The DHRS Archive

airport, although the name translates as 'the place of roaring tigers' on account of them overrunning the area at one time. The settlement gained a reputation in the heyday of the railway with the local population for its annual fair and with the Europeans for the golf, polo and tennis at the Bengdubi Club.

Leaving Bagdogra, the train was flanked on either side by tea, with the Kamalpur and Sannyasithan gardens being to the right and those of the Kadapany and Singijhora on the left. Two miles on, road and rail crossed the Telu River on a bridge of concrete piers as they nudged round the southern spur of the Dalkajhar Reserved Forest, a vast track of *sal* covering the foothills of the Himalaya. The large Deomani tea estate opened out to the north with the smaller Kristopur gardens and a sprawling jungle of *sal* to the south, and after crossing the Chenga River, the train approached the station of Hatighisa (473ft – 14 miles). The Atal and Dam Dim gardens lay beyond, after which the line ran for three miles through the less-manicured fields of mustard seed and jute as it crossed ten more bridges spanning perennial and seasonal rivers cutting their way from the brooding mountains. Passing the highest point on the line at 501ft and skirting the Satbhaiya tea gardens on the left, it was not long before the train swept round a left-hand curve and into Naksalbari (493ft – 17½ miles). It was an important stop for rice and timber brought in from nearby Nepal

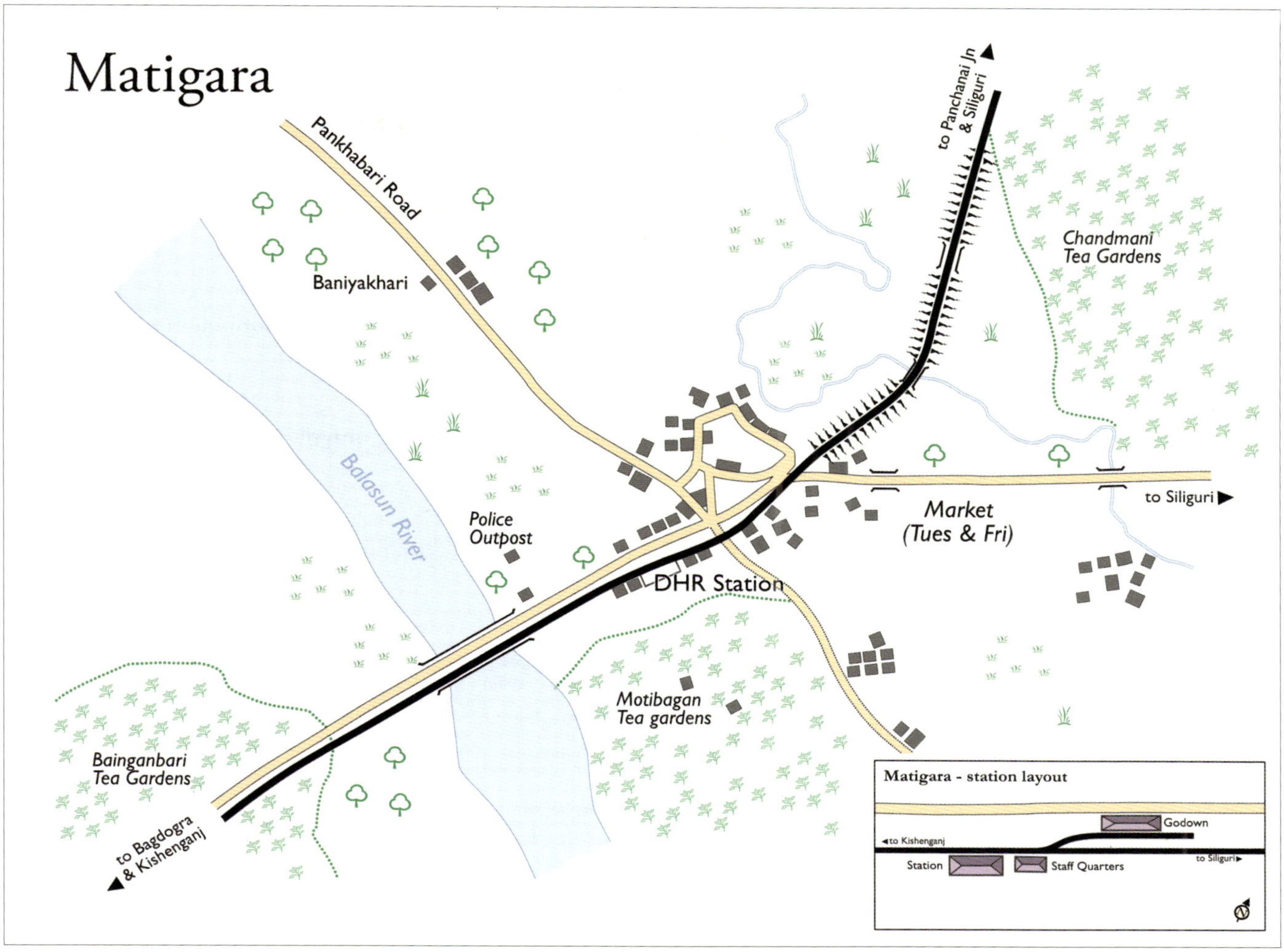

Believed to have been taken at Bagdogra in the late 1920s, this eclectic rake of coaches includes an early bogie travelling post office (third from right), next to which is a 1st Class four-wheeler.

Collection: Gwen Cattermull

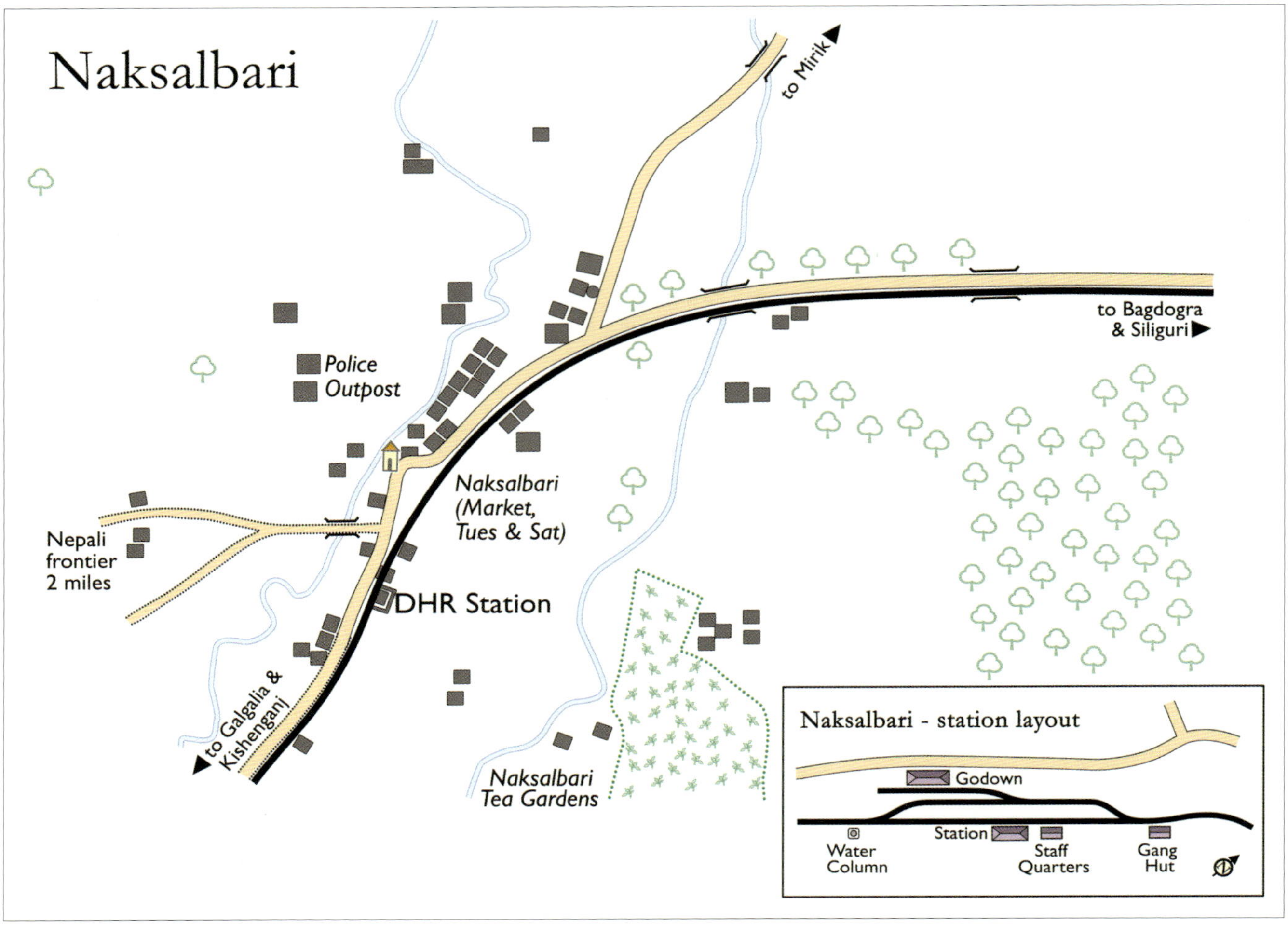

Repair work on bridge No.4 (it had no name) near Bagdogra, consisting of five spans supported by 20ft-long girders. The monsoon rains had completely scoured the foundations away, and it had to be totally rebuilt. This photograph shows the rail piles being driven into the bed of the river, upon which a footing of concrete was to be laid to secure the new piers.

Glynne Gladstone MSS

The DHR placed an order in 1913 with North British to built two 4-6-2 locomotives designed specifically for working the 70-mile run to Kishenganj. Designated as the 'C' Class and numbered 37 and 38 in the DHR stock list, they were superb machines that gave exemplary service. The top photograph is an unusual late-evening scene of No.37 running on the extension; the engines were subsequently renumbered 807 and 808 under the ISR scheme, the latter being seen in the lower illustration languishing in the yards at New Jalpaiguri in 1974.

Above: Kelland Collection
Below: Lawrence Marshall

and the station was on the southern side of the town, its name having come from the term Naksal, 'the forest hunting grove'.

The train was now running in a south-westerly direction away from the tea estates, with the Tukriajhar Reserved Forest covering the low hills rising to the east. By most accounts these would be seen as of little note, but in this land of vast flat horizons, the hills were a significant feature and followed the course of the railway at a discreet distance for nearly four miles. The railway came within a stone's throw of the Mechi River and the Nepalese border, and after cutting across a corner of the forest, the line veered due south away from the river and into fields of jute and tall grass. The area was now distinguished only by the small station of Batasi (373ft – 23½ miles), the nearest point of commercial interest being the last of the tea gardens lying two miles east of the railway and away from the potentially ruinous floods of the Mechi. Soon after leaving the station, the train was carried on an embankment for a mile and continued straight across open scrub until abruptly turning south-west and into the station of Adhikari (305ft – 26 miles), which served a scattering of isolated settlements and the sizeable market of Kharibari Hat, three miles away.

The route was now taking the train back in the direction of the Mechi, and after three miles it rose above the flood plain on an embankment. There were four bridges on this section, and the swollen river caused considerable damage to these over the years by under scouring the side abutments and sweeping away the central piers. In an effort to prevent further destruction, they were later rebuilt with shorter spans and supporting girders set on foundations of concrete piles. The train was obliged to head directly towards the river in order to reach the town of Bhatgaon Hat, and as it left the embankment by the final bridge, it crossed the border into Bihar and approached the station of Galgalia (273ft – 31 miles). Barely half a mile from Nepal, it had developed as a depot for the paddy brought across the frontier to Bhatgaon Hat, and the two rice mills that operated alongside the railway

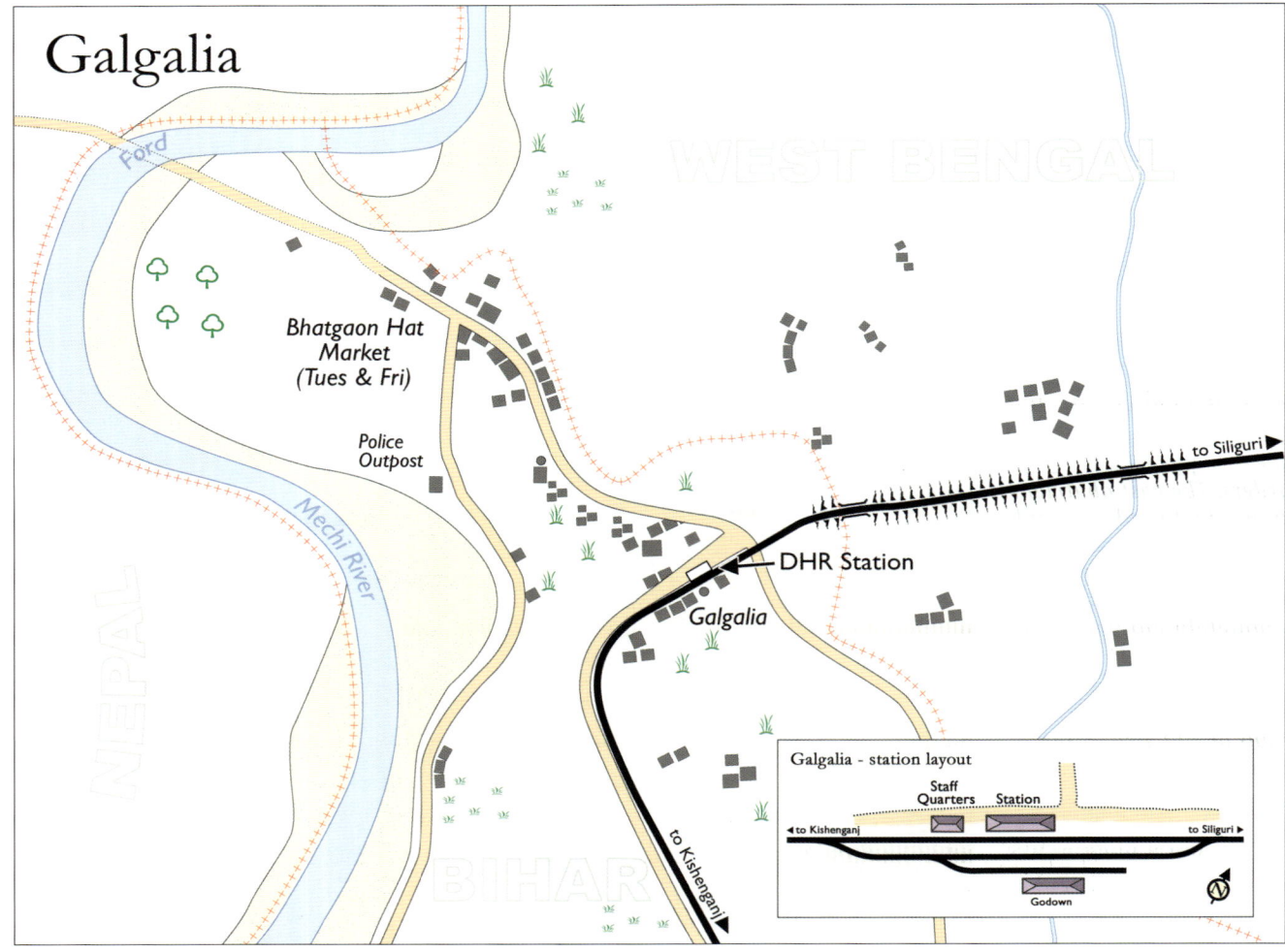

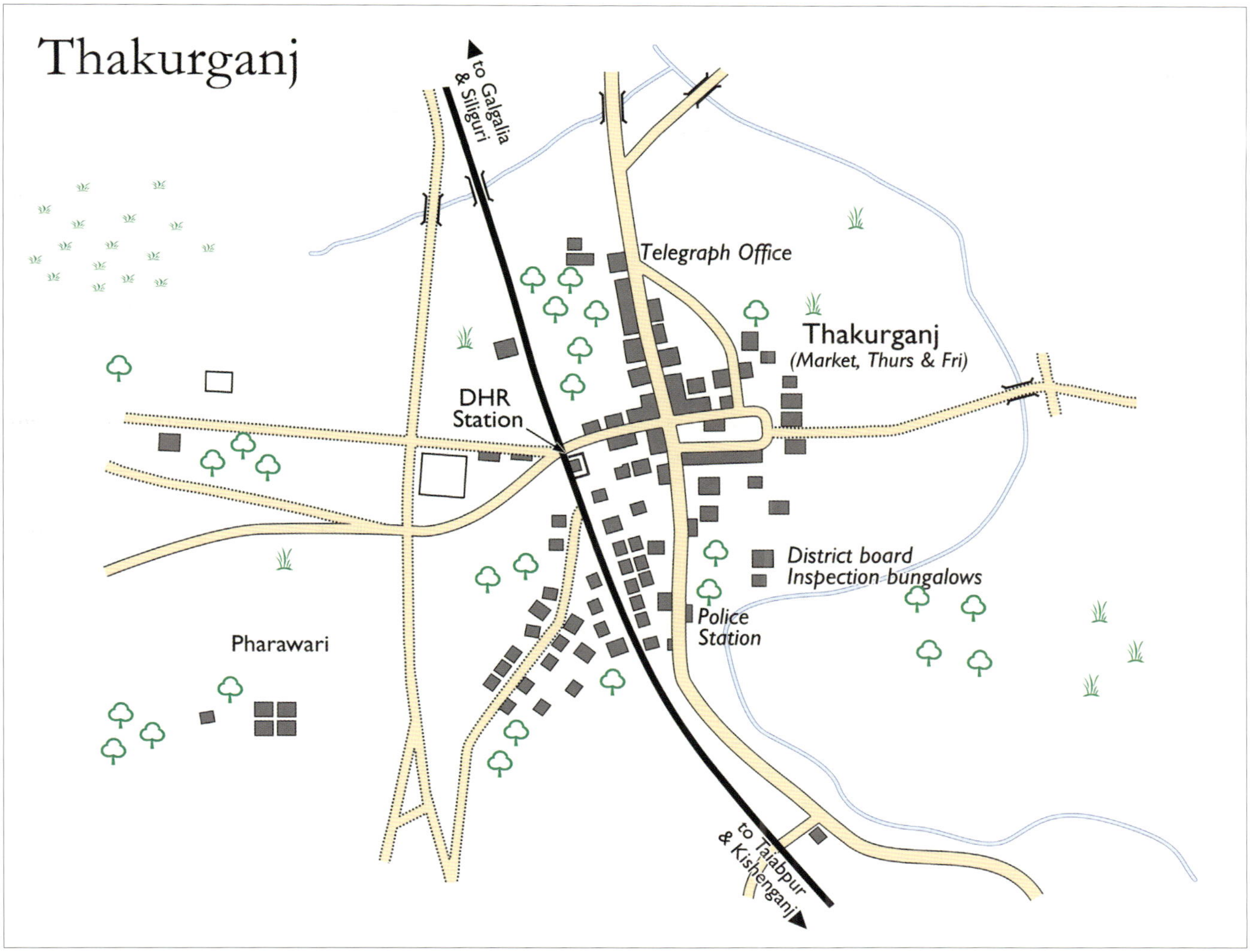

THE KISHENGANJ EXTENSION

Flood damage from the Mechi river near Galgalia. The bridge consisted of two spans supported by 30ft girders. The east abutment shown in the photograph had been under scoured and fallen forward, whilst the centre pier had been completely carried away by the river. The bridge was entirely rebuilt with two spans of 30ft and two spans of 20ft girders set on foundations of concrete piles.

Glynne Gladstone MSS

The girders of the ex-DHR crossing of the Laska River looking towards Siliguri in February 2005. The main highway can be seen to the left, and shows how close the railway ran to it.

The remains of the DHR bridge across the Telu River. The train veered away from the road at this point to avoid the Dalkajhar Reserved Forest, and the former railway embankment can be seen curving back to join the highway to Naksalbari. February 2005.

The godown and platform of the extension line at Adhikari (26 miles from Siliguri), the stack of rails belonging to the metre gauge that runs parallel to the former DHR trackbed. February 2005.

Looking north and standing on the former trackbed of the DHR line, local residents point out the site of the narrow-gauge station at Galgalia to Rajiv Lochan and David Charlesworth. The metre-gauge station is behind the photographer and on the opposite side of the track. February 2005.

The pillars of the former DHR bridge across the Mahananda form the base of the current road bridge, with the crossing for the metre gauge being seen beyond. February 2005.

Another photograph from the collection taken by George Cresswell, the General Manager of the DHR from 1906 to 1916. Looking upstream, it shows what may have been his inspection train (see also page 268) crossing the Mahanandi between Thakurganj and Taiabpur. Note the wooden 'baillies' in the river under the bridge.

The DHRS Archive

were able to export 14,000 tons a year and supply the whole of the district to Darjeeling and beyond. The area had also developed as a centre for the timber industry, and the records show that the railway was transporting approximately 1,000 tons of raw jute from the station every year.

Sensing danger from its proximity to the Mechi, the line backed off at ninety degrees in a south-easterly direction in three long straight sections, passing the halt of Piprithan (248ft – 34 miles) at the end of the first. The area was known locally as the Churli Milik, but for that it appeared no different from all the other fields of jute that baked under a pitiless sun. Thakurganj (234ft – 38 miles) came into view after four miles, with the station being constructed on the west side of the track. With a population at the time of 3,000, the town had grown as a centre for rice and for having a thriving market, along with the police, postal and telegraph services for the locality. It stood on a low plateau that overlooked the Mahananda River to the south-east and the impenetrable forests of Nepal to the west, and on a clear morning the distant summit of Mount Everest could be seen to the north.

Two miles after leaving Thakurganj, the train approached and then ran parallel to the outside of a bend in the Mahananda River. By maintaining the curve as the river straightened out, it was able to rise on an embankment and cross its unpredictable waters on a seven-span girder bridge. The river would often run dry in the winter and spring, and it was during this time that a line of wooden stumps that measured between 8 to 10ft long and 6 to 10in in diameter would be hammered into the river bed. Known as 'baillies', these would form the base to which a mesh of bamboo was attached and filled with boulders to protect the foundation of the pillars from scouring, although the photographic evidence suggests it was only partially successful.

Leaving the bridge, the railway curved back at ninety degrees to run parallel to the river bank and into the station of Taiabpur (230ft – 42 miles). The stop catered for three settlements that alternated along the line, the first being between the railway and the river bank on the approach to the station, after which four bustees (shanties of huts) stretched for half a mile on the opposite side of the track. Facing the last of these came the market town of Taiabpur itself hugging the left bank of the river, the train being carried on an embankment above the threat of flooding. Veering away, the embankment continued for two miles to a bridge across the Dauk, a major tributary of the Mahananda whose sluggish waters could be equally as temperamental during the monsoon rains.

THE KISHENGANJ EXTENSION

Panjipara Station, circa 1915. Approximately five miles from Kishenganj, Cresswell described the halt as a typical roadside station.

The DHRS Archive

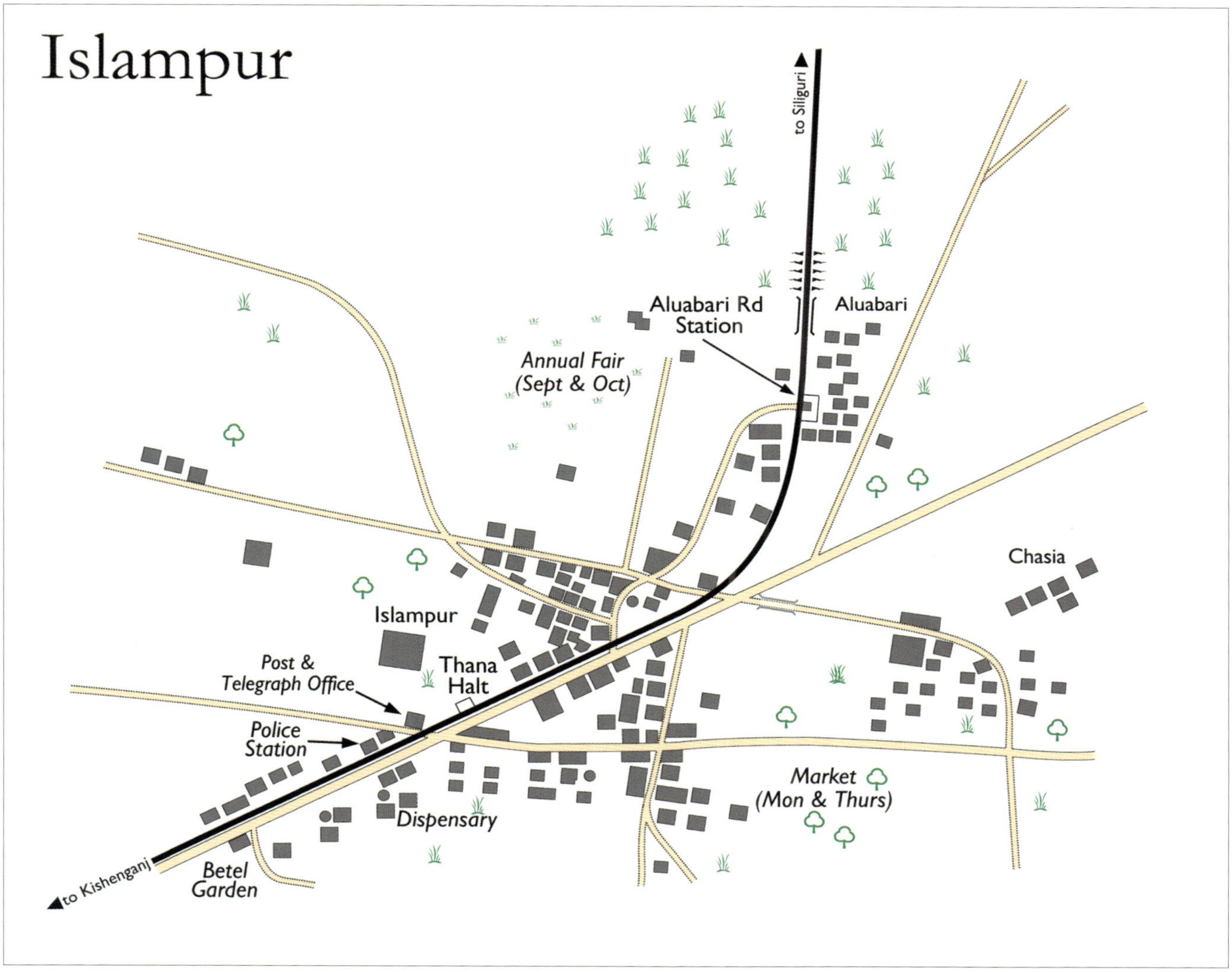

Islampur

Iron girders still bear witness the DHR crossing of the Laska River, the embankment constructed in 1949 for the metre-gauge Assam Rail Link being seen in the distance. February 2005.

The damage caused to the foundations of the bridges and the attempts at repair were still evident in February 2005 on the remains of the pillars that supported the DHR crossing over the Hulia River. This pillar is in the foreground of the picture below.

Looking across the columns of the Hulia bridge towards Bagdogra and Naksalbari, the large advertisement hoarding partially obscures the course of the railway running alongside the main highway.

Barely noticeable between two houses in February 2005, this short crossing in Naksalbari would have been in open country at the time that it took the DHR across the gully. The railway sleepers would have been laid directly on the ribbed steel and given excellent support.

A trio of semaphore signals at Adhikari looking towards Naksalbari. The one on the left was for the DHR, the other two still being in use for the metre gauge. February 2005.

The former quarters for the DHR staff at Galgalia, the Nepalese border being barely one mile away. February 2005.

Another embankment a mile beyond the river levelled the way for the train to approach Pothia (210ft – 47 miles), a secondary station that was close to the small market of Chilhamari. The original surveys had estimated the population of the area amounted to 400 persons to the square mile, and such was the popularity of the railway service that the village successfully petitioned the Directors of the Extension Company for their own station. The fields of jute gave way to bamboo soon after leaving Pothia, a short embankment leading the train to bridge the Burichana River before the straight run into Islampur, the next major settlement along the line. The station was sited on the approach to the town and referred to as Aluabari Road (215ft – 51 miles), taking the name from a small community nestling between the railway and the main Siliguri-Ganges highway coming in from the northeast. An annual fair was staged on the opposite side of the track during September and October, whilst the main town lay beyond the junction and had developed as an important collection point for jute.

Leaving Aluabari Road, the line turned to a southwesterly direction and followed the main road through the main part of the town, with an optional stop at Islampur Thana Halt for the local residents. Passing the offices of the District Board and a betel garden on the left, the train left the town for the final stretch to Kishenganj, shuffling along under a fringe of trees for 19 miles on the northern side of the road. The land beyond was so flat that the bamboo thickets and scrub appeared to stretch beyond the horizon, and most of the villages were little more than clusters of thatched huts surrounded by thickets of cane. Local markets were held adjacent to the first two stations at Gunjaria (196ft – 56 miles) and Dhantola (189ft – 58 miles), the farmers scratching a living from harvesting the jute and others somehow surviving amongst the parched swamps and reed beds. None was held at Gaisal Halt (59½ miles) or Ikarchala (60½ miles), after which a negligible change of direction took the road and rail to Panjipara Hat Halt and the market of Panjipara (172ft – 65 miles), the only settlement of any size along this section. The tributaries of the Mahananda River that lay to the right were often so listless that the sediment they had carried from the mountains had been deposited to create an area of dried-up channels and oxbow lakes. With the monsoon rains easily flooding the land, it had become a prime breeding ground for mosquitoes and malaria, and such was its reputation that a local proverb advised '*na zahar khayeh na makur khayeh, marna hai Purnea jayeh*', which translated means '*Do not eat poison nor any form of it; if you want to die go to Purnea.*'

The line clung remorselessly to the highway for the last five miles into Kishenganj, which at the time of the railway had grown to support a population of 15,000. There were two stations in the town for the DHR, the first being somewhat grandly known as Kishenganj City. It was built close to Kutubgunge, the site of the original market from which the town grew, and it was here that the engine shed and turntable for the 'Pacifics' were located. It was perhaps the more important of the two stations for the DHR, and the end of the run at Kishenganj Junction (150ft – 70 miles) was an extension that ran for a mile through the town to connect passengers with the metre gauge. The terminus was built alongside the road with a run-round loop and a siding, the station building being opposite the entrance to the EBR trains for Barsoi. The town did not have its own supply of electricity until after Independence. The stations for both gauges are remembered as being illuminated by the baleful gleam of Petromax lamps, burning pressurised kerosene, which hung from beams and wooden posts on the platforms. It is not clear from the records and contemporary maps, but it appears there was no

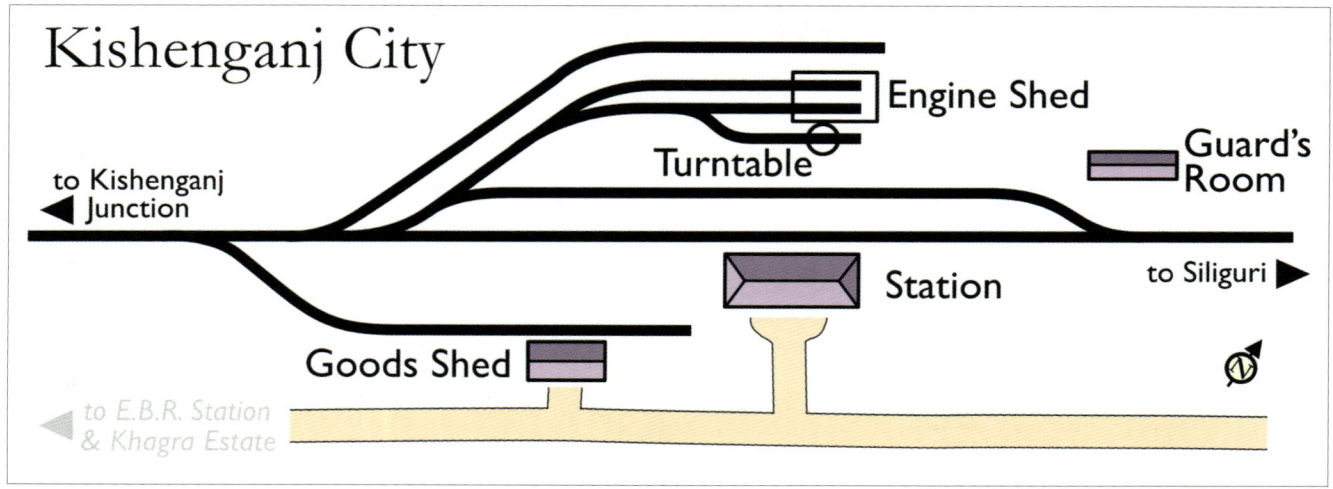

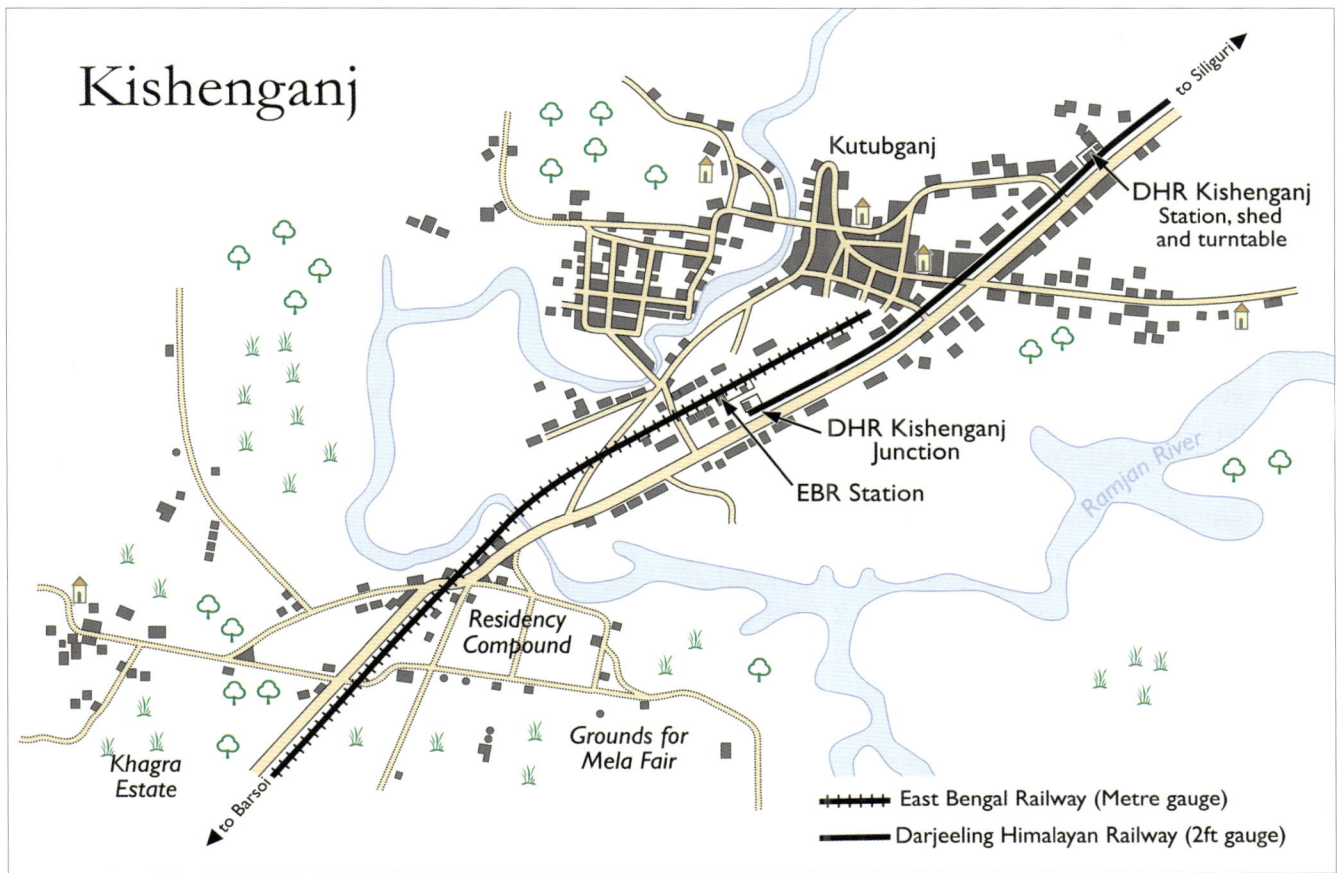

provision for the transhipment of goods, and what needed to be transferred was simply carried from the freight siding across the yard. Most of it was jute bound for Calcutta or rice for the hill stations, and as such it would have been taken direct to Siliguri.

The times for connections at Kishenganj made interesting reading, for it appeared there was a considerable allowance for the DHR running late. In 1939, the one train of the day from Siliguri was the 51 Mixed scheduled to arrive at 15.05, for which the EBR was content to wait until 16.58 before its own 246 Mixed for Barsoi departed. However, the metre-gauge 243 Mixed arrived at Kishenganj at 8.45, where it was thought that 30 minutes was sufficient to transfer to the DHR 52 Mixed for Siliguri waiting to depart at 9.15.[3]

The only other passenger trains on the narrow gauge were held overnight on the two running tracks at Thakurganj, there being no shed to accommodate the locomotives. The 56 Mixed departed at 5.10 and was due to arrive at Siliguri by 8.55, with the return service leaving as the 55 Mixed at 16.45 and arriving at Thakurganj at 20.22. The 53 Mixed departed Thakurganj at 5.15, and was due to arrive at Kishenganj by 8.32, the metre-gauge 248 Mixed being conveniently scheduled to depart at 9.30. For the return, the 223 Mixed on the metre gauge was timed to arrive at Kishenganj by 14.33, which could hardly be regarded as handy for the 54 Mixed to Thakurganj at 17.00, however attractive a 2½-hour doze in the afternoon sun may have appeared.

It was a half-mile walk from the station to the grounds of the Residency, where the stage was set every January for the annual Khagra Mela. The huge fair would run for several weeks and attracted large numbers of passengers and merchants travelling to Kishenganj by the DHR. Just about everything and anything was brought for sale, from Bata shoes and chill-proof vests to dromedary camels from Rajasthan and elephants caught in the jungles of Bengal and Assam. The market spread across acres of the open compound, whilst the animals would be tethered under the shade of the mango trees. The elephants were always regarded

---

[3] The 246 Mixed on the EBR had the dispensation to wait a further 30 minutes to ensure that a connection was made, and in return the DHR had the authority to delay the departure of its 52 Mixed for an hour.

Looking towards Matigara and Siliguri, the masonry pillars leading to the DHR bridge across the Buri Balasan were still much in evidence in February 2005. The former trackbed has now become a service road for a nearby settlement, the sloping embankment (top left) being the edge of the main highway.

The remains of the DHR bridge and embankment at Kumartoligachh, looking in the direction of Galgalia. In a land where everything is recycled, it is either a testament to its solid construction or an illustration of its remoteness that such a structure has remained over 55 years after its last use. February 2005.

Right: *The ex-DHR bridge parallel to the metre gauge across the Dauk River. February 2005.*

The same bridge at Kumartoligachh as on the opposite page (bottom) looking towards Aluabari Road and Kishenganj. February 2005.

The superb ex-DHR water tower at Aluabari Road. It received its supply from a nearby well (still extant), and the opening for the pipe that fed water to the locomotives can be seen beneath the corner of the tank.

as something special, and the air of mystique was reflected by their owners conducting negotiations in silence with their hands under a blanket, their fingers and joints representing the different monetary values.

Stalls, sideshows and even canvas cinemas would be erected, and amongst the many attractions was an exhibition of talking human heads apparently attached to the bodies of animals and reptiles. The illusion of a woman's head appearing on the body of a cobra and a man's on the body of a jackal was all done with mirrors, but cleverly connived and enough to induce awe to the more susceptible. Jugglers and magicians wandered around merchants trading silks from Benares, carpets from Kashmir and gemstones from Jaipur, along with gods to worship, *thankas* to inspire and jewellery to flaunt. The undoubted highlight was the big-top circus, and the bands playing 'Show Me the Way to Go Home' and 'Lay That Pistol Down, Babe' competed enthusiastically with the narcotic rhythms of the sitar and tabla beating to the more languid pace of Indian life. The circus and cinema would have their own generators, but gifted with the ability to make their music heard above all else, the locals would use old car-batteries to power their amplifiers and ensure the loudspeakers were blaring throughout the day. The air would be heavy with sandalwood and spices, which percolated through the smoke billowing from small braziers and open fires keeping vast cauldrons of curry on the boil. Everybody was catered for, with itinerant dentists pulling teeth, ear-cleaners inserting picks, ayurvedics pedalling cures, shamans possessing spirits, naked sadhus renouncing materialism, astrologers forecasting wealth, barbers shaving pilgrims, flutes charming snakes ... it was India indulging in all its array of gaudy fantasy.

It was good business for the railway, and the annual traffic returns within two years of opening showed that 76,478 passengers and 27,920 tons of goods were carried, giving the new Company gross earnings of Rs211,449. The fortunes of Siliguri began to grow, and the astute quickly began developing buildings and property nearby, particularly around Matigara with storehouses for the jute, which many anticipated would treble in output with the opening of the railway.

The success of the extension line was evident, and in February 1918 *The Englishman* reported that the railway had made a number of detailed surveys with a view to converting the section from Kishenganj to Islampur to metre gauge. The plan was for this to connect with a new metre-gauge railway that was being surveyed from Islampur to Siliguri via Titalia, which would provide a direct route of 36 miles as opposed to 50 miles by the two-foot gauge. Known as the Dinajpur & Purnea District Railway Surveys, an additional reconnaissance was made for a branch line to run from either Titalia or Ramgunja to Jalpaiguri and at the same time extend the two-foot gauge from Islampur to Dinajpur via Lahiree Hat. The proposal included a line branching from Lahiree Hat to Haldibari, all of which would add approximately 80 miles to the DHR extension.

Nothing further materialised from the studies, and with the figures for 1919–1920 showing that 327,000 passengers and 46,000 tons of freight were carried, the two-foot-gauge line continued to produce a healthy return. The following table illustrates that this did not diminish over the years:

Year	No. of Passengers	Tons of goods
1929 – 1930	653,000	44,000
1934 – 1935	381,000	45,000
1939 – 1940	379,000	64,000
1940 – 1941	351,000	56,000
1941 – 1942	401,000	49,000
1942 – 1943	459,000	50,000
1943 – 1944	402,000	45,000

In 1943, Jimmy Shaw, the works manager at Tindharia, travelled to Assam to inspect the locomotives and rolling stock of the Jorhat Railway. The Indian Government had taken it over in 1937, and after converting one section from two-foot to metre gauge and closing down the rest, had kept the old stock in the hope they would eventually find a customer. Shaw subsequently recommended the purchase of four of its locomotives for the Kishenganj branch, three of them being the 0-4-2 tank engines built by Andrew Barclay between 1925 and 1929, and the fourth either the Fowler 0-4-2 tank of 1887 or more likely, the 4-6-0 that came from Kerr Stuart in 1913. However, the DHR Directors did not wish to proceed with his advice, and the branch continued to be dependent on the two 'Pacifics' working most of the freight traffic and the 'B' Class for the passenger services.

The monsoon rains in September 1944 caused damage to several bridges between Matigara and Galgalia, the swollen rivers tearing away at the foundations and wing walls. Temporary repairs were made with old sleepers protecting the river banks, along with sand-filled gunny bags and boulders. By November the work had commenced on strengthening the foundations by driving vertical piles of rails into the river bed, which gave stability to the concrete bases supporting the stone and metal piers.

The dramatic changes brought by independence in 1947 gave a completely different emphasis to the importance of the area. New frontiers were drawn across the map that resulted in Assam being dependent on a corridor barely twelve miles wide sandwiched between Nepal and East Pakistan, and with the only rail link to the northern territory of West Bengal being the Kishenganj extension, the political machinations left that untenable.

The Railway Board awarded Karnail Singh the post of chief engineer of the Assam Rail Link Project (ARLP) in November 1947; his brief was to ensure the Province was connected by rail to the rest of India as quickly as possible. A survey of the area was immediately undertaken, which resulted in his recommendation for the construction of four new lines to connect with the isolated railway systems that ran across the Dooars, the eighteen 'doors' of Bhutan. Strictly speaking, the name related only to the eleven gorges and passes that opened into Bengal and the seven into Assam, but it had become the generic name for the area that included the adjacent plains.

The new Indian government gave the work top priority, and two of the lines to be constructed were to follow the routes of the DHR extensions as far as possible. Work began on the Kishenganj branch on 13th April 1948, where sections of the trackbed could be easily upgraded with new bridges and embankments. The work progressed at an astonishing rate and the first passenger traffic was able to run on the metre gauge to Thakurganj by 1st July 1948 and Naksalbari by the end of the month. This became the terminus for the DHR for the next year and was run as a joint station with the ARLP, for the conversion work from here on was going to involve planning a new route.

The problem was that a considerable part of the old line ran alongside the road in tramway fashion, and that would have made running a faster and more demanding service impractical. A new alignment was laid further back from the highway, and the opportunity was taken to allow the metre gauge to make a more direct approach into Siliguri and terminate at a new station on the northern side of the town. The two-foot gauge was finally closed on 8th December 1949, and the first metre-gauge train steamed into the new station named Siliguri North the following day. The first freight train also ran into Assam on the same day, a remarkable achievement by any standard, but when the terrain it had crossed was considered, it was nothing short of a miracle.

The two 'Pacific' locomotives found themselves redundant with the closure of the branch, and as they were unsuitable for the climb to Darjeeling, were relegated to working the section from Siliguri to Sukna. Even then there were problems, for the Bissel-truck under the cab was designed to trail and not lead, and with no turntable at Sukna, there was little option but to run in reverse back to Siliguri. This led to derailments, and it was thought that the solution lay in making solid the pivot from which the wheels moved laterally. However, the modifications caused damage to the track, particularly when crossing the points, and despite realignments and alterations to the permanent way, most of their work was confined to empty-carriage working. Both machines were simply too good to scrap, but with little left for them to do by the end of the 1960s, they were to be found laid up at the back of New Jalpaiguri shed. Luckily they managed to survive the cutter's torch, and No.807 is now preserved in Bombay at the Nehru Science Centre, whilst No.808 is mounted on a plinth at the Northeast Frontier Railway headquarters at Maligaon.

The Khagra Estate at Kishenganj was dissolved by the new government under the Land Acquisition Act, although it did not include the nationalisation of the weekly markets and annual fairs. In fact the settlement of these cases was to go on for years, and Nawabzada Syed Zainuddin Hossain Meerza was allowed to manage the Khagra Mela until the case was due to be heard at the Supreme Court in Delhi. However, the Indian Government pulled the rug from under his feet at the last minute by amending the Land Reforms Act to include their acquisition. Four hundred years of history were thus wound up as the merchants and contractors sat on a huge carpet under a shiamana (marquee) in the Residency compound and put in their bids for the various sites. It left the former owners virtually bankrupt, for the revenue from the fair was almost as much as that from the entire estate.

The roadside stations along the line were absorbed into the land, as are all things in India, and at first glance little appears to remain. However, a surprising amount can be observed with a little detective work, for the metre gauge between Matigara and Naksalbari was laid on a course further away from the road than the DHR and crossed the rivers on newly constructed bridges.

A curving footpath to the north of the Panchanai Bridge marks the beginning of the former trackbed of the extension, but this peters out and becomes lost across the plains and enveloping shacks of Matigara. The end piers of the DHR Balasan Bridge can still be seen adjacent to the metre gauge, whilst the pillars of those across the Laska, Buri Balasan and Hulia run parallel to the road and remain distorted in their own decay. The curving embankment and bridge supports that crossed the Telu between Bagdogra and Hatighisa are still evident, whilst another short bridge can be found in its entirety sandwiched between the shanties and houses in Naksalbari.

The route from here to Aluabari Road was divorced from the road, and as there was no problem with laying the metre gauge alongside the DHR, the same earthworks were generally used unless a more sympathetic curve was needed. The corrugated surface adjacent to the metre gauge at Batasi and Adhikari stations bear witness to where the sleepers of the extension line were once laid, the latter having a derelict DHR signal marking the course close to two fine working semaphores erected for the Assam Rail Link. The site of the DHR station at Galgalia can also be determined across the scrub from the walled-in rice and salt stores, whilst the former staff quarters still stand on the opposite side of the metre-gauge tracks.

Kishenganj Extension timetable, 1939

A final scene so typical of the Kishenganj extension. Looking north towards Galgalia, the DHR ran along the embankment seen trailing into the middle distance between the waving palms and plantain. The area was very susceptible to flooding, which caused considerable trouble for the railway over the years but was greatly appreciated by the boy and his water buffalo in February 2005. Despite the innocence of the scene, the area was equally vulnerable to marauding dacoits, several gangs having just been encountered less than a mile away.

Galgalia is just inside the frontier of Bihar, and from here on care must be taken by those seeking evidence of the DHR. At one time a seat of great learning and the cradle of Buddhism, the State has become a dejected land of squalid bustees, caste wars and decaying reputations. Five hundred years ago the area was known for its lawless mobs of dacoits, relieving travellers of their possessions in exchange for their lives, and the situation appears to have changed little up to the present day. Bihar is now regarded as being somewhat anarchic, and whilst researching for this chapter, several such gangs were encountered and were intent on securing a payment. Wielding large bamboo staffs with blades bound to the ends, their mood was heightened by the frenzied beating of drums, and one way or another they guaranteed that our vehicle would stop.

It is therefore with some caution that one strays across the dust-blown brickworks to the south of Galgalia, but reward will come as it is possible to drive along the former DHR trackbed on embankments and find the remains of more bridges. The ribbed course of the line can again be seen buried beneath the grass as it runs through the station at Thakurganj,[4] whilst its lifted rails can still be found rusting amongst the stacks of those from the more substantial metre gauge. Although it was regarded by the DHR as the major intermediate town on the line, today it is little more than a mass of single-storey huts and a scattering of deserted stone buildings occupied only by ghosts from the Raj. The road crossing the Mahananda River to the south has been laid on the piers of the DHR bridge, the sharp curves of the line leading to and away from the crossing being defined by sweeping embankments. The air of fascinated unease continues through the shacks and bustees that muster as Taiabpur, with the station surrounded by the confusion to the east. The River Dauk flows beyond and is the second major river to cross on this section, the stumps of the old railway bridge still poking through the water alongside the metre-gauge viaduct.

A hidden gem can be found amongst the back alleyways of Islampur, where the DHR ran alongside Aluabari Road to the station. It was here that the splendid locomotive water tank and supply well was purchased by a local man at auction following the closure of the line, for no other reason than the fact that he loved it. It is fenced off from the road that the railway once accompanied, the nearby wooden station building having been dismantled and the foundations used for a house. Beyond Islampur, the road to Kishenganj has become an arterial highway and little remains to indicate the DHR once ambled along its northern side. The town itself has lost its grace and is now sprawling and grubby, but amongst the desperation it is still possible to find the turntable pit close to the station that the railway rather haughtily referred to as Kishenganj City.

Kishenganj and Aluabari Road have also risen in stature with the coming of the broad gauge from Calcutta in the 1960s, and today they are connected by the direct route to New Jalpaiguri and Assam. Tragedy hit the line in 1999 when hundreds of lives were lost near the once-tiny DHR halt at Gaisal. The broad-gauge Brahmaputra Mail and the Awadh-Assam Express collided head-on and fifteen carriages piled into each other. Most of those who lost their lives on the Mail were personnel from the Indian Army, the Border Security Force and the Central Reserve Police Force. There was speculation that a massive explosion had taken place causing the accident, although it was later found to be the result of defective signalling.

Few could raise an eyebrow about the suspicion, for the area had become no stranger to subversion. Indeed, it was from the rail side village of Naksalbari that the murderous Naxalite[5] terrorist movement took its name in 1967, the Maoist cell having influenced the political complexion of North Bengal to this day. The proximity of the frontiers has also given considerable military significance to the airport at Bagdogra, and the Indian Army now has huge bases nearby in the terai forests. Further evidence of the unease became apparent in 2002 when it was reported that a top-ranking Inter-Services Intelligence operative and four accomplices were arrested at Matigara, during which a large number of arms, ammunition and maps of vital installations were seized from them.

It is not without reason that a troubled spectre is said to haunt this land.

---

[4] In 2005, the Stationmaster at Thakurganj advised that two of the original DHR benches had recently been identified and sent to Darjeeling for preservation.

[5] Taken from the recognised spelling of the town at the time.

Chapter 11

The Teesta Valley Extension

The Teesta Valley branch veered off to the north-east from Siliguri, and was altogether an extraordinary affair, for it terminated at an obscure hamlet that was over a mile short from anything that could be regarded as a reasonable railhead. The contract sanctioning the construction of the line stated it would terminate at the '*Tista Bridge Bazar*', which suggests that the intention may have been for the station to be close to the river crossing. Contemporary maps show the market was located adjacent to the bridge, and whether it was technical or financial difficulties that prevented the track being laid to this point is not known, but to everybody except the Company, the terminus at Gielle Khola 1½ miles away was a puzzling choice. Indeed, the first murmuring to build the line in 1909 moved the *Indian Railway Gazette* to comment in its column 'En passant':

> '*To the outside observer it is not quite clear that the proposal to link up Siliguri to the Teesta Bridge augurs so well (in relation to the Kishenganj extension), but it must doubtless promise well enough to the minds of the railway authorities, otherwise these would never have mooted the project.*'

In construction terms, it was a much more ambitious project than the Kishenganj line, and the railway had its eye focused on the merchandise passing through the bazaar of Kalimpong. Situated 4,000ft above sea level, the hill town held the key to commerce from Tibet and Sikkim, and was the starting point of the trade routes to Lhasa and Gangtok. Trains of pack ponies would regularly arrive in the market square with Tibetan wool and oranges from Sikkim, which alone could amount to 20 tons a day.

It had not always been a peaceful place. It was part of the lands belonging to the Rajas of Sikkim until the ending of the 17th century, when the Bhutanese took control and established an administrator at a fort in Dunsong, about 10 miles north east of Kalimpong. Following the rigours of their annual tax-collecting duties, the Bhutanese officials would gather on the relatively flat ground of the ridge by Rinkingpong Hill to engage in field sports; the name Kalimpong is derived from the Lepcha '*The Ridge Where We Play*', although scholars also advise of the Tibetan translation '*Stockade of the King's Ministers*'.

The Sinchula Treaty of 1865 was signed with the British to end thirty years of frontier tensions and skirmishes, which resulted in the Bhutanese retreating and Kalimpong becoming part of the British Indian Empire. This brought an air of stability to the region, and by the dawn of the 20th century, the annual trade of the bazaar had climbed to 5 lakh maunds, approximately 10,000 tons. The Government published figures to show that trade with Sikkim had almost doubled between 1905 and 1908, and there was talk that a copper industry would soon be developed.

It was enough to whet the appetite of the DHR Directors to consider a rail link to Siliguri along the trade route that led down the valley of the River Teesta, one of the great Himalayan mountain rivers that cut across Sikkim. Its source lies at 17,500ft in Lake Chalamu and is fed by the melt-water of the snows and the fearsome Zemu Glacier. Its temperament becomes unpredictable when it is met by the Great Rangeet River, where their combined fury has gouged a deep valley for twenty miles through thick forests to the Sevoke Pass. The foothills flatten abruptly beyond, and the swollen river

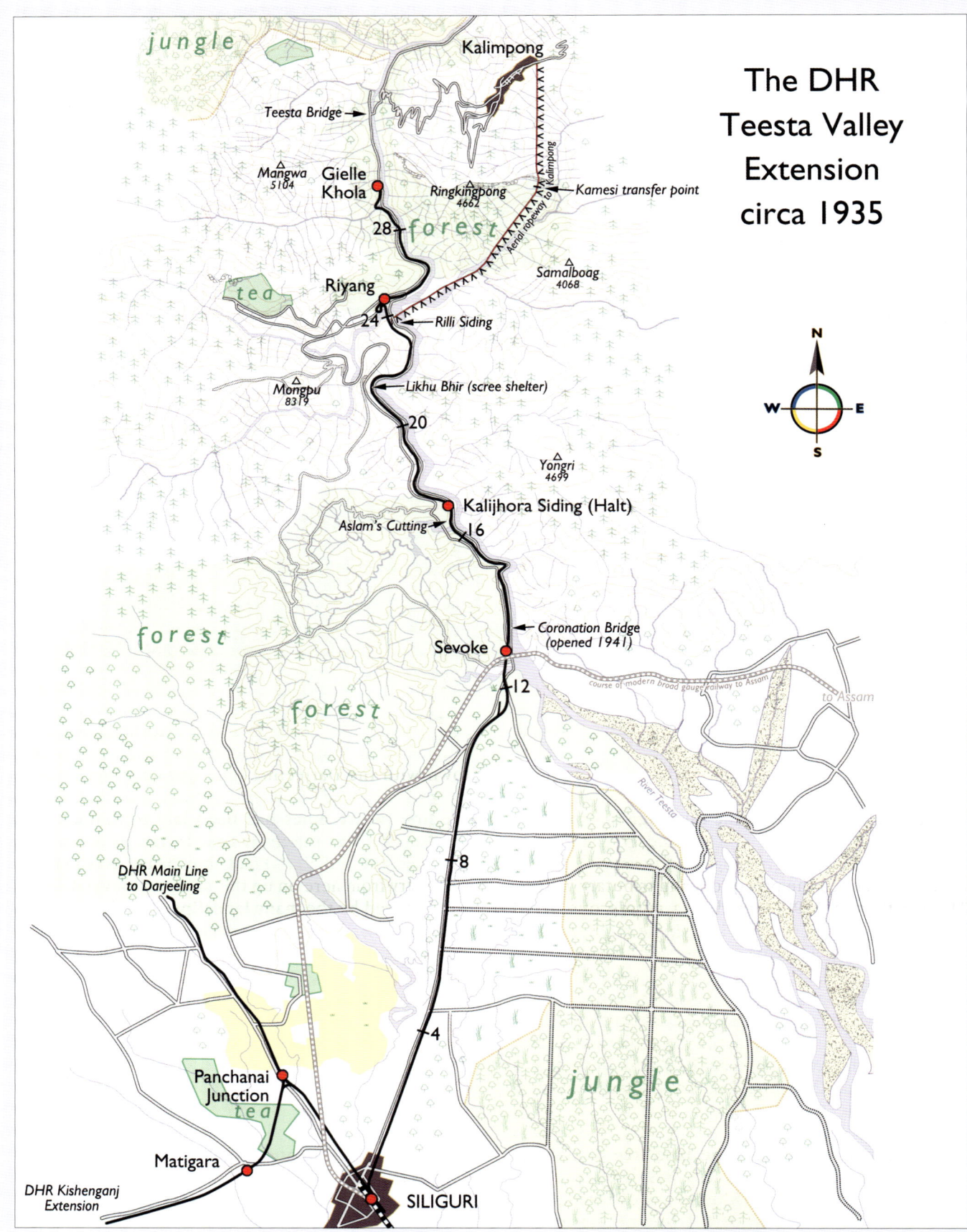

An early photograph showing the revetments and rock cuttings that were required to provide communications up the Teesta Valley.

Institution of Civil Engineers

empties into the mighty Brahmaputra as its crosses the torrid plains and the Bay of Bengal.

The old trade route had been improved by the Madras Sappers in 1888 as part of the campaign to drive back the Tibetan invasion of Sikkim, and girder bridges now replaced the sagging logs and twisted cane that formerly spanned the precipices and tributary valleys. The weather in 1899 turned to a murderous mood and 27$^{1}/_{2}$ inches of rain fell in a single night, causing disastrous landslips that crashed into the swollen rivers. Vast tracts of forest were swept down in the wake and the banks of the Teesta and its feeders rose between thirty and fifty feet in a night, totally destroying the road. A new route was constructed some 300ft above the river by the Public Works Department at a cost of Rs432,888, and was not completed until 1908-09.

The Government provided the land free of cost for the DHR Extensions Company, and the trackbed was in effect to be the residue of the old trade road destroyed in 1899. The DHR Directors agreed to sanction Rs3,500 to build a new station to be called Siliguri Road, which would provide a junction in the town with the Darjeeling line. Construction initially progressed ahead of schedule and by 16th March 1914 the first twelve miles had been laid to Sevoke. This first section was relatively easy to lay, as much of it followed the old Cart Road, but heavy blasting was necessary from here on up the valley and several delays were caused by the many landslips of shale and rock. The First World War also interfered with the delivery of the materials for bridge construction, and it was just over a year before the next ten miles were opened to Riyang on 1st May 1915.

The crossing at Riyang was a major exercise of civil engineering in its own right, for a 300ft-long embankment that was 20ft high had to be laid to divert the flow of the river. Set on a foundation measuring 100ft at the base and 30ft at the top, it was protected with wire bolsters to prevent the erosion of the hillside. The old PWD suspension road bridge was abandoned and the piers left standing, for the river now cut in from behind and the Department was unable to make

Taken from Cresswell's original record of the construction of the Teesta Valley extension, these notes describe the work undertaken to divert the flow of the Riyang River to protect the left-hand bank. A train from Siliguri would approach from the right-hand side of the photograph, and after crossing the river, climbed the hillside by a series of sweeping bends before entering Riyang Station.

The DHRS Archive

A second extract taken from Cresswell's notes illustrating the construction of Riyang Station and the rest bungalow. Looking in the direction of Gielle Khola, the railway ran through a short section of tropical forest before it opened out on a ledge 100ft above the Teesta river for the final 4½ miles to the terminus.

The DHRS Archive

THE TEESTA VALLEY EXTENSION

A construction team and train at milepost 28½ in August 1915. The five miles between Riyang and Gielle Khola was the most demanding section of the entire line for the civil engineers.

The DHRS Archive

> 29th mile –
> A difficult corner to get into the Gielle Valley. Some 30'ft had to be blasted back to get round from where the man is standing, and a heavy retaining wall built where marked × now completed (latter in April)

Cresswell's description of the work involved at the 29th mile to enable a trackbed to be formed into the valley of the Gielle River. After crossing this tributary of the Teesta, the terminus of the line was to be cut into the hillside seen in the middle distance.

The DHRS Archive

The official records submitted to the Government show that the tightest radius on the line was 100ft. However . . . .

. . . . Cresswell noted that this photograph of a works train in 1915 was cautiously pushing a 66½ft-long girder for bridge construction round an 80ft curve.

The DHRS Archive

Sevoke Station circa 1915. The photographer was facing Gielle Khola, and it is not clear if the line was still under construction or had been open to the public at the time it was taken. The locomotive is unusually facing downhill towards Siliguri, and appears to be waiting for the bogie flat-bed wagon and two open four-wheelers to be shunted into a siding.

The DHRS Archive

an embankment sufficiently strong to divert the river back again. The railway bridge had three spans, two being deck-plate girders that carried the train over the rocks and the third a 100ft pony-truss crossing the main river. The southern abutment was cut into the river bank and lined with Portland cement to stop the erosion of the river, whilst the northern one was a pier built on an enormous boulder.

The 7½ miles that followed tested the skills of the engineers to the limit in order to keep the gradient at a maximum of 1 in 100. A series of sweeping bends were cut into the hillside beyond the bridge to enable the line to scale 150ft above the river and enter the station of Riyang. From here a ledge had to be blasted from solid rock for the trackbed, which at first passed through a dripping forest before entering the rawness of an open gorge. Over 30ft of one particularly difficult corner was dynamited away in order that a shelf could be formed for the railway to enter the Gielle Valley and cross the final torrent. Retaining walls 10ft deep and some 20ft thick were set into the valley sides as the bridge was approached, for torrential rain had swollen the river to the extent that it had crushed one of the pier-heads with the boulders it dragged along. The river was crossed on a 60ft deck-plate girder span, and after rounding the final bluff, the train ended its journey in the middle of nowhere.

This final section was opened on 29th September 1915, but despite the plans to continue, Gielle Khola was to become the terminus of the line and was optimistically referred to by the railway as Kalimpong Road Station. It was true the station was on a road that would eventually lead to Kalimpong, but the town was on the other side of the suspension bridge that spanned the Teesta 1½ miles up the valley, followed by a climb of 3,000 feet on a tortuous 6-mile mountain track.

The intention was to lay a further 34 miles of rail to Gangtok, the capital of Sikkim. A preliminary survey was made during the winter months of 1917–18, which was to include a girder bridge across the Teesta near the confluence with the Great Rangeet River, replacing the 300ft-long suspension bridge built in 1880. The intermediary stations were planned at Melli (3 miles from Gielle Khola), Tarkhola (9 miles) and Rangpu (14½ miles), where a large siding was to be laid for railway stock and the development of a copper mine. It was from here that an endless chain of people, carrying baskets of oranges during the winter months, would slowly stumble along a narrow path to Kalimpong Road. One observer noted at least a thousand men, women and children staggering by with loads that weighed anything up to 160lbs, choking on dust that turned their skin white as it matted into a plaster with their sweat. The path was no more than a narrow ledge high above the river in parts and could only be negotiated by sidestep, whilst the nights were spent fighting for shelter from the frozen winds and fever-laden mists that haunted these gorges.

The railway was to continue beyond Rangpu to Sankokhola (24½ miles) before finally entering Gangtok. It would have required new retaining walls to be built, for the monsoon rains had previously brought down massive land falls and dislocated all traffic, particularly at the 1st, 3rd and 5th mileposts.

Once the railway had left Siliguri, it ran alongside the Sevoke Road for approximately five miles in open countryside before entering the terai forests. A Down train from Gielle Khola is seen returning on this section, circa 1915.

The DHRS Archive

An Up train bound for Gielle Khola passes through the cutting after leaving the company of the road near the 11th milepost from Siliguri.

The DHRS Archive

It was expected that trains would be steaming into Gangtok by 1925, but the project never progressed, and to this day Sikkim is still without a railway.

Nevertheless, it was possible to take the only train of the day as far as Gielle Khola, and it usually departed from Siliguri (393ft above sea level) shortly before the 'Mail' was due to leave for Darjeeling. Both trains shared the same track for half a mile to a junction, after which those bound for Darjeeling veered to the left and the service for the Teesta Valley to the right. The route may still be traced today by turning right along the Hill Cart Road before the level crossing and following the right-hand side of the road to the crossing at the fork in the road (currently opposite the Venus Hotel).

The original line to Darjeeling ran into Siliguri Road Station beyond the junction and continued on the right-hand side of the Hill Cart Road, whilst the train bound for Gielle Khola set off towards open country. The residential quarters for the DHR staff nestled between the two diverging lines, whilst the locomotive shed and coal store were to the right of the Teesta Valley line and close to the present Kanchenjunga Stadium. The whole area is built up today with concrete racks of shops and shacks, and the train would have run along what is now the right-hand side of the Bidhan Road. It was barely half a mile before the main highway to Sevoke and Sikkim was approached, whereupon the line curved to the right to run alongside the road and cross the shimmering flood plains of the distant Teesta.[1]

The hamlet of Salugara was passed five miles after leaving Siliguri, after which the train left the open fields and entered the enveloping terai forests, a section that was feared as being the haunt of tigers, rhinos, elephants and black panthers. The black caterpillars were among its less threatening residents, but their appetite for the wooden sleepers was such that the locomotive occasionally lost adhesion on this section and had to be halted in order that the crew could scrape them off the wheels and track. Continuing

---

[1] Formerly Tista, in Nepali an abbreviation of Trisrota, 'The Three Currents', on account of the river dividing into three channels that followed independent courses to the Ganges and Brahmaputra.

A Down train of open four-wheeled trolleys approaches the bridge over the Sevoke River, circa 1915. The road crossed the river further downstream at the time and was out of sight from the photographer.

The DHRS Archive

The new concrete road bridge across the Sevoke River ran parallel to the railway, and a 'B' Class with a Down train of flat wagons can be seen leaving from the far side.

Collection: Nigel Plackett

A mixed train bound for Gielle Khola waits at Sevoke station. The chassis of the toast-rack coach is showing signs of sagging in the centre, and the general condition of the rolling stock suggests this undated photograph was taken in the late 1930s.

Collection: Peter Tiller and Marilyn Metz

The daily Up mixed bound for Gielle Khola running on the ledge cut into the side of the Sevoke gorge. The composition of the train illustrates the comparative demands for the transportation of goods and passengers, whilst the last vehicle is a travelling post office. The white hexagons painted on the bottom left-hand side of the freight wagons bore the initials DH or DHR at the top, and the stock number, load and tare at the bottom.

Collection: Peter Tiller and Marilyn Metz

under the canopy of huge trees alongside the road, the train eventually swung sharply away to the right to venture out on its own and descend by a less severe gradient to the Sevoke River. A short siding was passed on the left at the 11th milepost, and the train ran through a deep cutting before turning back sharply to the left to cross the road and approach the girder bridge on an embankment. The river broadened out and settled to a slower pace before it passed under the railway and road bridges, after which it loosened itself into the Teesta.

The train ran into Sevoke station ('The Gate of the Winds', 13 miles) just after crossing the bridge. This marked the point where the line entered a constricting gorge that the Teesta had scoured through a mass of granite. The winds can become viciously cold hereabouts, blowing from early evening through to the next morning as they descend from the Himalaya and cause dense clouds of mist to form as they meet the hot air of the plains. It was an unholy place for fever, and the only sign of habitation in the area was a small settlement of fifteen huts to the right of the station. These were occupied by hillmen from Darjeeling who worked on the permanent way, along with the passing tradesmen from Sikkim with furs and copper, Tibetans with ponies and chow dogs, and the Gurungs (shepherds) with their flocks bound for the market at Matigara.

The foundation stone for a road bridge across the gorge was laid in November 1937 by Sir John Anderson, the retiring Governor of Bengal, and the railway passed beneath the abutments set on the left-hand bank (going upstream). The hollow-box construction in reinforced concrete was built to the design of John Chambers, and being 563ft long with a central span of 276ft rising 173ft above the level of the river, it was said to be the first bridge in India of such magnitude. Named in commemoration of the accession to the British throne by George VI in 1937, the Coronation Bridge was finally opened to road traffic on 12th March 1941 by the new Governor of Bengal, Sir John Herbert.

The train joined the course of the abandoned trade route as the gorge became less constricted, running on a ledge above the river and surrounded by superb scenery. Thick forests rose all around, and as the Teesta crashed over boulders it had brought down the valley in its more spiteful moods, the railway twisted and turned for five miles to negotiate massive outcrops of rock. The Andheri Jhora ('The Dark Torrent') had to be crossed, a fearsome tributary of the Teesta that had scoured its course in a dark and densely forested gorge. A bridge was constructed 60ft above the river bed, but its furious waters had torn down the central pier of the bridge before its construction had even been completed and delayed the opening of the railway by four months.

The road and railway came close together at the end of this section and crossed the Kali River on two separate girder bridges, the train running at a higher level in order that it could pass over the road on the far side and enter the confines of Aslam's Cutting. The sides here were near vertical in places and it appears that part of it subsequently caved in, for a former Permanent Way Inspector advised that a 50-yard long tunnel was formed at the northern end. This opened out and led to Kalijhora siding ('The Black Torrent', 17 miles – 550ft), where a small halt served the construction engineers' bungalow and a scattered settlement that had taken its name from the coal seam nearby at Daling.

The Sweti Jhora was the next tributary to cross, after which the railway ran on a reinforced ledge about 20ft above the river, with the old PWD road some 30ft higher. Both were cut from an almost perpendicular scarp on the outer edge of the river, but with the railway running at a lower level, it was able to take advantage of the flatter areas on the inside bends where the Teesta flowed slowly and had deposited sediment. Government-sponsored plantations of the cinchona tree clung to the hillside until the approach to Likhu Bhir, a viciously steep slope and a particularly dangerous area for falling stones. A Head Mate employed on the permanent way had been killed when passing by with his work gang, and the railway constructed a wooden avalanche roof over the track at this point as a safety measure. Beyond here and close to the 22nd mile, an embankment

Looking upstream in the direction of Gielle Khola, the railway can be seen running on a ledge on the opposite bank as it passes under the newly completed Coronation Bridge. Below: *Rare shot of the railway in the near foreground, passing beneath the Coronation Bridge during construction.*

Pat Orr

was built from the river's edge to enable the train to negotiate a 100ft curve round a bluff of some extremely hard quartz that had proved too hard and expensive to tunnel. The scenery was spectacular, and with the towering Himalaya gathering in the near distance, outcrops of rock poked through the thick vegetation like the bare bones of the earth.

The line was obliged to stray away from the bank of the Teesta in order that it could approach a favourable crossing point of the tributary Riyang River. A short siding veered off to the right to serve Rilli ('The Swirling River', 23¾ miles), which in 1930 became the lower station of the ropeway constructed to transport goods to Kalimpong. Built on a spit of low land formed by the confluence of the rivers, it had taken the name from a tributary valley on the opposite bank of the Teesta, and the station was distinguished only by a shed for transferring freight from the railway to the suspended cradles. Shortly after passing the siding, an embankment led the train to the bridge across the Riyang (the 'Spread Out' or 'Shallow River'), and the size of the massive boulders strewn along the banks was evidence of the destructive power the river possessed when gorged on the monsoon rains.

The station of Riyang (25 miles – 625ft) was on the far side of the river, and was approached by three sweeping curves that tightened to 100ft radius as the train fought with the contours to climb the side of the valley. Bark from the cinchona tree would be collected here, along with drums of crude petroleum ether for the production of quinine, a lifesaver in these malaria-infested lands. The station was set on a ledge high above the river, giving the impression of being half in a cutting and half on the bank, whilst a rest bungalow with three rooms and a large veranda was built approximately 100 yards further up the line. Known to those working on the railway as the 'Honeymoon Lodge', the bungalow was in a stunning location and much sought after for an overnight stay. A cook and a night watchman were always

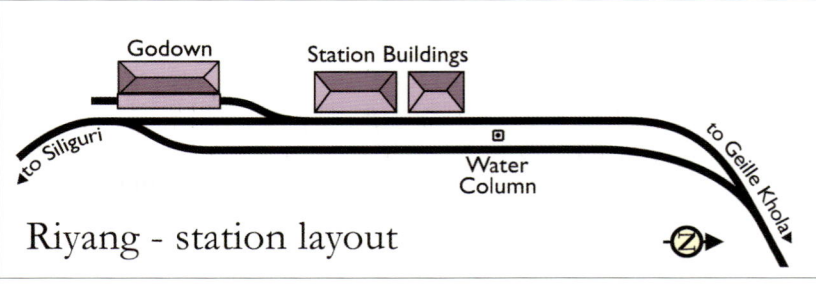

The DHR bridge across the Andheri Jhora. The two spans were 60ft and 30ft in length, and crossed at a point that was 60ft above the thickly forested gorge. The central pier was torn down by the river before its construction was completed and delayed the opening of the line by four months.

The DHRS Archive

A 'B' class at the head of a rake of second-generation bogie stock waits to cross the bridge at Kalijhora, circa 1930. Although it did not have the benefit of the Himalayan skyline, the beauty of the Teesta Valley extension was superb and the civil engineering exceeded that of the climb to Darjeeling. However, without a logical railhead its traffic never really matched expectations, and there were only sufficient travellers to require one mixed train a day. The annual passenger returns for the extension at the time totalled 23,000 (Darjeeling 258,000 and Kishenganj 653,000) and freight 28,000 tons (Darjeeling 80,000 and Kishenganj 44,000).

Above: *Road and rail cross the tributary valley of the Kali river on the approach to Aslam's cutting. Both bridges have since gone and a new bridge has been built in more recent times for the road at a higher level.*

Collection : Amanda Williams

A 'B' class working hard with a train across the Kalijhora Bridge. Aslam's Cutting was beyond the small footbridge (seen behind the spectacle plate of the locomotive), whilst the road on the far side would have passed under the railway at the level of the lower storehouse.

on call, and such was its peaceful seclusion that on a moonlit evening, tigers would pass close by on their way to the banks of the Teesta to drink.

Leaving Riyang, the train entered a short section of tropical forest that soon gave way and opened to awesome scenery, the railway outwitting the demand for tunnels and crossing numerous embryonic streams and rivers spilling into the Teesta. It would take 30 minutes of running time to cover these final $4^1/_2$ miles, and with the surrounding mountains soaring over 4,500ft, the line crossed the road for the final time and gripped a ledge blasted from a near-vertical rock face over 100ft above the river. The valley of the Gielle Jhora was the last obstacle to cross, and a five-mph speed limit was imposed as the train traversed a 60ft girder bridge over its rock-scarred river bed. Returning to the side of the Teesta, the train steamed into the terminus (710ft), and it had taken $3^1/_4$ hours to cover the 30 miles from Siliguri.

The suspension bridge lay $1^1/_2$ miles further upstream, and one can feign little surprise to learn that it had a somewhat bizarre history. It started as a precarious crossing that had been woven and plaited from the large canes that grew on the hills, but the structure was frequently swept away by floods. The Department of Public Works subsequently put up a temporary wire bridge in 1877, until it gave way just as a local carrying a heavy load was crossing the river. One of the two piers was condemned in 1879 and orders were given for it to be dismantled, but unfortunately they took down the wrong one! The bridge was finally completed in 1881, after dispelling the macabre rumours of the need for the heads of children to be laid in its foundations. It

The railway approached Aslam's Cutting immediately after leaving the bridge crossing the Kali River. Landslides subsequently caused it to fill in at the far end, and a 50-yard tunnel was built to protect the railway from further slippage. Encroaching vegetation and rock falls have made the cutting barely discernible today.

The DHRS Archive

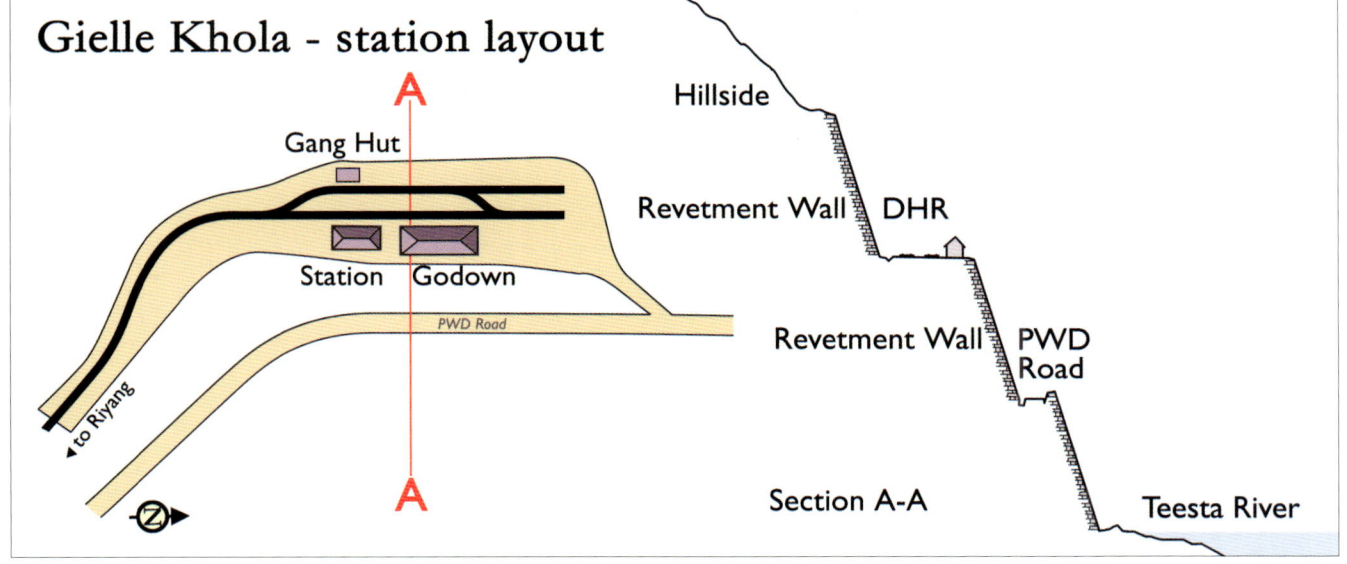

The wooden scree shelter built close to the steep hillside known as Likhu Bhir, approximately halfway between Kalijhora and Riyang.

Collection: Gwen Cattermull

took eighty coolies, walking one behind another, three days to carry the 465ft long steel cables the eighteen miles from Jor Bungalow to the Teesta Valley. The new bridge had a single span of 300ft, which was 20ft above the highest floodwater, and the twin piers became a useful purchase for attaching Buddhist prayer flags. It survived until 1933 when it too was replaced by a sturdier crossing, which managed to survive the fury of the river for a further twenty years.

The Teesta Valley line was primarily intended for goods traffic, and the returns for 1916 showed 15,589 tons were transported over its rails, supplemented by 48,071 passengers; the gross earnings for the year amounted to Rs121,480, which was just over half that achieved by the Kishenganj branch. The Company tried to develop the line as an attraction for the tourist, and a brief description of the scenic delights appeared in the official guide published in 1921. There was no doubt that the journey was extremely picturesque as it twisted like a convulsive snake up the valley, but it suffered from the fact that it did not really lead to any place where a traveller would willingly spend more time than was necessary for the return trip.

Rumer Godden wrote evocatively of the journey in her book 'Rungli-Rungliot':[2]

'I took another train, like the train of an amusement park, and puffed away through the foothills of the Himalayas. The trees dripped, hanging orchids dripped, the creepers dripped, the banks at the edge dripped, and the carriage dripped inside as well as out. We crept along at the edge of the Teesta River, up the valley, and the river looked as if it might flood again; it was wide and deep and incredibly swift, neither green nor grey in the rain swell but celadon, between low banks of grey-white stones all made smooth by the water. After the rains, in the winter, the river would be blue; first a chalky blue and then a blue with a grape-green tinge from the ice water. It is a dangerous cruel river, as cruel as it is beautiful, and the hill people say it has to take a life a year.

On either side of the gorge rise the mountains, and, at the far end, they part to show the snow peak Kabru. The little train stopped and started and made an amount of noise far beyond its size. The engine had a high, flat-topped funnel and bulging coal bunkers, it was painted spinach-green and a coolie stood on the ledge in front of it as it went along; occasionally he stepped off and walked. The first- and second-class carriages were empty, and the third-class were so full that people sat on the window ledges, on the luggage, on each other, and luggage and children oozed out of the corners and openings. All along the train, blowing into my window as I sat in solitary state, was an overpowering smell of biris; a biri is a little evil-smelling cigarette rolled in its natural leaf; every hillman, woman and child smokes them.

After a great many hours, the train crossed a red bridge over another river with deep fish-pools, looped the loop, and arrived panting at my station, which was a collection of tin-roofed huts in the middle of the forest; but it had a stationmaster in full uniform, with a whistle and a green flag, and a small-size grey car that had come to meet me and drive me twelve miles on a hairpin track up the precipices and gorges of the mountain to the tea estate.'

[2] Copyright: IPC + Syndication

Riyang Station was hidden amongst the trees and situated on a ledge cut into the hillside. A train bound for Siliguri can be seen descending the first of the three sweeping curves that would take the line to the level of the river crossing.

The DHRS Archive

An unidentified 'B' Class taking water at Riyang. The mongrel nature of the Class can be seen as the wing-tanks and supporting stays from the coal bunker to the cab would indicate the locomotive was built by Sharp, Stewart & Co., whilst the extended smokebox, twin safety valves, cylinder design and piston tail rods were later modifications.

Collection: Peter Tiller and Marilyn Metz

A long train descends through the tropical forest as it approaches Riyang.

By permission of The British Library (472/8 150)

Below: *A Down freight is led over the bridge spanning the Gielle Khola by a 'B' Class. Cresswell reported that the pier was ground away by boulders after the river rose about 20ft above the temporary bridge, originally a single span of 40ft and rebuilt with one of 60ft. The first bogie vehicle illustrates the wagon for carrying livestock well, with a side ramp that could be lowered for the animals.*

The DHRS Archive

Taken in February 2005 from a similar position to the previous photograph, the course of the railway can be discerned cut into the rock face on the right-hand side and leading to the remains of the abutment of the bridge across the Gielle Khola. Following the profile to the right of the photograph would lead round the bluff of rock and into the site of the former station.

The following returns show that the tonnage of goods carried was between 63% and 81% of that achieved by the Kishenganj extension, the main imports being grains and other food supplies along with salt and building materials, whilst the exports were the oranges, cardamoms, potatoes, timber and wool that were the trade of Sikkim and Tibet; the passenger traffic proved to be but a fraction of importance:

Year	No. of Passengers	Tons of goods
1919 – 1920	34,000	29,000
1929 – 1930	23,000	28,000
1934 – 1935	12,000	30,000
1939 – 1940	16,000	50,000
1940 – 1941	15,000	43,000
1941 – 1942	19,000	40,000
1942 – 1943	36,000	38,000
1943 – 1944	56,000	29,000

Despite the initial optimism, it had become inevitable that the track was not going to be extended any further beyond Gielle Khola, and it was realised that the interests of the railway would be best served by some means of a direct link with Kalimpong. A survey was made in 1925 for a freight ropeway to connect the bazaar to the line, and it was found the folds of the mountains were such that the practical base would be at Rilli, shortly before the river crossing to Riyang station. The Kalimpong Ropeway Co. Ltd was formed in 1928 and commissioned its design and construction to The British Ropeway Engineering Co. Ltd of London. The authorised capital was initially 5 lakh rupees, the whole of which was issued and subscribed, but this was subsequently increased to 20 lakh to cater for any future extensions that might be deemed. The ropeway was formally opened in September 1930 by Lady Stephenson, the wife of the acting Governor of Bengal, and the first carrier to arrive brought her a basket of flowers.

The responsibility for the management of the ropeway was placed in the hands of Messrs Gillanders Arbuthnot & Co., with the DHR tasked as the working Agent. It was operated in two parts, the lower section running for $4^{1}/_{2}$ miles from a base adjacent to a siding off the railway to an angled station at Nazeok, after which it crossed the Rilli River for a second time as it ascended to Kamesi, 2,500ft above sea level. Freight was transferred at this point to the second section, which climbed the remaining 1,600ft to Kalimpong in $2^{1}/_{2}$ miles by one straight line; the total journey time was $1^{1}/_{2}$ hours. The tallest trestle was 139ft high and each carrier could take a load of 10cwt; with carriers arriving every three minutes, the equivalent of ten tons per hour could be transported. A separate ropeway was suspended from the far side of the freight yard at Kalimpong up the slopes of Deolo Hill to Dr Graham's Home, the school founded in 1900 as a home for orphans and now internationally known as having inspired many similar establishments for the handicapped and destitute.

A 72hp oil engine supplied the power to drive each section of the main ropeway, one sited at Kamesi and the other at Kalimpong, and the loads were carried on small platforms suspended from the cable. These were automatically lifted off the rope and carried on overhead rails into each station for stacking or unloading, similarly to many present-day ski-lifts. Each platform was designed to carry 8 maunds with a double being available for special loads up to 13 maunds, and

The site of the lower station of the ropeway at Rilli Siding in February 2005. The ropeway would have spanned the Teesta to an angled station at the summit of the lower hill, centre right, after which it crossed the Rilli River to the hillside at Kamesi in the middle distance. Freight would then be transferred to a second section that climbed to Kalimpong, close to the distant crest line.

these were lowered on the rope at 3-minute intervals to ensure an equal load distribution being carried at a speed of 10 miles per hour.

It proved to be an efficient and economical means of transport, with the charges levied depending on the classification of goods, although it never amounted to more than 6 annas per maund. This compared favourably with the bullock carts and coolies who commanded a rate between 8 annas and Rs1-4 (1 rupee + 4 annas) for a similar load depending on the time of year, and that was for goods that were obliged to travel a further 4 miles to the terminus at Kalimpong Road. The downward freight comprised mainly bales of Tibetan wool, oranges and timber, with the returning platforms carrying food-grains, brick-tea, cloth, and building materials, although many of the elderly residents of Kalimpong still recall their mischief as children by stealing a ride and terrorising the staff with their acrobatics. Betty Shaw remembered the trepidation of standing at the embarkation point and watching her husband James travelling on one of the platforms, hanging on with one hand as it swayed above the gorge whilst he inspected the pulleys and pylons. Staff would be sacked if caught taking a ride following an accident when a coolie jumped on, the extra weight creating a strain until the platform slid back, hit the one behind and threw him to his death.

A fire destroyed the upper station and a considerable quantity of goods in 1939; the Directors agreed they would assist the Ropeway Company by forgoing the remuneration due for 1938/39, although this was subsequently amended to half the figure at the next Board meeting. The repair was put into effect straight away, and by the following year 17,000 tons of goods were being carried on the ropeway, although the conditions of the Second World War tested the ability of all the transport systems in the area to handle the increased traffic. This confused many of the figures, which rose to 18,000 tons in 1941–42 and dropped to 11,000 tons only two years later. Nevertheless, its success gave rise to debates on the ropeway being extended to the north into Sikkim and south to connect with the railway at Sevoke, with branches at Mangpu for the cinchona factory and others that would serve the surrounding area producing tea, timber and charcoal.

Indeed there were further ambitions for the Teesta Valley line, for the DHR Extensions Company suspended a wire ropeway across the river near Sevoke. It was projected this would eventually become a suspension bridge and provide a connection to Mal, a terminus on the Bengal Dooars Railway. It was reasoned this would shorten the time for the journey to the Darjeeling area and would attract traffic from the tea plantations, but again it came to nothing and left the DHR to continue its business, as it does to this day.

The construction of ropeways may have helped to overcome some of the difficulties posed by the weather, and in particular the monsoon rains that could transform the Teesta into a menacing torrent. The railway was at its most vulnerable running close to the bottom of the valley, and it became almost

A loaded carrier on the ropeway to Kalimpong about to leave the exchange sidings at Rilli. Note 'Q' on the side of the freight wagon, denoting 'Quick turn-around for Victory', an adaptation of the 'V for Victory' slogan seen on main-line stock during the Second World War.

Paddy Smith

Both the rail and road bridges at Sevoke were brought down by the monsoon rains in 1937. Looking in the direction of Gielle Khola, the proximity of the road can be seen on the far side.

Collection: Nigel Plackett

The collapsed road bridge at Sevoke (see photograph page 299). The location was difficult to recognise in 2005, for the river had since swept away the embankments leading to the bridge and broadened the flood plain. The current road bridge crosses the river further upstream, to the left of the photograph.

Nigel Plackett

An unidentified 'B' Class running close to the Teesta River as it descends the valley with a ballast train for repair work.

Nigel Plackett

Although the location was not recorded, the lay of the land suggests this repair work was being undertaken at the Sevoke breach in 1937. The receding waters of the Teesta can be seen fanning out in the middle distance.

Collection: Pat Orr

Lilian, wife of the Resident Engineer, George Batterbury, and a friend on an inspection of the repair work in the wake of the devastation caused by the 1937 rains.

Collection: Pat Orr

The Sevoke Causeway

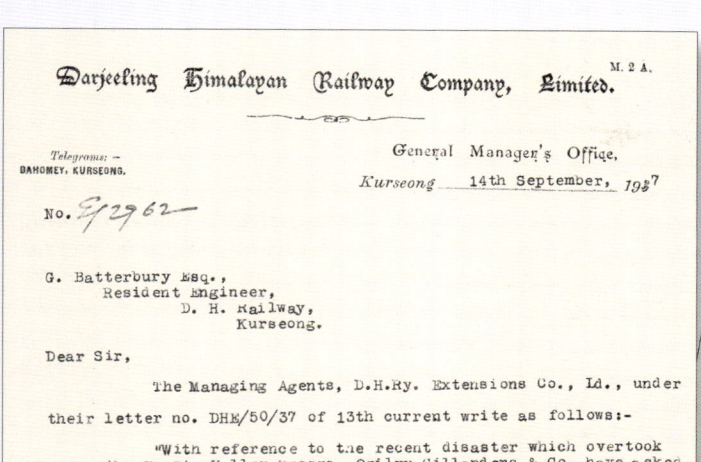

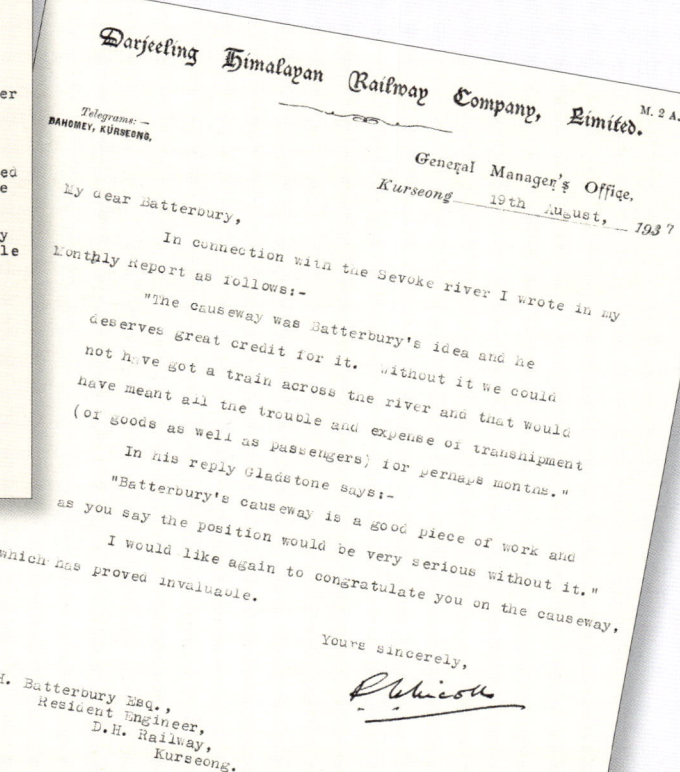

The repair work undertaken by George Batterbury was clearly inspirational and deservedly appreciated by the Directors and Management alike, as indicated by these two letters.

Collection: Pat Orr

An evocative picture of a 'B' Class running through the gushing water of the Sevoke river as it negotiates the temporary causeway. The steep drop from the embankment that approached the bridge can be seen in the background, as can the rails suspended above the river.

Glynne Gladstone MSS

an annual challenge for the engineers to divert the floodwaters away from the bridges and embankments. Heavy rain fell incessantly for three weeks during August 1937, causing numerous landslides across the tracks in the valley. Attempts were made to check the force of the river with boulders, but the raging waters tore down the girder bridge that took the railway across the river Sevoke near its confluence with the Teesta, leaving the tracks hanging in the air and the service suspended for an indefinite period. George Batterbury had been the Assistant Engineer in charge of the surveying and construction of the branch, and had since been promoted to the post of Resident Engineer. He conceived the elegant solution of laying a causeway of caged boulders across the river as it began to recede, which necessitated a short but steep climb to the original embankment that led to the bridge; it was built with remarkable speed and trains were running again by the end of August. The rains continued unabated, and on 5th October it was reported that the causeway itself was now under two feet of water and that the down 'Kalimpong Mail' was held up at Sevoke, the post having been transferred and brought to Siliguri by road.

The scheduled service of one train a day continued throughout the time of the Second World War, although the returns show that the number of passengers carried rose quite dramatically. The branch had settled into expecting an annual average of 15,000, but the returns in 1943 showed there were 36,000, and 56,000 the following year. However, the charming letter written to Sir Charles and Lady Tennyson by their daughter Margot in March 1947 recalled that the journey to Kalimpong was still fraught with hazards:

'Thursday morning we changed at the foot of the hills into a little toy train, the carriages painted in black and white checks and the second class carriages fitted with absurd moth-eaten armchairs. Ours must have been one of the few lavatories on the train because at every stop there was a queue to get into it. We began through rather meagre, scrubby forest. The homes and people at once struck us as extraordinary changed. The houses of course made of wood and often painted were stuck up on high stilts. Whilst already the small Bengal features were expanding into the Mongolian. Soon hills were towering round us, and the vegetation had become more profuse and varied. The train wound round the river course at about 100ft above it. A beautiful river, grey sand, delicately marked by the waters fingers, lining it either side, in the river great boulders were basking, smoothed into great shapes by the rushing torrent that pour over them in the rainy season. Eventually we debouched from the train (imagine the embarrassment when Tibetan

TEESTA-VALLEY EXTENSION.

UP TRAINS.		41 Up Mixed.		DOWN TRAINS.		42 Down Mixed.*	
Stations.		H.	M.	Stations.		H.	M.
B. & A. Ry. Train ...Arr.		6	40	Gielle Khola ... ...Dep.		16	
Siliguri Junction ...Dep.		6	57	Riyang ... ... "		16	40
Siliguri Road ... "		7	1	Rilli Siding ... ... "		17	5
Sevoke ... ... "		7	57	Sevoke ... ... "		18	23
Rilli Siding ... ... "		9	11	Siliguri Road ... ... "		19	8
Riyang ... ... "		9	25	Siliguri Junction ...Arr.		19	10
Gielle Khola ... ...Arr.		9	55	B. & A. Ry. Train ... Dep.		20	20

*From 1st June to 30th September, 42 Down will leave Gielle Khola at 15-30 arriving Siliguri at 18-38 hrs.

Teesta Valley Extension Timetable 1942

'B' Class No.40 in an undignified predicament along the bank of the Teesta in 1946. Cables and hawsers can be seen in place to right the locomotive to haul it clear of the breach and to allow a temporary repair to be undertaken. The locomotive was one of the Baldwin trio and subsequently renumbered 793 under the ISR scheme.

Betty Shaw

Below: *It is a rare occasion to have a photograph of the underside of any steam locomotive. Clearly visible are the well tanks with their cover plates, and in the middle what looks like a rectangular-shaped balancing pipe, profiled to achieve clearances.*

women porters, not unusually sturdily in appearance, jumped forward to carry our heavy baggage. In one trunk we were carrying almost a whole library!). We then got into a taxi for the last 10 miles to Kalimpong. The gradient must have been at least 1 in 3, and alas we soon discovered that not only had our taxi's battery run down, but there was a block in the petrol feed and a leak in the radiator and one cylinder missing. Every 100 yards we had to stop to refill the boiling radiator and once we stopped we had to back down the precipice to get the engine started. At last after 2½ hours we arrived.'

Kalimpong must have been a wonderful escape from the dying days of the Raj, and for some reason it began to attract more than its fair share of the arcane and those tottering on the edge of sanity, including two elderly ladies who took up residence and insisted they were reincarnations of Joan of Arc. It surprised few to find that a princess lived nearby who claimed to receive a daily supply of orchids delivered on a silver tray by a gentleman wearing gloves, whilst another resident asserted her cat was really the rebirth of her late husband. Her lodger was in complete fear of the animal and counselled the assistance of tantric lamas, whose prescription for peace required him to evict the creature without inflicting harm. This was not an easy matter, for the cat put up a spirited fight as it was bundled into a bag, but eventually it was packed off to a new residence some forty miles away. The air of tranquillity did not last long, for the animal was heard outside one night during a thunder storm, and tried to force its way back in, despite the doors and windows being barred. The cat was found dead in the relief of daylight, but the lamas returned to chant prayers and blessings before a ceremonial cremation, although the precaution of witch traps was conscripted as a contingency measure against any demons that might come howling through the night. If all else failed, the Mother of the Universe could have been consulted, for she also conveniently lived in the town, and would grant those who sought her guidance the gift of the *'fourth dimension'*, a blessing so subtle that many were to remain unaware of its effect.

Nevertheless, the effect of Partition placed a new political emphasis on the area, and the second stage of the new Assam Rail Link Project was to run from Siliguri to Sevoke, after which it would cross the Teesta and continue eastwards to Bagrakot. The route of DHR extension was unsuitable, for it threaded the streets of Siliguri and ran close to the road for much of the way. A new trace was surveyed from the recently constructed Siliguri North station that would cut through the forest and permit an approach to Sevoke at right angles to the Teesta, approximately 700 yards south of the gorge.

The cyclone that tore through Darjeeling over the weekend of 10th–11th June 1950 was no less forgiving in the Teesta Valley, the river having been swollen by

Sevoke Station in February 2005. It is now a private dwelling, but despite the years since the closure of the railway, the distinctive fretted woodwork fringing the end gables is still evident (see photograph on page 296).

one-third of the annual average rainfall in two days. It snapped off the new bridge for the Assam Rail Link at Sevoke in its fingers, leaving the central section standing after having washed away both ends. The river at this point at normal flood level is about 900ft wide, but the devastation had broadened this to 1,600ft. There was a hill on the right bank, which along with the approach to the bridge was swept away; the left bank had been mainly thick forest, but this was dragged into the torrent along with 760ft of track. Engineers had measured the maximum known flow of the river to be approximately 200,000 cu.ft of water per second, but during these floods it had risen to 650,000 cu.ft and was flowing at about 20mph. The water rose 10ft above the DHR line in the valley, which had been laid 10–15ft above the maximum known flood level.

It had been the worst flood for over 30 years, with the first obstruction across the railway just north of the Coronation Bridge and major slips occurring with increasing frequency until the 23rd mile beyond Riyang, where most traces of the track had disappeared for a mile. All signs of the road, rail and the settlement at Gielle Khola had collapsed into the river, as had most of the bridges along its course. The ropeway to Rilli was torn down, and with this artery severed, Kalimpong was cut off from the world and the stocks of food fell dangerously low. A new footpath was

Above: *The pillars of the soaring viaduct over the Andheri Jhora have become camouflaged by vegetation, but the stonework can still be identified by climbing down to the level of the river (see photograph on page 303). February 2005.*

Looking downstream to the confluence with the Teesta River, the pillars of the DHR bridge across the Riyang River could still be seen in February 2005, despite 55 years of monsoon rain and devastation. Rilli Siding and the ropeway to Kalimpong would have been on the spur of land to the right of the gap between the first two pillars.

discovered from Siliguri, allowing packs of mules to scale the path and transport 25 maunds of food a day. Twenty people had been killed at one blow when a collection of bustees perched on the hillside outside the town were undermined by water, and five hundred more had to be billeted in the Town Hall.

Mr K.C. Bakhie, the Chief Commissioner of Railways, reported to a Press conference on 26th June that work was under way rebuilding the new metre-gauge bridge at Sevoke, and it was anticipated the Assam Rail Link would be restored by the middle of August. He feared the two-foot-gauge extension up the valley would have to be abandoned, for although it was possible to rebuild the line if entirely new alignments were found and constructed, he advised '... *that is an expensive affair*'.

Life and business in Kalimpong came to a standstill and the price of commodities escalated. Repeated demands for restoration of the ropeway fell on deaf ears and the Government of Bengal appeared indifferent. Following representations from Indian woollen mills facing a shortage of raw materials due to increased demand from overseas, the Government of India imposed a ban in July 1950 on exports of all types of wool. America had become the biggest buyer of Tibetan wool since the 1930s, and the Kalimpong wool merchants faced financial ruin. Despite the protests, there was simply not enough money to make the repair of the railway a viable option and the Teesta Valley never saw its train again.

It was the same year that China invaded Tibet, and in the wake of the tragedy came an exodus of monks, traders and hill-farmers making their way over the ice-razed passes by the old trading route to Kalimpong. The build-up of communist forces along the Sikkimese frontier closed the area to foreign visitors in the 1960s, and the old cart road up the Teesta Valley became a strategic lifeline for the military.

In 1966, a new 1,470-metre ropeway was built across the Rilli and Teesta rivers, the cost of 2½ lakh rupees being donated by the Swiss Technical Co-operation Organisation. It was installed by the Lasso Ropeway Company of Basel, Switzerland, and is owned by the Samthar Co-operative Multipurpose Society Ltd (SAMCO). With a carrying capacity of three tonnes per hour each way, it carries agricultural and forest produce from the Suruk, Samthar, Sinji and Yangmakun Khasmahal forest blocks. India was invited to take over the administration of Sikkim in 1975 and an air of enforced stability was established. The road from Siliguri was rebuilt and a new crossing was made across the river just to the south of the old suspension bridge to maintain the crucial link with Ghum and Darjeeling.

As with the Kishenganj extension, there is little immediate evidence of the Teesta Valley line today. The growth of Siliguri has made it difficult to visualise the course it ran as it left the town, but the train would have passed in front of the Siliguri and Darjeeling Medical Stores, which are perversely next to each other and display their addresses as 'Road Station'. The right-hand side of the Sevoke Road provides a good approximation of where the track was laid for the next three miles, and the imposing Cindrella Hotel is a useful marker to indicate where the train would have been leaving the open fields and passing through the scattering of shacks known as Salugara.

The forest would have closed in beyond here, but the first signs of surviving civil engineering do not appear until Sevoke, where a pier of the old railway bridge still remains on the northern bank of the river. The mood of the Sevoke River could be as perverse as the Teesta, and over the years the configuration of the land hereabouts has changed considerably. A long embankment led the DHR above the flood plain to Sevoke station, whilst the road originally crossed the river at a point close its confluence with the Teesta before a new concrete bridge was built parallel to the railway. The embankment has since become absorbed into the land, and the broad-gauge line that has replaced the metre-gauge Assam Rail Link passes directly over its buried course on the approach to its crossing of the Teesta. The station is now a house and can be found just beyond the broad-gauge level crossing, the fretted weather-boarding fringing the ends of the roof revealing its ancestry.

The ledge on which the train ran through the Teesta gorge can be discerned in many places, particularly as it passes under the Coronation Bridge. The stone columns of the bridge that soared across the Andheri Jhora remain, but they have become so entangled by vegetation that they can only be properly seen by climbing down to river level. The current road alignment at Kalijhora easily confuses the former layout of the railway, but Aslam's Cutting is just discernible through the dense growth of shrubs and trees, although more of it has become filled in over the years with falling rocks and earth slips. Beyond here a discrete line in the vegetation indicates where the trains once ran across the alluvial spits of land on the inside bends of the river, and this is most distinctive at Rilli, the site of the transhipment siding and base of the ropeway to Kalimpong. The upper terminus of the ropeway in Kalimpong is now a school, and the staff occupy the former manager's house and engine room. Two of the winding wheels have been set in concrete outside, and the godowns for storing the freight remain further up the hillside.

Back at river level, the piers of the crossing at Riyang still poke above the turbulent waters and the sweeping loops that scaled the opposite hillside to the station pass through what is now a fish farm. A family occupies the old explosives store for the railway higher up the hillside, and the site of Riyang station can be traced amongst the scattering timber houses that cower beneath the canopy of the forest. The bridge abutments in Gielle Khola still cling to the hillside, and the course of the line to the terminus can just be made out as a fragile ledge cut from the eroded rock face. Little remains of Kalimpong Road station, although the water tank that filled the locomotives became immured in a landslide and was later restored for the use of the small community still there. The work was unsuccessful, and it remains out of use and encased in concrete.

There has been talk in recent years of a new line being laid up the valley, but most of it has been based on extravagant political promises that were quickly forgotten. However, the strategic importance of the route for Sikkim is clear, and for that alone the valley had to surrender its serenity for its security, a choice in which there was no alternative.

Looking upstream towards Gielle Khola, this private house at Riyang was once the explosives store of the DHR. The line had climbed up the side of the valley from the bridge by three sweeping curves, the site of the station now being hidden in the forest to the left. February 2005.

Chapter 12

Great Expectations

There was a collective sigh of relief across the world when the award by UNESCO was announced. At the same time, some rather worried looks were being exchanged at Northeast Frontier Railways headquarters, where certain elements had stuck to the belief that the railway would never qualify for accreditation and would at last be able to shut up shop for good.

So the DHR passed into a new era of ownership, for the NFR had become the guardians of a World Heritage Site, and with that came a new set of responsibilities. By definition, heritage is what is inherited, and in this case it was a steam railway. It was only the second railway in the world to receive the award, the first being in Austria.

The European line had been built between 1848 and 1854 to link Vienna with the Adriatic by crossing the Semmering, the lowest of the great passes across the Alps. This 41km line was recognised as one of the celebrated feats of civil engineering during the pioneering phase of railway construction, and was the first to cross a European mountain range, passing the summit through a tunnel some 1,564 yards long. The gradient of the line averages at 1 in 47 with a maximum at 1 in 40 for four kilometres, and to achieve this 15 additional tunnels, 16 viaducts, 11 iron bridges and 118 arch bridges were constructed. The railway was electrified long ago and the quality of the workmanship of the civil engineering has allowed it to be in continuous use as a main line to the present day. The question of motive power had not been part of the World Heritage equation in the Austrian case.

When it came to the DHR criteria, UNESCO stated the following in its justification for inscription:

• Criterion (ii): The Darjeeling Himalayan Railway is an outstanding example of the influence of an innovative transport system on the social and economic development of a multi-cultural region, which was to serve as a model for similar developments in many parts of the world.

• Criterion (iv): The development of railways in the 19th century had a profound influence on social and economic developments in many parts of the world. This process is illustrated in an exceptional and seminal fashion by the Darjeeling Himalayan Railway.

The brief description of the DHR that appeared in the 23rd Session of the UNESCO World Heritage Committee declared:

'The Darjeeling Himalayan Railway is the first, and still the most outstanding example of a hill passenger railway. Opened in 1881, it applied bold and ingenious engineering solutions to the problems of establishing an effective rail link across a mountainous terrain of great beauty. It is still fully operational and retains most of its original features intact.'

The World Heritage Convention had been established in 1972 with the objective of protecting and preserving historical and valued buildings, along with geographical sites of exceptional beauty and fragility. In 1999 there were 582 World Heritage Sites, 21 of them being in India, including the Taj Mahal, the Agra Fort and Fatehpur Sikri. It had been agreed that

Despite all the attempts to modernise the railway over decades, there was no denying that the DHR was a 19th-century transport system whose preservation was of international importance. Making that economically possible was the greatest challenge the Railway had to face, as exemplified by the solitary passenger trying to catch up with the two-coach Mixed near Rangbhul in January 2002.

John Clemmens.

applications for inscription would come from national governments, and where it related to a cultural site, the assessment would be made by the International Council on Monuments and Sites (ICOMOS). The criteria would focus on evaluating the fixed assets of a site, and would therefore protect the structure in the location in which it was built. The DHR now presented UNESCO with an anomaly, for the permanent way and buildings had received protection as its fixed assets, but the rolling stock had not. And more to the point, it said nothing about steam, and Indian Railways saw this as a chink of light in helping to overcome the running costs of the line ... it could introduce diesels.

However, it was not widely publicised that immediately following the two criteria under which UNESCO had inscribed the DHR as a World Heritage Site, the report also stated that:

> 'The Committee drew the attention of the State Party to the recommendations of ICOMOS concerning (a) the creation of a heritage conservation unit (b) the establishment of a buffer zone along the length of the railway line and station, and (c) the establishment of an adapted management plan. All these issues could be examined by the Bureau at its twenty-fifth session in 2001.
>
> The Observer of Germany underlined the importance of retaining steam trains within the site. The Committee was assured by both ICOMOS and the Observer of India that, despite the movable character of the steam trains, they would most certainly remain in use due to their importance as a tourism attraction. The Observer of India, in thanking the Committee for its decision, drew the attention of the Committee to the importance of preserving its unique site, which was the first industrial heritage site in Asia to be inscribed on the World Heritage List.'

The UNESCO recommendation of creating a heritage conservation unit and a buffer zone was interpreted in conflicting ways by those charged with its implementation. The relationship the railway has with the communities that have grown alongside the track in Siliguri is undoubtedly part of its history, but for some it was seen as an encroachment that should be removed. Where there are shacks there are stalls, and No. 788 is seen working through the bazaar just after leaving Siliguri Town in February 2002.

Peter Jordan

The Asian Institute for Transport Development had submitted a report to Indian Railways in December 1998 on how it saw the future of the DHR being secured. It had already successfully turned round the fortunes of the Kalka-Simla line, although it had to be acknowledged that whilst the two railways did indeed scale the flanks of the Himalaya, they were radically different. The climb to Simla was on a dedicated course specifically engineered for the railway, whereas the DHR clung remorselessly to the road and ran through the middle of towns and villages. The report recommended that the steam locomotives should be replaced by diesels and based at Siliguri, where a metre-gauge diesel shed already existed, and the procurement of '... *a few steam locomotives may, however, be only considered if commercially justified for short trips or excursions as tourist attractions*'.

Indian Railways certainly had appreciated the importance of the 'B' Class in helping the DHR retain its unique identity, and the Materials Management Department had previously invited tenders for the construction of three new 'B' Class to replace its worn-out motive power. The specifications were demanding, but such was the interest that a number of companies had risen to the challenge, including Alan Keef Ltd of Ross on Wye, Herefordshire, and the Boston Lodge Works of the Ffestiniog Railway in Wales. Both had built new locomotives and renovated existing engines for customers in many parts of the world, and nobody could question the excellence of their engineering.

However, the most attractive option in the eyes of Indian Railways appeared to come from Sulzer Winpro, which now had the business of the Swiss Locomotive and Machine Works in Winterthur. SLM had built the original 0-8-2T rack and adhesion locomotives for the metre-gauge Nilgiri mountain railway, and had recently been pursuing an order to construct four new machines for the line. Indian Railways also regarded the company as the only commercial enterprise in the world that was still actively involved in the design and manufacture of new steam engines.

During the 1980s SLM had become aware of a growing demand for the replacement of the steam engines they had originally built for a number of European rack-and-pinion lines. With this in mind, the company made a conscious decision to get back into the market, and in the early 1990s constructed eight new 0-4-2 tank engines for mountain railways in Austria and Switzerland. By embracing modern construction techniques, they produced state-of-the-art oil-fired machines that were highly efficient and could be operated by one man if necessary. Improved operational readiness was made possible by fitting modern boiler insulation, which would allow the locomotives to be kept in steam overnight, whilst an external electrical heating device could be remotely controlled by telephone and enable an unattended machine to be put into steam from cold.

It sounded as though the solution had been found that would suit everybody, at least until the price was quoted for a new 'B' Class. Unit costs in Switzerland are very high, and equated to $2^{1}/_{2}$ to 3 times that of the UK. The accountants at IR reeled in horror, and had barely recovered from the shock when Sulzer Winpro announced that it was selling the steam business of SLM to Hug Engineering, a company making ceramic catalysers for diesel engines. Hug also owned a machine-building company, which worked partly for its catalyser business and partly as a supplier for the rolling-stock industry. A new company, Dampflokomotiv und Maschinenfabrik AG DLM (Steam Locomotive and Machine Works Ltd) was formed under Roger Waller to continue with the development and marketing of modern steam engines. DLM secured its first order with the modernisation of '*Breithorn*', a rack steam locomotive owned by the Brig-Visp-Zermatt-Bahn, a profitable metre-gauge mountain line that climbed in the shadow of the Matterhorn in Switzerland. DLM also expressed its intention to tender for other new locomotives, including resurrecting those for the Nilgiri rack line in southern India.

Nevertheless, it had unsettled Indian Railways to the extent that the decision was made not to pursue the matter any further with tenders for a 'B' Class and to opt for dieselisation. It was anybody's guess where the future lay with the remaining fourteen steam engines still on the railway, although Tindharia took the curious decision to rebuild '*Baby Sivok*'. It appeared that implicit faith had been placed in the brass plate attached to the side of the cab that bore the date 1881, for this had erroneously been interpreted as the year of its construction. Once recorded in the ledgers it had become immutable, a convenient fact that had given it a stubborn authority when a local compilation of the railway's history was being made ... and what better locomotive could there be for the historic steam train run for tourists from Darjeeling to the Batasia Loop?

The truth was that the tiny locomotive was a contractor's engine purchased around 1911 to assist with the construction of the Teesta Valley extension, where it had been perfectly at ease with gradients that did not exceed 1 in 100. After a somewhat secretive career, it had been sent to the Indian Railways Centenary Exhibition in 1953, where it carried the

The reasons behind returning 'Baby Sivok' to working order may not have been historically sound, but it was certainly a delight to see the locomotive in steam. Unfortunately the expectations were far above the capability of the design, and it now enjoys an honourable retirement in the railway museum at Ghum.

Peter Jordan

date plate 1881 to record the opening of the DHR. Since then it had weathered the elements by being mounted on a plinth outside the station at Siliguri Junction, from which it was now duly removed and taken to Tindharia for overhaul. It finally raised steam on 14th January inside the works, but once outside on the main line, its limitations became immediately apparent on the 1 in 28 gradient. The mischievous truth had been pushed too far with the claim it had been one of the original locomotives, and the dream of it doing battle with trainloads of excited trippers to Batasia quickly faded. It caused a certain amount of embarrassment within NFR circles, but in the ever-optimistic spirit that pervades Tindharia, the problem was turned into an opportunity by introducing a '*Man Your Own Locomotive Programme*', whereby it could be hired for the day in order to be driven light to Agony Point and back.

So it was that two 400 HP Sury & Naire four-wheeled diesel hydraulic locomotives were brought on broad-gauge well-wagons to New Jalpaiguri. They had been built by the SAN Engineering & Locomotive Company of Bangalore and given the Indian Railway classification NDM6. Designed with a working speed of 32kph across the plains and 16kph on the mountain section, they were fitted with airbrakes and equipped to run in multiple-unit, although it was not foreseen this would initially be the working practice. A wry smile crept over the lips of those who had read their history, for long ago in 1879, Prestage had the same ambitions with the first steam locomotives. The question of flange friction on the loops with the rolling stock had not been a factor then, but in time the Garratt would illustrate the operational limitations imposed by this unique railway.

SAN had been given the contract to build six locomotives for the Matheran Light Railway and Nos. 601, 602 and 603 were already in service at Neral. The Railway Board subsequently allocated the funds to completely refurbish two of the original German NDM1 B+B diesels built by Arnold Jung in 1955 and still running on the MLR, which one can only surmise would release two of the new NDM6 locomotives for the DHR. No.604 arrived at New Jalpaiguri in December 1999 already dressed in the blue livery of the NFR, whilst No.605 was delivered on 27th February 2000 painted in the red associated with the Matheran Light Railway.

The new diesel-hauled service was inaugurated on 21st May 2000, and barely ten days had passed when the Down service overturned on a curve at Dhungekuthi, near Mahanadi. The train had been descending with four coaches, which had a combined carrying capacity of 69 passengers. However, the word was passed around that it had been estimated that 123 were indeed riding on the train and, with the Hill Cart Road being completely blocked, all traffic was suspended for several hours. Four people were hurt, and pride at NFR headquarters was severely bruised. It was feared that the ripples could spread to the highest level in the Ministry, and with that in mind, the search was on for an answer, if not the reason.

It was time for the Indian Steam Railway Society to take a lead. Formed in October 1999, its distinguished membership included Mr R.C. Sethi as its President, who had retired as a General Manager of Indian Railways, and Mark Tully[1] as Vice-President. The Society saw the move to dieselise the DHR as a betrayal of its heritage and brought the matter to the attention of the Southeast Asia Regional Office of UNESCO. The reply was encouraging, for it was agreed that the continued use of steam locomotives along the line was a major component of the 'universal value' of the site. They also found merit in the claim that the introduction of new diesel locomotives along the system would greatly diminish the significance and value for which the railway was inscribed as a World Heritage Site. The report was forwarded to the World Heritage Centre for evaluation, and representations were made to the Indian Government on the appropriate actions that were to be taken.

[1] Now Sir Mark Tully

Having just been delivered, the two new diesels wait in the locomotive shed at New Jalpaiguri to be commissioned into service. With the wooden panels still in place to protect the cab glass in transit, the red livery of No.605 gives away the fact that it was originally destined for the Matheran Light Railway.

Peter Jordan

No.782 makes a spirited approach to the Dilaram road crossing with a two-carriage Mixed in January 2002. The importance of retaining steam trains in terms of heritage on the DHR was now being championed across the world as IR faced the challenges that the status of World Heritage brought with it.

John Clemmens.

The debate regarding the motive power for the line was taken up by the Indian Press, followed by an article that appeared on 7th June 2000 in a major national newspaper in the UK. Its readers were informed that the World Heritage status of the railway had been placed in jeopardy by a programme of modernisation that had not been properly thought through, and highlighted its concern with the proposal made by Indian Railways to replace the steam engines with diesel.

The DHR Society responded and stated that:

'... the economic case for retaining steam on the DHR was overwhelming, and that not for the first time diesels had been tried, and crucially all have proved vastly inferior to the vintage 'B' Class steam that have served the railway with distinction'.

The stakes were now running high and the Indian Steam Railway Society drafted a letter and sent it direct to the President of India.

The question of pride had to be overcome with the introduction of the diesels, for it could not be seen that the tail was wagging the dog. In July it was reported that only one of the diesels was in use, and was running on alternate days with steam on the main service from New Jalpaiguri to Darjeeling. It was also said that the diesels were derailing at a higher frequency than the steam ever did, but it was only the major incidents that were being recorded to avoid too many political embarrassments. Considerable care now had to be taken when negotiating some of the more pronounced curves, particularly those just beyond the water stop near Rangtong, and it was clear that the diesels were inherently flawed in design when it came to the question of the centre of gravity. It was no accident that the 'B' Class was designed with well-tanks, which allowed for over a ton of water to be carried at, or below, axle level. The assurances given to UNESCO by ICOMOS and the *Observer of India* that the steam trains would most certainly remain in use had been somewhat inconvenient, and this information was still not in the public domain. With time running out for the reinvigoration of steam, it was feared that the disposal of the engines could be presented as a *fait accompli*.

On a more positive note, a rake of eight coaches was seen being prepared for service that had been refurbished in a style that was quite unlike anything seen before. The imaginative work had been undertaken by Marksman, a Siliguri company that specialised in the interior design of commercial properties, and each coach was to reflect aspects of Gorkha, Buddhist and Rajasthani cultures. The interiors were an extravaganza of tapestry and cane latticing, and with the seating arranged in a one-by-two layout, loudspeakers would entertain the passengers with the sound of music as their train climbed every mountain. These splendid vehicles were now being held back from regular service until the official visit by the President in the late autumn, but there were no doubts regarding where the Railway Board saw the market now lay. The drive was on to attract the tourists.

There were also new people knocking on the door, and it was announced that the post of Area Manager was to be upgraded to Additional Divisional Rail Manager to reflect the heritage status of the DHR. Mr Ranier thus replaced the position Mr Roy had held at New Jalpaiguri, whilst Mr Chakraborty, the Assistant Mechanical Engineer who had steered the railway through some of its leanest years, was to retire on 31st August. There had already been 31 previous AMEs appointed since independence, and it was said that the less charitable saw it literally and metaphorically as a siding to any further career advancement. However, Mr Chakraborty loved the line and was committed to its survival, but he had been obliged to take a number of difficult and sometimes controversial decisions in order to keep one of the world's most demanding railways running on a shoestring budget. In a land where everything is recycled, many had suggested that during his time, the soul of Colonel Stevens[2] had indeed been alive and well in Tindharia!

The difficulty of working the line also made the DHR the ultimate challenge for preserved railways of the same gauge in other parts of the world to test the mettle of their own locomotives. A number of exchanges had been taking place with such railways in Europe, although the fact that some of the engines were privately owned must have helped with the decision-making process. The first proposal with the DHR was bold and imaginative, for the Ffestiniog Railway in North Wales offered '*Linda*' as an exchange for a 'B' Class.

Built in 1893, '*Linda*' was one of three 0-4-0 saddle tanks supplied by Hunslet of Leeds for the Penrhyn Railway in North Wales. Acquired by the Ffestiniog, the

---

[2] The name of Colonel Holman F. Stevens RE (1868–1931) had become synonymous with some of the most delightful and evocative light railways that ever ran in the UK. Although the Colonel's autocratic style had not endeared him to everyone, there was no denying that the lines under his management had survived by his thrift in operating them with stock that others would have long discarded.

engine was extensively rebuilt by Boston Lodge as an oil-fired 2-4-0 saddle tank and tender, and in this form had given exemplary service with hauling passenger trains. It was also significant that the locomotive was the direct descendant of *Charles*, which had been built in 1882 alongside the four DHR 'A' Class sub-contracted to Hunslet, and similarities in the two designs had suggested one may have influenced the other. The exchange sadly foundered, as a detailed examination of the operating conditions revealed that they were not as compatible as initially suggested, and IR were unable to witness the possibilities of modern steam technology applied to a locomotive of a similar design and vintage as the 'B' Class on its home territory.

The next in the frame for consideration of locomotive exchanges were *Chaloner* and *Pixie*, two privately-owned engines operating on the 2ft-gauge Leighton Buzzard Railway in England, The LBR had provided the home for the ex-Matheran Light Railway Orenstein & Koppel 0-6-0 tank engine Indian Railways had donated to the National Rail Collection, and it would be the ideal stablemate for a visiting 'B' Class. At the same time, the DHR Heritage Foundation was arranging for a splendid gala of events in November 2000 to celebrate a relaunching of the railway following the UNESCO inscription, and it was suggested that *Chaloner* and *Pixie* would make a worthy attraction.

Built in 1877, *Chaloner* was one of a number of delightful vertical-boilered 0-4-0s designed and built by De Winton & Co. of Caernarfon to cross the lightly laid tracks of the slate quarries in North Wales. Built by Kerr Stuart in 1922, *Pixie*, as its name may suggest, was a diminutive 0-4-0 saddle tank and had spent much of its working life with the Devonshire County Council working a roadstone quarry. Neither locomotive made it to India, although three years later another exchange was announced that would offer two L.B.R. locomotives the possibility of climbing to Darjeeling.

No. 779 nosing its way through the Siliguri bazaar with a DHRS chartered special. The town had grown around the railway, so the idea that a 40-metre 'clearway' could be established around the DHR was liable to inflame an already tense political situation. There had been an influx of refugees seeking sanctuary since the civil war in East Pakistan, and removing them as part of a 'beautification project' was seen as nothing else but an insensitive action against an established community.

Peter Jordan

'Green Hills' waits patiently at Rangtong whilst passengers are entertained by a group of local traditional dancers known as Hamron DHR Sanghi. The refurbishment and landscaping of the station was designed by Shasheesh Prasad and Peter Tiller, and particular attention was paid to the detail of the finials and decorative timberwork of the roof. Although the whitewashed concrete revetments on the opposite side of the track did not display the same degree of grace, their presence was crucial to help stabilise the topsoil on the side of the cutting.

The proposals helped to create a culture of mutual cooperation, and a number of retired administrative and workshop managers from Indian Railways took up the cause of steam and came to the UK to assess the viability of building new steam locomotives to the pattern of the 'B' Class. The Indian Railways Board also issued another invitation to bid for three oil-fired steam locomotives for the DHR, and a number of visits were made to the railway from various workshops to see if they could rise to the challenge.

The ink was barely dry on the invitation when a row blew up regarding the encroachments by the side of the railway between New Jalpaiguri and Siliguri. *The Times of India* reported on 16th October 2000 that the whole status of World Heritage was being put in jeopardy with the battle lines being drawn between the Railway Administration and the Siliguri Municipal Corporation. There were now four organised and several unorganised markets that abutted alongside the track, in addition to the ever-enveloping shacks, and the Northeast Frontier Railway Divisional Headquarters at Katihar was planning for a 40-metre 'clearway' on both sides of the line to be maintained as part of the '*beautification project*'.

As Mayor of Siliguri, Bikash Ghosh felt that the forcible removal would be an '*anti-people action*', for they did indeed have municipal water lines, roads, street lighting and even licences for the traders. He argued that the Government should be turning its attention to the removal of the encroachments on railway land in the Gar, Jadavpur and Kasba districts of Calcutta, and claimed that the proposed evacuation of the DHR land was not for the development of the railway but for real-estate promotion to cover its budgetary deficits. Mr G. Dev of the Trinamool Congress[3] supported the development plans, although he thought the railways

---

[3] A political party founded by Ms Mamata Banerjee for Trinamool workers (grassroots workers) to encourage Congress to disassociate itself from the Communists.

Tindharia station in 1981, and as the locomotive takes water, one passenger appears to be so excited at boarding the train that the idea of a carriage door seems too much to cope with. The wooden balustrade between the platform and the train was later replaced by an unattractive concrete wall, but this has since been removed and the original features returned as part of the refurbishment programme during 2001–2002.

Peter Jordan

should also be sympathetic to the plight of slum dwellers and small businessmen, and suggested that the municipal corporation could devise a rehabilitation plan for them. However, the CPI(M) leaders argued that the DHR authorities had failed to improve the tracks to allow for an improvement in the train service and that the decision to introduce diesel engines did not reflect the spirit of retaining the railway in its original form.

The dispute could not have flared up at a more difficult time, for the celebrations to commemorate the first anniversary of the DHR being designated as a World Heritage Site were being staged from 12th to 26th November. Organised by the Friends of the DHR, two special trains had been chartered to run in tandem with guests that included the Alliance for Nature, one of the principal organisations in Austria that had campaigned for the UNESCO inscription of the Semmeringbahn. The festivities culminated with a visit by the Railway Minister Ms Mamata Banerjee on 26th November, and 'Baby Sivok' was hauled up to Ghum from Tindharia the day before by No.791 to be part of the new exhibition site.

The Minister unveiled a plaque in Darjeeling to proclaim the DHR as a World Heritage Site, and to the huge delight of the assembled crowd, declared that the Teesta Valley line was to be restored. The euphoria did not last long, for less than three months later the harsh reality of politics was in play again with further unrest in Darjeeling. *The Calcutta News* reported that Subhas Ghising had suffered serious head injuries during a grenade attack on 10th February 2001 near the Makaibari Tea Estate. Returning to Darjeeling from Bagdogra airport on the Pankhabari Road, his five-car convoy was ambushed by armed gunmen with AK-47 rifles, during which two security guards and two assailants were killed. The GNLF called for an indefinite strike, as a protest against the attack, and with all the shops and markets closed and all transport shut down, the police stated that it had

With the mist hanging high in the trees, an Up special chartered for the DHRS storms along the new course cut into the hillside beyond Pagla Jhora following the devastation in 1998. One section of the extensive work undertaken to abate the force of the monsoon rains can be seen in the background. The second coach is No.149 'Tenzing Norgay', the superb dining car rebuilt in 2001 by the Motibagh Narrow Gauge Workshop in Nagpur.

John Clemmens

No. 780 'Green Hills' shunts stock from the school train over the inspection pit at Darjeeling station. The town was to host the Stakeholders' Workshop in January 2002, where a strategy was discussed and agreed that would encourage those who lived and worked in the area to support the future of the DHR. It was a complex task that would have to empathise with many factions and interests, and at the same time allow for the development of a conservation plan that would ensure the survival of the railway.

John Clemmens

paralysed normal life across the Darjeeling district. It was suspected that the assault had been orchestrated by the Gorkha Liberation Organisation (GLO), a breakaway faction of the GNLF who had warned of the consequences if a separatist movement was not instigated to declare Darjeeling a State.

Ms Banerjee informed the Press that the incident had vindicated her party's position that law and order in West Bengal had reached its nadir, and joined the GNLF in demanding an investigation. However, the People's Democracy, an organ of the CPI(M), reported on 25th February that following surprise raids and interrogations, the police had arrested a number of armed agitators affiliated with the Trinamool Congress. In her speech on the Indian Union Budget fifteen days later, the Minister sought to appease her critics by repeating the announcement that the:

> *'Restoration of Teesta Valley narrow-gauge line from Sevok to Gillikhola has been a long standing demand of the people of Sikkim and North Bengal. I have also decided to take up the restoration of this important railway line during the year 2001–2002.'*

But a lot of water had flowed under the Teesta Bridge since 1950, and there was no shortage of sceptics who questioned if such a pronouncement would ever become a reality. Nevertheless, a number of local initiatives with the DHR began to mature in 2001, the most significant being the report that Peter Tiller had prepared for Indian Railways on the refurbishment of the stations. With the exception of the termini, the stations were contemporary with the opening of the line, but their use in recent years had declined with the changing fortunes and traffic on the railway. The report highlighted that this trend could now be reversed by the introduction of the 'faster' diesel service (which still did not match the steam-operated service when the locomotives were kept in top condition) and the potential promotion offered by the heritage accreditation. The stations could now take on a new role with tourist information booths, souvenir shops and modern waiting and toilet facilities sympathetically accommodated, whilst the tea stalls would be upgraded or converted into cafeterias.

Tindharia had previously been a major stop, where locomotives hauling trains from NJP were exchanged for others already prepared in the shed with a loaded bunker and full water tanks. Its importance to operation had diminished following the introduction of diesels, but it remained a key location for travellers, as it was the first stop after three reverse sidings and the Chunbatti loop. Like most of the DHR stations, it had suffered some cosmetic trauma over the years and the slabs of concrete positioned between the raised platform and the track contributed nothing to its appeal. They were replaced by an attractive wooden balustrade, which was complemented by the renewal of a number of decorative trimmings and features to the eaves. The roof and guttering was overhauled, the ubiquitous tangle of wiring inside was unravelled and replaced, and the flaking coats of paint stripped from the outside stonework. Indeed the whole area was tidied up, and various shacks and sheds whose use had long been forgotten were taken down and removed.

A substantial amount of clearing up had also been completed at Kurseong, and the turntable was found still intact under a vast mound of ash and rubble in the yard. This was exhumed, cleaned and painted, along with two historic goods vans that had previously been dumped in a siding. The paint was removed from the stonework on the ground floor walls at Ghum and the platform was flattened to one level, whilst the advertisement hoardings and squatter shop were removed. The decorative timber to the station canopy was to be returned, along with the gables and finials, and indeed the footbridge. A temporary exhibition on the refurbishment programme was established on the ground floor of the station building, illustrating the World Heritage status of the railway and historic artefacts from the surrounding area. Plans were now in hand to rebuild the goods and locomotive sheds, and the first floor of the station building was to form a permanent museum of the railway and the part it had played in the growth of the area. The plan would allow the ground floor to become a cafeteria, and the station yard would be the home to larger exhibits like '*Baby Sivok*'. It was anticipated that additions to the collection would include the frames of the 'A' Class that was still languishing amongst the scrub in Siliguri, the van and water wagon from Darjeeling and the restored bolster wagon rescued from Kurseong yard.

It was heartening to see, but the powder keg that was political life continued to smoulder when *The People's Review* reported that on 17th August a secret meeting had been held in Siliguri by leaders of Maoist and left-wing parties to discuss the drafting of the '*people's constitution*'. By contrast, the Dalai Lama spent seven days in the town in early November to attend the inauguration of the Sed-Gyved monastery, although any pretence of peace was short-lived when later that month *The Hindustan Times* advised its readers that 300 Maoist insurgents had slipped through the Siliguri corridor unnoticed. Their declared goal was

The Railway Children

Above: *The plight of children living in the wretched shanties that line the railway tracks in India inspired the development of the Siliguri Project, which was to give hope to many whose lives could extend little beyond the charity of others. Four such lads stand on the remains of 'A' Class No.11 still rusting away in the scrub near Siliguri Junction in 2002.*

Peter Jordan

A wide variety of ingenious trolleys have been made and passed on to successive generations, comprising little more than a flat wooden base running on ball-bearing races. They are held in place on the track by additional wheels set horizontally, and work remarkably well for carrying water containers and supplies, as well as being great sport for the children.

Nick Lera

the establishment of a 'Greater Nepal' and, having faced pressure from the Nepalese security forces, it reported that they were in search of safe sanctuaries in the Siliguri and Darjeeling districts. The guerrillas had opened a Darjeeling-Sikkim unit in Siliguri with the resolve to launch an armed revolution, and support for the 'liberation movement' in Darjeeling, Sikkim and the Dooars. To gain support, the Maoists were said to be contacting disgruntled politicians of the GNLF, ex-servicemen of the armed forces, and the police were faced with the difficulty in identifying them from everybody else.

It was clear that the revival work on the DHR would require an overall strategy and coordinated plan of action that acknowledged and respected everybody's interests, but it was equally apparent there had been a number of conferences held in recent years and that the fine words needed translation into action. To address the challenge, Indian Railways held a Stakeholders' Workshop in Darjeeling during January 2002 under the somewhat wordy theme *'Capacity Building and Sustainable Development of the DHR'*. It was coordinated by Rajesh Agrawal, the Director of the Indian National Rail Museum in Delhi, and the stakeholders were defined as all interested local groups, residents, and the administrative and government bodies that included Indian Railways and the Darjeeling Gorkha Hill Council.

The problems of the DHR had been rehearsed and voiced many times, and the purpose of the workshop was to devise and agree on a strategy that would sustain the livelihood, development and environment of the railway and its neighbouring communities. It was a move that finally appeared to be addressing some of the points raised by ICOMOS in February 2000 with the World Heritage inscription. Everybody at the workshop recognised the heritage potential, but the problem was to focus and coordinate the projects in

The metre-gauge rails from New Jalpaiguri to Siliguri Junction had been lifted by February 2003 to make way for the conversion to broad gauge. Concrete sleepers for the new track can be seen in the foreground as a DHRS special charter headed by No. 782 'Mountaineer' scurries close to the Western City bypass.

John Clemmens

Ex-DHR No.794, looking resplendent in her painted jewels as the 'Matheran Queen', departs from Neral Junction on the Matheran Hill Railway in February 2003. Following the success of the DHR, a submission was being prepared for the line to be considered as a World Heritage Site, but the devastation caused by the monsoon in July 2005 put its future in the balance.

Mike Walls

such a way that those who lived and worked in the area would see the tangible benefits of supporting the venture. The Lepcha Association also made a presentation for the revival of the Teesta Valley line, which may have been somewhat ambitious had it not been for the announcement made by Mamata Banerjee less than a year before. The railway was an important part of the community and the opportunities for tourism in this magnificent valley were undeniable, but there were one or two eyebrows raised with the claim that the transportation of troops was included as one of the immediate benefits it would bring.

A number of discussion groups were formed to explore the most constructive ways of achieving the objectives of the workshop and present the findings as recommendations to Indian Railways. It was determined that the area that was embraced by the World Heritage Site was the vicinity around the railway track that would reflect the heritage value of the journey, including views of mountains, vegetation, buildings and roadside bazaars. Once identified, it would need the involvement and agreement of the Darjeeling Gorkha Hill Council, the Government of Bengal, Forestry, Public Works, Water Board and all municipalities to ensure that the area was protected from violation. It was recommended that the conservation and management of the DHR be controlled through a unit based in Kurseong and directed by a Chief Executive Officer (CEO) who would report directly to the Secretary of the Railway Board. It was essential for the unit to be empowered to work with the heads of all the local agencies and to form business partnerships, requiring an active working mechanism to direct the CEO and the unit on a broad spectrum of community issues.

The Conservation and Management Unit (CMU) would consult and exchange information with a forum of stakeholders convened by the Darjeeling Gorkha Hill Council. The forum would be in equal partnership with Indian Railways, and as such it was agreed that all parties would take responsibility for contributing finance and effort. The DGHC committed itself to the provision of a secretary and full-time administrative officer, and would support local groups in the World Heritage area and assist stakeholders with direct partnership projects.

It was essential to adhere to a time-frame to maintain the impetus of enthusiasm, and it was agreed that the development of the conservation plan should be achieved in twelve months. For this a set of criteria had to be developed by the stakeholders and the CMU that would enable all the aspects of heritage to be recognised. This would identify the fixed and moveable items of heritage, the conservation areas and the more intangible aspects that reflected the history and culture. Although they would be connected, it was agreed that the conservation management plan would take precedence over the asset management and development plan that IR presented to the workshop. It was also crucial to identify what could be offered to the local population, the schools and colleges, and all the visitors, including a constructive framework to market the attractions for the tourist.

The reality was that the work carried out at Kurseong the previous year had already deteriorated, with ash creeping back across the turntable and the rails and sleepers removed. The two freight wagons had also been shunted back to a derelict siding and earth was piling up round the sides. The garden around the station sign at Tung was now overgrown and neglected whilst the paint was peeling from the sign and made it unreadable. Ballast was noted as being simply thrown over the track further along the line, and whoever was responsible clearly did not know what to do with it! The felony at Ghum was even more disappointing, for the natural stone walls, so carefully restored over the previous two years had since been covered in orange paint.

It was going to be a roller-coaster ride of progress and disappointments, but for many the most uplifting aspect of the workshop had been the list of those who wanted to take part in the discussions. By name and association, the line is immediately linked with Darjeeling, but the Siliguri Project for the railway children was a reflection of the concern that so many held for the future. Inspired by the work of David Maidment after being deeply moved by the problem of children living on railway premises, the group had been working in partnership with local charities since 1995. Amongst its many achievements, the organisation had constructed seven bamboo schools alongside the tracks in Calcutta and 300 children were now receiving food, health care, non-formal education and counselling, whilst their parents were actively encouraged to send them to mainstream education and not to scavenge and beg. A similar project had been initiated in 1999 on the land adjacent to the marshalling yards at New Jalpaiguri and was now being extended to the children living around the station at Siliguri Town and alongside the narrow-gauge tracks. The civic authorities had given permission to build a school and the charity funded local teachers, social workers, doctors and a nutritious meal every day, as well as encouraging people to be sympathetic to the needs of the children and their long-term development.

Indian Railways was definitely listening to the workshop, and indeed was looking for ways of introducing steam back to all four of its current hill railways. The rack sections of the Nilgiri Railway were still operated by the original 0-8-2Ts, the magnificent Kalka-Simla line had one of its own 2-6-2Ts restored to work steam specials, and No.794 was taken from the DHR and overhauled for service on the Matheran Hill Railway. It was not the first time that a DHR locomotive had been used on the line, for one of the 'A' Class had been sold to Matheran back in 1906 and had remained in service for twenty years. The main locomotive fleet had comprised four 0-6-0 tank engines built by Orenstein & Koppel of Berlin, which had been fitted with the Klien-Linder system of articulated axles to cope with the severe curvature of the line. They were eventually retired in favour of diesel traction in 1982, but all four were thankfully placed in preservation. The intention was to restore one to full working order, but as an interim measure, No.794 was a much easier and less costly project for the resumption of a steam service for tourists and was duly prepared at the Parel workshops.

The first test train ran on Saturday, 31st March 2002, with No.794 coupled to three coaches at Neral and setting off around mid-day for the 19km climb to Matheran. With a strange locomotive to operate, it is not surprising the crew encountered problems along the way, and it came to a halt in a cutting halfway between Jummapatti (5.69kms) and Water Pipe (11.57kms). It was found to be running low on water, and after some time discussing the situation, the train backed down to Jummapatti, where the only means of filling the tanks was from temporary water storage tanks. There was no alternative but to use a siphon hose and buckets, and it took about an hour to fill the tanks and get the boiler water levels and steam pressure back to acceptable levels, after which No.794 ran around its train to return downhill to Neral. The

Railway Minister, Nitish Kumar, paid a visit on the 7th May and No.794 was duly decorated with flowers and bunting to celebrate the occasion. The announcement was made that steam would be available for charter and that consultations were under way with Maharashtra Tourism Development Corporation to include steam as part of a package.

As part of the celebrations commemorating 150 years of Indian Railways, the DHR ran two special steam-hauled trains on 23rd August to recreate the opening of the service from Siliguri to Kurseong in 1880. They were flagged off from Sukna by 95-year-old Gorey Buchey, who had retired from working on the permanent way in 1965. Unfortunately there had been a landslip at Pagla Jhora three days earlier and the trains were not able to go beyond Tindharia, but Mr V. Nanda, the General Manager of NFR, was in attendance and reaffirmed the commitment that fresh investments were to be made to the track and that the service to Darjeeling would be improved in many ways. Although there had been a loss of Rs8 crore in the past year, the tremendous potential for tourists had been recognised and seven special chartered trains, plus thirteen chartered coaches, had alone generated approximately Rs10 lakh in the past two years.

The assurance had already been underpinned by the announcement made earlier in March that the contract to build three new 'B' Class locomotives had been awarded to the Golden Rock Workshop at Tiruchirappali on the Southern Railways division of IR. The estimated price for the prototype equated to approximately £235,000, and this figure would drop by 25% to £188,000 for the production locomotive. The design was to incorporate oil-firing, and Golden Rock collaborated with the Tiruchirappali Engineering College Science & Technology Entrepreneurs Park with a research project, conducted initially on the Nilgiri rack line. Locomotive No.37395 had been converted to burn oil, although for some reason that appeared to bypass logic, the simple and well-tried systems that had been developed in other countries over many years were not considered. Instead a supplementary diesel engine was fitted in what had been the rear coal bunker, and this was to provide the power for the oil fuel injectors. It was a novel if somewhat cumbersome design, and its questionable elegance was not enhanced by the fitting on an ungainly saddle tank for oil ahead of the cab. It was found that the performance of the locomotive improved from four to six carriages when working the rack section, although it was reported to be a very complicated system and that the Locomotive Foreman had advised more modifications were needed for it to run successfully.

Nevertheless it looked technically if not cosmetically encouraging, and 'B' Class No.787 was shipped from New Jalpaiguri to Golden Rock to be modified for burning oil. The conversion work included two small independent Villiers diesel engines being mounted each side of the running board under the coal bunker to provide the rotational power for feeding the burners and air scavenging. The locomotive was returned to the DHR in October and trials began in earnest the following month. The initial results were disappointing, and it was reported that the locomotive was consuming 30 litres of fuel per hour on the plains section. On this basis, a calculation had been made that showed it could use up to 2,800 litres for the return journey to Darjeeling, which was ten times the amount required by the diesels! The main problem lay with attaining the correct balance between air and fuel to achieve full combustion, but there was doubt that once that had been overcome, a system could be devised that would operate at the high altitudes on the line. However, the tests were terminated when the driver got badly burnt, after which the locomotive was returned to Golden Rock to consider the options. Nobody seemed to be questioning whether the conversion to oil-firing of an original locomotive was a breach of world heritage status.

The restoration of the DHR four-wheeled coach at the National Rail Museum in Delhi was seen as a very positive move towards preserving the heritage of the railway. It had been in a somewhat sorry state, with the timbers slowly rotting away after being left out in the open for many years. It came as the initiative of Peter Tiller and was funded through contributions made by the DHRS in the UK. As a Society member in Delhi, Virgil Miedema negotiated the contract with the New Era Construction Company of New Delhi, who undertook the overhaul of the chassis to running condition before fully refabricating the bodywork to a very high standard.

The future of the New Jalpaiguri-Siliguri section of the DHR came under the spotlight again with the conversion of the metre-gauge tracks to 5ft 6in. Important broad gauge trains like the Darjeeling Mail, the Sealdah - NJP Express and the Kanchenjunga Express would now go straight to the station at Siliguri Junction, from where it was feared passengers could make easy connections at the nearby bus stand and travel by road to Darjeeling. The DHR platform was certainly closer than the buses, but the time factor was still a concern and answers were needed as to why the steam trains were able to complete the journey in a little over five hours 50 years ago whilst the new diesels were taking at least seven. The diesels also needed a high level of maintenance and the sanding equipment was not always working properly, resulting in the exhausted steam fleet being summoned into service at the last minute. Indeed one was being regularly kept in steam at Kurseong to relieve the diesel from working the through service from NJP to Darjeeling and then return to the plains at the head of the down train.

The year 2003 opened on a high note, at least for DHR enthusiasts in the UK. Two of the original four 'B' Class locomotives that were introduced to the DHR in 1889 still survived, with No.18 (latterly ISR 777) cosmetically restored at the Delhi Railway Museum and No.19 (latterly ISR 778) preserved in the USA. The American machine had been purchased by Elliott Donnelley in September 1960 for use on his Ampersand, Reset and South Eastern Railroad in Lake Forest, Illinois,[4] where it became known as 19B. It is not clear whether it was used in steam at Lake Forest, but in time it was transferred to the La Porte County Historical Steam Society at Hesston in Indiana after Mr Donnelly became its Chairman. The Museum decided to change the focus of its interests in 2002 and, as a consequence, 19B was to be sold. It was purchased by Adrian Shooter, the Managing Director of Chiltern Railways, one of the most successful train-operating companies in the UK. The locomotive was loaded into a container on the shores of Lake Michigan and shipped via Felixstowe to Tyseley Locomotive Works, the engineering subsidiary of the Birmingham Railway Museum Trust. With a well-equipped workshop that rebuilds and maintains steam locomotives to main-line standards, 19B was placed in the care of Bob Meanley, the Engineer-in-Chief, for a complete rebuild. It was delivered 18 months later to the Beeches Light Railway, the privately owned line Adrian Shooter had built to incorporate a number of DHR features. With gradients of 1 in 22, severe curves and a station modelled on Gayabari, No.19 made a splendid sight in the Oxfordshire countryside, and has since been allowed to flex its muscles on the Ffestiniog Railway amongst others.

Indeed, it appeared that a second 'B' Class might make a debut on UK shores, for the idea was resurrected for

Purchased from the Hesston Museum in Indiana by Adrian Shooter, No.19 was shipped back to the UK to be restored to full working condition. It is seen here being unloaded from its container at Tyseley on 19th January 2003, after which it was placed in the hands of Bob Meanley, the engineer in charge of the locomotive works.

a locomotive exchange between IR and the Leighton Buzzard Railway. An agreement in principle was made for '*Chaloner*' and '*Alice*' to be operated by LBR crews on the DHR during the early part of 2004, which would bring substantial publicity to the line and dovetail neatly into the programme of developing the potential for tourism. Built by Hunslet in 1902, '*Alice*' was the first of a Class of 0-4-0STs that had spent most of their lives working high in the galleries of the Dinorwic slate quarries in North Wales. Cannibalised to keep

---

[4] The name was derived from Mr Donnelly's association with the printing industry.

The suspicion that the railway could be privatised spread like wildfire through the hill communities, and political action was threatened if there were any moves to reduce the staff. It resulted in the Darjeeling Himalayan Railway Protection Committee being formed in February 2003, and the demand was made for the provision of more steam engines to make the service viable. Despite the introduction of diesels, the early morning Mixed had continued to be hauled by steam, and No. 782 'Mountaineer' is seen with the two-coach train and a gravity trolley near Rangbhul.

John Clemmens

her sister locomotives running, *'Alice's'* remains were rescued from her shed on Elidir mountain after the quarry closed and lowered down derelict inclines to be saved from the scrap-man's torch. It took many years before the locomotive could be restored, and it was not until 1993 that her owner commissioned Boston Lodge Works to return her to full working condition. In return, IR would send a 'B' Class to Leighton Buzzard, where it would have the beguiling prospect of working in tandem with the ex-Matheran Hill Railway 0-6-0T.

The agreement had been facilitated by the Ministry of Tourism, and the intention was for the LBR locomotives to undertake a week of hauling revenue-earning trains on the level section between Siliguri and Sukna, and for tests to be conducted to assess their ability on the climb to Rangtong and back. The scheme had received the staunch support of Mr Ashwani Lohani, who had been a past Director of the National Railway Museum in Delhi before moving on to become the Director of Tourism for the Government of India. He had a been a driving force behind the renovation of *'Fairy Queen'* and of the DHR achieving its World Heritage status, and more recently had become responsible for all activities relating to steam traction on Indian Railways.

However, there had since been a change in personnel at Tourism, and IR advised that it had misunderstood the original basis of the exchange. The locomotive exchange sadly foundered, but quite where the problem lay was open to debate. It appeared that the DHR was still having some operating difficulties with the two diesels and thus was already stretched to provide the motive power to maintain the service. One of the 'B' Class had also been placed out of use with the oil-firing experiments, and with No.794 working on the Matheran line, there must have been some reluctance to part with another working locomotive.

The difficulties were not confined to the Railway, for the number of tourists from overseas had dropped since the terrorist outrage of 11th September 2001, when two aircraft were flown into the twin towers of the World Trade Center in New York. There were now escalating tensions with the Iraq crisis, and the few who did travel to Darjeeling during the early part of 2003 reported that the hotels were virtually empty. However, there was still a feeling of optimism as it was not yet the season for Indian tourists, who could be guaranteed to flock to the hills as the temperatures on the plains soared.

Nerves also began to fray over the question of whether the control of the railway should be handed over from NFR to the Indian Railways Catering and Tourism Corporation (IRCTC), a public-sector company set up and fully owned by the Ministry of Railways to promote domestic and international tourism. Opposition was being voiced by the Kurseong branch of the Mazdoor Union and the political parties, particularly over the question of any reduction in manpower at Tindharia. There was also concern over the possible closure of the railway printing press at Kurseong, and the Darjeeling Himalayan Railway Protection Committee was formed to begin an awareness campaign in February 2003 that demanded the immediate filling of vacant posts. Under the watchword Darjeeling Ko Sano Rail Bachao (Save the Darjeeling toy train), it was critical of the Railway Board for doing little to upgrade the service and demanded the provision of more steam engines *'to make services viable'*. The Mazdoor Union held a convention the following month to express its support *'in thwarting the victimisation of railway employees in the hills'*. The GNLF felt that nothing had been achieved to improve the railway in the two years since being declared a World Heritage Site and claimed that there was a *'nefarious motive'* to shut down the railway industry.

Whether it was by design or coincidence, it was not long before IR made the announcement that it was to introduce a Sunday service between Siliguri and Agony Point, a move more than welcome as it covered some of the most interesting sections of the line. In fact IR felt that with track improvements and air-braked carriages, the new locomotives being built could haul four carriages and reduce the journey time from NJP to Darjeeling to $4^{1}/_{4}$ hours. It sounded impressive, but the renewed permanent way left much to be desired and those who knew the railway intimately felt that such a schedule was too ambitious.

The problem was that ex-broad-gauge sleepers had been made available for use, but by the time the work had been contracted out and passed down to those undertaking the task, it had been thought that it would be economical to saw them in half for the narrow gauge. This resulted in sleepers being laid for 30kms that were 1.24 metres wide instead of 1.44 metres, which only compounded the incidence of rough riding and derailment. The building up of the road surface to

---

Opposite: *No.804 drifts down through the terai forest towards Rangtong in February 2005. Its ancestry from the Raipur Forest Tramway can be seen with the curved profile of the coal chute and the splayed-out support for the rerailing beam on the saddle tank.*

compensate for landslips had also caused a noticeable increase in the climb as the railway approached many of the crossings. This gradient had been measured as 1 in 16 at certain points, which made the locomotives susceptible to a loss of traction at a crucial moment when ascending, whilst the problems with effective braking on a downhill train were only too apparent.

It was feared that the conversion of metre gauge on the NJP-Siliguri Junction section to 5ft 6in would mean that the DHR would now have a new main-line connection, and as such the final 5½ miles of narrow gauge could be closed. The metre-gauge diesel facility at Siliguri Junction was certainly redundant, and it was decided to take advantage of this and resite the DHR locomotive depot from NJP. The projected demolition of the old shed again raised the question of the security of the fixed assets of the line, for it appeared that some were regarding the more recent history of the railway on the plains as being less worthy than that of the climb to Darjeeling. High-ranking voices were claiming that the NJP-Siliguri section was not included in the World Heritage inscription, although the original submission was quite clear that it had been. It appeared that the background to this section was less well known, and with it being steeped in modern politics, its heritage value had not yet retreated into the safety of the history books.

A new bridge was built across the Mahananda between Siliguri Town and Siliguri Junction to accommodate the broad gauge, the old one being simply cut up and dropped into the river until it could be retrieved in the dry season. It came as some relief when it was noted that a track for the DHR was being laid between the 5ft 6in rails, which at least preserved the line to the original 1879 terminus at Siliguri Town. The section beyond to NJP appeared to be in a much more vulnerable position, and although World Heritage status did not allow for selective closures, the rumour machine began to run in top gear when the bulldozers were seen in action at NJP and tearing up the two-foot gauge. However, the anxieties were finally put to rest when it was noted towards the end of 2003 that the former DHR platforms were being rebuilt to accommodate additional broad-gauge tracks and a new island platform serving the narrow gauge was being built on the northern side close to the booking office.

The section from Siliguri Junction to Sukna also saw some improvement work with a new road crossing constructed alongside the old Panchanai Bridge, which had previously carried all traffic including the railway. It was not before time, for safety had been stretched when a 17¼-tonne diesel had rumbled past the 7½-tonne weight limit each day! The station building at Sukna began to look particularly spruce when it was given a fresh coat of paint, which was complemented by the planting of shrubs and seedlings in the garden. The programme to build a relationship between the railway and local communities took a positive turn with the installation of a computer facility that provided access points to the Internet, which opened up opportunities for education and the development of trade. Information, Communication and Technology centres were also to be provided at Kurseong, Ghum and Darjeeling, all as part of the UNESCO-funded initiative, and these would be maintained with the assistance of young trained volunteers from the neighbourhood.

Anxieties regarding the funding of the IT project were later expressed by Ian Pringle, who was in charge of the UNESCO heritage sites in India. He visited Sukna whilst on an inspection of the progress being made with the DHR project aimed at eradicating poverty, and had cause to remind those responsible that the funds were not to provide a free service simply because the area was designated as being below the poverty line. The principle behind all the initiatives was that they should become self-sustaining, and it was recommended that self-help groups should be formed from local residents to take over the management and ownership of IT centres and develop strategies towards this goal.

Concerns were also being expressed elsewhere about the eviction of folk who had settled on railway land, whilst the demolition of the station tea stall was ill-advised. It had been a feature at Sukna for over fifty years, and it was shameful to displace its owner to a cramped section of a storage building at the north end. An act of sacrilege was also committed outside the station with the removal of the weighbridge, for it had been historically significant to the story of the railway and the Hill Cart Road, and in terms of heritage had been in its original position. It was to be taken to Ghum for the outside display, but had broken in transit and was now dumped in the yard.

A number of the 'B' Class began appearing from Tindharia paint shop with names applied to their cab sides, with No.786 becoming '*Ajax*', No.788 '*Tusker*', No.791 '*Horatio*', No.792 '*Hawkeye*', No.802 '*Victor*', and No.806 somewhat curiously as '*Queen of Hills*'.[5] The two diesels were bestowed with the names '*Maverick*' and '*Buccaneer*', but unfortunately the carriages they should have hauled had stood unused in the NJP yard for two years. They had come from the

The bridge across the Panchanai River three miles north of Siliguri was shared by rail and road, but a weight restriction of 7½ tonnes was imposed as a measure to control the constant pounding from overloaded lorries. The locomotives were twice as heavy as the limit, but there was no alternative for No.782 'Mountaineer' but to ease its train over the old bridge on an Up special to Darjeeling in January 2003. Note the new road crossing under construction to the left of the photograph.

John Clemmens

IR workshops at Mysore, three of them being rebuilds in 2000 from DHR stock dating from 1968 and 1990, and three constructed new in 2001. However, all had a number of shortcomings that included an absence of a fail-safe for the braking system, an alarming prospect for any railway, let alone one that scaled the flanks of the Himalaya. It was also claimed that metre-gauge air-brake equipment had been fitted and that the new diesels did not have sufficient power to operate the system, whilst others suggested that the contractors had not allowed for the fact that the loading gauge on the DHR was more restricted than the other 2ft-gauge railways, which brought back memories of the diesel trials in the late 1950s.

It seemed that no sooner had IR climbed a ladder on its game plan with the DHR than a snake would appear and take it sliding back down again to its starting point. *The Times of India* ran a feature, on 26th May 2003, to advise that UNESCO was unhappy with the

---

[5] Brass nameplates were already being carried by 779 *'Himalayan Bird'*, 780 *'Green Hills'*, 782 *'Mountaineer'*, and 804 *'Queen of the Hills'*. All the locomotives eventually received names, although the list issued by Tindharia did not always match those that had been painted on the cab sides!

change from the train being hauled by steam to diesel, the report stating that:

> 'DHR is turning out to be a white elephant for the railways, which says revenues generated were way below maintenance costs. The biggest reason for tourists shunning it for their journey to Darjeeling is that it takes seven hours to cover a distance that by road can be reached in half that time. Diesel locos have cut the journey by two hours, but haven't still managed to attract many passengers. DHR's annual cost for running the toy train is Rs90 million, but revenues generated are just Rs4.5 million. The railway has thus reportedly decided to stall all plans of expanding/upgrading the toy train service owing to lack of funds. It wants organisations like UNESCO to adopt DHR.'

Nobody could deny that the relationship the railway had with the Press had been fickle since its earliest days, but it did not come as a welcome comment to those trying to cope with the problem at Rail Bhavan in Delhi and NFR headquarters in Guwahati. Their shoulders must have sagged even more when the monsoon rains turned into a spiteful mood on 8th July and caused a number of landslides in the area, particularly around Sonada, Ghum and Simana, near Darjeeling station. One report claimed they had been the worst since 1968, although the casualties were lighter, but there were questions to be asked as to why it caused yet another wave of damage at Pagla Jhora after the extensive work undertaken in 1998. About 70 metres of road and rail had been washed away, and on 23rd July *The Statesman* reported that despite the recommendations of the Landslide Expert's Committee, the culverts were only about 1.5 metres wide and had been constructed to a poor design. This was refuted by the engineers responsible, who advised that no culvert could have coped with the boulders brought down by the sudden rush of the torrent. The Geological Survey of India had recently

A Down train ambles between Tindharia and Rangtong in 1998, but despite the innocuous setting, it was one of three areas identified where the soil had become persistently unstable. Local communities had found and excavated some thin seams of coal, which in turn had allowed water to seep through and undermine the bedrock, causing subsidence and landslides in July 2003.

Despite the introduction of diesels, it was clear that the railway could not compete with the road when it came down to the journey time to Darjeeling and was failing to attract more custom. The new locomotives certainly made the train service more reliable, but the nettle had yet to be grasped that an investment to rebuild the existing fleet of steam locomotives would reflect the spirit of heritage and adventure and attract a new generation of tourists. No.791 is seen here pounding its way through the upper reaches of the terai forest in March 1999.

identified Kurseong, Pagla Jhora and Tindharia as 'sinking zones' of persistent soil instability, pointing to chronic weaknesses in the soil and vegetation cover, whilst concern was raised with the claim that settlements in the area might disappear completely in 75–100 years.

Jeeps were used to bring essential supplies to Kurseong via the teeth-clenching road that bypassed Gayabari, whilst Darjeeling could be approached only by picking the way over the boulders and damage of the road that runs via Mirik; it was estimated that the repair to this road alone would cost Rs5.10 crore. Apart from Pagla Jhora, most of the damage on the Hill Cart Road occurred between Rangtong and Tindharia, which had been made worse by locals mining the tiny coal-seams. Although barely a few centimetres thick, the removal of the soil on the surface had created hollows and exposed the underlying sandstone. This had in turn allowed water to seep through to the feldspar and assist with its decomposition to form clay minerals and act as a lubricant to sliding rock. The estimate for the repair was given as Rs4.2 crore, excluding Pagla Jhora, and an official of the National Highways was reported to have thought that the area was relatively stable. In fact there had been a long history of it being just the opposite, including loops 1 and 2 having been destroyed and a fissure over 300 yards long appearing beneath the station yard at Tindharia.

The relief committee in Kurseong demanded that a Bailey bridge should be constructed immediately as prices of essentials were rising fast, whilst it was reported that consideration was being given to the construction of a tunnel at Gidapahar due to the virtual collapse of the Hill Cart Road. The GNLF organised a demonstration against what they called the failure of the authorities on the matter and planned to call a strike, but it was withdrawn after the branch President visited the site and saw that work was indeed under way. Three bulldozers had been employed, but posters were being put up by the Hill Transport Joint Action Committee threatening an indefinite transport strike if the road failed to open by 10th August. Quite how this would have helped matters was open to debate, but it was another illustration of the political sensitivities in the area.

A positive development came in October with the arrival at Tindharia of Paul Atkins and John Bancroft from the UK. The DHR Heritage Foundation had brokered a deal earlier in the year for them to work with the DHR management over three one-month periods to rehabilitate the rolling stock and improve the infrastructure. Paul Atkins was a public transport logistics consultant and John Bancroft a technical mechanical consultant, and they were given a wide-ranging brief to produce a no-holds-barred report that included assessing the potential for freight transport, a six-hour timetable for a steam-operated service from NJP to Darjeeling, the viability of the oil-firing designs and suspension systems for the rolling stock. It was agreed that to meet these objectives, their attention would focus on a high-quality renovation of 'B' Class No.791 and a set of coaches, along with the production of a business development plan to increase the passenger numbers and revenue.

The workshop staff at Tindharia was enthusiastic about the project, and made it clear that they were willing

No.788 approaches Rangbhul with the early morning Up Mixed from Kurseong in January 2002. There could be few places left in the world where such a delightful steam-hauled local passenger service could be found on a working railway in the 21st century. It was an integral element of its World Heritage appeal, and it was reported that the operating staff understood the custom this could bring, whilst the management was focused only on its economy and modernisation.

John Clemmens

to support any initiative that would help the Railway. It was a promising start, but it was soon found that their spirit was not to be so readily shared by the middle management. Indeed, it took considerable persuasion in motivating the Additional Divisional Rail Manager (ADRM) to secure the safety of the four 4-wheeled vans, which were lingering at the back of the now-derelict locomotive shed at NJP. There was something poetic when one was found still loaded with boxes of toilet seats from its last commission to haul freight! The wagons were eventually taken to Tindharia by road on the back of the workshop pick-up, although they were loaded upside down on their roofs and consequentially damaged in transit. Two bogie vans were also rescued, but it was found that they were too long to be moved by road and were placed in storage in the shed at Siliguri Junction to hopefully await transportation by rail.

Perhaps the most historic artefact was the remains of 'A' Class No.11, but despite representations having been made over recent years regarding its importance to the DHR heritage, it was still being left to decay and destruction at Siliguri Junction. Again the management seemed somewhat bewildered why it should now be treasured, and it was with some reluctance they finally arranged for it to be dragged from its grave in the scrub and taken by road to the protection of Tindharia locomotive shed.

As ever, the monsoon damage on the Hill Cart Road was repaired, and the train service resumed in time for a ten-day festival to be held in Darjeeling during November. It was put together by the Darjeeling Gorkha Hill Council, the Town Municipality, and the State Tourism Department, along with support from the railway, the tea industry and citizens' groups. It was also the golden jubilee of the Himalayan Mountaineering Institute, and thousands of tourists came to the town to join in the festivities, with many travelling on the DHR. One of the most welcome aspects was the drive to clean the town up, and work began with many of the buildings receiving a fresh coat of paint. The authorities declared that the tidying would continue after the event, and Pasang Bhutia, the chairman of Darjeeling municipality, told the Press he was determined *'to make sure nobody calls Darjeeling a dirty town any more'*.

The carnival showcased much of what had become part of the town's heritage, and ranged from painting and photographic exhibitions, tea-drinking ceremonies, and ethnic food festivals, to jazz and rock concerts, a two-kilometre run for 'Darjeeling and peace' and a meeting of nations playing chungi, a local game using a football made of leaves. Such was the success of the festival that the organisers declared that it would become an annual event, but the coin was still in the air as to whether it would heal any of the differences between the cultures of the hills and those of the plains. Nevertheless, it had been an encouraging sight to see the local Nepali-speaking Gurkhas, Bengalis and Punjabis dancing on the Mall every evening.

The Statesman News Service advised on 30th December 2003 that the Indian Railway Catering Tourism Corporation had taken over the reins of the DHR from Northeast Frontier Railways. The reality was that it had taken responsibility for the management and development of tourism on the DHR, for the Indian Railways Board had recognised that the future of the railway lay with tourism, and as such the railway would benefit from the management skills of the IRCTC. Privatisation had been considered, but the scale of subsidy required in the immediate future ruled that out, whilst a joint initiative with paid and volunteer labour had also been extensively debated. This had worked well on preserved railways in other countries, but for India there was the fear that it would snag with volunteers unwittingly undermining the pride of labour that was inextricably entwined with caste.

In order to make chartering a train more popular, the IRCTC announced it would cut the cost to Rs30,000, almost one-third of the previous rate. The New Year was to open with a special run commissioned by the Calcutta tour operator Bon Voyage, with No.802 'Victor' hauling a three-coach train to Kurseong. It was somehow fitting that it was the first time an Indian concern had chartered a train on the first railway that had been built by money wholly subscribed in India, some 125 years ago.

It reflected the mood of optimism that also accompanied the announcement, made at the beginning of 2004, that the first of the new oil-fired 'B' Class steam locomotives had been completed at the Golden Rock workshops. With the running number 1001, it had been awarded the name *'Snow Chariot'/'Himrathi'* and was now waiting to be flagged off by the Railway Minister. No.787 had also undergone further modification following the somewhat unfortunate trials in 2002, and it was hoped that these locomotives would herald the way to a new era of motive power for the railway. However, what evolved was sadly a cumbersome and charmless design that was not enhanced by the fitting of an ungainly fuel tank ahead of the cab. Both locomotives had two enormous air cylinders attached to the saddle tank and were surrounded by a mass of industrial valves and piping, all of which appeared to be over sized and out of proportion. No.1001 even

With the whistle blowing to announce its departure, No. 786 prepares to leave Darjeeling with a Down train in January 2003. Hotel bookings during the winter months tended to be dependent on overseas travellers, but the ten-day festival staged in the town during November 2003 brought tourists from many parts of India, giving a tremendous boost to trade and the opportunity for the railway to operate to its full capacity.

John Clemmens

had its chimney attached to the smokebox at an angle that was out of perpendicular, and the stone-guard bolted beneath the front buffer was wide enough to have distinct amputatory tendencies.

The Railway Minister eventually flagged off No.1001 along a siding round the back of Golden Rock, after which it was put back under wraps whilst No.787 was sent on a lorry to the DHR for further trials. It fared no better than the original test run, and the din created by the two diesel generators and exhaust was deafening. No.787 was soon dumped unloved and unwanted at the back of Siliguri shed, and the consensus of opinion was that the experiment had been an ingenious but perverse attempt at reinventing the wheel. The successful oil-fired conversions previously made to historic locomotives on the Ffestiniog Railway had not compromised their original exterior form or dignity, and it was far from clear why IR had not taken up the offer of their expertise.

Problems also began to surface during the second period of the project to renovate No.791, for the spares listed at the end of the first stage had not even been ordered. The consultants returned from the UK in April 2004 to begin reassembling the locomotive, but very little had been done during the interim period and various items of workshop equipment remained out of use awaiting repair. On 2nd July, *The Statesman* advised that the contract had been abruptly terminated at the end of the second period after the report had raised some '*uncomfortable truths*'. The departure of the two consultants had come shortly before that of the ADRM responsible for the DHR and the General Manager of NFR. The report had shown there were failures on the part of middle-management staff to carry out their agreed responsibilities, whilst the NFR betrayed its credibility by counter-charging the consultants had strayed outside their terms of reference. However, *The Statesman* also pointed out that '*One could also add a lack of appreciation and understanding of the World Heritage concept on part of the Indian Railways to this list.*' The five-yearly review of the DHR by UNESCO was also due, and the initial recommendations that had been made by ICOMOS had focused on producing a management plan, creating a heritage conservation unit, and establishing a buffer zone along the length of the railway line. None had yet been met.

The objective of having a buffer zone along the railway was to reflect the heritage value of the journey, and the 2002 workshop had determined this was to include the views of mountains, vegetation, buildings and roadside bazaars. Subsequent conferences had seen this concentrating on the town of Darjeeling, which was now being referred to as a World Heritage Area. It was in reality no more than a descriptive term for the areas beyond the line itself and its buffer zone; it had no official status, and the erroneous impression had been created that the town of Darjeeling had been acknowledged as a World Heritage Area by UNESCO. Nobody denied that the objectives were highly laudable, but when it came to declarations being made that included the rehabilitation of the water, waste and sanitation supplies, the generation of women's empowerment and employment, and the making of Bagdogra into an international airport, there were fears that too many diversions had been created from the primary objective of conserving the railway, which at times appeared to have been mentioned as little more than an afterthought.

The rebuild of No.791 was finally completed without further input from the consultants, and all agreed that when it was returned into service, it was indeed a fine locomotive. It was without doubt the most reliable engine, and was able to haul a three-coach train with ease, whereas its sisters often struggled with two. Early in 2005, the SAN diesel No.605 '*Buccaneer*' blew a cylinder liner, which necessitated the removal of the power unit in order that it could be sent away for repair. As a result, the daily through service was hauled by No.604 '*Maverick*' as far as Kurseong, after which No.791 '*Horatio*' took the train on to Darjeeling. The steam locomotive worked faultlessly, no time was lost …. and it was coal-fired.

It only added to the confusion with No.787, for there appeared to be no coordinated thinking with regard to the oil-firing issue. The Press began to report that two new machines had in fact been built at Golden Rock, and following the trials with No.787 they were now being modified with steam atomised burners developed by Bharat Heavy Electricals Ltd in an attempt to reduce the deafening noise. The large cylindrical compressors were to be said to be hidden from view and '*economisers*' introduced in the smoke box to enhance the efficiency of the boiler. It was claimed that the oil-firing system was necessary following apprehension from the Forest Department that a flying spark or hot cinder from a coal-fired locomotive could trigger a forest fire … the fact that none ever had did not seem to enter into the equation.

However, on 8th November 2004 the editorial of *The Statesman* reported that:

'After visiting the unique facility that has now acquired world heritage status, the

Parliamentary Standing Committee on Railways has strongly recommended the reintroduction of coal-burning steam engines, so that the railway operated in the manner that had marked it special even before it acquired antique value. . . .

The experiments with diesel-fired boilers had obviously failed to re-create that magic, hence the toy train not living up to its potential as a tourist attraction. Whether the century-old railway's loco shed at Tindharia, or indeed any other unit in the country is capable of turning out engines of the DHR's original class and style is for technical experts to ascertain, but the import option should not be ruled out.'

Indeed, the editorial reflected a profound understanding of the DHR by also stating that:

'The Committee is to be applauded for its display of sensitivity to something as intangible as nostalgia.'

There was a sting in the tail, for the Committee had also suggested that an alternative road should be constructed between Siliguri and Darjeeling, but as *The Statesman* pointed out, this would rob the DHR of its unique flavour, even though it would speed up the trains. The report wisely advised that money would be better spent shoring up the embankments to avert the landslips that bring both rail and road traffic to a halt each monsoon, delightfully rounding off with the observation that *'The Pagla Jhora can never be tamed, but a little method could be induced into its madness.'*

Tindharia certainly had to induce a little method into the madness of the new oil-fired locomotive when it was delivered from Golden Rock in March 2005, for it was noted that no oil-ways had been drilled in the pins and bushes of its valve gear and motion. Questions were also being asked about the NJP – Siliguri Junction section again, despite the new platforms constructed at NJP and the dual-gauge tracks laid across the Mahananda Bridge. No trains were allowed to run due to opposition being voiced to the closure of roads to allow trains to pass. The only crossing of any consequence was the Hill Cart Road at Siliguri Town, but a flyover was being constructed here and the one DHR train passing daily in each direction did not realistically constitute a major traffic problem. The broad gauge demanded a more frequent use of the crossing, but the employment of a 2,600hp WMD2 diesel with three coaches as the shuttle between NJP and Siliguri Junction did not appear to make a great deal of economic sense. It was a role ideally suited to a 400hp NDM6 diesel on the DHR, although hands were raised in despair at a heritage conference when a District Magistrate from Jalpaiguri strongly advocated that coloured lights should be set up for 7kms along the section from NJP in order *'to beautify it'*. From this it appeared that there was still a long way to go with understanding the meaning of heritage, but thankfully the students at Mahbert High School, near Sukna, were able to think with more clarity. Encouraged by their innovative Principal Nelson Petrie, they had made a pledge to keep the DHR stations at Sukna and Rangtong as free from litter as possible, a move that deserved nothing but the highest praise.

It was also clear that the problems the railway had been facing would not be properly resolved until the ownership of the railway had been settled once and for all. With the DHR internationally recognised as one of the most important industrial heritage sites in the world, the position of its Chief Executive Office would become a highly prestigious and respected assignment. Once appointed, the CEO could devise and implement a proper management plan for conservation and heritage that focused on the railway and not be diverted by such foolish frippery as fairy lights being strung along part of its course. Indeed, UNESCO's cultural head, Mr R.P. Perera, told the Press in July 2004 that *'Our association with the DHR will continue as long as the DHR retains the status of a World Heritage Site, which depends on how well it is managed in the coming years.'*

And that, as it has been since the days of Franklin Prestage, is where the shoe will always pinch.

Afterword

In 1999 an international committee from the United Nations agreed that the DHR was to be designated as a heritage site of world importance. There were just over 500 such sites, and every one had been inscribed by UNESCO as being of universal significance to all humanity. The DHR is the first in Bengal and the first industrial World Heritage Site in Asia. It is entitled to the same degree of respect and dignity as the Pyramids of Giza, the historic centre of Florence, and the Tower of London.

The concept of heritage presents its own challenges, and when it comes to the DHR it should reflect the creative genius of the original engineers, along with the technical, economic and social development of the railway. Heritage is a two-way process between the past, present and future, which means that things are kept as they originally were and not altered to how the task would be undertaken today. If the site has been inscribed as being of world importance, there comes with it the responsibility to ensure that it is achieved to a world standard. It does not imply that the standard of one country is better than that of another, for there is an international model of best practice, and the character of the country is to be found in its location, not by how it is maintained or decorated.

The challenges the DHR faces today are nothing new, and the answers to its problems have been rehearsed many times in the past. Indeed, a wide range of solutions has been offered in recent years, but nothing can effectively be implemented until the ownership of the railway is addressed and settled. Once this has been achieved, the appointment of a dedicated Chief Executive Officer is crucial, and charged with the responsibility and budget for all matters relating to the railway, the foundation will have been laid to enable a coordinated strategy for recovery to be developed that will focus on the Railway itself.

By its nature, the DHR is a linear site, and with such a diversity of culture, religions and politics along its 55-mile length, care must be taken to ensure that it does not become a political football and attract conflicting interests. Concern has been expressed that too many diversions have been created at recent workshops that are liable to attract ulterior agendas, losing sight of the fact that it is the Railway that has been listed as a World Heritage Site. Attention needs to be directed towards properly sorting out the civil engineering, the permanent way and the rolling stock before anything else, for without them there is no railway. Those who hold a genuine interest in the DHR will want to become part of it, and will not simply regard it as a means to promote their own cause.

Those working on the Railway are dedicated to its survival, and questions were raised at the 127th Working Committee Meeting of the Railway Employees Union held in Kurseong on 27th June 2005. A memorandum was issued that included revoking the ban on recruitment and for the modernisation of Tindharia Workshop, which should become self-sufficient in manufacturing locomotive parts and coaches. Demands were made to stop the reported move that would close down Kurseong and Tindharia locomotive sheds, along with the proper control of encroachment on railway land, the installation and improvement of housing and facilities for the railway staff. There was also strong support for the continued use of steam engines as their importance for the tourist industry was fully recognised.

The challenges of running a railway across a geologically unstable terrain that passes through a city, a forest, and several village bazaars can never be overestimated. Its world importance as a unique example of a hill passenger railway had been recognised by UNESCO but not by those charged with its management at the time that No. 782 'Mountaineer' was caught pounding through the terai in January 2003. The forest had been the haunt of wild animals since the earliest days of the railway, and despite the encroachment of traffic in more recent years, an elephant crossing was still to be found nearby.

It is inevitable that questions are raised with regard to the interpretation that the Railway Board makes to the DHR being a World Heritage Site. Fault lines were seen in its management during 2003 when it was found that there were 27 firemen but only 6 drivers, and it appeared that little effort had been made to redress the balance with a programme of basic training. A minimum of 7 drivers were required to maintain the timetable, and the only training that had been available was on metre-gauge diesels. Although the locomotive crews understand steam, it is clear that the management does not. The timetable of the steam-operated local train from Kurseong to Darjeeling is programmed for diesels, and with no allowances being made for water stops, it cannot help but always be late. The problem has been compounded by the bore of the pipes on the water towers being too small, and as a consequence it takes three times as long to fill the locomotives than is necessary. To add to the iniquities, most of the telephones were found not to work and locomotive crews had to guess where the other trains might be, whilst the sanding mechanism on the new diesels was faulty and prevented them from working the service efficiently.

The project with rebuilding No.791 highlighted further weaknesses in the system, for there was a severe delay with delivering the parts. It seemed almost impossible to obtain injectors, and it was found that those on the existing 'B' Class were so worn that they could not lift water from their well-tanks. This had plagued the locomotives of late, for it meant that only the water in the saddle tanks could be used and had been a fundamental cause of the frequent stops. New boilers were delivered from the Golden Rock workshops, but they had to send their technicians to Tindharia when it was found they leaked badly round the rivets. Added to this, work awarded to contractors had generally been disastrous, with no spares being provided or made available, and these problems are all compounded by a fundamental lack of understanding of the meaning of heritage. It seemed as though there was little cultural communication, along with a failure to appreciate the benefits of awarding the initiatives to local contracts. To make matters worse, the stores at Tindharia could not obtain the correct oil to lubricate the locomotive cylinders and were obliged to use thinner SAE 50 diesel oil, causing the piston rings to wear out after three months, whereas their life should be six to seven years.

It appears all too easy to lay the troubles on the doorstep of those managing the DHR, but as uncomfortable as it may be to read, it has to be recognised that there is an inherent problem with the bureaucratic structure of the Indian Railways Board. The practice of senior staff being rotated every two years has led to a culture that places a greater emphasis of concern on career advancement rather than the actual railway they are attached to. This is exacerbated by the DHR being a very vernacular railway, for it highlights the dichotomy between management and practical experience. The workshop staff is unable to rise to any position of influence without a qualification in English, and although it is not necessarily the fault of any individual, it does lead to management doing the correct thing in accordance with the system rather than the right thing for the railway.

Vision is a quality of leadership, and that brings with it a sense of belief and technical innovation. The DHR needs another Franklin Prestage or a George Cresswell, and one only needs to consider what Geoffrey Plackett and James Shaw achieved during the time of war to see where answers can be found. They were faced with huge demands being made on an exhausted and outdated railway, and not only was it fighting for survival, it was faced with a world war being fought near its doorstep, union unrest, political and religious insurgence, and the demise of the Raj. The DHR and its staff rose magnificently to the challenge through their inspired leadership, with ten passenger trains being run every day with an additional four services if ordered, along with the demand to transport children to their boarding schools, military personnel to the cantonments, and wounded troops in specially built ambulance stock. Built into this was the capacity for an additional forty-one goods trains if ordered, whilst six mixed passenger trains were maintained on the 70-mile-long Kishenganj extension and two along the 30 miles of the Teesta Valley (with eight more for freight if required). In 2005 there was one through passenger train in each direction, the early-morning 'Misteen' mixed from Kurseong to Darjeeling, the weekend steam specials to Agony Point and the occasional Joy Train from Darjeeling to Ghum, which only highlights that the more recent practice of make-do-and-mend, glazed over with management spin, has done the Railway no good at all.

The fact that the Railway is losing money has made it appear as something of a poisoned chalice, but anybody who passes such a judgement is making a mistake of the highest order. World Heritage sites are not commercial enterprises designed to make a profit, and the culture needs to be established that recognises a deficit in its returns is never regarded as failure. The DHR was indeed once a profitable business, but times have changed and its raison d'être has shifted to it being a unique example of industrial archaeology that is of world importance. It is a living museum, and one that can still play its part of being a viable public transport system.

There are difficult challenges to face, for the buffer zone as outlined by UNESCO is the area around the railway that is managed in order to conserve the heritage value of the journey. It was never intended to be a fixed tunnel of space around the trackbed from which everything should be cleared. Removing rubbish and debris is one thing, but demolishing the shacks and bazaars that buttress the line is not going to encourage the local population to become involved and respect the railway. The key word is 'sustain', for the people who live and work on the railway are there every day, and the lights do not only go on when the tourist visits. Indeed the stakeholders' workshop had agreed that the World Heritage site not only included the mountains and vegetation but the buildings and roadside bazaars. All the sites were to be protected from violation, which left many wondering just how the construction of the concrete rest house on the outer edge of Agony Point had been authorised.

Quite what constitutes the buffer zone is still open to debate in India. Few would doubt that the views of the Himalaya from the train would be part of the zone, but it would be harder to contend that the 50 miles between the observer and the mountain was part of the World Heritage Site. The town of Darjeeling is not part of the site, but it should not be denied that a control over the pollution from traffic and the dumping of rubbish would make a much-valued contribution to improving the area. Such initiatives would neatly dovetail into a project that would enable the DHR to become a hallmark in the mainstream of tourism, and in order to sustain that, the visitor should want to return. To encourage this, a culture of respect for the environment by the community needs to evolve. I stood at Darjeeling station one morning and became engaged in a conversation about the screes of litter thrown down the hillsides, but I was simply told not to look there if I did not like it. Plastic and polythene are not biodegradable, and the visitor is not going to feel attracted to return if the future prospect is more indiscriminate dumping of waste and rubbish.

The environment needs to be controlled, and such action is possible, as seen by the Government initiative with the Taj Mahal, perhaps the most famous World Heritage Site in India. The coke-based industries of Agra were polluting the atmosphere to the point of eroding the marble, and although the political will to take countermeasures was slow, new industries within a 10,000-square-kilometre buffer zone were banned. The Government went on to ban vehicles from entering the precincts of the Taj and restricted parking within a 500-metre radius of the building, whilst the Supreme Court ordered nearly 300 industries within the area to relocate or switch to an environmentally safe fuel.

A return to freight being transported on the DHR would not only make a difference in the income generated by the railway, but more importantly help with the preservation of the Hill Cart Road. The effect of the continual pounding of lorries on a geologically unstable road that was built for bullock-cart traffic cannot be overestimated. However, such a solution would not be without contention, for it is feared that reducing the traffic of private hauliers would be seen as taking work away from the area and driving a wedge between local people and the railway. This would cut across the ethos of sustaining employment, although it could be counterbalanced to a degree by an increase in work with transhipment at Siliguri and transport from the DHR stations. The hill station of Matheran owes its peace and tranquillity to a complete ban on motor vehicles, and a measure of control in Darjeeling may not be quite as far-fetched as it initially appears.

There is a genuine affection in the hills for the railway, providing that it does not trespass on the people's livelihoods. An initiative to popularise the line and encourage local involvement with its preservation was underaken by Marilyn Metz and Peter Tiller on behalf of the Education Group of the DHRS in September 2005. There was a very positive response to the presentations they made to the teachers and students at several schools in Darjeeling, the focus being to develop a range of study material about the DHR and the role it has played in the history of the area. An active awareness of the railway and its place in the community would help stimulate an appreciation of its heritage value and could prevent potentially damaging developments from taking place.

Further projects, from reforestation programmes to the introduction of a mobile health clinic on the line, could also help to address some of the material needs of the community. Trees had already been planted at Upper Pagla Jhora and Gidapahar by the Darjeeling Himalaya Railway Lovers' Forum, which was formed in 2003 by several prominent citizens and social workers of Darjeeling in collaboration with the Federation of Societies for Environmental Protection (FOSEP). Their main objective has been to educate people along the DHR on the importance of the railway and how they can assist with sustainable development. Such programmes should be loudly applauded as they would make a significant contribution to the improvement of the area, whilst the role that the tea gardens could play in the regeneration of the area would be immense, for the industry has become synonymous with the name of Darjeeling itself.

Domestic tourism is crucial to the success of the railway and every effort should be made to ensure the fares are priced accordingly. Returns made in recent years indicate that barely 4½% of the tourists visiting Darjeeling are from overseas, and most of them travel to the sub-continent between November and March. The railway has to survive throughout the year, and whilst many visitors from the West are prepared to pay a premium for steam-hauled trains, there is a danger of placing the experience beyond the means of many Indians travelling to Darjeeling. Chartered specials have their rightful place in the DHR equation and should be actively encouraged, but with the focus on national tourism, the foreign visitor would benefit from the experience of India and not a manicured parody.

However hard one tries to argue the case, the DHR was and always will be a roadside tramway. It is potentially a long journey by rail to Darjeeling, but the problem could be turned into its own solution if a reliable steam-hauled train is introduced with comfortable carriages equipped with refreshment facilities. Indeed, in October 2004 NFR inaugurated a special weekend service to Agony Point based on the proposals submitted by Rajendra Baid of the Cindrella Hotel in Siliguri. With a packed breakfast on the train and a hot lunch at Agony Point, it has been a brave start, and one that could pave the way for a through service hauled by steam that turns the journey into an adventure. A stop at Tindharia would be ideal for some tea, followed by lunch at Kurseong in the renovated station restaurant 'Glenary's Junction'. A short stop at Ghum for tiffin and the museum would be the preparation for the final descent to Darjeeling, where the station itself could become the perfect site for a hotel and restaurant. It is true that the building was clumsily abused in 1983 by the addition of an ugly rest house, but its removal and a sympathetic coat of paint would soon restore the station to its former elegance.

The Darjeeling Steam Tramway Company changed its name to the Darjeeling Himalayan Railway in 1881, but despite all attempts at denying its relationship with the road, it has remained a tramway. The distinctive fretted cap to the chimney identifies the locomotive as No.779 'Mountaineer' nudging through Kurseong Bazaar in 1999, running close enough for the passengers to make purchases from the shops and stalls that fringe the track.

India travels at a different pace from the West, but the traveller should be able to depend upon the service. The lead needs to be taken to establish the confidence that a train will indeed run, for what better way could there be to convey the spirit of romance and adventure than a steam train climbing the Himalaya?

The problems of determining what constitutes the 'site' of the DHR can be seen in this superb photograph of No.795 negotiating a small village near Ghum adjacent to the Hillman's Free Church in January 2002. The intimacy with the houses is an essential ingredient for many travelling on the railway and a matter of great debate for those with the responsibility of ensuring its heritage is preserved.

John Clemmens

The income generated would help to subsidise the local service, and that is where the diesels would have a rightful place in the operation. A dedicated DHR management would also have the wisdom to discuss with the communities a service that is tailored to their needs, and not be obliged to operate one that has been directed by a bureaucrat in Delhi.

As ever, the solutions appear simple and straightforward to the West, where economists of the East often believe the answers are to be found. But India exists in several centuries simultaneously, and as the gurus stand and stare at the altar of consumerism, those reflecting on the matter of caste are looking over their shoulders. It not only dictates occupation but the interaction with members of other castes, which in the past has invited the suspicion that there is always somebody else to blame and that 'it is not my job'. It is said there are 3,000 castes and 25,000 sub-castes in India, and although it is regarded by many as a burden to progress, it is seen by others as providing a sense of community and purpose to people's lives. The system has disappeared as far as the Indian Constitution is concerned, but the links between thousands of years of tradition within Indian society and Hindu beliefs have ensured that caste consciousness remains deeply rooted among the people. At its most pitiless are the untouchables, who are considered too impure and polluted to rank as worthy beings; they are seen as deserving only the lowest of jobs, which include toilet cleaning, garbage removal ... and maintenance. Herein might be the root of the problem with the apparent reluctance of the DHR management to understand the need for basic maintenance of the railway. Caste would define the task as something disreputable, but waiting until something breaks or falls to bits is not only uneconomic and inefficient, it is incompatible with the concept of conservation and heritage.

It is true that the Raj came to immure itself from its own nightmares with India by creating an indigenous way of life, but it was from this perspective that it was able to defer to the traditions and culture and not encroach on religious beliefs. As non-Hindus the British were without caste, but the absence of spiritual probity was not seen as an impediment to their management skills. As with any successful relationship, there was mutual trust and respect, and it was from this that a substantial core of improvements evolved with lasting benefits ... law and order, a judicial system,

Two little girls wait for the chance of some hot water from No.804 'Queen of the Hills' at Sukna. The driver appears quite unconcerned with the effect it could have with the questionable electrics attached to the down pipe.

and an impartial administration. The consequences of the British rule in India were often mixed, and whilst it has become fashionable to attach colonial clichés to the time, few can deny that the railways were one of the greatest legacies that united the sub-continent.

So the memories of those whose lives this extraordinary Himalayan railway has touched should never be lost, for they are the foundation of its heritage. Like India itself, the frustration of getting things done can be exasperating to the point of defeat ... until, that is, you see one of the incomparable 'B' Class weaving its ambitious way through the tormented forests of the *terai*. All is forgiven as the train wrenches itself into impossible loops and thrashes up staggering reverses to gain height, after which it ploughs through village bazaars and upends the stalls as there is nowhere else for it to go ... dishevelled, audacious and totally endearing. It is an enchanted railway, and when the locomotive whistle heralds the final approach to Darjeeling, you are in the company of the highest mountains on earth and the thundering might of Kanchenjunga soaring ahead.

'The Iron Sherpa' has truly transported you *'Halfway to Heaven'*.

'Halfway to Heaven' indeed, as No. 779 pauses on the top section of the Batasia loop.

Peter Jordan

Bibliography

A Concise History of Darjeeling (1922)   E.C. Dozey
A Winter in India (1883)   Rt Hon. W.E. Baxter MP
An Active Life (1963)   Dr Frederick Barnardo
At Home in India   Mrs Herbert Reynolds
Bengal Past & Present (1908)
     Calcutta Historical Society
British Social Life in India (1937)   Dennis Kincaid
Building the Railways of the Raj   Ian J. Kerr
Calcutta (1971)   Geoffrey Moorhouse
Darjeeling, a Favoured Resort   Jahar Sen
Darjeeling and its Mountain Railway (1921)
     DHR Co.
Darjeeling at a Glance (1944)   Dr K.C. Bhanja
Darjeeling Gazetteer (1947)   Arthur Jules Dash
Darjeeling Gazetteer (1980)   -
Darjeeling Ropeway Prospectus (1936)   -
Darjeeling Ropeway Souvenir Opening (1939)   -
Darjeeling Route Guide (1913)   Geo. Robertson
Exotic Indian Mountain Railways (1984)
     R.R. Bhandari
Harrow on the Hooghly (1994)   John Lethbridge
Himalayan Adventure   J. Thomas
Himalayan Journals (1849)
     Sir Joseph Dalton Hooker
Hobson-Jobson (1886)   Sir Henry Yule & A.C. Burnell
India Britannica   Geoffrey Moorhouse
India Called Them (1947)   Lord Beveridge
Indian Locomotives (Parts 1–4) 1863–1990
     Hugh Hughes
Indian Pictures (1881)   Rev. W. Urwick
Kalka-Simla & Kangra Valley Railways (1983)
     R.R. Bhandari
L.Mandelli, Darjeeling Tea Planter & Ornithologist
     Fred Pinn
Land of the Thunderbolt (1923)   Lord Ronaldshay
Light Railways (1896)   J.C. Mackay
Lines of Communication   J. Thomas
Loco Profile No.23 – Darjeeling Tanks   Brian Reed
More Tramps Abroad   Mark Twain
Permanent Way (1976)   M.F. Hill
Picturesque India (1890)   W.S. Caine
Rains, Landslides & Floods in the Darjeeling Himalaya   Leszek Starkel & Subhasranjan Basu
Rail Transport Museum of Delhi Guide   -
Rungli Rungliot–Thus Far and No Further (1946)
     Rumer Godden
Sikkim and Darjeeling: Division and Deception
     Dr Sonam B. Wangyal
Steam Locomotive Design, Data & Formulae (1936)
     E.A. Phillipson
Summoned by the Bell (2003)   Stanley Vernon Prins
Thackers Business Directory (1864–1948)   -
The DHR Illustrated Guide for Tourists (1896)
     DHR Co.
The Diaries of Alistair Crowley (1905)   -
The Festiniog Railway (Vols 1 & 2)   James I.C. Boyd
The Forests of India (1926)   Prof. E.P. Stebbing
The General Rules for Indian Railways (1906)   -
The Highlands of India (1887)
     Major-Gen. D.J.F. Newall RA
The Road to Destiny: Darjeeling letters 1839 (1986)
     Fred Pinn
Through Tibet to Everest (1927)   Captain J.B.L. Noel
Trains at a Glance
Indian Railways Timetables
Travelling to Darjeeling in 1830 (2000)   Fred Pinn
Under the Old School Topee (1990)   Hazel Craig
Up in the Clouds (1878)   Mary H. Avery

Magazines/Newspapers:
Continental Modeller
Continental Railway Journal
Indian Railway Study Group newsletters
Narrow Gauge World
Railway World
Steam Railway
The Darjeeling Mail
The Engineer
The Indian Railway Gazette
The Indian & Eastern Engineer
The Locomotive Railway Carriage & Wagon Review
The Narrow Gauge
The Railway Magazine
The Calcutta Gazette
The Englishman
The Friend of India
The Hindu
The Hindustan Times
The Independent
The People's Review
The Statesman
The Telegraph of India
The Times of India.

Index - Volume 1

A

Addis, Robert Bawn 133,143,148
Adhikari 274,277,281,288
Agarwal, Mr B.K. 254
Agarwal, Mr V.K. 254
Ager, John 189
Agony Point 60,66,78
Agrawal, Rajesh 336
Agreement for the Darjeeling Tramway 36
Alan Keef Ltd 324
Alcard 168
All-India Muslim League 122
Allen, W. 59
All- India Gorkha League 215
Aluabari Road/Islampur 279, 282,290
Ambulance Train 179,180
Ampersand, Reset & South Eastern Railroad 340
Amusement Club 110
Anderson, Sir John 170,173,301
Andheri Jhora 301,317,319
Annand, A.E. 48,59
Anniversary, 125-year 13
Arbuthnot, Mrs 92
Arnold, Frederick William 102
Asian Institute for Transport Development 324
Aslam's Cutting 301,305,319
Assam-Bengal Railways 116
Assam Rail Link Project 209,210,211,214,215, 218,287,316
Assam Railways & Trading Co. 239
Atkins, Paul 348
Austin 7 163
Avadh Tirhut Mail 227
Awami League 239

B

Bagdogra 269,271,290
Bagley, F.R. 152
Baid, Rajendra 357
Baker, General Sir William 29
Bakhie, K.C. 319
Balasan Bridge 214,288
Balasan River 268
Baldwin Locomotive Co. 131
Balsun Valley 128
Bamjee, Dinshaw 195
Bancroft, John 348
Banerjee, A.T. 134
Banerjee, K.N. 59
Banerjee, L.N. 59
Banerjee, Major 217
Banerjee, Ms Mamata 330,334,337
Banerjee, S.K. 211

Bangladesh 207,239
Barnard, Mr 94
Barnardo, Dr Frederick 139
Baroda & Central India Railway 37
Baroda and Central India Railway Regiment 174
'Baron Bounder Bill' 110
Barrie, David 253
Barry, Mr 133
Barsi Light Railway 42
Basu, Bistu 212,213
Batasi 274,288
Batasia Loop 139,165,172
Batasia Loop Reverse Siding 172
Batterbury, George 12,130,133,262,269,314
Baxter, Rt. Hon. W.E. 66
Beau Site 167,168
Beeches Light Railway 340
Bellow, Mr F.D. 49
Bengal-Assam Railway 210
Bengal Dooars Railway 116,310
Bengal Secretariat 123
Benn, William Wedgwood 163
Bernard, Mr 133
Bewick, Mr 47
Beyer Peacock & Co. 121,123
Bhutia, Pasang 349
Bhuttacharjee, K.C. 59
Bibra, J. 59
Biswas, Dr S.K. 188
Blake, Mr 133
Blasting boulders 98
Blue Devils 75
Bojaxhiu, Agnes Gonxha 195
Bombay 174
Bomdila 231
Boscolo's hotel 106
Bose, Sauri 188
Boseck & Co, J. 102
Boston Lodge Works 72,258
Brighton Pavilion 135
British Engineering Ropeway Co. 171
British India Steam Navigation Co. 174
British Ropeway Engineering Co. Ltd 309
British Surveyor General of India 144
Broad gauge 129
Bruce, Brigadier-General H.C. 144
Bruce, Lady Elisabeth 90
Buchey, Gorey 339
Buffer zone 351,356
Bunsgopal 59
Buri Balasan 288
Buri Balasan Bridge 284
Burma Railway 148

Burrat, S.N. 59
Bury, Colonel Howard 144

C

Calcutta Exhibition 69
Calcutta News 331
Calorex 239
Calthorpe, E.R. 42
Cameron, Colonel H.A. 152,161
Campbell, Dr 21,23
Campbell, Bessie 16
Cape Government Railways 73
Capitol Cinema 165,198,217
'Captain La-Di-Da Fitz-Fop' 110
Cary, Sulyard Bernard 32,42,63,69,74, 82,85, 107,115
'Castelton' 92
Caste system 40,41,154,359
Causeway 313
Central Railway 219
Central Reserve Police Force 290
Chakraborty, Mr 328
Chamber of Princes 134
Chatterjee, J.G. 59
Chatterji, M.L. 59
Chief Engineer of Bengal 76
Chinese labour 43
Chittarajan Das 157
Chowdry, R.G. 59
Christison, G.W. 117
Chuckerbutty, M.L. 59
Chucrobutty, K.N. 59
Chunbatti 43,44,45,65
Chunbatti loop 135
Churail, the 205
Churchill, Winston 161,163
Chuttackpur siding 106
Cindrella Hotel 319,357
Cinerama 222–225
Clarendon Hotel 40,43,47,48,51,86
Claudius, R.B. 59
Cleminson, James 53
Clubside Motors 217
Coaches
   1st Class bar saloon 180
   2nd generation bogie 142
   Buffet saloons 178
   Cleminsons 41,55,60,61
   Everest 221
   First bogie coach 118
Communist Party of India 191,193,207
Communist Party of India (M) 235,236,331
Congress 170,175,193,243

Conservation and Management Unit 337
Cooper, R. Elliott 133
Cork & Bandon Railway 37
Coronation Bridge 173,301,302,319
Coronation Durbar 121,122
Corps of Army Schoolmasters 161
Coupland, Mrs 92
Cowley, Henry 188,194,211
Craggs, B.C. 131
Craig, Gordon 191
Craig, Hazel 202
'Craigmount' 92
Cresswell, George Belben 115,116, 130,132
Crimson, T. 59
Cripps, Sir Stafford 176,191
Crompton, Colonel R.E. 26
Crowley, Alistair 114
Crown Prince of Germany 121
Curzon, Lord 75,111
Cyclone, 1899. 93,96

D

Dak Bungalow 31
Dalai Lama 127
Dalhousie, Lord 28
Dalrymple, Col 47
Damookdeah Ghat 129
Dampflokomotiv und Maschinenfabrik AG DLM 324
Darjeeling 16,19,21,23,43,55,70,87,91,103, 111,157,162,165,173,215,217,221,234, 243,331,349,351,356
Darjeeling Bazaar 101
Darjeeling Bullock Cart Train Company 26
Darjeeling Darpan 146
Darjeeling Gorkha Hill Council 249
Darjeeling Himalayan Railway Co. 63
Darjeeling Himalayan Railway Extensions Co. 127,261,262
Darjeeling Himalayan Railway Protection Committee 343
Darjeeling Himalayan Railway Society 253,328
Darjeeling Himalayan Railway Supporters Association 253
Darjeeling Himalaya Railway Lovers Forum 356
Darjeeling Ko Sano Rail Bachao 343
Darjeeling Mail 176
Darjeeling Ropeway Co. 172,173
Darjeeling Station 84,112,146,148,174,190,192, 201,231,244,258
Darjeeling Steam Tramway Company 33,55,59
Das, Chittarajan 160
Dastur, Syed Khan 265
Dauk 278
Dauk River Bridge 284,290
Davenport & Co. 213
Davison, Norman 168
Decauville 121
Delaram Tea Estate 40

Deolo Hill 309
Derbyshire & East Coast Railway 133
Dev, Mr G. 330
Dhantola 282
Dhasraty, Mr S. 254
DHR Heritage Foundation 249,348
Diamond Jubilee of Queen Victoria 87
Diesel Trials 178,227,244,325,326
Dikshit, Banshidhar 12,192,222,237,239,268
Dinajpur & Purnea District Railway Surveys 286
Dinapore 129
Dining-car special 11
Dinshaw Sorabjee & Co. 195
Diocesan School 98
Disraeli, Prime Minister 25
Donnelley, Elliott 340
Dooars Railway 89
Dow Hill School 205
Drum Druid Hotel 40
Dupuis 163
Durely Chine 221
Durrell, Lawrence 127
Durrell, Louisa 127
Durrell, Samuel 127
Dutta, J.N. 59
Dyer, Brigadier-General 140

E

Earthquake, 1897. 87,89
Earthquake, 1920. 139
Earthquake, 1934. 164
Earthquake, 1935. 171
East Coast State Railway 133
Eastern Bengal Railway 26,27,63,129,160
East India Company 15
East Indian Railway 25,37
East Pakistan 215,239
Eden, Sir Ashley 47,55
Education Group, DHRS 356
Edwards, H. 37,59
Edward VII 111,121
Edward VIII 144
Electric lighting 128
Elgin, Countess of 90
Elgin, Lord 90
Elkins, A.J. 172
Ellis, Bruce 12,170,171
El Nino 254
'Elysia' 167,168
Emmanuel, Colonel 213
Emperor Humayan 265
Empress of India 25,106
Engineer's bungalow, The 264
Essex Road 168
Everest 144
Everest Expedition 132,149

F

Fairlie, Robert 37,53

Fares 37,70,164
Federation of Societies for Environmental Protection 356
Feltwell, Messrs Hurt and 75
Feng, Yang 127
Fenton, Bessie 16
Ffestiniog Railway 29,31,53,72,258, 324,328
Field Columbian Museum 83
Fishers Ltd, Messrs 148
Fitzgerald, Dr Ronald 254
Fluff to Feather 219
Forestry branch 148–150
Freight bypass route 218,232
Friends of the DHR 252,331
Fripos Restaurant 221
Fullerton Hodgart & Barclay 174

G

Gaekwar of Baroda 41
Gaisal 290
Gaisal Halt 282
Galgalia 274,277,281,288
Gandhi, Indira 243,248
Gandhi, Mohandas Karamchand 140, 144,155,15 6,157,161,163,207
Gandhi, Rajiv 249
Gangtok 131,297
Ganguli, B.C. 232
Garrard, George Mingay 73,133
Garratt, Herbert William 123
Gel Jhora 130
Geological Survey of India 110,173
George V 121
Ghising, Subhas 331
Ghosal, M.L. 59
Ghose, J.N. 59
Ghosh, Bikash 330
Ghum 94,120,244,334,338
Gielle Jhora 305
Gielle Khola 291,297,308,317,320
Gillanders Arbuthnot & Co. 61,69,86,109,132, 164,211,214,309
Gladstone, Thomas 191,192
Glenary's Junction 357
Goenka & Co. 172,173
Goenka, N.C. 171
Going Home Day Specials 202
Golden Rock Workshop 339, 349,351,355
Gold Medal, Rescue 1899. 102
Gorabari 233
Gorai Bridge 63
Gorakhapur 236
Gore, D.J. 59
Gorkha Hill Council 337
Gorkhaland 243,244
Gorkha Liberation Organisation 334
Gorkha National Liberation Front 243,248,249, 347
Gorkhas, The 15
Gorkhastan 207,243

Gottwaldt, Alfred 249
Gouldsbury, Frank 16
Government Inspector of Railways 131
Government of India Act, 1919. 139
Government of India Act, 1935. 170
Government Steam Train 26
Grahams Home 309
Grand Hotel 131
Grand opening 53
Grant, Captain James 16,17,18
Great Eastern Hotel 81
Great Game 77,123
Great Indian Peninsular Railway 24
Greer, Mr 90
Gunjaria 282
Gupta, Dr 191,212
Gurkha Recruiting Depot 129
Gymkhana Club 198

H

'Halfway to Heaven' 11,360
Hall, Major King 89
Harcourt, F.H. 59
Hardie, Keir 122
Hardinge Bridge 26
Hasimara Tea Co. 213
Hatighisa 270
Heal, Elizabeth Anne 39
Henderson, Mr J.C. 217
Herbert, Captain James Dowling 17,18
Herbert, Sir John 301
Heritage Conference 258
Heritage Foundation 254
Hill Cart Road 25,33,35,103,123,128,139,143,
    152,233,237,239,242,255,298
Hill Transport Joint Action
    Committee 347
Himalayan Mountaineering
    Institute 349
Hindu Extremists 135
Holguette, Denis 198,212,214
Holkar & Sindia Neemuch State Railway 37
Home Rule League, 1916 135
Honeymoon Lodge 302
Hooghly River 42
Hooker, Dr Joseph 23
Horse racing 199
Houghton, James 59
House of Gladstone 61
Howrah-Amta Railway 178
Hudson & Redwood, Messrs 172
Hughes, John 73
Hulia River Bridge 280,288
Humayan 15,265
Hume, Colonel, Royal Engineers 116
Hume, Allen Octavian 85,111
Hunslet Engine Co. 64,148,328
Hurdwar Dehra Branch Railway 61
Hydroelectric schemes 128

I

Ikarchala 282
Improvement Fund 148
India General Navigation and Railway Co. 212
Indian cavalry 135
Indian Engineering 75
Indian Medical Service 21
Indian Molasses Co. 174
Indian National Congress 111,122,140
'Indian Odeon' 193
Indian Railway Catering Tourism Corporation
    349
Indian Railways Catering and Tourism
    Corporation 343
Indian Railways Centenary 219
Indian Steam Railway Society 326,328
Indian Tea Association 128,231
Indian Water Transport Co. 174
India Pale Ale 155
India Public Works Department 86
Industrial Training Institute 236
Institution of Civil Engineers 27,42,69,74
Institution of Mechanical Engineers 86
International Council on Monuments & Sites
    254,323
Irvine, Andrew 132,144
Islampur 128,286,290
Islampur Thana Halt 282

J

Jackson, William Henry 83
Jalapahar 161,179
Jalpaiguri 26,28
James 32
Jelap Pass 144
Jet curves 66
Jinnah, Mohammed 207
John, Col St. 47
John King & Co. Ltd 148
John Stagg 93,96
Jor Bungalow 50
Jorhat State Railway 185,286
Joy Ride Railway 221
Jummapatti 338
Jung, Arnold 226,325

K

Kahn, A.W. (Telu) 183
Kalijhora 319
Kalijhora Bridge 304
Kalijhora siding 301
Kalimpong 130,291,309,310,316,319,320
Kalimpong Road Station 297,310,320
Kalimpong Ropeway Co. Ltd 309
Kali River 305
Kalka-Simla Railway 120,324
Kanchrapara workshops 129
Katapahur 129

Kathmandu valley 77
Kendal, Felicity 199
Kennedy, Hall and 48
Kennedy, J. 48
Kenyon, Eustace 71
Kerr, Mrs Linberry 185
Khagra Estate 266,287
Khagra Mela 283
Khan, A. 59
Khan, Telu 195
Khandwa-Aleola-Basim Railway 133
Kilburn & Co. 90,212
Kings Shropshire Light Infantry 161
Kirby, Robert 148,152,172,174
Kirkness, L.H. 164
Kishenganj 12,15,26,117,127,128,214,261,283
Kishenganj City 282,290
Kishenganj Extension 265
Kishenganj Station 263,282
Kishenganj timetable 1939. 288
Kitson, Mr 47
Knights-Errant 183
Kohat-Bannu Railway 133
Kumar, Nitish 339
Kumartoligachh 284
Kurseong 43,49,87,88,131,147,156,166,168,
    334,338
Kurseong & Terai Tea Company 48
Kurseong Amusement Club 168,169,183,211
Kurseong station 88
Kushalgarh-Kohat-Thal Railway 133
Kutubgunge 266,282

Kydd, W.J. 165

L

Lady Minto's Nursing Association 117
Lal, Group Captain 217
Land Acquisition Act 235,287
Landslide Experts' Committee 346
La Porte County Historical Steam Society 340
Larkin, A.S. 173
Laska River 276,280,288
Lasso Ropeway Company 319
Lawrence, Sir John 120
Lawrence, T.E. 223
Lebong 36,117,199
Lee, Dr Robert 254
Leigh, Vivien 127
Leighton Buzzard Railway 329,340
Lepcha Association 337
Leroux, Colonel 179
Likhu Bhir 301,306
Lily of Lebong 110
Lindsay RE, Major 27
'Little House, The' 169
Lloyd, Captain 17,19
Lloyd, T. 59
Locomotives
    'A' Class 80,138
    'B' Class 80,81

'C', Class 80,85
'Ajax' 344
'Alice' 340
'Baby Sivok' 221,264,324,325
'Breithorn' 324
'The Climber' 73,86
'Chaloner' 329,340
'Fairy Queen' 343
Garratt 121,123,131,222
'Linda' 328
NDM-1 Class 226,227,244,325
NDM6 326
No.1 Class 46,80
No.1B 78
No.2 Class 44,46,63,73,80
No.9 222,264
No.11 138,222,349
No.15 69
No.17 78,219
No.18 340
No.19 340
No.22 264
No.25 188
No.28 'Jervis Bay' 179,182,189
No.39 228
No.40 315
No.42 213
No.46 119
No.47 153
No.48 221
No.53 186,228
No.604 'Maverick' 351
No.605 'Buccaneer' 344,351
No.704 227
No.777 233
No.779 'Mountaineer' 248,329,357
No.779 'Himalayan Bird' 345
No.780 'Green Hills' 246,330,333,345
No.782 'Mountaineer' 252,327,345,354,357
No.786 'Ajax' 344,350
No.787 339,349,351
No.788 'Tusker' 242,344,348
No.790 229
No.791 'Horatio' 351,344,355
No.792 'Hawkeye' 255,344
No.793 230
No.794 337,338
No.795 246
No.802 'Victor' 344,349
No.804 'Queen of the Hills' 343,345,359
No.806 'Queen of Hills' 251,344
No.1001 'Snow Chariot/Himrathi' 349
Oil-firing 330,339,351
Pacifics 222,287
'Pixie' 329
Superheated 0-6-0 148
'Tiny' 47
Walford diesel 178,219
ZDM-1 Class 226,227,244,325
ZDM-1 diesel 223
Lohani, Ashwani 343

London, Brighton & South Coast Railway 116
Longview Tea Co. 154
Loop No.1 64,249
Loop No.2 64,76,85,184
Low, Mr H.M. 49
Fishers, Ltd, Messrs 148
Luard, Major 36
'Lulu, the Lily of Lebong' 110
Lytton, Lady 47
Lytton, Lord 33,35,47

M

MacDonald, David 127
MacNeill & Co. 123,212
Madras State Railway 72
Mahananda Bridge 43,57,64,71,76,82,85,344,352
Mahananda River 278,290
Maharajadhiraj of Burdwan 113
Maharajah of Burdwan 212
Maharajahs, The 134
Maharashtra Tourism Development Corporation 339
Mahatab Club 168
Mahato, Sagina 191
Mahbert High School 352
Maidment, David 338
Makaibari Tea Estate 331
Mallory, George 132,144
Manchu Qing dynasty 123,127
Mandelli, Louis 82
Mansfield, Dr 100
Manufacture of sacks 131
Maoist insurgents 334
Marsden, W. 59
Martin, C. 59
Martin, J. 59
Martin, Joe 188,196,211,212
Martin, Messrs 48
Martin, W.R. 48
Mary, Tom Tom 205
Matheran Hill Railway 183,325,338
Matigara 269,290
Mayo, Lord 29,31
Mazdoor Union 191,193,239,343
McConville, Beryl 179,181
McPherson, Mrs 92
Meanley, Bob 340
Mechi River 275
Meiggs, Henry 66
Messurier, Colonel A. Le 56,75
Metropolitan Carriage & Wagon Works 134
Metz, Marilyn 356
Miedema, Virgil 339
Military Road 20,21,25,217,237
Miller, J. 59
Mirik 269
Mitchell & Co., Thomas 40,41
Mitchell, K.G. 164
Mobedjina, M.F. 211
Mohammed Ali Jinnah 175

Molesworth, Guilford 31,36
Monro, W. 59
Monsoon, 1909 120
Monsoon, 1927 158
Monsoon, 1944 286
Mookerjee, N.L. 59
Mookerjee, R.K. 59
Motor car, The 160,161,163,172
Motor Vehicle Run 175
Mountbatten, Lord 144,207
Mount Hermon School 177,202,203
Mubaya, Mr 211
Munday, Bella 183
Munro's chemist shop 205
Muslim League 140,175,193
Mutual Improvement Fund 139

N

Naidu, Ms Padmaja 234
Naksalbari 128,214,215,235,269,270,281,287, 288,290
Nanda, Mr V. 339
Napier, Lieutenant 20
Nash, J. 59
National Rail Museum, India 66,254,339,340
Naxalbari 236
Naxalites 236
Nehru, Jawaharlal 161,207,221,231
Nelson, W. 59
Nepalese Extension 76,79
New Jalpaiguri Station 232,233
New Lebong Road 36
New Siliguri 232
Nicolls, Reginald 161,168,172
Nilgiri Railway 74,324
Noel, Captain J. 144
Nolan, Mr, Commissioner in Darjeeling 91,106
North-Eastern coalfields 239,240
North Bank Express 227
North Bengal State Railway 33
North British Locomotive Co. 131,152
North Eastern Railway 219
Northeast Frontier Railway 226
Northern Bengal State Railway 27,32,35,43,61
North Wales Narrow Gauge Railways 53
North Western Railway 133
NWR Volunteer Rifles 161

O

O'Flaherty, R. 59
O'Malley, L.S. 131
Ogilvy Gillanders & Co 61,132
Oil-fired locomotives 330,339,351
Orange Valley Tea Estate 154
Order of Precedence 155,182
Ordham, Miss 92
Orenstein & Koppel 338
Oroya Railway 66
Orr, Pat 12
Osprey, The 129

P

P&O steamers 87
Pagla Jhora 76,80,97,100,165,205,346
Pakistan 207
Palace on Wheels 249
Palden Thondup 242
Panchanai 266
Panchanai Bridge 344,345
Panchanai Junction 266,268,269
Pangborn, Joseph Gladding 83
Panjipara Hat Halt 282
Panjipara Station 279
Parliamentary Standing Committee 352
Pelican, The 169
Penrhyn Railway 328
People's constitution 334
People's Democracy 334
People's Review 334
Perera, R.P. 352
Petrie, Nelson 352
Phillips, J. 59
Piggott Chapman & Co. 127
Pinecote 168,171
Pinnell, L.G. 165
Piprithan 278
Pitty's funeral 194
Plackett, Geoffrey 12,168,173,183,188,191,194
Plackett, Nigel 12
Planters' Club 155,164,179,183,193
Planters' Association 217
Plaza Cinema 199
Pliva, Mr 177
Poradah Junction 26
Porpoise, The 129
Post Master General of Bengal 117
Potala Palace 127
Pothia 282
Prasad, Shasheesh 258
Prasadjote 235
Prestage, Franklin 26,32,33,47,55,63,69,72,79,
   80-82
Prince Albert 111
Prince of Wales 113,144
Pringle, Ian 344
Pugh, Miss 92
Pul Bazaar 171

Q

Queen's Hill School 164
Queen Mary 122
Queen Victoria 25,87,111
Queen Victoria's Jubilee 89
Quit India campaign 176

R

Radical Democratic Party 191
Railcar 143
Railway Board, The 254
Railway Children, The 335
Railway Electrical Engineers 165
Railway Gang Case 133,135
Railway Volunteers 161
Raipur Forest Tramway 61,185
Rangoon-Mandalay Railway 12
Rangtong 152
Ransome 26
Reset and South Eastern Railroad 340
Reverse sidings 65
Reverse No.1 67
Reverse No.2 66,67
Reverse No.3 66,67
Reverse No.4 66
Reynolds, Mrs Herbert 57
'Richmond Villa' 92
Rift Valley 80
Rilli 302,317,319
Rilli, exchange sidings 309-310
Rink Cinema 198
Riyang 293,294,297,302,317
Riyang Station 294,307,320
Roband, Reverend 185,194
Roberts, Keith 170
Roberts' Hotels 40
Robertson, Leslie 86
Robertson, Mr Andrew 202
Robert Stephenson & Co. 148
Robert Stephenson & Hawthorn 182
Robinson, W.H. 59
Roddy, P.R. 37
Ronaldshay, Lord 147
Ropeway, aerial, tea 152
Ropeway, aerial, Darjeeling 171
Ropeway, aerial, Kalimpong 171,310,320
Ropeway, aerial, Sukna 206
Rouhrey, G. 59
Rowlatt Commission 139
Roy, Dr B.C. 218
Roy, G.C. 59
Royal Engineers 175
Royal Indian Engineering College 133
Royal Orient 249
Royal Proclamation, 1917 135
Royal Titles Bill 25
Ruhman, Golam 59
Ruikingpong Timber Compartments 123
Rumsey, Herbert Gordon 41,39,40,65
Rumsey, Lily 65
Rungpo 133
Runjo Valley Tea Association 48

S

Sahibgunj station 25
Salesian College 237
Salugara 298,319
Samthar Co-operative Multipurpose Society Ltd 319
Sanatorium for convalescence 31
SAN Engineering & Locomotive Co. 325
Santahar 129
Sarstedt, Bert 194,211,212
Satow, Mike 66
School specials 202
Sed-Gyved monastery 334
Semmering Railway 321
Sethi, R.C. 326
Sevoke 311,313
Sevoke Causeway 313,314
Sevoke gorge 301
Sevoke Station 296,300,301,316,319
Shah, Sher 265
Shah of Persia 265
Sharma, Prem 254
Sharp, Stewart & Co. 60,63,80
Sharpe, J. 59
Shaw, Betty 12
Shaw, James 12,174,177,178,179,183,188,
   191,193,195,196,206,210,211,212,
   213,286,310
Shaw, Mrs Shuldham 92
Sherston 166,168
Shooter, Adrian 340
Signal Engineers Committee 165
Sikkim 242
Siliguri 28,31,43,129,148,207,209,211,226,230,
   235,244,329,334
Siliguri Junction 214,218,233,238,339,344
Siliguri Municipal Corporation 330
Siliguri North 215,218,287
Siliguri Project 338
Siliguri Road Station 146,196,293,298
Siliguri Town 344
Simla 81,86
Simms & Head 26
Simon, Sir John 161
Sinclair, James 12
Singell Tea Company 48
Singh, Karnail 211,287
Sinking zones 347
Smith, A.K. 133
Smith, Mr H. Babbington 90
Smith, S.A. 188
Sonada 245
Sonada Brewery siding 106
Sorabjee's refreshment room 203,205
Southern Punjab Railway 61
Spooner & Co. 37,72,73
Spooner, Charles Easton 29
Spooner, George Percival 37,42
Spooner, James 29,72
Spooner, Thomas John 72
St. Joseph's School 170
St. Peter's School, York 133
Stableford & Co. 148
Stagg, John 93
Stakeholders' Workshop 333,336
St Andrew's Colonial Homes 202
Stanton RE, Colonel 32,47,55
Saw mills, steam 39
Stephen, Mr A. 143
Stephenson, Lady 309
Stephenson, Sir Hugh 160

Stevens, Colonel Holman F. 328
Stink express 120
St Joseph's College 164
Stoppard, Kenneth 177
Stoppard, Sir Tom 177
St Paul's School 164
Straussler, Dr Eugene 177
Sukna 43,344
Sulzer Winpro 324
Sury & Naire 325
Sweti Jhora 301
Swiss Locomotive & Machine Works 324

T

Taiabpur 269,278,290
Takdah 129
Tambur valley 77
Tata Iron & Steel Co. 133
Taylor, Colonel 41
Tea, transportation 154
Tea estates 21,22,31
Tea Planters' Association 130
Teesta Bridge 239
Teesta Forestry Division 123
Teesta River 291
Teesta Valley 12,117,127,130,168,171,215, 218,261,291,331,334,337
Teesta Valley Timetable 314
Telu River 276,288
Tenduf, Sherab 249
Teresa, Mother 195
Thacker's Business Directory 131
Thakurganj 278,283,290
'The Baron, The Butcha and The Bap' 110
'The Concise History of the Darjeeling District' 131
The Darjeeling Tea Research & Development Centre 31
The Pioneer Hotel 81
Thomas, Lowell 223
Thomas Mitchell & Company 40,41
Tibetan monasteries 127
Tibetan Passes 123
Tiger Hill 144
Tigers 169
Tiller, Peter 258,334,339
Tindharia Office 56
Tindharia school 123
Tindharia station 119,331,334
Tindharia works 125,127,188,194,353
Tingri Dzong 144
Tiruchirappali Engineering College 339
Tonic water 155
Track 29,41,42,76,85,139,222,254,343
Trinamool Congress 330,334
Troop trains 187
Tully, Sir Mark 10,13,326
Tung 149,157,338
Turner, E.R. & F. 73
Twain, Mark 120

Tyler, Captain 29
Tyseley Locomotive Works 340

U

'Under the Old School Topee' 202
UNESCO 254,258,321,323,344
Urwick, Reverend W. 31
Uttarkhand 215,243

V

Vacuum brakes 236,237
'Valley View' 168
Victoria School 205
Vizianagram-Raipur Railway survey 133
Voluntary Aid Detachment 179
Vulcan Engineering 174

W

Wagons
   Stableford flat wagons 148,151
Waite, Reverend Arthur 123
Walford Transport Ltd 178
Waller, Roger 324

War, 1914–18 128,136,137
Water tower, Aluabari 285
Wells, Vernon 161
Welsh Slate Company 73
West Pakistan 239
Whitton, John 65
Whitty, Irwine John 37,38,59,61
Williams, W.R. 59
Williams, William 72
Wilson, D & Co. 20
Wilson, President Woodrow 140
Windamere Hotel 177,193
Witch of Ghoom 202,203
Wolfe, Mr 133
'Woodcot' 170
Wood Hill hotel 185
'Woodland' 92
World's Transportation Commission 83
World Heritage Site 258,321,331,353,355,356
Wrekin College 173

Y

Young, Teddy 249
Younghusband, Colonel Francis 127

Darjeeling
55
Batasia Loop
Ghum
Jor Bungalow
50
Tiger Hill
Rangbul
Sonada
45
Dilaram
Tung
40
Old Military Road
Mahanadi
30
Pagla Jhora
Agony Point
4
25
3
6
5
Kurseong
35
Gayabari
Pankhabari Road
Pankhabari Road
N
E
S
W

DHR - GRADIENT PROFILE
+8000
8000
7000
6000
5000
4000
3000
2000
1000
New Jalpaiguri 480 ft
Siliguri Town 500 ft
Siliguri Junction 510 ft
Sukna 533 ft
Rangtong 1404ft
Chunbatti 2208ft
Tindharia 2822ft
Gayabari 3516ft
Mahanadi 4120ft
Kurseong 4864ft
Tung 5656ft
Sonada 6552 ft
Ghum 7407ft
Darjeeling 6812 ft
1 in30
1 in 24
1 in 32
1 in 28
1 in 29
1 in 26
1 in 35
1 in 28
1 in 35
1 in 33
kilometers 0 5 8 18 26 32 38 44 50 57 65 73 82 88
miles 0 3 5 11.25 16.25 20 23.75 27.5 31.25 35.5 40.5 45.5 51.25 55

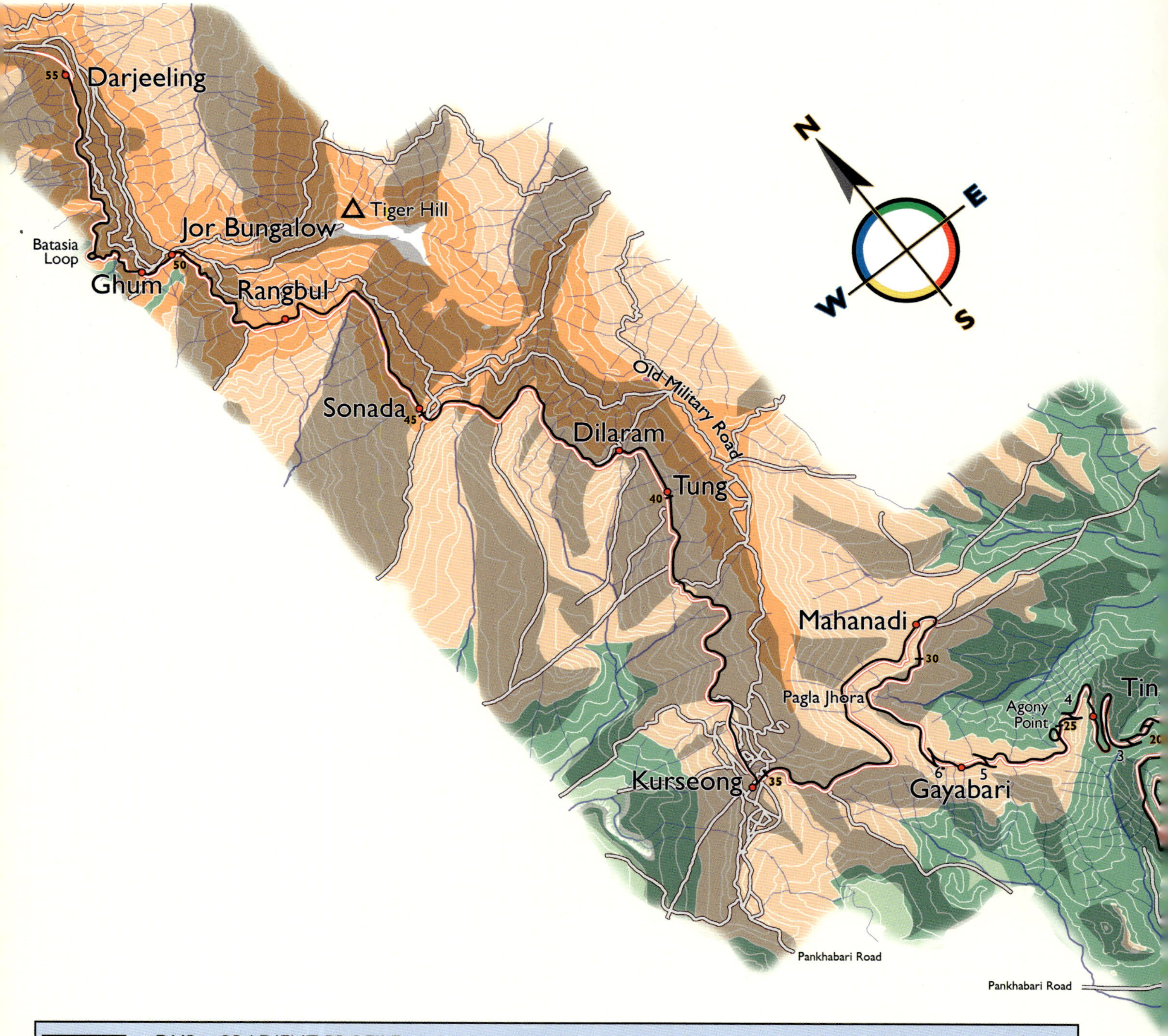

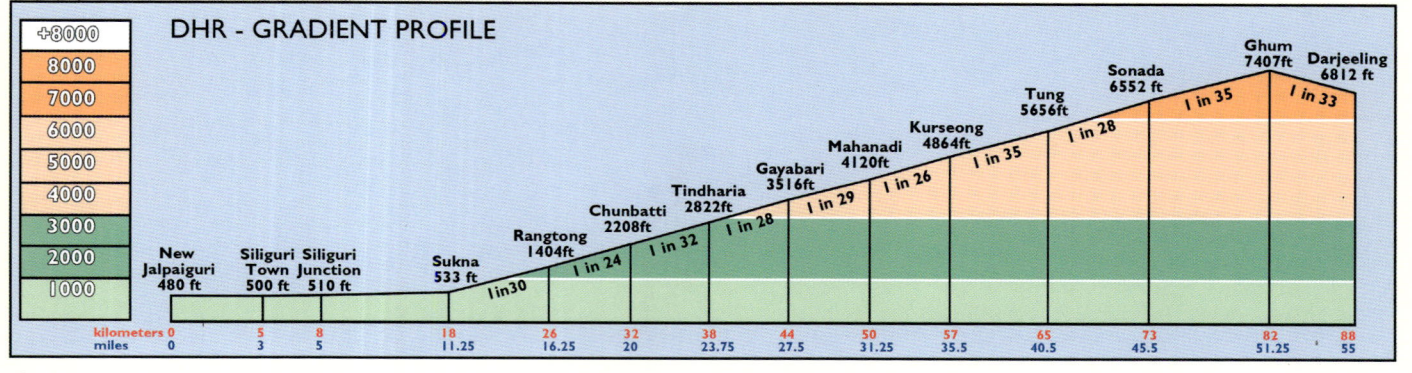